D0278491

Rethinking Political Violence

Series Editor
Roger Mac Ginty, School of Government and International Affairs,
Durham University, Durham, UK

This series provides a new space in which to interrogate and challenge much of the conventional wisdom of political violence. International and multidisciplinary in scope, this series explores the causes, types and effects of contemporary violence connecting key debates on terrorism, insurgency, civil war and peace-making. The timely Rethinking Political Violence offers a sustained and refreshing analysis reappraising some of the fundamental questions facing societies in conflict today and understanding attempts to ameliorate the effects of political violence.

This series is indexed by Scopus.

More information about this series at
https://link.springer.com/bookseries/14499

Ewelina U. Ochab · David Alton

State Responses to Crimes of Genocide

What Went Wrong and How to Change It

palgrave
macmillan

Ewelina U. Ochab
IBAHRI
London, UK

David Alton
Parliament of United Kingdom
London, UK

ISSN 2752-8588 ISSN 2752-8596 (electronic)
Rethinking Political Violence
ISBN 978-3-030-99161-6 ISBN 978-3-030-99162-3 (eBook)
https://doi.org/10.1007/978-3-030-99162-3

© The Editor(s) (if applicable) and The Author(s), under exclusive license to Springer Nature Switzerland AG 2022
This work is subject to copyright. All rights are solely and exclusively licensed by the Publisher, whether the whole or part of the material is concerned, specifically the rights of translation, reprinting, reuse of illustrations, recitation, broadcasting, reproduction on microfilms or in any other physical way, and transmission or information storage and retrieval, electronic adaptation, computer software, or by similar or dissimilar methodology now known or hereafter developed.
The use of general descriptive names, registered names, trademarks, service marks, etc. in this publication does not imply, even in the absence of a specific statement, that such names are exempt from the relevant protective laws and regulations and therefore free for general use.
The publisher, the authors and the editors are safe to assume that the advice and information in this book are believed to be true and accurate at the date of publication. Neither the publisher nor the authors or the editors give a warranty, expressed or implied, with respect to the material contained herein or for any errors or omissions that may have been made. The publisher remains neutral with regard to jurisdictional claims in published maps and institutional affiliations.

Cover illustration by Wilfredo Benitez

This Palgrave Macmillan imprint is published by the registered company Springer Nature Switzerland AG
The registered company address is: Gewerbestrasse 11, 6330 Cham, Switzerland

This book is dedicated to all victims and survivors of genocide.
Past. Present. Future.

FOREWORD

For most of us, the term 'genocide' will be forever associated with the atrocities of the Nazi concentration camps and the deliberate effort to exterminate the Jews during World War II.

We all know too well what happened in the late 1930s and 1940s. Although I am a Scot of Catholic background, I am married to a man whose mother was a Jewish refugee from Vienna. She and her sister, both highly trained doctors, fled Austria after the Anschluss. They were able to bring their mother from Austria with the help of the British Quaker community who sponsored her. We still have among family papers her passport, which bears the stamp 'J' for Jew. They came to this country fleeing persecution and would have been sent to concentration camps had they remained in their home.

We always link back to the Nazi atrocities to remind ourselves about the past and to use this past to shape our future. However, despite this remembered history, we still fail to learn the lessons that would ensure such atrocities do not happen again.

Genocide is a word that carries incredible weight, and its importance cannot be diluted.

'Genocide' has a specific legal meaning and the alarming truth is that, while genocidal violence has been perpetrated on a number of occasions around the world since Word War II, there is often resistance to using the terminology and a refusal to recognise genocide as genocide, because it carries inconvenient legal responsibilities.

The 1948 Genocide Convention defines genocide as, *'[acts] committed with intent to destroy, in whole or in part, a national, ethnical, racial or religious group.'*

The genocides in Central Africa—the Congo, Rwanda, the Sudan, and Uganda—proved to us that genocides were not a thing of the past. Only a few years ago, we watched as Daesh perpetrated horrific atrocities against the Yazidi and other religious minorities. The Yazidi were perceived by Daesh as primitive because their religious observance was not of the Abrahamic tradition; they were seen as sub-human and, as a result, Daesh felt at liberty to reduce this people to nothing. Men and boys were slaughtered by beheading. Captured Yazidi women and girl children were used as sex slaves, raped and raped over and over again, and then sold on to other abusers. To this day, over 2700 Yazidi women and children are still missing.

In 2016, I met for the second time the Yazidi Member of Parliament, Vian Dakhil. She has been trying to draw the world's attention to the plight of her people. I heard her account of spending time with the families, now in refugee camps, and the descriptions of their experiences. She says it is hard to find words for what happened. There are girls whose young bodies are so torn they will never be able to have a proper family life when they grow into adulthood. In 2019, I went myself to the refugee camps in Northern Iraq where many Yazidi are now sheltering. It broke my heart just listening to the women. Some had borne children but had left them behind in Syria because their Yazidi families could not accept the offspring of such violation and destruction. The tears of these victims were testament to their immeasurable pain.

So we are talking about genocide. We are talking about the destruction of a people and their ability to procreate, and the destruction of family. That is at the heart of crimes that are currently happening. Some of the girls violated in these outrages are as young as seven, eight, or nine. A few who have escaped are suffering from the most severe trauma. Doctors are visiting the refugee camps to work with the girls, but they do not have the facilities so cannot help with the terrible traumatic effects—not just physical but mental. Some women feel that they can never be intimate with anyone ever again in their lives. Mrs Vian describes the mass graves that she has visited, the beheadings of children and the crucifixions; she cannot understand why Western Governments are not being more vociferous about these horrors and naming them as genocidal atrocities.

Genocide requires a very high evidential burden. All of us lawyers working in the field know that the crimes have to surmount a number of vaulting bars. However, these acts do just that. The constitutive acts of killing, causing bodily or mental harm, raping, preventing reproduction, and the forced transferring of people from their land, all meet the legal requirements of genocide, so we should not be in any doubt that we are dealing with genocide here. Commentators express regret that because the perpetrators were Daesh—non-state actors—they cannot be held accountable for genocide, a crime where the accused must be a nation state. The perpetrators can be accused of crimes against humanity but not genocide. It is clear to me that we have to break the cycle of inertia that we have heard described. The Genocide Convention creates a duty upon states to prevent genocide. Are there nations that should be held to account for failing to prevent the Yazidi genocide?

It did not stop there and we did not learn anything from the atrocities perpetrated against the Yazidis.

Only a couple of years later, we have observed the atrocities perpetrated by the Burmese military against the Rohingya Muslims in Myanmar, a community that is unwelcome in the country and considered illegal immigrants for decades. Mass murder, physical and mental torture, and rape and sexual violence are only a few examples of the atrocities unleashed against the community and resulted in over 800,000 people fleeing across the border to Bangladesh. Their pain and suffering continue to this day.

Again, we have not learned anything from the atrocities.

In 2018, we started hearing stories of mass incarceration in so-called re-education camps in Xinjiang, in China. In fact, they had nothing to do with re-education but were the early stages of a genocidal campaign against the Uyghurs and other Turkic minorities in the region. Evidence of killings, torture, rape and sexual violence, forced abortions, forced sterilisations, separation of children from their parents, forced labour, and much more followed.

On the egregious crimes against the Uyghur, I have heard directly the testimonies of those who have suffered, especially exiled women who have been sexually abused and raped, sterilised or forced to terminate pregnancies. Some have been separated from children, who are sent to remand homes to be deracinated—denied their religion and culture. I have seen the aerial photographs showing the destruction of mosques and burial grounds. I have heard evidence from well-connected academics of forced labour, of the large numbers held in labour camps and the coerced movement of villagers to work in other parts of China.

These are some examples of genocidal atrocities from recent years. Three chances for us to put the lessons from the Nazi atrocities to work and to act. However, we failed again and again.

We have not only failed to identify situations where there is a serious risk of genocide, we have also failed to act to prevent these crimes taking place. We allow the perpetrators to get away with genocide, again and again, usually because we want to avoid any diplomatic fallout or because we fear the economic consequences for ourselves.

I welcome this important book by my friends and colleagues, Dr Ewelina Ochab and Lord Alton. It is an important contribution to a much-needed debate about the failure of the international community to live up to its responsibilities and identifies the blocks in securing justice, without which there can be no peace.

London, UK   Helena Kennedy
December 2021   Baroness, QC

Acknowledgements We would like to thank all those who provided comments on the drafts of this manuscript, including Rebecca Tinsley, Aarif Abraham, Anton' de Piro, Jessica Templeman, Erin Rosenberg, David Campanale, Lela Gilbert, and Fr. Samuel Burke OP.

OUTLINE

Chapter 1 provides an introduction into the topic of genocide and some of the recent events that have shaped the thinking behind this book.

Chapter 2 explains the fundamentals of genocide. It briefly outlines how the concept came into being and how it progressed into a Convention which imposed duties upon states. It explains the principles of international law and jurisprudence on genocide and provides some areas for consideration when engaging with genocide. It then addresses the often-neglected question of genocide determination and considers how some states have approached the issue.

Chapters 3–6 analyse the four previously mentioned cases of recent genocide: the Daesh atrocities against religious minorities in Syria and Iraq, the Burmese Military's genocide against the Rohingya Muslims, the genocide of Christians in Nigeria, and the Chinese Government's genocide against the Uyghurs in China. These chapters examine some of the available evidence of the atrocities, the steps taken to suppress the atrocities, and steps taken to investigate these crimes and to prosecute the perpetrators. The analysis of these case studies—which examines the challenges and responses in each instance—is followed by recommendations which flow from these examples.

Chapter 7 considers some of other situations that show risk factors of genocide and require urgent response. We further consider some other cases of concern: the situations in NagornoKarabakh (the 'slow burn' continuation of the Armenian Genocide), the man-made catastrophe of

Tigray, and North Korea declared to have committed crimes against humanity by a UN Commission but where the eradication of religious minorities may fall within the definition of genocide.

Chapter 8 attempts to answer the question of why the perpetrators have been able to get away with genocide. It begins with an analysis of the failures to prevent genocides focusing on the lack of comprehensive monitoring mechanisms, the lack of analysis and determination mechanisms, and the issue of responses manifesting the 'too little too late' approach. This assessment, which draws on the analysis of the cases discussed in Chapters Three to Six, identifies the areas requiring urgent change or improvement to ensure that states' responses to genocide are up for the game.

It identifies the urgently needed responses required to address these challenges and to ensure that we can better address the legacy of failure in responding to genocide. It focuses on four aspects, including genocide risk factors monitoring, genocide analysis and determination, informed genocide responses, and investigations and prosecutions. Each recommendation draws on the authors' experience of engaging states and international bodies on the issue of genocide.

CONTENTS

ABBREVIATIONS

CCP	Chinese Communist Party
CoI	Commission of Inquiry
Daesh	Al-Dawla al-Islamiya al-Iraq al-Sham (Islamic State of Iraq and the Levant)
ICC	International Criminal Court
ICJ	International Court of Justice
ICTR	International Criminal Tribunal for Rwanda
ICTY	International Criminal Tribunal for the former Yugoslavia
IICoISAR	International Independent Commission of Inquiry on the Syria Arab Republic
IIFFMM	Independent International Fact-Finding Mission on Myanmar
IIIM	International, Impartial and Independent Mechanism
IIMM	Independent Investigative Mechanism for Myanmar
UDHR	Universal Declaration of Human Rights

CHAPTER 1

Introduction

In 1948, when the UN Convention on the Prevention and Punishment of the Crime of Genocide (the Genocide Convention) was being drafted, it was seen as a way to ensure that the world would 'Never Again' witness atrocities of the kind committed by the Nazis. However, while the immense scale of the loss of life seen during World War II has (arguably) not been matched since, acts of genocide and atrocity crimes have continued to be perpetrated. Since that war, we have witnessed genocide in Cambodia, Rwanda, Bosnia, Darfur, Northern Iraq, and now in China, Burma, Nigeria, and Tigray. This is not an exhaustive list.

As we write, terrible atrocities and war crimes are being committed in Ukraine. Some of the Kremlin's supporters have justified Putin's War with arguments which come perilously close to eliminating whole groups of people. President Biden has called it genocide. As they read the exacting thresholds required for a declaration of genocide, readers can reflect on whether the horrendous atrocities in Bucha and elsewhere in Ukraine may meet the criteria set out in the Genocide Convention. However, what is abundantly clear is that in Ukraine—and Tigray—terrible atrocities are occurring and if those responsible are to be held to account we must be unrelenting in systematically collecting and preserving the evidence.

The response to these atrocities has always been inadequate, sadly demonstrating that the noble ideals of the Genocide Convention are

© The Author(s), under exclusive license to Springer Nature
Switzerland AG 2022
E. U. Ochab and D. Alton, *State Responses to Crimes of Genocide*,
Rethinking Political Violence,
https://doi.org/10.1007/978-3-030-99162-3_1

insufficient on their own. Whenever a genocide has taken place, there is a collective wringing of hands; world leaders repeat the tired and pious platitude that 'Never Again' must not be allowed to happen all over again. In reality, the promise to break the relentless and devastating cycles of genocide has not been kept. In recent years, things have arguably deteriorated.

Recall that in 2014, Daesh unleashed genocide against religious minorities in Syria and Iraq. Then, in 2017, in quick succession the Burmese military launched a genocidal campaign against the Rohingya Muslims in Myanmar and harrowing reports emerged of ever-growing atrocities against Christian minorities in Nigeria. By 2018, we were shocked once more—this time by reports from China of a genocidal campaign against the Uyghur Muslims. The end of 2020 brought us news of atrocity crimes in Tigray—where rape and starvation have been deployed as weapons of war.

We believe that the word 'genocide' should never be used lightly, inappropriately, or for rhetorical purposes. But in each of these cases of mass atrocities, all within the last few years, we will argue that the high legal bar in the definition of genocide has indeed been met. Yet, in each instance, the world's response has been utterly inadequate, making little difference to the targeted communities. Taken at face value, this does not offer much hope for the future.

Why have we have failed to rise to the ambitions of those who drafted the Genocide Convention? We cannot simply accept that there is nothing which can be done to prevent mass atrocities; the challenge is to recalibrate our response so as to deter future genocides—and, at the very minimum, where they do occur, to respond differently and more effectively. Against the backdrop of these frequent and recurring mass atrocities, these questions manifestly warrant urgent consideration—especially when considered alongside the growing impunity of perpetrators.

Our failure to act inevitably results in further mass atrocities. There is no question about it.

While the word genocide should not be used for rhetorical effect, neither should we allow it to become a word which dares not speak its name. It has its origins in the work and experiences of the Polish Jewish lawyer, Raphael Lemkin, whose story we tell. Having studied the mass murder of Armenians, Assyrians, and others, Lemkin then experienced the brutal murder of over forty members of his extended family. He wanted to use a word which described graphically and succinctly the deadly cutting of the human family, severing apart groups of people, slaughtered because of ethnicity, religion, or difference. Hence *genos* and *cide*.

Although this word, genocide, should not be used inaccurately, we should not hesitate to use it whenever and wherever all elements of the crime are present. Moreover, where the elements of genocide are not all established, this should not conclude the conversation. Crimes against humanity, war crimes, and other atrocity crimes are invariably harbingers—canaries in the mine—warning us of even worse to come.

This book has become necessary because of the lamentable failure of the international community to predict, prevent, and punish genocide, as well as to protect the victims of this heinous crime. It has been made urgent by the increasing role of authoritarian states in subverting and controlling international institutions, creating the conditions for impunity and worse. And it has become necessary because of the craven and sometimes duplicitous position of governments that place a higher premium on their business, trade, and diplomatic links with genocidal states than on their duties under the Genocide Convention.

The position of the UK Government has been to insist that declarations of genocide are not made by politicians but by the international judicial system—yet there has been no referral of any evidence by the UK Government to any international judicial systems. And, while this macabre game of pass the parcel of responsibility continues, people are being ruthlessly targeted, along with their identity, their culture, and their history.

This book doesn't set out to excoriate one country. But it does ask pertinent questions about our alliances, about our trading partners, about our values—and how we should respond. It is unsurprising that among those who so strongly supported our calls, during the passage of the 2021 Trade Act, to limit trade with states credibly accused of genocide, was the British Board of Jewish Deputies. They know their history. They remember Hitler's willing business partners, companies like IBM which were complicit while Jews saw their businesses sequestrated and were forced into concentration camps. IBM was just one company among many.

We also know well the monstrosities committed by Stalin—not least during the Holodomor in Ukraine. We didn't see fundamental change in Eastern Europe solely by deploying more and more Cruise and Pershing missiles; change also came through the Helsinki Process. It did not come by ignoring the Kremlin's depredations in its Siberian gulags or through business as usual. In facing today's authoritarians we must never forget how change occurred. Can you imagine mid-twentieth-century leaders of Western democracies treating Soviet Communism as if it was just another trading partner?

This book has its origins in those twentieth century experiences, but it also has roots in the genocide in Northern Iraq, where both authors took first-hand accounts of what befell Yazidis, Christians, and other minorities.

But, unapologetically, it has been written against the disturbing backdrop of the shocking treatment of the Uyghur population in Xinjiang, the use of slave labour, the mass incarceration of a minority group, reports of forced organ harvesting of Falun Gong practitioners and others, the penetration of our national security infrastructures, the obscuration of the origins of COVID-19, the dismantling of democracy and the rule of law in Hong Kong, and the subversion of international institutions.

Although this book is not about one country and not about China alone, it is being published shortly after the finding of genocide in Xinjiang against China's Uyghur population by the Independent Uyghur Tribunal, which was chaired by Sir Geoffrey Nice QC, and painstakingly collected evidence and interviewed witnesses throughout 2021.

Prior to this finding, in April 2021, the UK House of Commons passed an all-party motion declaring events in Xinjiang to constitute a genocide.

Paradoxically, the Chinese Government has achieved the rare feat of uniting parties across the UK's political spectrum, both sides of the aisle in the US Congress (along with outgoing and incoming US Presidents), the sometimes-disparate G7 nations as well as the Dutch Parliament and Canadian House of Commons—bringing them to an understanding that the Chinese regime's ambition is to create a world safe for authoritarianism and that genocide or crimes against humanity will not be obstacles in its path.

Academics and lawyers have reached the same conclusion with one report by over 50 international lawyers who say that that Xinjiang is a genocide and that every single one of the criteria in the Genocide Convention has been met.

Attempts to silence such assessments have led to Chinese sanctions against lawyers and Parliamentarians (including one of the authors) while broadcasters like the BBC have faced a ban in China because it dared to broadcast the testimonies of courageous Uyghur women who described conditions in the concentration camps—including their forced indoctrination, rape, and public humiliation by camp guards.

What is happening in Xinjiang is ruthless and barbaric. It is part of the Chinese Government's long history of cruelty, drawn from the same playbook as the Cultural Revolution and the destruction of Tibetan identity, religion, and culture. Dominic Raab, then the UK Foreign Secretary, told the UN Human Rights Council that what is afoot in Xinjiang is *'on an industrial scale'* and *'beyond the pale.'* Quite so. But while we decline to give these events a name, is it to be business as usual? Elizabeth Truss, the Foreign Secretary, has said that a genocide is underway in Xinjiang. But, simultaneously, Ministers in the same Government justify the promotion of trade deals with the very regime accused of genocide and of using slave labour.

In response to questions at a 2021 hearing of the House of Lords International Relations and Defence Select Committee, key witnesses (including a former Chancellor of the Exchequer, the UK's former National Security Adviser, and the former Head of the Foreign Office on China) declined to say whether trade should continue with a state accused of genocide. One said there wasn't enough evidence, and another said the question was too political. One rejected the suggestion that Britain should distance itself from China owing to its human rights record, saying '*I see no British prosperity without a trading relationship with China.*' And finally, one said: '*There are many countries in the world with appalling human rights records with which we have had an economic relationship over many decades, and that has been a traditional position of the UK.*' But should it be?

Tellingly, the UK's Integrated Review (Global Britain in a Competitive Age, published in March 2021), which set out the UK's future security, defence, development, and foreign policy, along with its vision of the UK's role in the world over the next two decades, is also silent on the question of genocide and atrocity crimes. Trade is simply singled out in the Review as standing '*at the heart of Global Britain.*'

But when asked whether we should trade with states accused of genocide, Global Britain risks holing its nose, doing business as usual with whomever greases our palm.

Yet genocide is not one of those '*on the one hand this and on the other hand that*' questions: no balance needs to be struck.

Global Britain requires a stable business environment in its potential trading partners. British businesses cannot be expected to engage with countries disrupted by conflict and insecurity. If a country is abusing human rights law, it is quite likely it is also ignoring other international rules-based norms such as property law, contract law, and intellectual property law. In other words, countries with wretched human rights record are dubious places to do business. The UK Government owes a duty of care to British businesspeople (and taxpayers) not to pretend that trading in an unstable country will be without great risk.

We should not accept the counterargument that trade brings liberal democracy. It hasn't in China or Saudi Arabia; it didn't when the West was heavily involved in Iran; and Canada's decades of trade with Communist Cuba moved the Castro brothers not one jot.

This is not a new debate. Two hundred years ago that foremost champion of free trade, Richard Cobden, the great northern radical, said that free trade was not more important than our duty to oppose both the trade in human beings and the trade in opium. On the latter, he forced a four-day parliamentary debate and with bipartisan support defeated the government.

Genocide is no different. Knowing where and when a great nation must draw a line—as Coden did—is a challenge we lay down. The book's central purpose is to demonstrate the shortcomings of existing responses to genocide and to provide proposals on how these shortcomings might be addressed. We draw on the recent experience of genocide to suggest a change. We consider the purpose and effect of recent legislative attempts to amend the Trade Act (2021) with a widely supported Genocide Amendment, which was laid before Parliament by Lord Alton.

The book begins with an explanation of the fundamentals of genocide and with an outline of four recent cases of genocide which we analyse in detail.

We then endeavour to answer the question of why perpetrators have been able to get away with genocide. This includes an analysis of multiple failures to prevent genocides, focusing on the lack of comprehensive monitoring mechanisms, methodology to determine genocide, and our wholly inadequate 'too little, too late' approach.

This assessment, which draws on our analysis of the case studies, identifies the areas requiring urgent change or improvement to ensure that the responses of states to genocide are fit for purpose. We focus on several aspects, including genocide risk factors monitoring, genocide analysis and determination, informed genocide responses, investigations, and prosecutions. Each recommendation draws on the experience of the authors in engaging states and international bodies on the issue of genocide.

May 2022

PART I

Genocide as the Crime Above All Crimes

CHAPTER 2

Genocide as the Crime Above All Crimes

This chapter explains the fundamentals of genocide. It briefly outlines how the concept came into being and how it progressed into a convention imposing obligations upon states and responsibilities on individuals. It further explains the basics of the international law relating to genocide, providing some pointers for consideration when engaging on the issue. The chapter then explains the formal definition and meaning of genocide under Article II of the UN Convention on the Prevention and Punishment of the Crime of Genocide (the Genocide Convention). Lastly, it engages with the neglected question of who determines genocide and considers how some states have approached the issue of genocide determination and response.

1 The Crime Without a Name

Raphael Lemkin, a Polish lawyer of Jewish descent, once said that his awareness of mass atrocities had first been stirred when, as a 12-year-old, he read Henry Sienkiewicz's description in 'Quo Vadis' of Nero throwing Christians to the lions.[1] Twenty years later, in 1933, Lemkin

---

[1] Raphael Lemkin (ed. Donna Lee Frieze), *Totally Unofficial* (Yale University Press, 2013) 1.

© The Author(s), under exclusive license to Springer Nature Switzerland AG 2022
E. U. Ochab and D. Alton, *State Responses to Crimes of Genocide*, Rethinking Political Violence, https://doi.org/10.1007/978-3-030-99162-3_2

9

had been working on defining other international crimes, such as the crime of barbarity and the crime of vandalism. This was prior to his work on the concept of genocide, and before the most egregious crimes of the Holocaust (in which 49 of Lemkin's relatives were murdered) were yet to be committed. Lemkin gave these definitions:

> Whoever, out of hatred towards a racial, religious or social collectivity or with the goal of its extermination, undertakes a punishable action against the life, the bodily integrity, liberty, dignity or the economic existence of a person belonging to such a collectivity, is liable, for the offense of barbarity, to a penalty of... unless punishment for the action falls under a more severe provision of the given Code

and

> Whoever, either out of hatred towards a racial, religious or social collectivity or with the goal of its extermination, destroys works of cultural or artistic heritage, is liable, for the offense of vandalism, to a penalty of... unless punishment for the action falls under a more severe provision of the given Code.[2]

Lemkin sent the proposal and accompanying reports for the Fifth Conference for the Unification of Penal Law in Madrid, happening in October that year. Despite initial challenges, including the Minister of Justice banning Lemkin from attending and heavy criticism of his proposal in the press,[3] Lemkin's proposal was considered at the conference, starting the discussion around the topic of crimes specifically targeting whole communities.[4]

The horrific actions of the Nazis during the 1930s and 1940s added a shocking new dimension to Lemkin's understanding of mass atrocities and also to the urgency of the issue. Several years later, at an event at the Hotel Pierre in New York, Lemkin said that he began to seek a word to capture the severity of the Nazi atrocities after hearing Churchill's

---

[2] Raphael Lemkin, 'Acts Constituting a General (Transnational) Danger Considered as Offences Against the Law of Nations' Presented at the 5th Conference for the Unification of Penal Law in Madrid (14–20 October 1933).

[3] As Lemkin described, 'In an article being widely discussed in Warsaw, the newspaper wrote that I was acting solely for the protection of my own race.' Ibid., 23.

[4] Ibid., 23–24.

radio broadcast in which he stated that the Nazis had committed '*a crime without a name*.'[5] As Lemkin later wrote:

> New conceptions require new terms. By "genocide" we mean the destruction of a nation or of an ethnic group. This new word, coined by the author to denote an old practice in its modern development, is made from the ancient Greek word *genos* (race, tribe) and the Latin *cide* (killing), thus corresponding in its formation to such words as tyrannicide, homicide, infanticide, etc. Generally speaking, genocide does not necessarily mean the immediate destruction of a nation, except when accomplished by mass killings of all members of a nation.[6]

Lemkin proposed a definition of genocide as:

> It is intended rather to signify a coordinated plan of different actions aiming at the destruction of essential foundations of the life of national groups, with the aim of annihilating the groups themselves. The objectives of such a plan would be disintegration of the political and social institutions, of culture, language, national feelings, religion, and the economic existence of national groups, and the destruction of the personal security, liberty, health, dignity, and even the lives of the individuals belonging to such groups. Genocide is directed against the national group as an entity, and the actions involved are directed against individuals, not in their individual capacity, but as members of the national group.[7]

Lemkin's definition was a direct response to the Holocaust. Between 1941 and 1945, some six million Jews, including two thirds of Europe's Jews, were exterminated in concentration camps, in gas chambers, in pogroms, and mass shootings.[8] Auschwitz, Dachau, Treblinka, and others were the charnel houses of Hitler's murderous infamy. It all began with

---

[5] Winston Churchill, Radio broadcast, 24 August 1941.

[6] Raphael Lemkin, *Axis Rule in Occupied Europe: Laws of Occupation. Analysis, Proposals for Redress* (Carnegie Endowment for International Peace: Washington DC, 1944) 79.

[7] Ibid.

[8] See, for example, Jack R. Fischel, *Historical Dictionary of the Holocaust* (Rowman & Littlefield Publishers, 2020); Timothy D. Snyder, *Bloodlands: Europe Between Hitler and Stalin* (Vintage Books: London, 2011); United States Holocaust Memorial Museum, *Holocaust Encyclopedia* (2017).

Hitler's isolation of Jews, the boycotting of their businesses, the Nuremberg Laws,[9] Kristallnacht (the night of the broken glass) and, sensing that his Final Solution would carry no consequences, it ended with mass murder.[10] Hitler had asked '*Who, after all, speaks today of the annihilation of the Armenians?*'—and precious few did, or even cared.[11] The mass murder of Jews occurred alongside the killings of disabled people, Roma, gay men, political and religious dissidents, ethnic Poles, Russian civilians, and prisoners of war.[12]

Lemkin's definition of genocide was influenced by the crimes of the Nazis and referred to their methods, including attacks on political and social institutions, religion, culture, language, economy, and lives.[13] He went on to explain why these methods were pertinent to the definition of genocide. Indeed, he stressed that even less serious sounding acts such as confiscation of property had great significance:

> The confiscation of property of nationals of an occupied area on the ground that they have left the country may be considered simply as a deprivation of their individual property rights. However, if the confiscations are ordered against individuals solely because they are Poles, Jews, or Czechs, then the same confiscations tend in effect to weaken the national entities of which those persons are members.[14]

Lemkin not only coined the word genocide and proposed a definition, but went further with his analysis, considering the damaging effects of

---

[9] Nuremberg Laws, including the Law for the Protection of German Blood and German Honour and the Reich Citizenship Law, were antisemitic and racist laws enacted in Nazi Germany on 15 September 1935.

[10] See for example: Saul Friedländer, *Nazi Germany and The Jews, Volume 1: The Years of Persecution 1933–1939* (Phoenix: London, 1997); Joseph Goldstein, *Jewish History in Modern Times* (Sussex Academic Press, 1995); Reimund Schnabel, *Macht ohne Moral* (Roederberg Publishing: Frankfurt, 1957); Raul Hilberg, *The Destruction of the European Jews* (Yale University Press, 2003).

[11] Adolf Hitler, Speech, 22 August 1939. Cited in Louis P. Lochner, *What About Germany?* (Dodd, Mead & Co.: New York, 1942) 1–4.

[12] United States Holocaust Memorial and Museum, 'Documenting Numbers of Victims of the Holocaust and Nazi Persecution' (4 February 2019).

[13] Raphael Lemkin, 'Genocide as a Crime under International Law' (1947) 41 *American Journal of International Law* 145.

[14] Ibid.

genocide and impunity of the perpetrators upon the targeted communities, along with the collateral effects on international peace and security more broadly. As he emphasised:

> The practices of genocide anywhere affect the vital interests of all civilised people. Its consequences can neither be isolated nor localised. Tolerating genocide is an admission of the principle that one national group has the right to attack another because of its supposed racial superiority. This principle invites an expansion of such practices beyond the borders of the offending state, and that means wars of aggression.[15]

Lemkin also noted the very contagious nature of a crime which, if permitted to flourish in an environment of impunity, sends a dangerous message to others intending to commit their own genocidal acts, especially the eradication of minorities:

> The disease of criminality if left unchecked is contagious. Minorities of one sort or another exist in all countries, protected by the constitutional order of the state. If persecution of any minority by any country is tolerated anywhere, the very moral and legal foundations of constitutional government may be shaken.[16]

This is the ultimate case for acting to prevent such atrocities, suppress them when they occur, help the victims, and prosecute the perpetrators: in order to ensure that those responsible do not believe that they can get away with genocide. Impunity merely begets further crime. Lemkin believed that the response to genocide needed to be international—that it would require 'international co-operation to liberate mankind from such an odious scourge.'[17]

After devising the terminology, definition, and intent, Lemkin built international consensus at the newly created United Nations. He proposed that the UN should promulgate the treaty on genocide and incorporate the following principles:

---

[15] Raphael Lemkin, 'Genocide- A Modern Crime' (1945) 4 *Free World* 39–43.

[16] Ibid.

[17] Ibid.

– Genocide to be recognised as an international crime:

> The crime of genocide should be recognised therein as a conspiracy to exterminate national, religious or racial groups. The overt acts of such a conspiracy may consist of attacks against life, liberty or property of members of such groups merely because of their affiliation with such groups...[18]

– Genocide to be criminalised by domestic penal codes:

> The crime so formulated should be incorporated in every national criminal code of the signatories. The defendants should be liable not only before the courts of the country where the crime was committed, but in case of escape shall be liable as well, before the courts of the country where they are apprehended.[19]

– Liability to be extended to a broad range of perpetrators:

> The liability for genocide should rest on those who gave and executed the orders, as well as on those who incited to the commission of the crime by whatever means, including formulation and teaching of the criminal philosophy of genocide. Members of government and political bodies which organised or tolerated genocide will be equally responsible.[20]

– Genocide to be addressed by individual criminal responsibility and state responsibility:

> Independently of the responsibility of individuals for genocide, states in which such a policy obtains should be held accountable before the Security Council of the United Nations Organization. The Council may request the International Court of Justice to deliver an advisory opinion to determine whether a state of genocide exists within a given country before invoking, among other things, sanctions to be levelled against the offending country. The Security Council may act either on its own initiative or on the basis of petitions submitted

[18] Raphael Lemkin, 'Genocide' (1946) 15 *American Scholar* 227–230.
[19] Ibid.
[20] Ibid.

by members of interested national, religious or racial groups residing either within or without the accused country.[21]

– Genocide to be addressed by joint and complementary efforts:

A multilateral treaty for the prevention and punishment of genocide should not preclude two or more countries from entering into bilateral or regional treaties for more extensive protection against genocide...[22]

In October 1946, Lemkin joined the UN General Assembly meeting held at Lake Success, New York, where he worked with representatives of states in establishing agreement around the concept and on affirmation of the different legal principles involved. The proposed resolution was then referred to the Legal Committee for discussion.[23] Lemkin reported that:

The preamble referred to the destruction of racial, religious or national, groups in the past and stressed the losses to humanity in the form of cultural and other contributions. It further stated that genocide is a denial of the right of entire human groups in the same sense that homicide is a denial to an individual of his right to live, and that such a denial is contrary to the aims and purposes of the UN. In its part the resolution of the assembly called upon the Social and Economic Council to prepare a report ... to declare that genocide be dealt with by national legislation in the same way as other international crimes such as piracy, traffic in women and children, and others.[24]

Due to the overwhelming support for the resolution, Sir Hartley Shawcross, Member of Parliament for St. Helens, and later Lord Shawcross, who had been Chief Prosecutor at the International Military Tribunal in Nuremberg, proposed that the Legal Committee should declare genocide an international crime without further review by the Social and Economic Council. On 11 December 1946, after some

[21] Ibid.

[22] Ibid.

[23] Ibid.

[24] Raphael Lemkin, 'Genocide as a Crime under International Law' (1947) 41 *American Journal of International Law* 145–151.

amendments by the Legal Committee and its sub-committee, the Legal Committee unanimously adopted the Resolution on the Crime of Genocide.[25] Among other things, it affirmed that:

> Genocide is a crime under international law which the civilised world condemns -- and for the commission of which principals and accomplices, whether private individuals, public officials or statesmen, and whether the crime is committed on religious, racial, political or any other grounds -- are punishable;
>
> [it] invites the Member States to enact necessary legislation from the prevention and punishment of this crime;
>
> [it] recommends that international cooperation be organised between states with a view to facilitating the speedy prevention and punishment of the crime of genocide.[26]

The combined work resulted in the resolution defining genocide as:

> A denial of the right of existence of entire human groups, as homicide is the denial of the right to live of individual human being; such denial of the right of existence shocks the conscience of mankind, results in great losses to humanity in the form of cultural and other contributions represented by these human groups.[27]

However, Lemkin's efforts were by no means concluded with the passage of the 1946 Resolution on the Crime of Genocide by the UN General Assembly. His persistence and single mindedness led, on 9 December 1948 (one day before the Universal Declaration of Human Rights was ratified), to the unanimous adoption by the UN General Assembly of the UN Convention on the Prevention and Punishment of the Crime of Genocide (the Genocide Convention), which entered into force on 12 January 1951. The Genocide Convention not only introduced the

---

[25] UN General Assembly, The Crime of Genocide, 11 December 1946, UN Doc. A/RES/96.

[26] UN General Assembly Res 96(I) (11 December 1946) UN Doc S/RES/91(I).

[27] Ibid.

definition of genocide but also imposed obligations upon ratifying states requiring them to prevent and punish the crime.[28]

The other side of the story

While the work of Lemkin greatly contributed to the adoption of the Genocide Convention, the idea of the nameless crime that ultimately became the crime of genocide emerged from the work and thinking of Polish, Austrian, and Russian legal thinkers in the 1920s and 1930s, including Andrei Vyshinsky, Aron Trainin, Vespasian Pella, and Henri Donnedieu de Varbes. Their work further contributed to developing the jurisprudence surrounding the crime through the International Military Tribunal in Nuremberg 1945–1946.[29]

While Lemkin led the work that resulted in the Genocide Convention, he was ultimately side-lined from the drafting process.[30] This, and associated political pressures, resulted in the Genocide Convention, significant achievement though it was, falling short of what Lemkin had intended. Anton Weiss-Wendt, a Norwegian academic and historian, commented that '*due to political pressure, the final outcome may be described as arrested development, not the natural progression of humanitarian law Lemkin hoped for.*'[31] These political pressures came from all sides, including the Soviet Union and the United States—these states showing little will to codify genocide as an international crime.[32] Indeed, '*Soviet negotiators fought tooth and nail against the establishment of an international criminal court and the inclusion of political groups among those protected by the convention. Simultaneously, they construed the cultural aspect of genocide so as to target colonial powers, especially Britain.*'[33] The fact that the Soviet Union ultimately supported the resolution on genocide was

[28] See Sect. 2 and 3 of this chapter.

[29] Anton Weiss-Wendt, *The Soviet Union and the Gutting of the UN Genocide Convention* (The University of Wisconsin Press, 2017) 5.

[30] Ibid., 5.

[31] Ibid., 5.

[32] Ibid., 7.

[33] Ibid., 7.

because that country identified the Convention as a response to the infamies of Nazism.[34]

At the drafting stage, various aspects of Lemkin's definition of genocide were removed piece by piece, moving away from an identity-based crime towards one focused on biological destruction.[35] Apart from narrowing the scope of the definition from what Lemkin had envisioned, the drafters of the Genocide Convention successfully wrote their own genocides out of the law. Furthermore, the introduction of the threshold of specific intent to the definition of genocide was aimed at making it almost impossible for any case to reach it. As Lemkin said, they wanted '*non-enforceable laws with many loopholes in them, so that they can manage life like currency in a bank.*'[36] The final text of the Genocide Convention was a compromise document supported by the great powers; a text that meant that the great powers would not be held accountable for their own crimes.

As a result, the Genocide Convention became only a shadow of what Lemkin had intended it to be—a powerful mechanism to equip states to prevent genocide. The shortfall from this ideal resulted in Lemkin falling into a deep depression. He spent the rest of his life trying to get genocide criminalised domestically.

2   GENOCIDE AS WE KNOW IT

The Genocide Convention provides a legal definition of genocide in Article II:

> Genocide means any of the following acts committed with intent to destroy, in whole or in part, a national, ethnical, racial or religious group, as such:
>
> (a) Killing members of the group;
> (b) Causing serious bodily or mental harm to members of the group;
> (c) Deliberately inflicting on the group conditions of life calculated to bring about its physical destruction in whole or in part;
> (d) Imposing measures intended to prevent births within the group;

[34] Ibid., 7.

[35] Ibid., 19.

[36] Raphael Lemkin (ed. Donna Lee Frieze), *Totally Unofficial* (Yale University Press, 2013) 217.

(e) Forcibly transferring children of the group to another group.[37]

The main elements of the definition are briefly considered below. We do not set out to comprehensively assess the whole range of jurisprudence, emanating from decisions and judgements of courts and tribunals, but rather outline some of the main elements and issues. The footnotes indicate where a fuller account of some of the jurisprudence may be found.[38] Our brief explanation is aimed at equipping the reader with some basic knowledge of the different elements and manifestations of genocide.

We now consider the protected groups, the prohibited acts (*actus reus*), and the mental state (*mens rea*).

2.1   The Protected Groups

Genocide is a crime perpetrated against a group, targeting group identity, and not against an individual. Indeed, in the International Criminal Tribunal for the former Yugoslavia (ICTY) case of Radovan Karadžić (who served as the president of Republika Srpska during the Bosnian War and was later convicted of genocide, crimes against humanity, and war crimes) the judgement emphasised that '*the crime of genocide pertains to the destruction of a race, tribe, nation, or other group with a particular positive identity, not to the destruction of various people lacking a distinct identity.*'[39]

Writing on the differences between genocide and crimes against humanity,[40] Philippe Sands asked '*Does it matter whether the law seeks to*

---

[37] This definition of genocide is mirrored in Article 6 of the Rome Statute, (the treaty which in 1998 established the International Criminal Court, came into force in 2002 and has 123 State Parties).

[38] See for example: William A. Schabas, *Genocide in International Law. The Crime of Crimes* (Cambridge University Press: Cambridge, 2009); Marco Odello and Piotr Łubiński (eds.), *The Concept of Genocide in International Criminal Law Developments After Lemkin* (Routledge, 2021); Paul Behrens and Ralph Henham (eds.), *The Criminal Law of Genocide. International, Comparative and Contextual Aspects* (Routledge, 2016); Philippe Sands, *East West Street* (W&N, 2017).

[39] *Prosecutor v Karadžić*, Judgment, IT-95-5/18-T (24 March 2016) 541.

[40] Crimes against humanity are international crimes defined in Article 7 of the Rome Statute of the International Criminal Court. Contrary to genocide, crimes against humanity do not need to target a specific group.

protect you because you are an individual or because of the group of which you happen to be a member?'[41] He drew on the work of Lemkin and Sir Hersch Lauterpacht QC, a prominent British international lawyer and judge at the International Court of Justice, commenting that: *'Despite their common origins, and the shared desire for an effective approach, Lauterpacht and Lemkin were sharply divided as to the solutions they proposed to a big question: How could the law help to prevent mass killing? Protect the individual, says Lauterpacht. Protect the group, says Lemkin.'*[42] While one should strive for both, as it stands international law imposes the duty to prevent genocide, and as such, the targeting of a group is a crucial consideration.[43]

The Genocide Convention articulates four types of groups the convention exclusively applies to: national, ethnic, racial, and religious groups. For the definition of genocide to be met, one would have to ensure that the targeted people are both from a distinct group and one of the four that are identified.

There are two ways to establish this: either by applying objective criteria,[44] or on the basis of subjective identification. The subjective test to determine whether the group qualifies within Article II determination depends on whether the *perpetrator* believed that the victims belonged to a national, ethnic, racial, or religious group. In the ICTY case of Goran Jelisić, the Bosnian Serb policeman, who described himself as *'the Serb Adolf Hitler'*, the Tribunal found that *'it is more appropriate to evaluate the status of a national, ethnical or racial group from the point of view of those persons who wish to single out that group from the rest of the community.'*[45]

---

[41] Philippe Sands, *East West Street* (W&N, 2017).

[42] Ibid.

[43] See Sect. 3.1 on current attempts to introduce a duty to prevent crimes against humanity.

[44] *Nottebohm (Liechtenstein v. Guatemala)* (Merits) [1955] ICJ Rep. 4. See also: *Prosecutor v. Akayesu*, 511. The Chamber defined a national group as 'a collection of people who are perceived to share legal bonds based on a common citizenship, coupled with reciprocity of rights and duties.' According to the same judgement, an ethnic group is one who's 'members share a common language or culture', a racial group is 'based on the hereditary physical traits often identified with a geographical region, irrespective of linguistic, cultural, national or religious factors' and a religious group is one 'whose members share the same religion, denomination or mode of worship.' Ibid., 513–516.

[45] *Prosecutor v Jelisic*, ICTY-1-95-10, 70.

In another case referred to the International Criminal Tribunal for Rwanda (ICTR), that of Clément Kayishema and Obed Ruzindana (who were both found guilty of genocide), the Tribunal held that it was sufficient that a group was '*identified as such by others, including perpetrators of the crimes*'[46] and that the determinative factor was the perpetrator's subjective knowledge or belief about the group identity of the victims.

In the ICTR case of George Rutaganda (who was the second vice president of the Hutu Militia), the Tribunal made the very same point, saying that:

> the Chamber notes that for the purposes of applying the Genocide Convention, membership of a group is, in essence, a subjective rather than an objective concept. The victim is perceived by the perpetrator of genocide as belonging to a group slated for destruction. In some instances, the victim may perceive himself/herself as belonging to the said group.[47]

Interestingly, the judges also made the point that '*the concepts of national, ethnical, racial and religious groups have been researched extensively and that, at present, there are no generally and internationally accepted precise definitions thereof*.' That being so, one might conclude that for the purposes of the Genocide Convention, it is more sagacious to use the subjective perceptions of the accused rather than objective categorisation.

It is noteworthy that the four protected groups include neither social groups nor political groups. As such, the cases of Cambodian and North Korean atrocities, Mao's Cultural Revolution (still the largest state-sponsored crime in history), and Stalin's political purges and liquidation of the Kulaks may fall short of the legal definition of genocide in Article II of the Genocide Convention.

While the Genocide Convention specifically refers to just four groups, the drafters also considered whether political groups should be covered. This proposal, however, was opposed by the Soviet Union and others; it was therefore not included.[48] As a consequence (and notwithstanding the appalling and egregious atrocities in countries such as North Korea, which

---

[46] *Prosecutor v Kayishema and Ruzindana*, Judgment, ICTR-95-1-T (21 May 1999) 98.

[47] *Prosecutor v Rutaganda*, Trial Chamber I, ICTR 96-3 (6 December 1999) 56.

[48] Robert Gellately and Ben Kiernan, *The Specter of Genocide: Mass Murder in Historical Perspective* (Cambridge University Press: Cambridge, 2003) 267.

involve the specific targeting of political opposition for annihilation) the definition of groups within the Genocide Convention would not allow for acts against political groups to be deemed genocide. The UN Commission of Inquiry on Human Rights in the Democratic People's Republic of Korea found the North Korean regime to be *'without parallel'* and judged its actions to be *'crimes against humanity'* and *'unspeakable atrocities'*—but not genocide (although subsequent studies have reopened this question).[49]

2.2   Actus Reus: Prohibited Acts to Bring About Genocide

When we think of genocide, we think of the Nazi atrocities. We think of mass graves. We think of seeing bodies on the streets. Indeed, killing is often erroneously considered to be the ultimate determinant of genocide; it is but one of them. Killing is the most universally recognised prohibited act to bring about genocide. However, Article II of the Genocide Convention identifies four other prohibited acts that must always be considered. This preoccupation with killing might be understandable since the genocides of the past infamously employed this genocidal method. However, any inquiry into genocide must not stop there. In the ICTR case of *Akayesu*, the Tribunal stated that:

> Contrary to popular belief, the crime of genocide does not imply the actual extermination of group in its entirety but is understood as such once any one of the acts mentioned in Article II is committed with the specific intent to destroy "in whole or in part" a national, ethnical, racial or religious group.[50]

The five prohibited acts have been at the core of all modern genocides. While the manifestations of these five acts may be diverse, they ought to be strictly construed and interpreted in the light of the extant jurisprudence.

That said, the five prohibited acts do require specific discussion.

---

[49] See Sect. 2 in Chapter 7.

[50] *Prosecutor v Akayesu*, ICTR-96-4-T (2 September 1998) 497.

2.2.1   Killing Members of the Group

(Unlawful) killing is the most recognised prohibited act to bring about genocide and is understandably considered the most shocking, particularly since the killings concern whole communities, including the elderly, mothers, and children—non-combatants. The figures for genocidal killing over the twentieth century are monumental, amounting to many millions of deaths, with precise figures hard to calculate. There have been many other mass killings in the twentieth century that would *not* meet the definition of genocide, either because those killed were not part of a specific national, ethnical, racial, or religious group, or because of the lack of specific intent.

How many killings are required to meet the threshold?

Genocide as defined by the Genocide Convention and customary international law does not necessarily entail the immediate destruction of the group by mass slaughter; in fact, no killings at all are necessarily 'required' if at least one or more of the five prohibited genocidal acts are proven. Furthermore, as the Tribunal in the ICTY case of *Radovan Karadžić* confirmed 'a numeric assessment of the number of people killed is not required for the *actus reus* of genocide to be established.'[51]

Killing '*as an act of genocide requires proof of a result.*'[52]

2.2.2   Causing Serious Bodily or Mental Harm to Members of the Group

Causing serious bodily or mental harm to members of the group means '*an intentional act or omission which causes serious bodily or mental harm to members of the protected group and requires proof of a result*'[53] and may include torture, inhuman or degrading treatment or punishment, rape and sexual violence, serious injuries to external and internal organs.[54] The harm must go '*beyond temporary unhappiness, embarrassment or humiliation.*'[55]

---

[51] *Prosecutor v Karadžić*, Judgment, IT-95-5/18-T (24 March 2016) 542.

[52] Ibid.

[53] Ibid., 543.

[54] Ibid., 545.

[55] Ibid., 543.

For the purposes of Article II b, serious bodily or mental harm may flow from other acts that may not, in and of themselves, be prohibited acts of genocide—for example:

> Enslavement, starvation, deportation and persecution ... and by their detention in ghettos, transit camps and concentration camps in conditions which were designed to cause their degradation, deprivation or deny their rights as human beings, and to suppress them and cause them inhumane suffering and torture.[56]

Psychological harm, while not having to be permanent or irreversible, must result '*in a grave and long-term disadvantage to a person's ability to lead a normal and constructive life.*'[57]

Rape and sexual violence are acts constituting serious bodily and/or mental harm and, if perpetrated with the intent to destroy the group, would amount to genocide. For example, the Trial Chamber in the ICTR case of Édouard Karemera and Mathieu Ngirumpatse (two Rwandan politicians) found that '*the sexual assaults, mutilations, and rapes that Rwandan Tutsi women were forced to endure from April to June 1994 certainly constituted acts of serious bodily and mental harm*' under Article II b.[58] As affirmed in the ICTR case of Jean-Paul Akayesu, rape and sexual violence:

> certainly constitute infliction of serious bodily and mental harm on the victims, and are even ... one of the worst ways of inflicting harm on the victim as he or she suffers both bodily and mental harm... These rapes resulted in physical and psychological destruction of Tutsi women, their families and their communities. Sexual violence was an integral part of the process of destruction, specifically targeting Tutsi women and specifically contributing to their destruction and to the destruction of the Tutsi group as a whole.[59]

---

[56] *Attorney General of the Government of Israel v Eichmann*, 36 ILR 5 (District Court of Jerusalem, 1961).

[57] *Prosecutor v Karadžić*, Judgment, IT-95-5/18-T (24 March 2016) 543. See also *Prosecutor v Krstić*, Judgment, IT-98-33-T (2 August 2001) 513.

[58] *Prosecutor v Karemera and Ngirumpatse* (Trial Judgment) ICTR-98-44C-T (20 September 2006) 1609, 1666.

[59] *Prosecutor v Akayesu*, Judgment,, ICTR-96-4-T, 731.

This is particularly important since rape and sexual violence are often used as a deliberate military strategy for various purposes, including to demoralise an enemy. Notably, rape and sexual violence have a particular impact in rural, traditional communities. In Rwanda and Darfur, these practices destroyed family cohesion and the social fabric, acting as a second, long-term genocide. We know from the testimony of soldiers and victims that rape is used in a calculated and systematic way *because* it causes such long-term damage to whole societies—let alone to the survivors. This perception constitutes a significant shift from when rape and sexual violence were considered to be simply inevitable by-products of war. This has allowed for the prosecution of sexual violence in conflict as international crimes.

2.2.3 Deliberately Inflicting on the Group Conditions of Life Calculated to Bring About Its Physical Destruction in Whole or in Part

This prohibited act of genocide deliberately inflicts conditions of life that would, as a matter of objective probability, lead to death or physical or mental harm of the targeted people.[60] The methods of destruction do not need to immediately kill the members of the group, but ultimately aim for their physical destruction.[61] This provision *'does not require proof … that a result was attained; as such, it does not require proof that the conditions actually led to death or serious bodily or mental harm of members of the protected group.'*[62]

The Tribunal in the ICTY case of Radovan Karadžić confirmed that these methods can take the form of *'subjecting the group to a subsistence diet; failing to provide adequate medical care; systematically expelling members of the group from their homes; and generally creating circumstances that would lead to a slow death such as the lack of proper food, water, shelter, clothing, sanitation, or subjecting members of the group to excessive work or physical exertion.'*[63] The Death Marches of the Nazis are examples of conditions calculated to bring about destruction. Subjecting people in

---

[60] *Prosecutor v Karadžić*, Judgment, ICTY-95-5/18-T (24 March 2016) 546–548.

[61] *Prosecutor v Akayesu*, Judgment ICTR-96-4-T, 505.

[62] *Prosecutor v Karadžić*, Judgment, ICTY-95-5/18-T (24 March 2016) 546.

[63] Ibid., 547.

camps to starvation or heavy labour, or denying humanitarian access to communities in urgent need of such assistance would also qualify.

2.2.4   Imposing Measures Intended to Prevent Births Within the Group

The imposition of measures intended to prevent births within the group not only focuses on the ultimate result (that is, the reduction of births)[64] but also on acts leading towards such reductions, including '*sexual mutilation, the practice of sterilisation, forced birth control, and separation of the sexes and prohibition of marriages.*'[65] Similarly, rape and other forms of sexual violence are recognised as methods which may constitute genocide under this prohibited act.

This was affirmed in the ICTR case of Jean-Paul Akayesu, who was infamous for allowing the use of rape and sexual violence in his military advances. As a result, half a million women were raped. The intent behind the use of rape and sexual violence in that case was to breed out the Tutsi people and increase the numbers of Hutus—this, paired with the killing of the men, was a highly effective way of bringing about the destruction of the community in whole or in part. As noted in the judgement:

---

[64] International Criminal Court, Report of the Preparatory Commission for the International Criminal Court. Addendum. Part II, Finalised draft text of the Elements of Crimes, 2 November 2000, PCNICC/2000/1/Add.2, 7.

See also: Raphael Lemkin, 'Genocide as a Crime Under International Law' (1947) 41 *American Journal of International Law* 145–151. 'Fn 6. See especially statements by Sir Hartley Shawcross and Sir David Maxwell Fyfe for the British prosecution; and Champetier de Ribes and Dubost for the French prosecution, who elaborated at length and with great eloquence on the crime of genocide in the course of the Nuremburg proceedings. The concept of genocide was also used recently by the Chief of Counsel in subsequent Nuremberg proceedings, Brigadier General Telford Taylor, in the case against the Nazi doctors [offsite link] who [p. 148] experimented in order on human camps. In this classical genocide ease the defendants practiced experiments in order to develop techniques for outright killings and abortions, on one hand, and sterilisations and castrations on the other hand. The present writer calls the first "ktonotechnics" (from the Greek ktonos meaning murder) and the second "sterotechnics" (from the Greek steiros meaning infertility). Both "ktonotechnics" and "sterotechnics" were considered by the Nazi as very essential and served the purposes of genocide in its physical and biological aspects. As to various aspects and techniques of genocide see the writer's volume cited in Chapter, IX, Genocide. If and when "sterotecnics" achieves scientific character and is free of its genocidal purposes it could then qualify as sterology (the science of sterilisation).'

[65] *Prosecutor v Akayesu*, Judgment, ICTR-96-4-T (2 September 1998) 506.

In patriarchal societies, where membership of a group is determined by the identity of the father, an example of a measure intended to prevent births within a group is the case where, during rape, a woman of the said group is deliberately impregnated by a man of another group, with the intent to have her give birth to a child who will consequently not belong to its mother's group.[66]

The use of rape and sexual violence had a long-lasting impact on the victims: '... *rape can be a measure intended to prevent births when the person raped refuses subsequently to procreate, in the same way that members of a group can be led, through threats of trauma, not to procreate.*'[67]

As such, rape is not only used as a method of causing physical and/or mental harm to women, but also with the explicit aim of impairing ability to procreate either via that inflicted trauma, by utilising cultural taboos, or by forcible impregnation.

2.2.5 Forcibly Transferring Children of the Group to Another Group

Forcible transfer of children refers to the act of removing children from their families and communities and placing them with other groups. The term '*forcible transfer*' is to be interpreted widely. Transferring children from their families or communities to another group is '*not restricted to physical force, but may include threat of force or coercion, such as that caused by fear of violence, duress, detention, psychological oppression or abuse of power, against such person or persons or another person, or by taking advantage of a coercive environment.*'[68]

Such a removal of children from their families and communities, placing them with another group, is done in order to cut their ties with their communities, culture, and religion and thereby attack their group identity—and so prevent them from continuing to identify with their group as they grow up.

---

[66] *Prosecutor v Akayesu*, Judgment, ICTR-96-4-T (2 September 1998) 507.

[67] *Prosecutor v Akayesu*, Judgment, ICTR-96-4-T (2 September 1998) 508.

[68] International Criminal Court, Report of the Preparatory Commission for the International Criminal Court. Addendum. Part II, Finalised draft text of the Elements of Crimes, 2 November 2000, PCNICC/2000/1/Add.2, 8.

2.3   Mens Rea: Specific Intent to Destroy in Whole or in Part

Not all of the above discussed crimes amount to genocide. For these crimes to meet the legal definition of genocide, they must be carried out with the *specific intent* to destroy a protected group in whole or in part. Indeed, the key element to differentiate genocide from other international crimes is the intention to destroy a protected group. As Philippe Sands explains:

> For Lauterpacht, the killing of individuals, if part of a systematic plan, would be a crime against humanity. For Lemkin, the focus was genocide, the killing of the many with the intention of destroying the group of which they were a part. For a prosecutor today, the difference between the two was largely the question of establishing intent: to prove genocide, you needed to show that the act of killing was motivated by an intent to destroy the group, whereas for crimes against humanity no such intent had to be shown. I explained that proving intent to destroy a group in whole or in part was notoriously difficult, since those involved in such killings tended not to leave a trail of helpful paperwork.[69]

This element of specific intent means that genocide cannot be committed by accident or negligence. It is a crime committed knowingly and wilfully.[70] There must exist the intent to commit one or more of the prohibited acts specified in Article II of the Genocide Convention, as well as an intent to bring about the destruction of a group in whole or in part through that commission. The courts have held the word '*destroy*' to refer to physical or biological destruction.[71] This specific intent, the '*intent to destroy*', distinguishes genocide from other violations of international law, such as crimes against humanity and war crimes.[72] In the

---

[69] Philippe Sands, *East West Street* (W&N, 2017).

[70] See for example: International Law Commission, Report, 48th Session, 6 May–26 July 1996, Doc N A/51/10, 44.

[71] *Prosecutor v Krstic*, Judgment, ICTY-98-33-A 580.

[72] William A. Schabas, *Genocide in International Law: The Crimes of Crimes* (Cambridge University Press: Cambridge, 2009) 836. See also: Kai Ambos, 'What Does 'Intent to Destroy' in Genocide Mean?' (2009) 91 *International Review of the Red Cross* 834.

case of *Prosecutor v Akayesu*, Jean-Paul Akayesu[73] (the Mayor of Taba) was found guilty of genocide by the ICTR. The court noted:

> Genocide is distinct from other crimes in as much as it embodies a special intent or *dolus specialis*. Special intent of a crime is the specific intention, required as a constitutive element of the crime, which demands that the perpetrator clearly seeks to produce the act charged. Thus, the special intent in the crime of genocide lies in *'the intent to destroy, in whole or in part, a national, ethnical, racial or religious group, as such.'*[74]

In addition, the ICTY noted that, while the intent to destroy must extend to the entire group, the targeted group may be a smaller part of the whole—although it must be *'significant enough to have an impact on the group as a whole.'*[75]

Specific intent may be determined directly from the words or actions of alleged perpetrators, or indirectly inferred from the surrounding facts or circumstances in which prohibited acts were committed. *'In assessing evidence of genocidal intent, [a court] should consider whether "all of the evidence, taken together, demonstrates a genocidal mental state", instead of considering separately whether an accused intended to destroy a protected group through each of the relevant acts of genocide.'*[76] For example, in the ICTY case against Major General Radislav Krstić for his part in the Srebrenica massacres, the Tribunal concluded that this specific intent to destroy manifested as follows:

> The Bosnian Serb forces knew, by the time they decided to kill all of the military aged men, that the combination of those killings with the forcible transfer of the women, children, and elderly would inevitably result in the physical disappearance of the Bosnian Muslim population at Srebrenica ... as such and eliminated all likelihood that it could ever re-establish itself on that territory.[77]

---

[73] *Prosecutor v Akayesu*, Judgment, ICTR-96-4 (2 September 1998) 477.

[74] *Prosecutor v Akayesu* (Judgement) ICTR-96-4 (2 September 1998) 498.

[75] *Prosecutor v Krstić* (Appeal) ICTY-98-33-A (19 April 2004) 8.

[76] *Prosecutor v Karadžić*, Judgment, ICTY-95-5/18-T (24 March 2016) 550.

[77] *Prosecutor v Krstić* (Judgement) IT-98-33-T (2 August 2001) 595, 597.

Referring again to the ICTR case of Jean-Paul Akayesu,[78] the specific intent to destroy was inferred from the nature of the atrocities: '*in the absence of a confession from the accused, his intent can be inferred from a certain number of presumptions of fact.*'[79] The Tribunal concluded that in the case '*there is no doubt that considering their undeniable scale, their systematic nature and their atrociousness, the massacres were aimed at exterminating the group that was targeted. Many facts show that the intention of the perpetrators of these killings was to cause the complete disappearance of the Tutsi.*'[80]

This is of particular significance since it will not always be possible to identify specific intent—that is, to infer the actual intentions of the alleged perpetrators—from policies or laws established by the state, or from other official documents. The lack of such evidence, however, does not preclude the recognition of genocide, for the Tribunal clarifies that:

> ... it is possible to deduce the genocidal intent inherent in a particular act charged from the general context of the perpetration of other culpable acts systematically directed against that same group, whether these acts were committed by the same offender or by others. Other factors, such as the scale of atrocities committed, their general nature, in a region or a country, or furthermore, the fact of deliberately and systematically targeting victims on account of their membership of a particular group, while excluding the members of other groups, can enable the Chamber to infer the genocidal intent of a particular act.[81]

In the International Criminal Court (ICC) case of President Omar Hassan Ahmad Al Bashir's genocide in Darfur, the Pre-Trial Chamber considered a litany of evidence. This included official statements and public documents allegedly relating to genocidal policies, as well as the nature and extent of the acts of violence against members of the Fur, Masalit, and Zaghawa ethnic groups. However, evidence from intergovernmental reports and NGO reports on conditions within the camps for internationally displaced people (IDP) and alleged hindrance of humanitarian assistance were also considered as key components to establish genocidal

---

[78] *Prosecutor v Akayesu*, Judgment, ICTR-96-4 (2 September 1998) 477.

[79] Ibid., 477.

[80] Ibid., 118.

[81] Ibid., 477.

intent. In making the determination, reports used included those from the UN Security Council, United Nations Office for the Coordination of Humanitarian Affairs, HRW, press articles, USA Today, Médecins Sans Frontières, individual submissions,[82] including first-hand accounts and statements from Darfur taken in October 2004 by Rebecca Tinsley and Lord Alton (and described in The Independent on 18 October 2004).

We can conclude that in determining genocidal intent there is precedent for the courts considering the acts themselves, patterns of behaviour, and laws, as well as official and unofficial communications from the perpetrators and their organisations.

For a crime to be considered to be genocide, its ultimate aim must be the destruction of the protected group in whole or in part. Here, '*destruction*' means physical or biological destruction. As confirmed in the ICTY case of *Prosecutor v Krstic:*

> Customary international law limits the definition of genocide to those acts seeking the physical or biological destruction of all or part of the group... an enterprise attacking only the cultural or sociological characteristics of a human group in order to annihilate these elements which give that group its own identity distinct from the rest of the community would not fall under the definition of genocide.[83]

What does this phrase '*destruction could be in whole or in part*' actually mean? The Appeal Chamber in the Krstic case noted that the destruction of a portion of the group may be enough, in certain situations, for a finding of genocide:

> The numeric size of the targeted part of the group is the necessary and important starting point, though not in all cases the ending point of the inquiry. The number of individuals targeted should be evaluated not only in absolute terms, but also in relation to the overall size of the entire group. In addition to the numeric size of the targeted portion, its prominence within the group can be a useful consideration. If a specific part of the

---

[82] *The Prosecutor v. Omar Hassan Ahmad Al Bashir*, Decision on the Prosecution's Application for a Warrant of Arrest Against Omar Hassan Ahmad Al Bashir, ICC-02/05-01/09-3 (4 March 2009) 164–189.

[83] *Prosecutor v Krstic*, Case No. IT-98-33-A, Appeal Judgement, 19 April 2004, 25.

group is emblematic of the overall group, or is essential to its survival, that may support a finding that the part qualifies as substantial....[84]

When the destruction does not involve the whole group a specific intent to eradicate the *entire* group must still be present.[85]

3   THE DUTIES TO ADDRESS GENOCIDE—PREVENT AND PUNISH

Article I of the Genocide Convention incorporates the duty to prevent and punish genocide: '*the Contracting Parties confirm that genocide, whether committed in time of peace or in time of war, is a crime under international law which they undertake to prevent and to punish.*' While state parties to the Genocide Convention are bound to comply with the duties in the convention, as the ICJ has repeatedly stated, the Genocide Convention embodies principles that are also part of customary international law.[86] The ICJ has set this out with admirable clarity:

> The origins of the Convention show that it was the intention of the United Nations to condemn and punish genocide as '*a crime under international law*' involving a denial of the right of existence of entire human groups, a denial which shocks the conscience of mankind and results in great losses to humanity, and which is contrary to moral law and to the spirit and aims of the United Nations. The first consequence arising from this conception is that the principles underlying the Convention are principles which are recognized by civilised nations as binding on states, even without any conventional obligation. A second consequence is the universal character both of the condemnation of genocide and of the cooperation required '*in order to liberate mankind from such an odious scourge*'... The objects of such a convention must also be considered. The Convention was manifestly adopted for a purely humanitarian and civilising purpose. It is indeed difficult to imagine a convention that might have this dual character to a greater degree, since its object on the one hand is to safeguard the very

---

[84] *Prosecutor v Krstić* (Appeal) ICTY-98-33-A (19 April 2004) 12.

[85] Pieter N. Drost, *The Crime of State: Book II, Genocide* (A.W. Sythoff: Leyden, 1959) 83.

[86] Application of the Convention on the Prevention and Punishment of the Crime of Genocide (Bosnia and Herzegovina v. Serbia and Montenegro), Judgment, ICJ Reports 2007 (I), 110–111, 161. See also: *Akayesu*, 495.

existence of certain human groups and on the other to confirm and endorse the most elementary principles of morality.[87]

Ultimately, this means that a state is bound by the principles that (1) genocide is a crime under international law and (2) that states have obligations to prevent and punish the crimes, whether they ratified the Genocide Convention or not.

While the states are the duty bearers, international bodies (which consist of states) must play their role in addressing genocide. However, as we will show in subsequent chapters, international bodies have frequently neglected to predict and identify risk factors for genocide; they have failed to intervene, failed to deter, and failed to hold the perpetrators to account. While a proactive response by international bodies is desirable—and who could disagree with the oft-repeated hope that the world should stand united in addressing genocide—we know what has happened (or, rather, failed to happen) in reality.

Our position is that the duties to respond to genocide lie with states. They could act individually or collectively, including through the United Nations. But, as will be explained, that does not happen either.

3.1   The Duty to Prevent

The Genocide Convention imposes a duty to prevent genocide—and says no more than this. It is silent about how state parties are to implement their duty to prevent the occurrence of genocide and, tellingly, does not suggest how prevention should be achieved. The ICJ in its judgement in *Bosnia and Herzegovina v Serbia and Montenegro* clarified the duty to prevent, stating that the duty to prevent:

> … arise at the instant that the state learns of, or should normally have learned of, the existence of a serious risk that genocide will be committed. From that moment onwards, if the state has available to it means likely to have a deterrent effect on those suspected of preparing genocide, or reasonably suspected of harbouring specific intent (*dolus specialis*), it is

---

[87] Reservations to the Convention on the Prevention and Punishment of the Crime of Genocide, Advisory Opinion, ICJ Reports 1951, 23. See also: Application of the Convention on the Prevention and Punishment of the Crime of Genocide (Croatia v. Serbia), Judgment, ICJ Reports 2015, 95.

under a duty to make such use of these means as the circumstances permit.[88]

This means that triggering the duty to prevent does not have to—indeed, cannot—wait until genocide is already being perpetrated. States must act in advance and must act upon the serious risk of genocide.

The duty of third-party states to prevent genocide, which has the same trigger (knowledge of a serious risk of genocide occurring), is dependent upon their political ties and ability to influence the potential perpetrators. As the ICJ stated in its judgement in *Bosnia and Herzegovina v Serbia and Montenegro*:

> Various parameters operate when assessing whether a state has duly discharged the obligation concerned. The first, which varies greatly from one state to another is clearly the capacity to influence effectively the action of persons likely to commit, or already committing, genocide. This capacity itself depends, among other things, on the geographical distance of the state concerned from the scene of the events, and on the strength of the political links, as well as links of all other kinds, between the authorities of that State and the main actors in the events.
>
> The state's capacity to influence must also be assessed by legal criteria, since it is clear that every state may only act within the limits permitted by international law; seen thus, a state's capacity to influence may vary depending on its particular legal position vis-à-vis the situations and persons facing the danger, or the reality, of genocide. On the other hand, it is irrelevant whether the state whose responsibility is in issue claims, or even proves, that even if it had employed all means reasonably at its disposal, they would not have sufficed to prevent the commission of genocide. As well as being generally difficult to prove, this is irrelevant to the breach of the obligation of conduct in question, the more so since the possibility remains that the combined efforts of several states, each complying with its obligation to prevent, might have achieved the result — averting the commission of genocide — which the efforts of only one state were insufficient to produce.[89]

---

[88] *Bosnia and Herzegovina v. Serbia and Montenegro*, Application of the Convention on the Prevention and Punishment of the Crime of Genocide, International Court of Justice, 26 February 2007, 431.

[89] Ibid.

The duty to prevent is conduct-oriented, not result-oriented. As such, '*a state cannot be under an obligation to succeed, whatever the circumstances, in preventing the commission of genocide: the obligation of states parties is rather to employ all means reasonably available to them, to prevent genocide so far as possible.*'[90] Since the duty is conduct-oriented, '*it is irrelevant whether the state whose responsibility is in issue claims, or even proves, that even if it had employed all means reasonably at its disposal, they would not have sufficed to prevent the commission of genocide.*'[91] Ultimately, a state must act to prevent and has a duty to do so.

As set out in Article VIII of the Genocide Convention, states may '*call upon the competent organs of the UN to take such action under the UN Charter as they consider appropriate for the prevention and suppression of acts of genocide or any of the other acts enumerated in article III.*' However, there is no duty to report possible genocide or to call upon the competent organs of the UN to act. Even when (in accordance with Article VIII) a state calls upon the UN to act, the UN has discretion to decide how to respond to the call.

It is noteworthy that the duty to prevent under the Genocide Convention relates to the crime of genocide *only*. Other international crimes, such as crimes against humanity and war crimes, are subject to the Responsibility to Protect: a political commitment to prevent international crimes, but not a legal duty.[92] Currently, there is an attempt being made to introduce a legal duty to prevent crimes against humanity. On 10 November 2019, the UN Sixth Committee adopted Draft Resolution II on Crimes against Humanity, deciding to '*include in the provisional agenda of its Seventy-Fifth session an item entitled "Crimes against humanity" and to continue to examine the recommendation of the Commission.*'[93] At the time

---

[90] *Bosnia and Herzegovina v. Serbia and Montenegro*, Application of the Convention on the Prevention and Punishment of the Crime of Genocide, International Court of Justice, 26 February 2007, 430.

[91] Ibid.

[92] The 2005 World Summit Outcome Document, UN Doc. A/RES/60/1. Paragraphs 138 and 139. Available at: https://www.un.org/en/genocideprevention/about-responsibility-to-protect.shtml.

[93] UN General Assembly, 'Report of the International Law Commission on the work of its seventy-first session. Report of the Sixth Committee' (21 November 2019) UN Doc. A/74/425. The current draft states:

Article 3 General obligations

of writing this manuscript, the UN Sixth Committee was yet to revisit the topic.

3.2   The Duty to Punish

The Genocide Convention is clear that the duty to punish refers to the prosecution and punishment of the perpetrators for their role in genocide. Article III of the Genocide Convention states that the following should be punishable:

a. Genocide
b. Conspiracy to commit genocide
c. Direct and public incitement to commit genocide
d. Attempt to commit genocide
e. Complicity in genocide

Following from Article III, committing genocide is not limited to direct and physical perpetration of the crime, and may, for example, include close and personal supervision of the atrocities.[94] In the ICTR case of *Gacumbitsi*, the Appeals Chamber found that:

> In the context of genocide... "*direct and physical perpetration*" need not mean physical killing; other acts can constitute direct participation in the *actus reus* of the crime. Here, the accused was physically present at the

1. Each State has the obligation not to engage in acts that constitute crimes against humanity.
2. Each State undertakes to prevent and to punish crimes against humanity, which are crimes under international law, whether or not committed in time of armed conflict.
3. No exceptional circumstances whatsoever, such as armed conflict, internal political instability or other public emergency, may be invoked as a justification of crimes against humanity.

Article 4 Obligation of prevention
Each State undertakes to prevent crimes against humanity, in conformity with international law, through:

(a) effective legislative, administrative, judicial or other appropriate preventive measures in any territory under its jurisdiction; and
(b) cooperation with other States, relevant intergovernmental organizations, and, as appropriate, other organizations.'

[94] *Gacumbitsi v the Prosecutor*, ICTR-2001-64-A (7 July 2006) 59–61.

scene of the Nyarubuye Parish massacre, which he "*directed*" and "*played a leading role in conducting and, especially, supervising*". It was he who personally directed the Tutsi and Hutu refugees to separate--and that action, which is not adequately described by any other mode of Article 6(1) liability, was as much an integral part of the genocide as were the killings which it enabled.[95]

Conspiracy to commit genocide, an inchoate offence, concerns an agreement between two or more individuals to commit the crime.[96] In case of conspiracy:

> The existence of such an agreement between individuals to commit genocide (or "*concerted agreement to act*") is its material element (*actus reus*); furthermore, the individuals involved in the agreement must have the intent to destroy in whole or in part a national, ethnical, racial or religious group as such (*mens rea*).[97]

According to Article 25(3) of the Rome Statute, the crime of conspiracy is '*the commission or attempted commission of such a crime by a group of persons acting with a common purpose.*' The crime of conspiracy is punishable even if the result is not achieved.

Direct and public incitement to commit genocide involves:

> ... directly provoking the perpetrator(s) to commit genocide, whether through speeches, shouting or threats uttered in public places or at public gatherings, or through the sale or dissemination, or offer for sale or display of written material or printed matter in public places or at public gatherings, or through the public display of placards or posters, or through any other means of audio-visual communication.[98]

Direct and public incitement to commit genocide is a crime in itself—and it is not necessary to demonstrate that it in fact substantially contributed to the commission of acts of genocide.[99]

---

[95] Ibid.

[96] *Nahimana et al. v the Prosecutor*, ICTR-99-52-A (28 November 2007) 894.

[97] Ibid.

[98] *The Prosecutor v Akayesu*, Case No. ICTR-96-4-T (2 September 1998) 559.

[99] *Nahimana et al. v the Prosecutor*, Case No. ICTR-99-52-A (28 November 2007) 678.

An example is the role and power of Radio Milles Collines in Rwanda, through which the population was manipulated with hate speech in the years running up to the genocide.

The propaganda broadcast on Radio Milles Collines is an example of the centrality of euphemism in genocide, enabling those responsible to deny intent and responsibility. The Tutsi minority were repeatedly called cockroaches in Rwanda, and the audience was fed misinformation about the Tutsi for years.[100] As another example of euphemism, at the Wannsee Conference in 1942 attendees referred to '*The Jewish Question.*'[101]

Euphemism also plays a role when the international community denies knowledge of incipient genocide. Officials can claim, after the killing has begun, that no one could have known what was being prepared in a given country. '*We didn't know they were talking about murdering people when they talked about cockroaches,*' or '*We thought it was just a turn of phrase.*'

Even where genocide is not perpetrated, the perpetrator could be prosecuted for the crime of attempting to commit genocide.[102]

Complicity in genocide applies to a broad range of acts of assistance or encouragement that have '*substantially contributed to, or have had a substantial effect on, the completion of the crime of genocide.*'[103] As such, the accused must have acted intentionally and been aware that they were contributing to the crime of genocide (including all of its material elements).

How should the duty to punish be fulfilled? Article V places an obligation on states to introduce '*the necessary legislation to give effect to the provisions of the [Genocide Convention], and, in particular, to provide effective penalties*' for those responsible. Article VI further provides that:

> Persons charged with genocide or any of the other acts enumerated in article III shall be tried by a competent tribunal of the state in the territory of which the act was committed, or by such international penal tribunal as

---

[100] MIGS, 'Rwanda Radio Transcripts. The Role of Radio'. Available at: https://www.concordia.ca/research/migs/resources/rwanda-radio-transcripts.html.

[101] USHMM, 'Wannsee Conference and the "Final Solution"'. Available at: https://encyclopedia.ushmm.org/content/en/article/wannsee-conference-and-the-final-solution.

[102] *Nahimana et al. v the Prosecutor*, Case No. ICTR-99-52-A (28 November 2007) 678–679.

[103] *The Prosecutor v Semanza*, Case No. ICTR-97-20-T (15 May 2003) 395.

may have jurisdiction with respect to those Contracting Parties which shall have accepted its jurisdiction.

Lastly, the duty to punish is not limited to prosecuting perpetrators in domestic courts but also requires states to cooperate with international tribunals.[104] The ICJ clarified that:

> It is thus to the obligation for states parties to co-operate with the *"international penal tribunal"* (...) For it is certain that once such a court has been established, Article VI obliges the Contracting Parties *"which shall have accepted its jurisdiction"* to co-operate with it, which implies that they will arrest persons accused of genocide who are in their territory — even if the crime of which they are accused was committed outside it — and, failing prosecution of them in the parties' own courts, that they will hand them over for trial by the competent international tribunal.[105]

3.3 The Perpetrators

The duties to prevent and punish the crime of genocide apply to all cases of genocide, whether perpetrated by a state or a non-state actor. A state is to be responsible for its own acts and omissions in breach of the duties required by the Genocide Convention. These include: a duty not to commit genocide or to be complicit in the commission of genocide by other states or non-state actors, a duty to prevent genocide by using all means reasonably available to the state, a duty to punish perpetrators, and a duty to enact legislation to give effect to the provisions of the Genocide Convention.

While states are the primary bearers of the duty to prevent and punish genocide, states themselves can be involved in violations of the obligations under the Genocide Convention. Such violations might occur by way of legislation, policies, or administrative practices. Genocidal acts might be ordered, authorised, or implemented by the state. A state

---

[104] *Bosnia and Herzegovina v Serbia and Montenegro*, Application of the Convention on the Prevention and Punishment of the Crime of Genocide, International Court of Justice, 26 February 2007, 443 ff. See also: Dapo Akande, 'The Impact of the Genocide Convention on the Obligation to Implement ICC Arrest Warrants' in Richard H. Steinberg (ed), *Contemporary Issues Facing the International Criminal Court* (Brill, 2016) 78.

[105] Ibid.

may also become complicit in genocide by virtue of the state's passive support of acts perpetrated by non-state actors. The catalyst is in failing to respond to them adequately (or at all), or in failing to investigate or prosecute—thereby failing to fulfil the state's Genocide Convention obligations.

4   The Question of Genocide Determination

Of themselves, the duties which we have identified lead us to the question of whether states should conduct their own determinations of genocide (and also of other international crimes).

Genocide determination should not be confused and conflated with the determination of such atrocities by courts for the purposes of determining individual criminal responsibility (or by the ICJ to determine state responsibility).[106] The determination of criminal responsibility for international crimes would need to be decided by a competent court or tribunal for the prosecutions to stand.[107]

However, this does not mean that states cannot make their own *interim determinations* of such atrocities. This would be in order to inform their decisions concerning foreign policy and, prior to all such considerations, to determine whether their obligations under international law are engaged (and not to determine the criminal liability of an individual).

Such interim determinations of atrocities are crucial steps in informing a state's response to the atrocities under the duty to prevent and punish. The UN Office on Genocide Prevention and the Responsibility to Protect confirms that '*national legislative and executive authorities have sometimes characterised certain incidents or periods of violence as genocide, following processes that include political assessments alongside legal considerations. These characterisations cannot be treated as authoritative or determinative, at least beyond the states concerned.*'[108] Such an interim determination of genocide does not replace a determination made by international

---

[106] UN Office on Genocide Prevention and the Responsibility to Protect, 'When to Refer to a Situation as 'Genocide'? Guidance 1'. Available at: https://www.un.org/en/genocideprevention/documents/publications-and-resources/GuidanceNote-When%20to%20refer%20to%20a%20situation%20as%20genocide.pdf.

[107] Ibid.

[108] Ibid.

bodies or international judicial bodies. However, they are essential to any eventual determination being made.

The Genocide Convention does not require state parties to conduct their own genocide determination. However, the ICJ makes clear that the duty to prevent is triggered when the state '*learns of, or should normally have learned of, the existence of a serious risk that genocide will be committed.*' Clearly, a state must have effective monitoring and determination mechanisms in place. There is no ambiguity about that. Where states do not establish such monitoring and determination mechanisms, they may fall back to the specious argument of having insufficient relevant knowledge—and use this as a pretext to evade their responsibility to act. But this is contrary to the duty to prevent and the spirit of the Genocide Convention.

Another question arises when considering who else can determine genocide. Several states (including the United Kingdom, since the 1960s), have argued, that it is for '*international judicial systems*' to make the determination. In 1971, the UK Foreign Secretary, Sir Alec Douglas-Home, in answer to a question about genocide in East Bengal (Bangladesh) said that:

> ... in the case of genocide there must first be an accusation, and that must be dealt with first in the courts of the country concerned. Then it must be dealt with in a court under the auspices of the United Nations; but no such court has been set up. Therefore, any accusations of genocide fall on barren ground.[109]

Fifty years later, this same circular argument is used in replies from Foreign Office Ministers to questions from Lord Alton: '*It is a long-standing government policy that any judgements on whether genocide has occurred are a matter for the international judicial system rather than governments or other non-judicial bodies.*'[110] It is an elegant way of passing the parcel and becomes a convenient way of shifting responsibility to act.

This flawed, circular, repetitive argument neglects the fundamental principle that the state is the duty bearer under the Genocide Convention. States that are parties to the Genocide Convention must act to ensure that

---

[109] HC Deb, 2 August 1971, c1072.
[110] HC Dec, 20 April 2016, c959.

the determination is made by a competent body and that decisive steps follow, fulfilling the state's obligations to prevent and punish.

The self-serving reliance on international judicial bodies ignores the reality that some bodies have themselves become compromised by veto-wielding superpowers determined to prevent genocide cases being heard, cases in which they or their allies might be judged as being complicit in the crime.

The UN-established investigative mechanisms, *ad-hoc* tribunals, and the ICC often do not have the mandate to consider the situation and make relevant determinations. Historically, the UN Security Council (despite being reluctant to deal with the question of genocide) was sometimes able to take steps to ensure that such a determination was made. In the case of the mass atrocities in Bosnia and Rwanda, the UN Security Council established Commissions of Experts to collect and analyse the evidence and confirm whether the atrocities amounted to genocide. Once the Commissions of Experts confirmed their findings, the UN Security Council then proceeded to establish *ad-hoc* tribunals to deal with prosecution of the perpetrators.

Commissions of Experts, welcome as they are, accomplish their work long after the violence—and while their role is important in assembling the material with which justice may *eventually* be delivered, setting up these commissions should not be regarded as the limit of our responsibility, or an alternative to preventing ongoing genocide.

This approach changed with the emergence of the ICC.

The ICC was established with the express intention of removing from the UN Security Council the burden of requesting and overseeing the investigation and prosecution of international criminal law violations on an *ad-hoc* basis. However, since the ICC is a treaty-bound court, its jurisdiction is limited. The UN Security Council could refer situations to the ICC. But given the potential complicity and vested interests of certain states with permanent seats on the UN Security Council (and which hold power of veto), the suggestion that these states might refer themselves or their allies for investigation or prosecution borders on the absurd.

Another '*international judicial system*', the ICJ, could also engage with the making of a determination. However, to do so, it would have to be approached by one of the relevant organs—for example, the UN General Assembly, the UN Security Council, other competent organs, or specialised agencies. Alternatively, the ICJ could become relevant if the two states are state parties without reservation on the dispute resolution clause. This option has rarely been used and also requires the willing approval of states that might have a vested interest in deterring such an investigation.

The determination, and recognition, of mass atrocities is not merely a matter of good practice but derives from states' international legal duties—namely, the duties to prevent and punish the crime of genocide—and cannot be abrogated by referring to impotent, inadequate, or non-existent '*international judicial systems.*'

Gregory H. Stanton, former Research Professor in Genocide Studies and Prevention at George Mason University, conducted a study on the perception and effects of using the words '*ethnic cleansing*' or '*genocide.*'[111] His research convincingly argues that recognising mass atrocities that meet the legal definition of genocide as *being* genocide has resulted in a more comprehensive response, including the stopping of such atrocities. Referring to such crimes as '*ethnic cleansing*' did not have the same effect. Empirical research suggests that once a crime is named there is a difference in the way different international crimes are addressed by states.

We would wish to see proactive responses to all international crimes, and not only genocide. However, if, as Stanton argues, labelling international crimes (that meet the legal definition) as genocide can trigger action, then such a determination should be made without hesitation.

Treating genocide as '*the crime above all crimes*' is what Raphael Lemkin and the architects of the Genocide Convention intended. Genocide determination also plays an important role in addressing the issue of genocide denialism. Be clear: denying the occurrence of genocide is invariably aimed at denying justice to the victims and belittling their suffering.

There is no prescribed, defined way in which states should engage with genocide determination. But, as we have explained, in order to be able to fulfil their duties under international law, states must engage in making such an assessment and determination.

---

[111] Gregory H. Stanton, 'Weak Words Are Not Enough,' Testimony to the Subcommittee on Africa, Global Health, and International Organizations of the House Committee on Foreign Affairs (2015). See also: R. Blum R, G.H. Stanton, S. Sagi, E.D. Richter, 'Ethnic Cleansing Bleaches the Atrocities of Genocide' (2008) 18 *European Journal of Public Health* 204–209.

We have examined how four countries, the United States, Canada, the Netherlands, and the UK, approached genocide determination in the case of Daesh atrocities against religious minorities in Syria and Iraq.

4.1   The United States—Conducting Its Own Analysis and Determination

The US State Department conducts its own analysis and determination of genocide. In December 2015, former US Secretary of State, Hillary Clinton, said that although she had been reluctant to use the term '*genocide*' there was now '*enough evidence*' for her to use that word to denounce the murders of religious minorities by Daesh:

> What is happening is genocide, deliberately aimed at destroying not only the lives but wiping out the existence of Christians and other religious minorities in the Middle East in territory controlled by [Daesh].[112]

However, the determination of the atrocities as genocide did not follow for some months. First came significant civil society engagement aimed at ensuring that the evidence of the atrocities was before all those making the important considerations. Indeed, over subsequent months, Congress and the US State Department received a 300-page report detailing more than 1000 instances of Daesh deliberately massacring, killing, torturing, enslaving, kidnapping, and raping Christians, along with the findings of the International Association of Genocide Scholars.[113]

In March 2016, the US House of Representatives, by 393 votes to zero, declared that targeted beheadings, enslavement, mass rape, and other atrocities against Christians and other minorities to be crimes against humanity and genocide.[114] Shortly after, the then US Secretary of State, John Kerry, officially recognised the atrocities perpetrated by

---

[112] Hanna Trudo, 'Clinton Breaks with Obama Over 'Genocide' of Middle East Christians' (29 December 2015) Politico. Available at: https://www.politico.com/story/2015/12/hillary-clinton-christian-genocide-217215.

[113] IAGS, 'An Appeal to the United States Congress from Genocide Scholars'. Available at: https://anca.org/wp-content/uploads/2015/12/IAGS-An-Appeal-to-the-United-States-Congress-from-Genocide-Scholars.pdf.

[114] House Resolution 75. Available at: https://www.govinfo.gov/content/pkg/CREC-2016-03-14/html/CREC-2016-03-14-pt1-PgH1314.htm.

Daesh against religious minorities as genocide.[115] Kerry said that '*naming these crimes is important*'; that Daesh, in targeting these minorities with the purpose of their annihilation, is '*genocidal by self-proclamation, by ideology and by actions*'—in what it says, in what it believes and, indeed, in what it does. He called for criminal charges to be brought against those responsible.[116]

Although the US administration has been more proactive than any other country, successive US administrations have not had a prescribed policy on how to approach the question and have faced criticism for politicising this determination.[117] Most recently, the outgoing Trump Administration and the incoming Biden Administration both determined that depredations in Xinjiang, directed at the Muslim Uyghur population, constitute a genocide. The then Secretary of State Mike Pompeo said: '*I believe this genocide is ongoing, and that we are witnessing the systematic attempt to destroy Uighurs by the Chinese party-state*,'[118] adding that Chinese officials were '*engaged in the forced assimilation and eventual erasure of a vulnerable ethnic and religious minority group.*' His successor, Secretary Antony Blinken, is equally clear. He says: '*the forcing of men, women and children into concentration camps, trying to, in effect, re-educate them to be adherents to the ideology of the Chinese Communist Party, all of that speaks to an effort to commit genocide.*'[119]

However, the United States has been less clear in failing to make such a determination in the case of the Rohingya Muslims, despite overwhelming evidence in support of such a determination. First in 2022, and after significant campaigning of civil society, the US State Department formally recognised the atrocities against the Rihingyas as genocide.

[115] John Kerry, 'Remarks on Daesh and Genocide, US Department of State' (2016). Available at: http://www.state.gov/secretary/remarks/2016/03/254782.htm.

[116] Ibid.

[117] Todd F. Buchwald and Adam Keith, 'By Any Other Name. How, When, and Why the US Government Has Made Genocide Determinations' (2019) USHMM.

[118] See: https://2017-2021.state.gov/determination-of-the-secretary-of-state-on-atrocities-in-xinjiang/index.html.

[119] See: https://www.bbc.co.uk/news/world-us-canada-55723522.

4.2   Canada—Following the UN Determination

On 14 June 2016, the Canadian Parliament debated the issue of the Daesh genocide of religious minorities. 166 voted against and 139 in favour of recognising the atrocities by Daesh as genocide.[120] Parliamentarians opposed to the designation argued that such a recognition should have been made by an independent court and not by politicians. However, after a United Nations body, the International Independent Commission of Inquiry on the Syrian Arab Republic, released a report, ' "*They Came to Destroy*": [*Daesh*] *Crimes Against the Yazidis*,' which confirmed that the atrocities against the Yazidis amounted to genocide, the Canadian Government followed this recognition.

On 16 June 2016, Stephane Dion, the then Minister of Foreign Affairs, made a statement to the Canadian House of Commons confirming Canada's recognition of the Daesh genocide of the Yazidis. Dion called upon the UN Security Council to undertake urgent actions. As a follow-up the Canadian Government promised to send a fact-finding mission to Iraq to establish best practices for helping the Yazidis in Iraq.[121]

In October 2016, the Canadian House of Commons unanimously passed a motion recognising the Daesh genocide against the Yazidis and called upon the government to open the doors for the Yazidi refugees within the following four months.

4.3   The Netherlands—Obtaining Expert Opinions

The Dutch Parliament initially refused to engage with the question of genocide determination, relying on the argument that it is not for politicians to do so. In 2016, because of significant pressure from politicians, and, above all, from civil society, the Dutch Government requested an expert legal opinion on whether the Daesh atrocities amount to genocide and whether politicians could deal with the question of genocide determination. In December 2017, based on this legal opinion, the Dutch Government published a statement confirming that the Daesh atrocities

[120] House of Commons, 42nd Parliament, 1st Session, Number 72, 14 June 2016, http://www.parl.gc.ca/HousePublications/Publication.aspx?Language=E&Mode=1&Parl=42&Ses=1&DocId=8365546.

[121] House of Commons, 42nd Parliament, 1st Session, Number 74, 16 June 2016. See: http://www.parl.gc.ca/HousePublications/Publication.aspx?Language=E&Mode=1&Parl=42&Ses=1&DocId=8377402.

are likely to amount to genocide—and also clarified that politicians may determine genocide, if supported by evidence.

The opinion obtained from the experts further confirmed that politicians could and should engage with the question. Indeed, they should not be hindered in making such a recognition, simply because a court has not made such a decision. The expert opinion confirmed that both governments and parliaments could use the term *'genocide'* or *'crimes against humanity'*; however, they should act with caution and consideration with regard to two main issues. First, such a determination should be based on a thorough investigation establishing all of the facts. Secondly, while the determination of genocide (or crimes against humanity) by an international body is preferable, the lack of such a recognition should not prevent or delay domestic determinations.

The expert opinion emphasised the necessity and importance of determination of genocide as the first step towards fulfilling the obligation to prevent. However, the determination should not be seen as necessary to trigger the obligation. The obligation should be triggered when *'there is a reliable indication of a serious risk of genocide,'* even if there is a degree of uncertainty. The expert opinion concluded that genocide is not necessarily more severe than crimes against humanity, and so proposed not to distinguish between the two when considering the duty to prevent—thus triggering the duty to prevent whenever genocide or crimes against humanity are suspected.[122] However, it is important to note that there is no basis for this under international law.

---

[122] A translation of the key points from the Dutch Government's 22 December letter:

Parliaments, as opposed to governments, have a higher tendency to make findings regarding such situations of mass atrocities. According to CAVV and EVA, such a selective approach is politically risky.

Historical and current situations of mass atrocities should not be treated alike. The determination of "genocide" in historical situations is aimed at providing a degree of "comfort". On the contrary, in case of a current situation of such mass atrocities, the overriding objective is the prevention of the crimes or their escalation.

CAVV and EVA confirmed that parliaments should not be hindered in making such a recognition, only because a court has not made the decision. However, CAVV and EVA emphasised the difference between governments and parliaments making such recognition, with the parliamentary recognition bearing no particular weight under international law.

CAVV and EVA confirmed both governments and parliaments could use the term 'genocide' or 'crimes against humanity.' Nonetheless, they should act with caution and consideration to two main issues. First, such a determination should be based on a thorough fact-finding investigation. Second, while the international

4.4   The United Kingdom—Relying on International Judicial Bodies or Competent Courts

British Parliamentarians were very proactive in calling for genocide determination in the case of Daesh. In December 2015, 75 members of both Houses sent a joint letter to the Prime Minister calling on the government to recognise the Daesh atrocities as genocide. The former commander of the UK's armed forced and the former head of the UK's intelligence service were among those who signed the letter, which stated: *'there is no doubt in our minds that the targeting of Christians and other religious minorities by Daesh falls within that definition.'*[123] The letter insisted: *'this is not simply a matter of semantics. There would be two main benefits from the acceptance by the UN that genocide is being perpetrated.'*[124] The first is that those responsible would one day face a day of judicial reckoning. The second is that it would require the 152 states who have signed the

determination of genocide or crimes against humanity is preferable, the lack of such recognition should not prevent or delay domestic, or 'national,' determinations.

CAVV and EVA further considered the legal obligations flowing from the determination of 'genocide' under the 1948 UN Convention on the Prevention and Punishment of the Crime of Genocide, namely, to prevent and punish. They considered that the obligation to punish is broader than only conducting domestic prosecutions and includes the cooperation with international tribunals.

The obligation to 'prevent' is subjected to limitations of the UN Charter. The mere obligation is not equivalent to an obligation to engage in a military intervention or justify the use of force in another state.

CAVV and EVA explained that genocide is not necessarily more severe than 'crimes against humanity' and so proposed not to distinguish both at the prevention phase. This means that the duty to prevent should be triggered whenever 'genocide' or 'crimes against humanity' are suspected.

CAVV and EVA emphasised the necessity and importance of determination of genocide as the first step towards fulfilling the obligation to prevent. However, the determination should not be seen as necessary to trigger the obligation. The obligation should be triggered when 'there is a reliable indication of a serious risk of genocide,' even if there is a degree of uncertainty.

See: https://www.worldwatchmonitor.org/2018/01/netherlands-joins-un-security-cou ncil-shine-light-genocide/

[123] Letter from 55 Parliamentarians to Prime Minister David Cameron, 'Genocide Perpetrated by Daesh/ISIS Against Minorities' 21 December 2015. Available at: https://www.david-davies.org.uk/sites/www.david-davies.org.uk/files/rt_hon_david_ cameron_mp.pdf.

[124] Ibid.

convention to step up to the plate and, *'face up to their duty to take the necessary action to "prevent and punish" the perpetrators.'*[125]

Alongside that letter, a debate was triggered in the House of Lords when Lord Alton, along with Lord Forsyth and Baroness Cox, called a vote after the government refused to accept that Parliament could determine events in Iraq to be a genocide. Undeterred, the question was then put in a motion to the House of Commons. On 20 April 2016, the House of Commons overwhelmingly passed a motion moved by the Member of Parliament for Congleton, Fiona Bruce M, stating:

> That this House believes that Christians, Yazidis, and other ethnic and religious minorities in Iraq and Syria are suffering genocide at the hands of Daesh; and calls on the Government to make an immediate referral to the UN Security Council with a view to conferring jurisdiction upon the International Criminal Court so that perpetrators can be brought to justice.

Nevertheless, the UK Government did not act on the motion and has failed to make any determination of genocide. Indeed, the UK Government does not have any formal mechanism for genocide determination (even for a preliminary finding of genocide) and relies on the invocation of international judicial systems or competent courts. Ad nauseam, government ministers in both Houses repeat the mantra that:

> It is a long-standing government policy that any judgements on whether genocide has occurred are a matter for the international judicial system rather than governments or other non-judicial bodies.[126]

When asked by Lord Alton whether and how the UK Government would engage international judicial bodies on the issue of Daesh atrocities, they replied that *'we are not submitting any evidence of possible genocide against Yazidis and Christians to international courts, nor have we been*

---

[125] Ibid.

[126] See for example: Response to a WPQ for Foreign and Commonwealth Office UIN HL1255, tabled on 18 July 2016. Available at: https://questions-statements.parliament.uk/written-questions/detail/2016-07-18/HL1255.

asked to.'[127] This despite the fact that the duty to punish incorporates cooperation with international tribunals.

As for referring this matter to the ICC, a Foreign Office Minister said: '*I understand that, as the matter stands, Fatou Bensouda, the chief prosecutor (of the ICC), has determined not to take these matters forward.*'[128] This despite the fact that, in her address, the Chief Prosecutor clearly stated that: '*the decision of non-party states and the UN Security Council to confer jurisdiction on the ICC is, however, wholly independent of the Court.*'[129] This is a frustrating and circular argument, leaving unanswered the question of who is to engage on the issue of genocide determination.

When challenged about this the then Foreign Secretary, Boris Johnson MP, told the readers of The Daily Telegraph, that '*[Daesh] are engaged in what can only be called genocide… though for some baffling reason the Foreign Office still hesitates to use the term genocide.*'[130] However, seven years after the atrocities by Daesh, for the same baffling reasons, the UK Government has not engaged international judicial bodies to make such a determination.

To its credit, the UK Government led the work on the UN Security Council Resolution 2379 to establish an investigative mechanism into Daesh atrocities in Iraq, but did this without engaging on the issue of genocide determination (despite such an approach having been taken in the cases of Bosnia and Rwanda). This suggests that the UK's baffling position is that the determination is *not needed*, rather than that it is for international judicial bodies to do so. Otherwise, the UK would have been more proactive in seeking such a determination. The UK Government has not taken any steps to ensure that the issue is indeed considered by an international judicial body.

In subsequent chapters we analyse this further and consider a possible approach in the case of the Burmese military's genocide against the

---

[127] See: Response to a WPQ for Foreign and Commonwealth Office UIN HL4327, tabled on 8 December 2015. Available at: https://questions-statements.parliament.uk/written-questions/detail/2015-12-08/hl4327.

[128] House of Lords Debate, 16 December 2015, c2146.

[129] ICC, Statement of the Prosecutor of the International Criminal Court, Fatou Bensouda, on the alleged crimes committed by ISIS (8 April 2015). Available at: https://www.icc-cpi.int/Pages/item.aspx?name=otp-stat-08-04-2015-1.

[130] Boris Johnson, 'Bravo for Assad—He Is a Vile Tyrant, but He Has Saved Palmyra' *The Daily Telegraph* (27 March 2016).

Rohingyas. We outline how the UK could address the issue by implementing the provisions of the Genocide Determination Bill, or other legislative measures such as the Genocide Amendment to the Trade Bill 2021.

PART II

Genocides of Today

'Tolerating genocide is an admission of the principle that one national group has the right to attack another because of its supposed racial superiority.'

Raphael Lemkin

In his closing speech at the International Military Tribunal in Nuremberg, Sir Hartley Shawcross, the Chief British Prosecutor—and Raphael Lemkin's contemporary—trenchantly insisted that the rule of law was a guarantor against repeated cycles of atrocity crimes:

> In all our countries, when perhaps in the heat of passion or for other motives which impair restraint, some individual is killed, the murder becomes a sensation. Our compassion is roused, nor do we rest until the criminal is punished and the rule of law vindicated. Shall we do less when not one but 12 million men and women and children are done to death, not in battle, not in passion, but in a cold calculated deliberate attempt to destroy nations and races.[1]

Shawcross reminded his generation that, in the future, such tyranny and brutality could only be resisted, 'not based merely on military alliances,

---

[1] Sir Hartley Shawcross, Nuremburg War Crimes Tribunal, Nuremberg Trial Proceedings Volume 3, 12th Day, 4 December 1945. Available at: https://avalon.law.yale.edu/imt/12-04-45.asp.

but grounded, and firmly grounded, in the rule of law.'[2] As we have suggested in the preceding chapter, the firm foundations envisaged by Lemkin were never dug very deeply and have become decidedly shaky. The law which he put in place in 1948 has been honoured only in its breach.

Since entering Parliament forty years ago, and on over 300 occasions in the past twenty years, Lord Alton, in speeches, or Parliamentary Questions, has raised examples of genocide and the failure to respond adequately—repeatedly demonstrating how the law itself cannot deliver on the promise of Never Again.

In 1979, just weeks after being elected to the House of Commons, and perhaps in a portent of things to come, Lord Alton raised the atrocities occurring in Cambodia. He followed up questions and letters to Ministers in a long speech on 6 December 1979 and criticised the political establishment in the United Kingdom and United States as 'partners in crime' by failing to recognise Pol Pot's *'atrocious acts and barbaric acts'* for which the Khmer Rouge were responsible: *'The present government and their predecessors failed to speak up.'* He called for *'an international solution to save the needless bloodshed of yet more people in that troubled country.'*

Throughout the autumn of 1979, as reports of the atrocities appeared in the public domain the government had told him that the important thing was not the recognition or naming of atrocity crimes but the delivery of humanitarian aid. He had pressed Prime Minister Margaret Thatcher to directly raise the atrocities with Pol Pot's allies in China and to do so, during the visit to London of the Chinese leader, Hua Guofeng, and to call on the Chinese Communist Party (CCP) to disassociate themselves from Pol Pot.

The government failed to do that, but six weeks later they changed their mind.

David Alton said that what had really changed was that Chairman Hua's visit was behind them and he was safely back in Beijing—and that their change of mind was more to do with not having wanted to cause disruption to the visit than *'any compassionate or humanitarian motives.'* He said that nothing had changed since the Australian journalist, John

---

[2] Ibid.

Pilger, had written and produced earlier in the year the British Television documentary film, 'Year Zero: The Silent Death of Cambodia'.

David Alton told the Commons that Pilger had reported that Cambodia's survivors were 'mostly starving children. Words like "suffering greater than Biafra" look meaningless on the typewriter. It is impossible to describe the sound and frequency of the cries of emaciated and sick children...'

He said we had 'gone on for months and months talking about what we were going to do to distribute aid and how we were going to play our part. It seems to me like pure crocodile tears.' Cambodia's population had been 7 million in 1970. In 1979, it was 4 million. He warned that by the end of the year there might be only 2 million left.

He accused the government of 'twisting and turning like cats in a bag' and said that for the future they 'must wipe away some of the blood that is on the hands of successive governments who have failed to do anything to disassociate themselves from the bloody murders in Kampuchea.'

He described how at Tuol Sleng 'one of their extermination centres, about 12,000 people were brutally murdered ad then placed in incinerators. They suffered in the same way as people suffered at Auschwitz...we have taken too long before uttering the cries of condemnation murmured in the Chamber tonight.'

Cambodia–Kampuchea—and the Khmer Rouge proved to be an especially bloody milestone in tracing the post-war failure to prevent genocide. But as UK officials have encouraged Ministers of all persuasions to regurgitate the discredited mantra that we have laws and judicial mechanisms in place to deal with genocide and, therefore, all shall be well, it has proved to be an illusion at best and a self-serving deceit at worst. The decision of the current UK Foreign Secretary, Liz Truss, in November 2021, to break with this calculated and cynical posturing and to describe events in Xinjiang as a genocide—in the absence of any court determination—suggests that officials and Ministers—the ones who are expected to mouth these platitudes in the face of gross crimes—are increasingly unsustainable. In 2022, she and Boris Johnson privately agreed to re-evaluate the policy.

The following chapters will look at the genocides perpetrated, or attempted, in the twenty-first century, cases generally accepted to constitute genocide (such as the Daesh atrocities and the atrocities in Myanmar) along with atrocities that show the hallmarks of genocide but have not been recognised as such by states, international bodies, or an independent mechanism (as, for example, the crimes in northern Nigeria), or atrocities that have been developing before our eyes as we were writing this book (as the case of the atrocities against the Uyghurs). Each case study will contain information about the atrocities (correlating the example with the legal definition of genocide), followed by an analysis of the domestic and international responses to the atrocities.

CHAPTER 3

The Chinese Government's Genocide of the Uyghurs

1 Introduction

Through the nineteenth-century Opium Wars to the Rape of Nanking and the horrors of Mao Zedong, China has itself suffered gross human rights violations. Although in its legitimate excoriation of the unpardonable British role, it neglects to point out that among the opponents of the opium wars were notable Parliamentarians including William Gladstone, Benjamin Disraeli and the great free trader, Richard Cobden. He led a four-day House of Commons debate in which he said that, like slave trade, it was unconscionable for the UK to sustain the opium trade. His cross-party coalition defeated the government. The protection and promotion of human rights should be seen as a moral cause. It can never be in a nation's self-interest to see universal freedoms and values trampled upon.

Over the years, Lord Alton and others have challenged the UK Government in relation to human rights violations—not least about reports that up to one million Uyghurs have been sent to forced indoctrination camps. He has frequently asked what representations have been made to the Government of China on these issues.[1] In reply, the UK

---

[1] See for example, WPQ UIN HL10450, tabled on 9 October 2018.

© The Author(s), under exclusive license to Springer Nature Switzerland AG 2022
E. U. Ochab and D. Alton, *State Responses to Crimes of Genocide*, Rethinking Political Violence, https://doi.org/10.1007/978-3-030-99162-3_3

57

Government has admitted to 'serious concerns about human rights violations in Xinjiang and continued reports of the Chinese Government's
deepening crackdown; including credible reports of forced indoctrination
camps and wide-spread surveillance and restrictions targeted at ethnic
minorities.' They insisted that the UK had raised their concerns at the
UN Human Rights Council (of which China is a member).[2] But as the
years have passed evidence of severe human rights violations has accumulated. Mere dialogue with the very regime responsible for the atrocities is
an inadequate response to dire treatment of ethnic and religious groups
including the treatment of Uyghur Muslims, Christians, Falun Gong, and
Tibetan Buddhists. As we shall see, reports that Uyghur Muslims detained
in China have undergone unwanted blood, tissue, and DNA tests and
allegations of state-sanctioned organ harvesting from non-consenting religious prisoners of conscience, including Uyghur Muslims' demands more
than dialogue. The UK Government has repeatedly been made aware of
the issue.[3]

The appalling crimes committed by the Chinese Government against
the Uyghurs should be seen in the context of the enormities committed
by the CCP, with one estimate holding it responsible for the deaths of 50
million Chinese people over the decades. But, undoubtedly, the crimes
against the Uyghurs are an example of the most glaring state-authorised
atrocities in recent history. The ruling party, the CCP, stands accused
of designing, implementing, and systematically, ruthlessly committing
the atrocities. Holding China to account for crimes against humanity
and genocide is a challenge that the international institutions have not
been ready to address, despite the measures put in place in response to
state-authorised atrocities following the Holocaust.

Apart from the limitations of the international law and international
mechanisms, China's position as a twenty-first-century trading super-
power disincentivises opposition and it relies on the difficulty of finding
any state willing to jeopardise their lucrative trading and investment
relationships. This has led to craven self-interest dictating the world's
response. It has also revealed the depth and effectiveness of the Chinese
Government's subversion of UN institutions—most notably the UN
Security Council, the UN General Assembly, the UN Human Rights

---

[2] Ibid.

[3] See for example, WPQ UIN HC185636, tabled on 5 November 2018.

Council, and agencies such as the World Health Organisation—all of which appear increasingly 'wholly owned subsidiaries' of the Chinese Government. In turn, this has hollowed out a rules-based order based on the rule of law and liberal values. The Trump Administration correctly understood the Chinese Government's dismounting of international accountability and its subversion of the UN. However, it hesitated to name atrocity crimes in Xinjiang to be a genocide—and only did so one day before President Trump completed his term of office.

What word does best describe what is happening in Xinjiang?

What word comes to your mind when you hear evidence of a state involved in the destruction of a people's identity; involved in mass surveillance; involved in forced labour and enforced slavery; involved in the uprooting of people, the destruction of communities and families, the prevention of births, the ruination of cemeteries where generations of loved one had been buried? What word comes to mind when you hear of people being forcibly indoctrinated to believe that you, your people, your religion, your culture, never existed—and the certainty that through ethno-religious cleansing, you will cease to exist? Those whose signature is written across these monstrous crimes know that name well, but smugly sleep content, believing that corrupted and compliant self-serving institutions, combined with a loss of nerve in countries which have the privilege of democratic institutions, the rule of law, and human rights, have thus far enabled them to avoid international censure or the risk of being arraigned before a court of law on the charge of genocide.

And how easily we forget.

Recall how, in Europe, bureaucrats identified who was a Jew, confiscated property, used their victims as slave labour, scheduled trains to uproot them from their homes and communities, and deprived them of livelihoods and positions in society; and how German pharmaceutical companies tested drugs on camp prisoners, confiscated personal property, shaved heads, sent hair, jewellery, and other artefacts as trophies, and then made prisoners build their crematoria.

Genocides do not happen overnight. They emerge from a casual indifference to discrimination and persecution, and then from crimes against humanity, it seamlessly morphs into a full-blown genocide.

The current persecution of the Uyghur people began around 2008, when a Uyghur man died in police custody. This triggered protests in Western China. The following year, two Uyghurs were killed in South China, which precipitated rioting in the Uyghur homeland in Xinjiang

Province. During the violence, 197 Han Chinese died. The Chinese Government perceived the unrest as a direct challenge to its authority, and it responded with disproportionate brutality. Instead of trying to bring reconciliation and social harmony, a systematic campaign of repression began, aimed at eliminating the Uyghur culture and the Muslim faith. This has entailed the destruction of religious and cultural buildings, the demonisation of Uyghur people, the obliteration of all symbols of Uyghur identity, and the brutal 're-education' of an entire ethnic group. This ideological programming manifests itself in shipping Uyghur people across China to work as slave labour, dramatically reducing their birth rate, trying to stamp out religiosity, and devising an entire industrial-scale system aimed at brainwashing millions of people.

Paradoxically, the Chinese Government's actions betray how little the CCP leadership in Beijing actually believe their ideology is embraced by their citizens. If people must be forcibly indoctrinated, tortured, and terrorised into praising an institution, at most it can have a fragile legitimacy among its voiceless subjects. The treatment of the Uyghurs also reveals an authoritarian, unimaginative, and corporate mentality that assumes that this ruthless approach will genuinely convert people leading them to abandon their ancient beliefs and culture. The Chinese Government's campaign also betrays a naivety about the human spirit and a bewildering inability to grasp that its actions are counter-productive, pushing future generations of Muslims and Uyghurs into the arms of extremist ideologies.

In 2021, after examining the evidence, the House of Commons Foreign Affairs Select Committee report '*Never Again: The UK's Responsibility to Act on Atrocities in Xinjiang and Beyond*' said the government should '*respect the view of the House of Commons that crimes against humanity and genocide are taking place, and take a much stronger response.*'[4] The House of Lords International Relations and Defence Committee, on which Lord Alton serves, subsequently published its report on '*China, Trade and Security.*' In evidence, Charles Parton, a leading authority, told the inquiry: '*Xinjiang and the genocide—and it is genocide under the UN convention's description—have to be taken into account. This is not just about the sheer goodness and badness aspect but the reputation of companies of ours that are trading with those that are*

---

[4] See: https://committees.parliament.uk/publications/6624/documents/71430/def ault/.

producing materials through forced labour and benefiting from what is going on in Xinjiang.[5]

Each piece of evidence adds to the argument that the atrocities amount to international crimes, and highly likely, genocide. There is a cascade of chilling reports—examining everything from the Australian Strategic Policy Institute's compelling report '*The Architecture of Repression* to *Laundering Cotton*,' the joint report of Sheffield Hallam University and the Helena Kennedy Centre for International Justice; from the joint contribution of Dr Joanne Smith Finley and Dilmurat Mahmut on cultural genocide, which will appear in the forthcoming volume '*The Xinjiang Emergency*,' edited by Michael Clarke; to Dr Adrian Zenz's recent work on the use of population control, separation of families, sterilisations, and abortion to target the Uyghurs; and Darren Byler's book '*In the Camps: Life in China's High-Tech Penal Colony*.'

And then there are the courageous testimonies of the few escapees who risk their lives to break the great wall of silence; and brave decisions by broadcasters and newspaper editors not to be cowed into silence. CNN took the decision to broadcast an interview with a former Chinese police detective who described how Uyghurs had been pulled from their homes, with police officers '*handcuffing and hooding them, and threatening to shoot them if they resisted*.' And the BBC broadcast the testimonies of courageous Uyghur women who described conditions in the concentration camps, including their re-education, rape, and public humiliation by camp guards.

While writing this book, the writers met a Uyghur woman who told them that more than twenty members of her family have disappeared. We heard fearful concerns from witnesses to the Uyghur Tribunal that having given evidence their lives would be at risk and we have taken action to prevent Uyghur refugees from being repatriated to China.

In the face of all this, the response of the UK and international community has been profoundly disappointing. While Muslims around the world are outraged by the treatment of their co-religionists, their leaders have kowtowed to Beijing, seduced by the Belt and Road promise of loans, infrastructure projects, and personal inducements. Leaders of developing nations have been similarly co-opted and muted. At the same time, multinational corporations have set aside any scruples, intent on cashing in

---

[5] See: https://committees.parliament.uk/publications/7214/documents/75842/default/.

on China's phenomenal economic growth. Although their annual reports may boast of their corporate social responsibility projects, their words ring hollow as they disregard the consequences of supporting a supply chain based on slavery.

And the subversion of British institutions—notably great universities—has been sickening. The House of Commons Select Committee on Foreign Affairs is explicit: '*there are substantial research connections between the Chinese organisations responsible for these crimes and UK universities.*' Lamentably, UK institutions care far too little about the origins of dirty money, about the use of slave labour in Xinjiang, or about the nature of the CCP's genocidal state.

2   The Atrocities Against the Uyghurs

Since 2001, on over 400 occasions, Lord Alton has raised violations of human rights and crimes against humanity in the People's Republic of China—and what is happening in Xinjiang should be seen in this wider context. In 2008, in Parliament, he challenged the government to say whether the UK and China human rights dialogue—established in 1997—eight years after the Tiananmen Square massacre—was anything more than window dressing.[6] He wanted to know what benchmarks the UK Government had used to evaluate the success of that process—and asked where human rights figured in China's domestic policies and within its relationship with the rest of the world. He drew attention to the estimated 8000 executions of prisoners carried out annually; pointed to the Chinese Government policy of detention without trial and the wide use of 're-education through labour'; raised further concerns about the failure to implement the UN Convention against Torture and Other Cruel, Inhuman or Degrading Treatment or Punishment and denial of freedom of expression; said that 'internet censorship has intensified, with websites regularly closed down… The BBC news site is inaccessible, and broadcasts are jammed. At least 33 journalists and 50 internet users are currently detained in China.'[7] He continued:

[6] House of Lords Deb, 10 January 2008, c1026.

[7] Ibid.

What a tragedy that Microsoft, Google and Yahoo have all collaborated in the censoring of the web. Microsoft blocks words such as "freedom", "democracy" and "demonstration", while Yahoo deplorably decided to provide to the state information about Shi Tao, a journalist with Contemporary Business News in Hunan province. As a result, he was jailed for 10 years after he released to foreign-based websites an internal Communist Party document, while a Google search for the banned Falun Gong spiritual movement would direct users to a string of condemnatory articles.[8]

In 2009, Lord Alton had the opportunity to travel to Western China and Tibet (with the encouragement of the Dalai Lama) and during that visit met members of the Muslim community at the Great Mosque of Xining, the Dongguan Masjid Mosque, dating from the fourteenth century. One of the four largest mosques in Northwest China, it is the largest and most important mosque in Qinghai Province. Enlarged in 1946, it serves as a reminder of the religious pluralism, which existed within China before the coming of Chinese Communism. In 2019, it was reported that at Dongguan, the CCP had imposed their own officials to replace the Imam and that instead of religious teaching political indoctrination had taken its place.[9] Along with the emasculation of religious observance, even the outward appearance of religious buildings has been altered by the CCP. On a trip to the Nan Guan Mosque in Yin Chuan, the United Kingdom's deputy head of mission in China, Christina Scott, in a tweet, deplored the changes to the religious building, saying: 'Domes, minarets, everything gone. Of course, no visitors are allowed either. So depressing.'[10]

Following his 2009 visit, a report was presented to CCP officials entitled '*Tibet: Breaking the Deadlock*,' which examined the failure to promote reconciliation with the Dalai Lama or to respect religious liberty.[11] It

---

[8] Ibid.

[9] Yuan Wei, 'Party Ideology Replaces Quran in Xining's Dongguan Mosque' Bitter Winter (26 July 2019). Available at: https://bitterwinter.org/party-ideology-replaces-quran-in-xinings-dongguan-mosque/.

[10] Tom Williams, 'China Destroys Domes of Famous Mosques in Bid to Suppress Islam' Metro (2 November 2020). Available at: https://metro.co.uk/2020/11/02/china-destroys-domes-of-famous-mosques-in-bid-to-suppress-islam-13519937/?ito=cbshare.

[11] All Party China Group, 'Tibet: Breaking the Deadlock' (2009). Available at: http://jubileecampaign.org/wp-content/uploads/2009/10/final-pdf_tibet_report.pdf.

recognised that Deng Xiaoping had moved China away from the cruelties of the Cultural Revolution, recalling that in an encounter between the Dalai Lama and Mao Zedong in 1955 Mao had told him 'religion is poison.'[12]

The 2009 report warned that:

> Where a religion and its leaders are vilified, imprisoned, regulated, or driven underground, it turns the adherents of that faith into enemies of the state.
>
> The younger generation of believers, especially, are invariably alienated and radicalised. Their grievance becomes a *causus belli* against the state.
>
> We are mindful that membership of the ruling Communist party still requires a personal disavowal of any religious confession. Membership of the Communist Party of China is a means of social mobility and an informal prerequisite to appointment to political office. The effect of this party membership requirement, therefore, is the inability of religious people to occupy official positions and be duly represented in government as would otherwise naturally be the case.
>
> Furthermore, we are of the view that the tight controls upon religious institutions fail to strike a satisfactory balance between the legitimate regulation of civic institutions and the freedom to appoint and direct administrative and spiritual matters, according to the traditions and dictates of a particular confession.
>
> We were further concerned about restrictions on the extent to which religious expression is permitted and the "patriotic re-education" aimed at qualifying religious belief.[13]

Although, in 2009, there was plenty of evidence of previous attempts to eradicate religion—and religious adherents—and continuing attempts to 're-educate' believers—Deng Xiaoping's reforms had created a more hopeful atmosphere. In 2009, the same year as the visit and Report, the Golden Lampstand Church was built in Shanxi Province—one of the largest evangelical churches in China. In 2018, shocking footage smuggled out of China showed the dynamiting and demolition of the

---

[12] Ibid.

[13] Ibid., 12.

church.[14] But buildings have been the least of it. Over the last four years, we have been seeing report after report shedding light on new evidence of the atrocities perpetrated against the Uyghurs, and others—including Falun Gong practitioners and unregistered Christians.[15] These atrocities are discussed below.

2.1 Forced Incarceration and Indoctrination in 'Re-Education Camps'

Although the first signs had begun to appear over a decade ago, in October 2018, several news outlets reported that Muslims in China were being detained for 're-education' purposes. Knowing what this had led to during Mao Zedong's Cultural Revolution should have set alarm bells ringing. Indeed, it did not take long for the true meaning of this 're-education' to emerge: reports suggesting that China was forcibly converting Muslims by, among other things, forcing them 'eat pork and drink alcohol'[16] and doing so under the pretext of education.

In a letter to US Ambassador to China, Terry Branstad, dated 3 April 2018,[17] Senator Marco Rubio and Congressman Chris Smith cited credible reports that, at the time, between 500,000 and a million people were in or had been detained in the so-called re-education camps in China's Xinjiang Uyghur Autonomous Region. It alleged that this practice of forced indoctrination had become the largest mass incarceration of a minority population in the world today:

---

[14] Benjamin Haas, 'China Church Demolition Sparks Fears of Campaign Against Christians' *The Guardian* (11 January 2018). Available at: https://www.theguardian.com/world/2018/jan/11/china-church-demolition-sparks-fears-of-campaign-against-christians.

[15] See for example: China Tribunal, Judgment (2019).

[16] Gerry Shih and Dake Kang, 'Muslims Forced to Drink Alcohol and Eat Pork in China's 'Re-Education' Camps, Former Inmate Claims' *Independent* (19 May 2019). Available at:
   https://www.independent.co.uk/news/world/asia/china-re-education-muslims-ramadan-xinjiang-eat-pork-alcohol-communist-xi-jinping-a8357966.html

[17] Congressional Executive Commission on China, 'Chairs Urge Ambassador Branstad to Prioritize Mass Detention of Uyghurs, Including Family Members of Radio Free Asia Employees' (3 April 2018). Available at: https://www.cecc.gov/media-center/press-releases/chairs-urge-ambassador-branstad-to-prioritize-mass-detention-of-uyghurs.

Thousands are being held for months at a time and subjected to political indoctrination sessions. Many have reportedly been detained for praying, wearing "Islamic" clothing, or having foreign connections, such as previous travel abroad or relatives living in another country. Reports have emerged of the deaths of detainees in these centres, including the death of a well-known Muslim religious scholar who may have been held in such a facility, and there are reports that torture and other human rights abuses are occurring in overcrowded centres secured by guard towers, barbed wire, and high walls.

Initially, the Chinese Government denied the existence of such 're-education camps.' As evidence slipped out of China, the storyline changed and the Chinese Government said that camps did indeed exist but that they were for educational and training purposes. The treatment of over 1 million people in Xinjiang Uyghur Autonomous Region has rendered normal life for Muslims impossible. Among others, a briefing by CSW describes what it calls the, 'already critical level of fear... Disappearances can happen at any time, to any person, without warning. In such a climate of fear, many Uyghur Muslims have stopped public and communal religious observance and have broken off contact with relatives overseas.'[18]

Over the months, harrowing testimonies were provided by courageous young Uyghur women about the reality of the camps, among them Rahima Mahmut, who had made it her mission to translate and give voice to unspeakable and unconscionable violations. These stories are a rare glimpse into the tightly controlled and secretive world of Xinjiang—where at least one million Uyghur people are interned against their will. But there are other glimpses and other witnesses which do not give us the luxury of claiming we did not know, we weren't aware, and lamely asking, how could it happen?

Another rare escapee provided some answers to that question. Sayragul Sauytbay, a Chinese Muslim of Khazak descent, a teacher by background, was detained by the Chinese Government in 2017.[19] Four armed men

---

[18] CSW, 'China: Mass Arbitrary Detentions in Xinjiang Uyghur Autonomous Region (XUAR)' (October 2018).

[19] David Stavrou, 'A Million People Are Jailed at China's Gulags. I Managed to Escape. Here's What Really Goes on Inside' *Haaretz* (17 October 2019). Available at: https://www.haaretz.com/world-news/.premium.MAGAZINE-a-million-people-are-jailed-at-china-s-gulags-i-escaped-here-s-what-goes-on-inside-1.7994216.

pushed their way into her home, put a black sack over her head, bundled her into a vehicle, and took her to a camp where she was ordered to teach inmates. Ultimately, she escaped from China to Kazakhstan in 2018. Having given her testimony, which placed her life in mortal danger, she was given asylum in Sweden.

In a long interview which inspired a forthcoming biography by an Italian journalist, Sayragul described what she had seen and experienced in one of the Chinese Government camps. She told Haaretz that 'twenty prisoners live in one small room. They are handcuffed, their heads shaved, every move is monitored by ceiling cameras. A bucket in the corner is their toilet. The daily routine begins at 6:00 am. They are learning Chinese, memorising propaganda songs, and confessing to invented sins.'[20] The hands and feet of inmates were shackled all day: 'except when they had to write. Even in sleep they were shackled... They had to recite slogans from posters: Thank you to the Communist Party; I love Xi Jinping.'[21] The daily routine went on until midnight. She said there were about 2500 inmates, the youngest was 13, the oldest 84. She described torture with metal nails; fingernails pulled out; electric shocks and said, 'punishment is constant.'[22] 'Some prisoners were hung on the wall and beaten with electrified truncheons. There were prisoners who were made to sit on a chair of nails. I saw people return covered in blood. Some came back without fingernails.'[23] She described one elderly woman whose skin had been flayed. She said that the prisoners are used for medical experiments: 'some of the men become sterile.'[24]

The determination to erase religion and culture was also described by Sayragul: 'Meat was served on Fridays, but it was pork. The inmates were compelled to eat it, even if they were religiously observant and did not eat pork. Refusal brought punishment.'[25] Of course, the Chinese Government's objective is to erase any trace of Islam, to criminalise ethnic

---

[20] Ibid.

[21] Ibid.

[22] Ibid.

[23] Ibid.

[24] Ibid.

[25] Ted Regencia, 'Uyghurs Forced to Eat Pork as China Expands Xinjiang Pig Farms' *Aljazeera* (4 December 2020). Available at: https://www.aljazeera.com/news/2020/12/4/holdUyghurs-forced-to-eat-pork-as-hog-farming-in-xinjiang-expands.

identity, to eradicate minority languages, and to instil fear by arresting public figures or those representing culture and identity—such as singers, poets, and artists. The clock has been turned back by the CCP and Xi Jinping has embarked on his own version of Mao's Cultural Revolution.

Sauytbay knew that she had to speak for those who she had left behind. She said that she felt compelled to talk about what she had seen and experienced because, as she remarked, 'I cannot forget the eyes of the prisoners, expecting me to do something for them. They are innocent. I have to tell their story, to tell about the darkness they are in, about their suffering.'[26] In March 2020, Sauytbay was honoured for her bravery as among the year's 'Women of Courage.'[27] To this day, she continues to receive threatening phone calls telling her that she should think about the lives of her children. All so very reminiscent of the Gulag stories which Lord Alton heard during his early days as a young MP when travelling in the Soviet bloc, and of the behaviour of the KGB, the Securitate, the Polish UB, the Stasi, the Sigurimi, and all the other agencies of Secret Police empowered by Communist regimes to terrorise and subjugate whole populations—and which so many people in the West, at the time, were unwilling to believe could be true. Chinese Government apologists are no different.[28]

Despite international outcry, evidence suggests that the situation will continue to deteriorate. Among others, Australian Strategic Policy Institute (ASPI) reported that new camps are being built. Reportedly, between July 2019 and July 2020, there have been indications that at least 61 new suspected detention facilities are being constructed with satellite imagery suggesting that at least 14 facilities remain under construction.[29] Approximately 50% are higher security facilities. According to ASPI, this may suggest a shift in the camp's usage from lower security 're-education centres' to higher security prison style facilities. In addition, ASPI reports that satellite imaginary suggests that at least 70 facilities appear to have

[26] Matthew Walther, 'America's Consumer Paradise Means Hell on Earth for Chinese Muslims' *The Week* (23 October 2019). Available at: https://theweek.com/articles/873 455/americas-consumer-paradise-means-hell-earth-chinese-muslims?utm_source=links& utm_medium=website&utm_campaign=facebook.

[27] Ibid.

[28] Ibid.

[29] Nathan Ruser, 'Exploring Xinjiang's Detention System' (2020). Available at: https:// xjdp.aspi.org.au/explainers/exploring-xinjiangs-detention-facilities/.

had internal fencing or perimeter walls removed, and eight camps may have been closed. According to ASPI, 90% of the desecuritised camps were lower security facilities.

What happens inside these camps—designed to strip Uyghurs of their religious and ethnic identity and to replace it with absolute loyalty to the state—is gradually coming to light through eye-witness testimonies of the few who have been able to escape. Escaped Uyghurs attest to degrading treatment, torture, human trafficking, forced labour, forced sterilisation, and forced abortion: all of which need to be urgently assessed by an independent inquiry. As Chinese Government may well be preparing for further waves of forced mass incarceration of ethnic and religious minority groups, states and international institutions must urgently up their game to ensure that the allegations are adequately investigated and the crimes addressed.

Dominic Raab was not exaggerating when he told the UK House of Commons of persecution on an industrial scale.[30] Doubtless the then Foreign Secretary will have been given access to satellite imagery. Modern-day satellites can read car number plates from space and pin-point details and even people. In addition to the pictures that have been released, which show the general outline of camps, it would be instructive to know what further detail led Mr. Raab to say that what is happening is on an industrial scale. By some estimates, there are as many as 400 of these camps. According to Radio Free Asia, 'between March 2017 and February 2018, the [Xinjiang] government listed 5–10-million-yuan (US$760,000 to $1.52 million) tenders for contractors to build nine "burial management centres" that include crematoria in mostly Uyghur-populated areas throughout the region, according to a report listed on the official website of the Xinjiang Production and Construction Corps (XPCC).'[31]

The Chinese Government continues to deny the allegations. Their repeated claim that 're-education' is voluntary, and a welcome liberation, is part of a farrago of lies. In the face of all this, one of the greatest

---

[30] FCDO, Human rights violations in Xinjiang and the government's response: Foreign Secretary's statement (12 January 2021). Available at: https://www.gov.uk/government/speeches/foreign-secretary-on-the-situation-in-xinjiang-and-the-governments-response.

[31] RFA, 'Xinjiang Rapidly Building Crematoria to Extinguish Uyghur Funeral Traditions' RFA (26 June 2018). Available at: https://www.rfa.org/english/news/uyghur/crematoriums-06262018151126.html.

tragedies has been the silence of so many nations who share the religious beliefs of the predominantly Muslim Uyghurs. While witnesses such as Sayragul risk their lives, by giving their testimony, too many political leaders have been cowed into craven silence, fearful of the Chinese Government. Rabbi Mirvis is right to have described 'an unfathomable mass atrocity' but will we accept, like him that 'the responsibility for doing something lies with all of us?'[32]

2.2   Imprisonment and Enforced Disappearance

Separate from the internment camps, the Chinese Government is also using the formal criminal penal system to imprison Uyghurs at an alarming rate, though there is less data on this specific aspect.[33] In terms of both formal imprisonment (with lengthy sentences) and enforced disappearances, these acts target the Uyghur community specifically and may be referenced against the concept of 'substantial' part in the jurisprudence relevant to the destruction of the group. As reported in March 2021:

> There is a growing list of nearly 450 disappeared or imprisoned Uyghur intellectuals from 2016 to the present, including government officials, tech founders, prominent university professors, deans, medical researchers, doctors, journalists, editors, publishers, celebrated artists, poets, linguists, computer engineers, and the like.[34] Many of these guardians of Uyghur culture and identity are subjected to formal, often harsher prisons sentences, and even death sentences,[35] evidencing a deliberate government policy of specifically targeting prominent Uyghur leaders.[36]

The issue requires further consideration and investigation.

[32] Ephraim Mirvis, 'As Chief Rabbi, I Can No Longer Remain Silent about the Plight of the Uyghurs' *The Guardian* (15 December 2020). Available at: https://www.theguardian.com/commentisfree/2020/dec/15/chief-rabbi-silent-plight-Uyghurs-atrocity-china.

[33] Uyghur Human Rights Project, 'Detained and Disappeared: Intellectuals Under Assault in the Uyghur Homeland' (March 2019) 22.

[34] Ibid.

[35] Shepherd, Christian, 'Fear and Oppression in Xinjiang: China's War on Uighur Culture' *Financial Times* (12 September 2019).

[36] Newlines Institute, 'The Uyghur Genocide: An Examination of China's Breaches of the 1948 Genocide Convention' (March 2021) 40.

2.3   Rape and Sexual Violence

Evidence suggests that women are subjected to systematic rape and sexual violence in camps. According to a BBC investigation, 'women in China's "re-education" camps for Uyghurs have been systematically raped, sexually abused, and tortured.'[37] Their reporting includes testimonies of victims of gang rape. 'On an everyday basis the policemen took the pretty girls with them. The police had unlimited power. There were also cases of gang rape.'[38] Sayragul, who has been raising the issue of the situation in the camps, described a shocking incident in which one woman was publicly raped by police offers with inmates forced to watch:

> They took 200 inmates outside, men and women, and told one of the women to confess her sins. She stood before us and declared that she had been a bad person, but now that she had learned Chinese, she had become a better person. When she was done speaking, the policemen ordered her to disrobe and simply raped her one after the other, in front of everyone. While they were raping her, they checked to see how we were reacting. People who turned their head or closed their eyes, and those who looked angry or shocked, were taken away and we never saw them again.[39]

Sayragul said that 'It was awful. I will never forget the feeling of helplessness, of not being able to help her.'[40]

Among the testimonies obtained by the BBC, Tursunay Ziawudun, who fled Xinjiang to the United States, stated that 'women were removed from the cells 'every night' and raped by one or more masked Chinese men.'[41] She added that she was tortured and gang-raped three times in the camp. Torture and physical abuse were also common. She was

---

[37] Matthew Hill, David Campanale and Joel Gunter, '"Their Goal Is to Destroy Everyone": Uighur Camp Detainees Allege Systematic Rape' *BBC News* (2 February 2021). Available at: https://www.bbc.co.uk/news/world-asia-china-55794071.

[38] David Stavrou, 'A Million People Are Jailed at China's Gulags. I Managed to Escape. Here's What Really Goes on Inside' *Haaretz* (17 October 2019). Available at: https://www.haaretz.com/world-news/.premium.MAGAZINE-a-million-people-are-jailed-at-china-s-gulags-i-escaped-here-s-what-goes-on-inside-1.7994216.

[39] Ibid.

[40] Ibid.

[41] Matthew Hill, David Campanale and Joel Gunter, 'Their Goal Is to Destroy Everyone': Uighur Camp Detainees Allege Systematic Rape' BBC (2 February 2021). Available at: https://www.bbc.co.uk/news/world-asia-china-55794071.

subjected to abuse as well: 'They had an electric stick, I didn't know what it was, and it was pushed inside my genital tract, torturing me with an electric shock.'

There are more stories like that. Indeed, Qelbinur Sedik, an Uzbek woman from Xinjiang who was teaching Chinese in the camp, recalled one Uyghur woman saying that 'The rape has become a culture. It is gang rape and the Chinese police not only rape them but also electrocute them. They are subject to horrific torture.' Another woman, Gulzira Auelkhan, aged 40, incarcerated in camps for a year and a half, confirmed that guards would enter the holding cells and 'put bags on the heads of the ones they wanted.'[42] She testified that the very job she was forced to do was to 'remove their clothes (...) and handcuff them so they cannot move. Then I would leave the women in the room and a man would enter - some Chinese man from outside or policeman. I sat silently next to the door, and when the man left the room I took the woman for a shower.' She added that these men 'would pay money to have their pick of the prettiest young inmates.'[43]

These accounts of rape tally with testimonies which Rahima Mahmut brought before Members of Parliament. They tally, too, with an account by 30-year-old Ruqiye Perhat, who escaped to Turkey and described how she was repeatedly raped by guards, became pregnant twice and then forcibly aborted.[44] She told The Washington Post that 'Any woman or man under the age of 35 was raped and sexually abused.'[45] At a webinar on International Women's Day organised for the All-Party Parliamentary Group on Uyghurs by Dr Ewelina Ochab, Lord Alton repeated the testimonies of some of the women whose accounts have been recorded and which demonstrate that for them life will certainly never be the same and, for us, having heard their stories we cannot be complacent and indifferent, amble along as if nothing has changed in our way of thinking about the treatment of Uyghurs.

[42] Ibid.

[43] Ibid.

[44] Amie Ferris-Rotman, 'Abortions, IUDs and Sexual Humiliation: Muslim Women Who Fled China for Kazakhstan Recount Ordeals' Washington Post (5 October 2019). Available at: https://www.washingtonpost.com/world/asia_pacific/abortions-iuds-and-sexual-humiliation-muslim-women-who-fled-china-for-kazakhstan-recount-ordeals/2019/10/04/551c2658-cfd2-11e9-a620-0a91656d7db6_story.html.

[45] Ibid.

Following the reports of rape and sexual violence by the BBC, the Chinese Government responded by banning the BBC. Furthermore, in March 2021, a spokesperson for the Chinese Government sought to publicly denigrate the women and their testimonies. He impeached their good character, defenestrating and humiliating them, attempting to discredit their testimonies by public defenestration and by smearing their reputations.

2.4   Forced Sterilisations, Forced Abortions, and Other Forced Medical Procedures

Evidence suggests that the Chinese Government attempts to stop or severely limit reproduction by Uyghur Muslims. This is a specific indicator of genocide and was the criterion which led the Uyghur Tribunal to differentiate between other crimes against humanity which it found to have been committed in Xinjiang and the specific finding of the crime of genocide.

And for years, the red lights have been flashing.

The scale and gravity of these violations were underlined by a report published by Professor Adrian Zenz in June 2020 suggesting that Uyghur Muslim women have been subjected to forced sterilisation, significantly affecting the number of births within the persecuted minority group.[46] According to the findings, 'natural population growth in Xinjiang has declined dramatically; growth rates fell by 84% in the two largest Uyghur prefectures between 2015 and 2018, and declined further in 2019. For 2020, one Uyghur region set an unprecedented near-zero population growth target.'

The research found that 'documents from 2019 reveal plans for a campaign of mass female sterilisation in rural Uyghur regions, targeting 14 and 34% of all married women of childbearing age in two Uyghur counties that year. This project targeted all of southern Xinjiang, and continued in 2020 with increased funding.' It also found that 'by 2019, Xinjiang planned to subject at least 80% of women of childbearing age in the rural southern four minority prefectures to intrusive birth prevention

---

[46] Adrian Zenz, 'Sterilisations, IUDs, and Mandatory Birth Control: The CCP's Campaign to Suppress Uyghur Birthrates in Xinjiang' (2020). Available at: https://jamestown.org/product/sterilizations-iuds-and-mandatory-birth-control-the-ccps-campaign-to-suppress-uyghur-birthrates-in-xinjiang/.

surgery (IUDs or sterilisations). In 2018, 80% of all new IUD placements in China were performed in Xinjiang, despite the region only consisting up 1.8% of the nation's population.'[47]

In September 2020, Lord Alton raised the issue of Uyghur Muslim women being subjected to forced abortions and womb removals, of Uyghur children being separated from their parents and placed in orphanages, and of the treatment of those children while in such orphanages. The government replied:

> We are deeply concerned by reports of suppression of birth rates and the mistreatment of Uyghur children in China, including reports of children being forcibly separated from their parents and placed in state run institutions... On 25 September, at the UN Human Rights Council, I also raised serious concerns about the human rights situation in Xinjiang, including credible reports of forced labour and forced birth control in the UK's 'Item 4' national statement. It is noteworthy that the Chinese authorities' own figures show a drastic decline in birth rates in Xinjiang. These reports add to the growing body of evidence about serious and widespread human rights violations taking place in Xinjiang. We continue to raise our concerns at the UN, and directly with China.[48]

In response to the allegations, the Chinese Embassy in the United States tweeted that a 'study shows that in the process of eradicating extremism, the minds of Uyghur women in Xinjiang were emancipated and gender equality and reproductive health were promoted, making them no longer baby-making machines. They were more confident and independent.' The tweet aims to portray the forced sterilisations and forced abortions as emancipation of women. The post has since been removed by Twitter for violating Twitter's rules.

Forced abortion and forced sterilisation are a long-standing part of the CCP play book. For several decades, Lord Alton challenged the CCP's use of forced abortion as part of the one-child policy (part funded by UK aid programmes for 'reproductive rights'). One-child China has led to what Chinese writers have described as 'bare branches' and 'little emperors.' The origins and extent of the CCP created and enforced disaster began to seep out from behind the closed doors when, in 2013,

---

[47] Ibid.

[48] WPQ UIN HL8355, tabled on 22 September 2020.

an internal Communist Party document exposed the scale of this pernicious policy: over 40 years some 330 m abortions, 196 m sterilisations, and 403 m intrauterine devices inserted into women, often without their consent, had led to a massive imbalance between young men and women. This relentless targeting of female babies became known as *gendercide*—indirectly funded by British taxpayers under successive British governments. Challenge it and you were denounced.

During the 1990s, at one memorable meeting with a Minister in charge of International Development, the air was literally blue with undeleted expletives and four-letter words, as Lord Alton was accused of undermining development policies which relied on population control. During that meeting, he had raised the case of Gao Xiao Duan, a former Chinese family planning official, who, in 1998, described to a US Congressional Committee the horror of forced abortions of women, how babies had been murdered during delivery, and newborns drowned in paddy fields by officials.

After this intemperate Ministerial harangue, and during a subsequent visit to Beijing, Lord Alton met with Communist Party officials. The contrast with our own officials and Minister could not have been greater. Of course, the difference was that many of these officials had suffered too. Hardly anyone in China has been unaffected.

In private, some of those Chinese officials quietly encouraged Lord Alton to go on opposing the one-child policy. He specifically raised the case of Chen Guangchen, the barefoot, blind human rights lawyer whom Lord Alton campaigned for after Chen was imprisoned in 2006 for four years after exposing and leading protests against the coercive one-child policy.

This extraordinary and deeply patriotic man, who has no sight, had seen so clearly what his country's leaders have been blind to: not only was their policy an outrageous violation of human rights but the disastrous demographic effect. The cruel enforcement of the policy has opened the eyes of millions to the nature of the system—now cruelly perfected in Xinjiang.

Lord Alton told CCP officials that one day Chen Guangchen would be seen as a national hero. Chen's brave stand had opened minds and given people courage to speak out.

As Chinese micro-bloggers took up Chen's case and publicly questioned the policy, the bloggers began to ask deeper questions, too.

They were joined by brave lawyers, increasingly asking why a totalitarian political system be allowed to crush the spirit of a truly great people.

The one-child policy was seen as being the perfect image of a one-party system. In the absence of a free press, the bloggers—one of whom had five million followers—opened minds. By shining a light on horrifying stories, like that of a woman who was coercively aborted, and whose seven-month unborn baby was then left by her side on her bed, as a warning not to become pregnant again, millions have fundamentally questioned the nature of a one-party Communist state.

During the 2015 UK visit of China's President, Xi Jinping, Lord Alton again raised the coercive one-child policy in Parliament (along with other human rights issues including the arrest of lawyers) and referred to the distortions in population balance between the genders and the abuse of human rights. On his return to Beijing, President Xi said the CCP would allow parents to have two children but would still require Chinese women to obtain a birth permit and women would still be subject to forced abortions if they became pregnant without a birth permit. State-coercion and state-control remain at the heart of the policy.

And that is the policy which has been pursued again the Uyghurs of Xinjiang. And it isn't only women who suffer.

In a series of interviews with escapees, the journalist Ben Mauk, who has written for The New York Times Magazine, detailed accounts of medical treatments that led to male impotence, among other dire treatment, including gross punishments, water torture.[49]

Locking up and sterilising the men while forcibly aborting the women will, unless the conscience of the world is aroused, achieve the CCP's desired solution: the eradication of the Uyghur people.

2.5   Forced Labour

Corrie ten Boom in her memoir, 'The Hiding Place,' explains how after sheltering Jews from the Nazi regime, she was sent to Ravensbrück concentration camp. She describes her experience there as part of the forced labour used by Siemens in the camps where her sister and many

---

[49] See, for example: Ben Mauk, 'Weather Reports: Voices from Xinjiang' The New York Times (1 October 2019).

others died.[50] Eric Vuillard vividly brings the gravy train of big corporations to life in '*The Order of the Day*' which reconstructs a defining series of meetings in the run up to the World War II, companies which collaborated with the Reich.

It opens and closes with the twenty-four German patriarchs who are the titans of German industry. Their shameful willingness to aid and abet Hitler, to profit from the Reich, and from the slave labour of the concentration camps, generated phenomenal wealth—and became the foundation of their post-war success. From Krupp to Bayer, BMW, Daimler, IG Farben, Agfa, Shell, Schneider, Telefunken, and Siemens, fortunes were made in the hideous camps of Sachsenhausen, Buchenwald, Auschwitz, Ravensbruck, and the rest.

Like the political leaders who danced obligingly around Hitler, these tainted corporations—and the calculating machines which owned them—didn't give a tinker's damn about what was happening to the incarcerated Jews, and others. The play-acted fantasy meetings which Vuillard describes—from a Downing Street lunch for Ribbentrop to an encounter between Lord Halifax and Hitler—and the toadyism of aristocratic English neo-Nazis—have the feel of a Whitehall farce whose actors sleep walk into a world war.

The chapters which deal with the elimination of Austria, the treacherous collaboration of weak political and church leaders, are potent and deeply relevant today as we watch the ascent of the Chinese Communist Party. Learning again how quickly opposition was subdued and the population largely acquiesced as Jews were forced to scrub paving stones, and Nazi ideology became commonplace, is a sobering reminder of the thin veneer which separates us from tyranny.

The collaborating corporations which today turn a blind eye on slave labour in Xinjiang, to reports of appalling human rights violations, genocide, and atrocity crimes, and to the daily intimidation of Taiwan (as too many pretend it isn't happening) have any number of self-evident parallels.

The Holocaust saw state-sponsored mass enslavement on an appalling scale. Ironically, on the morning following Holocaust Memorial Day 2020, the United Kingdom committed to sign over up to 35% of the UK's 5G infrastructure to Huawei, a company that the government know

---

[50] Corrie ten Boom, *The Hiding Place* (Hodder & Stoughton, 2004).

actively partners with the Xinjiang Government to make the world's most dystopian system of governance possible. Is what happened at Ravensbrück, or in the Gulag Archipelago, so very different from the plight of these 1 million Uyghur Muslims, incarcerated and forced to work for nothing?

According to a report published by ASPI, between 2017 and 2019, the Chinese Government facilitated the transfer of Uyghur Muslims and other ethnic minorities from Xinjiang to factories in various parts of China.[51] According to ASPI, there are strong indications that some 80,000 Uyghurs have been forced to work in factories that form part of the supply chains of at least 83 global brands including:

> Abercrombie & Fitch, Acer, Adidas, Amazon, Apple, ASUS, BMW, Bosch, Calvin Klein, Carter's, Cerruti 1881, Dell, Electrolux, Fila, Gap, General Electric, General Motors, Google, H&M, HTC, Huawei, Jack & Jones, Jaguar, Lacoste, Land Rover, Lenovo, LG, Mercedes-Benz, Microso, Mitsubishi, Nike, Nintendo, Nokia, The North Face, Panasonic, Polo Ralph Lauren, Puma, Roewe, Samsung, Sharp, Siemens, Sony, Tommy Hilfiger, Toshiba, Uniqlo, Victoria's Secret, Volkswagen, Zara.[52]

The report says that these companies use forced Uyghur labour in their supply chains. They may well be in breach of laws prohibiting the importation of goods made with forced labour. Are these companies directly complicit? One of ASPI's researchers, Vicky Xu, says that the idea that Huawei is not working directly with local governments in Xinjiang is 'just straight-up nonsense.'[53] The 2018 announcement of one Huawei public security project in Xinjiang—as posted on a Chinese Government website in Urumqi—quoted a Huawei director as saying: 'Together with the Public Security Bureau, Huawei will unlock a new era of smart

---

[51] Vicky Xiuzhong Xu, Danielle Cave, Dr James Leibold, Kelsey Munro and Nathan Ruser, 'Uyghurs for Sale' (2020). Available at: https://www.aspi.org.au/report/uyghurs-sale.

[52] Ibid.

[53] Cited in The Telegraph, 'Human rights, Uighurs, and Huawei: It's Time for Helsinki with Chinese Characteristics' *The Telegraph* (28 June 2020). Available at: https://www.telegraph.co.uk/opinion/2020/06/28/human-rights-uighurs-huawei-time-helsinki-chinese-characteristics/.

policing and help build a safer, smarter society.'[54] This is not speculation, or evidence extrapolated from big data. This is straight from the horse's mouth. We all know that safer, smarter policing is a euphemism that would make George Orwell roll in his grave. Huawei is making huge profits from Xinjiang's unique techno-totalitarianism.

Among the International Labour Organisation (ILO), forced labour indicators relevant in the case of the Uyghur Muslims include:

- Being subjected to intimidation and threats, such as the threat of arbitrary detention, and being monitored by security personnel and digital surveillance tools;
- Being placed in a position of dependency and vulnerability, such as by threats to family members back in Xinjiang;
- Having freedom of movement restricted, such as by fenced-in factories and high-tech surveillance;
- Isolation, such as living in segregated dormitories and being transported in dedicated trains;
- Abusive working conditions, such as political indoctrination, police guard posts in factories, 'military-style' management, and a ban on religious practices; and
- Excessive hours, such as after-work Mandarin language classes and political indoctrination sessions that are part of job assignments.[55]

The report focuses on a number of case studies. For example, it alleges that in January 2020, around 600 ethnic minority workers from Xinjiang were employed at Qingdao Taekwang Shoes Co. Ltd., making Nike sneakers. It further adds that: 'At the factory, the Uyghur labourers make Nike shoes during the day. In the evening, they attended a night school where they study Mandarin, sing the Chinese national anthem and receive "vocational training" and "patriotic education." The curriculum closely mirrors that of Xinjiang's "re-education camps".'

The ASPI report calls upon other states not to turn a blind eye but to act together to 'increase pressure on the Chinese government to end

[54] Cited in Oscar Williams, 'The Issue Ministers Are Avoiding When It Comes to Huawei' *New Statesman* (22 January 2020). Available at: https://www.newstatesman.com/science-tech/2020/01/issue-ministers-are-avoiding-when-it-comes-huawei.
[55] Ibid.

the use and facilitation of Uyghur forced labour and mass extrajudicial detention, including through the use of targeted sanctions on senior officials responsible for Xinjiang's coercive labour transfers' and to 'review trade agreements to restrict commodities and products being produced with forced labour.' Such concerted action—especially if consumers themselves refuse to buy products originating from the use of Uyghur forced labour—is the only approach likely to bring to an end the Chinese Government's human rights violations, including its abuse of religious minorities.

Despite confirming credible evidence, the UK Government did not propose any steps to address the issue. In one wholly inadequate response the UK Government simply said that it would keep companies under review:

> Recent reports indicating that Uyghurs are being used as a source of forced labour add to the growing body of evidence about the disturbing situation that Uyghurs and other minorities are facing in Xinjiang. Section 54 of the Modern Slavery Act 2015 requires companies operating in the UK with a turnover of £36m or more to publish annual statements setting out what steps they have taken to prevent modern slavery in their organisation and supply chains. The Home Office keeps compliance under active review.[56]

In a Westminster Hall debate on 11 March 2020, Nigel Adams MP, the Minister for Asia, further confirmed that:

> We have also seen credible evidence to suggest that Uyghurs are being used as a source of forced labour in Xinjiang and across China, and that if individuals refuse to participate, they and their families are threatened with extra-judicial detention. (…)
>
> Our intelligence is that families are also obliged to host Chinese officials in their homes for extended periods, to demonstrate their loyalty to the Communist party. On the streets, Uyghurs and other minorities are continuously watched by police, supported by extensive use of facial recognition technology and restrictions on movement.[57]

[56] WPQ, UIN HL2408, tabled on 24 March 2020.

[57] Official Report, House of Commons, Westminster Hall, 11 March 2020, c149-50WH.

This has not been done yet. Some 180 human rights groups say that many of the world's biggest fashion brands and retailers, along with suppliers of PPE to the United Kingdom, and companies such as Huawei and Volkswagen are complicit in the forced labour and human rights violations of millions of Uyghur people in Xinjiang.[58] In November 2020, Bob Rae, Canada's ambassador to the United Nations, called on the UN to investigate the horrors of Xinjiang.[59]

Then, in early January 2021, the Foreign Secretary said that what is happening in Xinjiang is 'on an industrial scale'[60] (a phrase he also used in addressing the UN Human Rights Council in February 2021). He added: 'Violations include the extra-judicial detention of over a million Uyghurs and other minorities in political re-education camps. Extensive and invasive surveillance targeting minorities. Systematic restrictions on Uyghur culture, education and indeed the practice of Islam, and the widespread use of forced labour.'[61] The Foreign Secretary said that this is 'reminiscent of something not seen for a long time.'[62] Such echoes from a terrible past have also been heard in reports that 13 tonnes of human hair, taken from the shaved heads of Uyghur people, has been exported to be used in wigs by those who are equally comfortable wearing fashion items made by Uyghur slave labour.[63] How many heads would have had to be shaved

---

[58] Annie Kelly, "Virtually Entire' Fashion Industry Complicit in Uighur Forced Labour, Say Rights Groups' *The Guardian* (23 July 2020). Available at: https://www.theguardian.com/global-development/2020/jul/23/virtually-entire-fashion-industry-complicit-in-uighur-forced-labour-say-rights-groups-china.

[59] Raisa Patel and Rosemary Barton, 'Bob Rae Calls on UN to Investigate Evidence of Genocide Against China's Uighur Minority' CBC (15 November 2020). Available at: https://www.cbc.ca/news/politics/bob-rae-genocide-investigation-uighur-minority-1.5802920.

[60] FCDO, Human Rights Violations in Xinjiang and the Government's Response: Foreign Secretary's Statement (12 January 2021). Available at: https://www.gov.uk/government/speeches/foreign-secretary-on-the-situation-in-xinjiang-and-the-governments-response.

[61] Ibid.

[62] Ibid.

[63] Rebecca Wright, Ivan Watson and Isaac Yee, "Black Gold' How Global Demand for Hair Products Is Linked to Forced Labor in Xinjiang' CNN (October 2020). Available at: https://edition.cnn.com/interactive/2020/10/asia/black-gold-hair-products-forced-labor-xinjiang/.

to produce 13 tonnes of hair! Do the math! Ethan Gutmann's assessment is that at least **90,000**.[64]

In March 2021, Adrian Zenz published another report on the issue of forced labour, entitled 'Coercive Labour and Forced Displacement in Xinjiang's Cross-Regional Labour Transfer Program.'[65] The report concluded that:

> New evidence from the Nankai Report, other Chinese academic publications and publicly available government documents provides strong proof of the systemically coercive nature of Xinjiang's labour transfer programs and underscores a process-oriented approach towards designating such programs to be forced labour. These sources also show that the primary aims of labour transfers are not economic, but political and demographic.[66]

The report shed light on the forced displacement aspect of the Chinese Government's forced labour. This programme demonstrates how the forced labour scheme is not only economically motivated, but has an aim to break up the Uyghur community and reduce its density as a group in Xinjiang.

As we consider what academics have described as the world's worst incident of state-sanctioned slavery, we are duty bound to consider both the human costs and the dangers to the UK of placing so much of our critical national infrastructure into the hands of the Chinese Government. On 11 March 2021, during exchanges in the House of Lords, Ministers were reminded that the China Nuclear Power Group, which has been banned in the United States for 'stealing nuclear secrets,' owns one-third of the UK's Hinkley Point nuclear reactor. Whether the Chinese Government is acquiring the ability to turn off our electricity supplies or to use slave labour to flood our markets with cheap goods, it all forms part of the same determinations to acquire power and hegemony for its ideology. Just like the Jews and others forced to work for the Reich, the Chinese Government see Muslim Uyghurs as useful slaves of their state.

---

[64] Venus Upadhayaya, 'Seized Human Hair Products from Xinjiang Provide Evidence of Persecution' *The Epoch Times* (2 August 2020). Available at: https://www.citizensjournal.us/seized-human-hair-products-from-xinjiang-provide-evidence-of-persecution/.

[65] Available at: https://jamestown.org/wp-content/uploads/2021/03/Coercive-Labor-and-Forced-Displacement-in-Xinjiangs-Cross-Regional-Labor-Transfers-A-Process-Oriented-Evaluation.pdf?x46096.

[66] Ibid., 26.

The extraordinary thing is that we who care about safety standards, working conditions, minimum wages, and the rest are willing to buy goods that have been made in outrageous conditions and circumstances—while stupidly allowing our own industries and workers to be priced into oblivion through their inability to compete with prices that are only made possible by the use of slaves. We then become dependent as our resilience is weakened on a variety of fronts. China was the UK's third largest import market, and in 2019, more than 60,000 UK VAT-registered businesses imported goods from China worth about £46.4 billion.

The COVID-19 pandemic exacerbated the problem further. In a parliamentary question, Lord Alton established that in 2020–2021 more than 1 billion lateral flow tests had been imported from China—in addition to shed loads of face masks and PPE at a total cost of £10 billion to the NHS. In what circumstances were these products manufactured and why have secret procurement policies been allowed to disguise the identities of many of the companies and individuals who have been creating lucrative profits rather than creating UK manufacturing capacity? In a welcome move in April 2022, the UK Government pledged to 'eradicate' slavery in the NHS procurement, and incorporated an amendment moved by Lord Blencathra and Lord Alton to the Health and Care Bill before Parliament. Time will only tell whether action will follow words.

And what about the workers?

Over Easter 2019, Lord Alton met a group of Uyghurs who told him that British citizens are among the many families whose relatives have disappeared into these camps. That atrocities have been perpetrated against the relatives of British citizens should give the UK Government even more reason to act as it is a duty of the state to protect its people. But the UK is complicit in other ways. In 2019, Lord Alton challenged the government over reports that UK investors hold shares totalling £800 million in companies that supply CCTV and facial-recognition technology used to track Uyghur Muslims in Xinjiang. The Minister replied that it had 'not undertaken analysis of British investor shareholdings in Chinese surveillance companies. However, we are aware of the recent reports.'[67] Being 'aware' but unwilling to act is not worthy of a great nation.

Another issue concerns links to major commercial and service providers. In March 2020, in connection with Huawei and 5G, Lord

[67] WPQ, UIN HL17192, tabled on 16 July 2019.

Alton asked the government 'what assessment they have made in relation to their decision to award contracts to Huawei and other companies of the implications of the government of China's National Intelligence Law requiring Chinese organisations and citizens to support, assist and cooperate with the state intelligence work.'[68] He pursued the question by asking Huawei's compliance with the Modern Slavery Act. The government's response deftly dodged the question. Profiteering from the blood, sweat, and tears of enslaved Uyghurs is either a criminal offence under British law or it is not. Either it is a nice slogan and good public relations or we take it deadly seriously and refuse to profit from it. The more we learn about the realities of life in Xinjiang the more difficult it becomes to claim to be world leaders in opposing modern-day slavery while doing business as usual on the broken backs of Uyghurs.

Nor do we act in concert with our Five Eyes allies. In 2021, Lord Alton moved amendments to the Telecommunications Security Bill which would have required the UK Government to look at the bona fides of companies banned in other jurisdictions. He gave the example of Hikvision and cited the House of Commons Foreign Affairs Select Committee Inquiry which said that Hikvision was the company responsible for the cameras 'deployed throughout Xinjiang and provide the primary camera technology used in the internment camps.'

The same facial-recognition cameras are collecting facial-recognition data in the United Kingdom. The government was asked to prohibit UK organisations and individuals from doing business with companies known to be associated with the Xinjiang atrocities through the sanctions regime. But despite promises from Ministers to meet Hikvision and to consider what action to take, unlike the United States, which has banned Hikvision, the UK has failed to do the same.

The government also declined respond positively to Lord Alton's request that they carry out an audit of the UK assets of CCP officials, and why, under the Magnitsky sanctions regime, the UK sanctioned four lower-level Chinese officials for their repression in the Uyghur Region, but left out Chen Quanguo—the CCP's chief architect of the whole thing, whom the United States has sanctioned and who was also responsible for mass human rights abuses in Tibet.

[68] WPQ, UIN HL2408, tabled on 10 March 2020.

There is also an urgent need to be more vigilant in combatting the risk of the CCP and other authoritarian regimes using surveillance and artificial intelligence to subvert liberal democracy even, according to one recent report, using AI-driven smart toys to collect children's data.

2.6 Destruction of Religious Sites

Destruction of religious sides is not a genocidal method nor does it in itself suggest genocidal atrocities. However, as it is being used to destroy every sign of the religious group ever living in the region, it adds to the available evidence. According to ASPI, mosques across Xinjiang are being systematically destroyed. They report that:

> We located and analysed a sample of 533 mosques across Xinjiang, including 129 from Urumqi. Of those mosques, 170 were destroyed (31.9%), 175 were damaged (32.8%) and 188 remained undamaged (35.3%). Of the 404 mosques we sampled in other parts of Xinjiang, 148 were destroyed (36.6%), 152 were damaged (37.6%) and 104 were undamaged (25.8%)." ASPI further indicates that "across [Xinjiang] approximately 16,000 mosques have been damaged or destroyed and 8450 have been entirely demolished. The 95% confidence range of our regional findings is ±4% for the estimates of demolished, destroyed and undamaged mosque numbers.[69]

APSI says that 'the Chinese Government's destruction of cultural heritage aims to erase, replace and rewrite what it means to be Uyghur and to live in the [Xinjiang]. The state is intentionally recasting its Turkic and Muslim minorities in the image of the Han centre for the purposes of control, domination and profit.' This is not the first time allegations of this kind have been made. In the past few months, the media have reported the state-authorised destruction of churches and other places of worship across China. The allegations continue to be denied.

The new wave of destruction of mosques in China is relevant when we consider the ever-growing evidence of atrocities against Uyghur Muslims. While the Chinese Government bans any international observers or investigators, hoping to conceal the persecution in the detention centres, the

---

[69] Nathan Ruser, Dr James Leibold, Kelsey Munro and Tilla Hoja, 'Cultural Erasure' (2020). Available at: https://www.aspi.org.au/report/cultural-erasure.

very visible destruction of mosques in China tells its own story. In May 2022, the United Nations is to visit Xinjiang, however, it is not clear what would be the scope of investigations and whether unfettered access would be granted.

2.7   Religious or Ethno-Religious Persecution More Broadly

We have already described the campaign of Chen Guangchen, the blind self-taught lawyer, imprisoned in Shandong Province in 2005[70] after Chen exposed the mass forced abortion and sterilisation of thousands of women in Shandong. As Lord Alton said:

> China is the only country in the world where it is illegal to have a brother or a sister. Female foeticide has led to a population imbalance of 117 men to every 100 women, and that is leading to catastrophic social consequences. Human Rights Watch had said of Chen's case: "It was house arrest, physical abuse, and then 'disappearance'... His case is a textbook example of how little the rule of law really means in China".[71]

After Chen was finally released and allowed to leave the country, he travelled to London and was a recipient of the Westminster Award for Human Rights, Human Life and Human Dignity. He said that he was receiving the award on behalf of the millions who had suffered at the hands of the CCP.

Among those who had suffered the most were people with divergent political beliefs or religious faith. In 2008, Lord Alton had drawn attention to the infringement of political rights and religious liberties, to the situation in Tibet and in Western China:

> Tibetan religion is, of course, the root of Tibetan identity and that is why China wants to destroy it. There are over 100 million self-described Buddhists in China. They have been shown little tolerance. Nor have the Uyghur Muslims, the Falun Gong, or Christians.[72]

---

[70] Ibid. Edward Wong, 'China Arrests Activist Amid a Clampdown' *The New York Times* (6 January 2015). Available at: https://www.nytimes.com/2015/01/07/world/asia/guo-yushan-arrest-china-chen-guangcheng.html.

[71] Ibid.

[72] Ibid.

He referred to reports of the harvesting of organs of Falun Gong members, their incarceration in forced indoctrination camps, and the use of electro-shock therapy and torture to force adherents to recant their beliefs. He said that millions of underground Christians, Catholic and Protestant, have also faced persecution for their beliefs—with up to a dozen Catholic bishops incarcerated—under house arrest, in police custody, or in hiding; that forty of China's 100 Catholic dioceses were without a bishop; that thousands of members of the underground Catholic Church and members of various illegal Protestant house churches had been arrested and tortured.[73] He drew attention to the cases of imprisoned bishops—Lin Xili; Shi Enxiang; Xu Zemin; and Yao Liang—along with Tian Mingwei and Su Dean, two prominent Protestant leaders of large house church networks:

> We cannot and should not ignore such realities. As China flexes its economic muscle and enjoys unprecedented economic growth, there needs to be a commensurate change in the way it dispenses justice and deals with human rights. Change at home will influence its actions overseas and within the region—in its relations with Tibet and Taiwan, and in the way it deals with issues such as the repatriation of North Korean refugees.[74]

Some of these atrocities received a degree of attention and consideration. For example, in June 2019, the Independent Tribunal into Forced Organ Harvesting from Prisoners of Conscience in China (the China Tribunal), a people's tribunal, published its interim findings of the situation of Falun Gong practitioners in China, stating that:

> Forced organ harvesting has been committed for years throughout China on a significant scale and that Falun Gong practitioners have been one – and probably the main – source of organ supply. The concerted persecution and medical testing of the Uyghurs is more recent and it may be that evidence of forced organ harvesting of this group may emerge in due course. The Tribunal has had no evidence that the significant infrastructure associated with China's transplantation industry has been dismantled and

[73] Ibid.
[74] Ibid.

absent a satisfactory explanation as to the source of readily available organs concludes that forced organ harvesting continues till today.[75]

The China Tribunal concluded that crimes against humanity against the Falun Gong and Uyghurs have been proved beyond reasonable doubt.[76] However, since, no international body has followed up on the findings of the China Tribunal.

Christians have also been subjected to various methods of discrimination and persecution in China. The treatment complained of includes the closures of churches, the ban on the sale of bibles online, the removal of crosses, and the arrest of priests and worshipers. Reportedly, there are plans to 'contextualise' the Bible to make it more 'culturally acceptable' and Christian preaching is to be adapted to include the core values of socialism.[77] In early 2021, reports suggested that Christians have now been subjected to forced indoctrination in mobile 're-education camps.'[78]

Among the recent cases which Lord Alton has raised in Parliament are those of Zheng Zhan, a young Christian woman journalist and lawyer who was given a four-year prison sentence after going to Wuhan to discover the truth about the origins of COVID-19. At the time of writing, she is on a hunger strike and her life at risk. He has also raised the case of imprisoned Pastor, Wang Yi, of Early Rain Church. The UN Working Group on Arbitrary Detention has called for his immediate and unconditional release.

The situation of all religious minorities—and the daily breach by the Chinese Government of Article 18 of the Universal Declaration of Human Rights, setting out the right to freedom of religion or belief—requires full and comprehensive investigation and consideration to ensure that the responses address the issues at stake. Under Article 18 of the International Covenant on Civil and Political Rights (ICCPR), all people have the right to manifest religion or belief in a community with others, including in worship. The UN Human Rights Committee has clarified

---

[75] China Tribunal, Judgment. Available at: https://chinatribunal.com/final-judgment/.

[76] China Tribunal, Judgment. Available at: https://chinatribunal.com/final-judgment/.

[77] Report on China. Available at: https://www.opendoorsuk.org/persecution/countries/china/.

[78] Radio Free Asia, 'Chinese Christians Held in Secretive Brainwashing Camps: Sources' *Radio Free Asia* (1 April 2021). Available at: https://www.rfa.org/english/news/china/christians-camps-04012021081013.html.

that 'the concept of worship extends to... the building of places of worship.'

3 DO THE ATROCITIES AMOUNT TO GENOCIDE?

While, in recent years, we have witnessed these Mao-style instances of persecution of religious minorities in China, the treatment of the Uyghurs differs. Uyghurs, as an ethno-religious group, fall within the purview of the Genocide Convention's protected groups. The reports and testimonies we have recorded here suggest that Uyghurs have been subjected to a litany of atrocities, including killings, torture, inhuman and degrading treatment, and much more besides—all of which are detailed in genocidal methods described in Article II of the Genocide Convention. The systematic control of births appears designed to bring about the destruction of this religious minority community, in whole or in part, in contravention of Article II. Indeed, the evidence described by Adrian Zenz suggests that the Chinese Government has imposed measures intended to prevent births within the group in breach of Article II (d). The destruction of places of worship is also a fundamental violation of human rights which must not be ignored and add to the targeting of the religious identity of the community. Places of worship are an essential part of the right to freedom of religion or belief, enabling some form of religious manifestation.

Are acts by the Chinese Government perpetrated with the specific intent to destroy the protected group, in whole or in part? In 2019, the New York Times published over 400 pages of Chinese Government documents suggesting direct intent to destroy.[79] Each piece of evidence adds to the argument that the atrocities against the Uyghurs amount to international crimes, and highly likely, genocide. Indeed, more and more actors come to this conclusion.

On 19 January 2020, the then US Secretary of State, Mike Pompeo, officially recognised the atrocities as amounting to genocide and crimes against humanity, stating that:

---

[79] Austin Ramzy and Chris Buckley, "Absolutely No Mercy': Leaked Files Expose How China Organized Mass Detentions of Muslims' *The New York Times* (16 November 2016). Available at: https://www.nytimes.com/interactive/2019/11/16/world/asia/china-xin jiang-documents.html.

> After careful examination of the available facts, I have determined that the [People's Republic of China (PRC)], under the direction and control of the [Chinese Communist Party (CCP)], has committed genocide against the predominantly Muslim Uyghurs and other ethnic and religious minority groups in Xinjiang. I believe this genocide is ongoing, and that we are witnessing the systematic attempt to destroy Uyghurs by the Chinese party-state. The governing authorities of the second most economically, militarily, and politically powerful country on earth have made clear that they are engaged in the forced assimilation and eventual erasure of a vulnerable ethnic and religious minority group, even as they simultaneously assert their country as a global leader and attempt to remould the international system in their image.[80]

Mike Pompeo's incoming successor, Antony Blinken, immediately reaffirmed that decisions at his confirmation hearing in the US Senate.[81]

This was followed by similar formal recognitions made by the UK House of Commons, Canadian, Belgian and Dutch parliaments, among others.[82] In early 2021, lawyers from Essex Court Chambers published a legal opinion on the issue of genocide and crimes against humanity against the Uyghurs. Further evidence of crimes against the Uyghurs was published on 9 March 2021 in a landmark report by Newlines Institute for Strategy and Policy and which drew on a panel of more than 50 experts in international law. The first independent investigation into the allegations of genocide concluded that China is violating the Genocide Convention. The All-Party Parliamentary Group on the Uyghurs—of which Lord Alton is vice chair and the other author is the Secretariat of the APPG—has heard some profoundly moving and shocking testimonies of Uyghurs who have escaped from Xinjiang. Unequivocally, we agree with the conclusion of the British academic who has studied the evidence from Xinjiang and says that what is afoot points to 'a slow, painful,

---

[80] US State Department, 'Determination of the Secretary of State on Atrocities in Xinjiang' (19 January 2021). Available at: https://2017-2021.state.gov/determination-of-the-secretary-of-state-on-atrocities-in-xinjiang//index.html.

[81] BBC News, 'US: China 'Committed Genocide Against Uyghurs' BBC (20 January 2021). Available at: https://www.bbc.co.uk/news/world-us-canada-55723522.

[82] Canadian Parliament 23 February 2021; Dutch Parliament 25 February 2021.

creeping genocide.'[83] However, this determination is not universal yet, and indeed, many states continue to look away.

4   Responses to the Atrocities

The responses to the atrocities against the Uyghurs have been predominately symbolic. However, this started to change mid-2020 and at the beginning of 2021 when states began to take more proactive approaches.

4.1   Attempts to Prevent and Suppress the Atrocities

Attempts to prevent and suppress the atrocities have predominately focused on diplomatic engagement. Among others, in June 2020, nearly 50 UN independent experts raised their concerns and called for action. They urged the UN Human Rights Council to take steps to address the atrocities including by way of, among others:

> The establishment of an impartial and independent United Nations mechanism - such as a United Nations Special Rapporteur, a Panel of Experts appointed by the HRC, or a Secretary General Special Envoy - to closely monitor, analyse and report annually on the human rights situation in China, particularly, in view of the urgency of the situations in the Hong Kong SAR, the Xinjiang Autonomous Region and the Tibet Autonomous Region.[84]

By early 2021, these steps had not been taken, and given the powerful position of China at the UN, they are unlikely to be taken. In recent months the powerful position of China at the UN has been repeatedly demonstrated and ultimately means inaction in the face of atrocities against the Uyghurs. During 2021, the UN worked on a report on the situation in Xinjiang, but by 2022 the report had not been disclosed. In May 2022, the UN was due to visit the region, but it had not disclosed any information in relation to the scope of the investigation, nor the

---

[83] Joanne Smith Finley, Newcastle University, cited in AP, 'China Cuts Uyghur Births with IUDs, Abortion, Sterilization' AP (29 June 2020). Available at: https://apnews.com/article/269b3de1af34e17c1941a514f78d764c.

[84] UN HRC, 'UN Experts Call for Decisive Measures to Protect Fundamental Freedoms in China' (26 June 2020). Available at: https://ohchr.org/EN/NewsEvents/Pages/DisplayNews.aspx?NewsID=26006&LangID=E.

powers of those investigating and the terms of reference. It was not clear whether the investigators would have unfettered access nor whether they would be able to meet with victims and survivors, and anyone other than those identified by the Chinese Government.

When, in 2019, during a visit to Islamabad, Lord Alton raised the persecution of Uyghurs with senior figures and scholars, it was met with an embarrassed silence. Pakistan, like many other predominantly Muslim nations, has become over-dependent on the Chinese Government's funding of major capital projects. This has been orchestrated through the Chinese Government's Belt and Road Initiative, not inspired by generosity or altruism, but by the Chinese Government's needs for access to resources and its determination to turn countries like Pakistan, and many in Africa, into dependent compliant servile states.

In Islamabad and Lahore, Lord Alton took photographs of huge road-side fake posters purporting to show Muhammad Ali Jinnah, Pakistan's illustrious founder, clenching the hand of Mao Zedong in friendship. This distorted and fictionalised piece of propaganda is all about entrenching China's hegemony and exploiting Pakistan's desperate need for development and the need of powerful ally, united together in their antagonism towards India. And, as Julia Lovell describes in her outstanding book, 'Maoism: A Global History',[85] and in Dikotter's trilogy chronicling the Great Famine, the nature of Maoism and the Cultural Revolution,[86] the Chinese Government's objective is to use the same manipulative techniques throughout the world, with docile Western nations and international organisations all in their sights. Their Faustian Pact with developing nations is what guarantees compliant votes at the United Nations.

In July 2020, 22 ambassadors from permanent representation to the UN signed a letter to the UN Human Rights Council raising the dire treatment of Uyghurs in Xinjiang.[87] 37 other ambassadors—including those from Muslim nations such as Kuwait, Syria, Bahrain, and Saudi Arabia—jumped to the Chinese Government's defence: 'his bread I eat,

---

[85] Julia Lovell, *Maoism: A Global History* (Vintage, 2019).

[86] Frank Dikötter, *Mao's Great Famine, The Tragedy of Liberation, The Cultural Revolution* (Bloomsbury, 2019).

[87] Letter signed by 22 states. Available at: https://www.hrw.org/sites/default/files/supporting_resources/190708_joint_statement_xinjiang.pdf.

his song I sing.'[88] None of which inspires much confidence that countries which should be speaking out for the Uyghurs will do so. Nor does it inspire confidence in bodies like the UN Human Rights Council to see that China has been elected to seats on the Council. Not only will the Chinese Government silence and outvote voices raised on behalf of the Uyghurs, as a permanent member of the UN Security Council, China will veto any attempt to ensure justice for the Uyghurs. If ever there is to be justice, it will be because of the testimonies and evidence of victims and because the free world provides the victims and their communities with legal mechanisms to bring atrocities into the light.

While the UN has been reluctant to act, several states have taken steps to address some aspects of the atrocities, by way of imposing sanctions against some of those most responsible for the atrocities. Among others, on 9 July 2020, the US Secretary of State, Mike Pompeo, designated three senior CCP officials, Chen Quanguo, the Party Secretary of the Xinjiang; Zhu Hailun, Party Secretary of the Xinjiang Political and Legal Committee; and Wang Mingshan, the current Party Secretary of the Xinjiang Public Security Bureau for their involvement in gross violations of human rights. The designation means that the three individuals and their immediate family members will not be able to enter the United States. Pompeo further placed visa restrictions on 'other CCP officials believed to be responsible for, or complicit in, the unjust detention or abuse of Uighurs, ethnic Kazakhs, and members of other minority groups in Xinjiang.' These designations and visa restrictions were in addition to the US Department of the Treasury's Global Magnitsky Designations of the Xinjiang Public Security Bureau and four current or former officials of the People's Republic of China—Chen Quanguo; Zhu Hailun; Wang Mingshan; and Huo Liujun—for their roles in serious human rights abuse. Pompeo stressed that 'Before ramping up the CCP's campaign of repression in Xinjiang, Chen oversaw extensive abuses in Tibetan areas, using many of the same horrific practices and policies CCP officials

---

[88] Tom Miles, 'Saudi Arabia and Russia Among 37 States Backing China's Xinjiang Policy' Reuters (12 July 2019). Available at: https://www.reuters.com/article/us-china-xinjiang-rights-idUSKCN1U721X.

currently employ in Xinjiang.'[89] The United States also sanctioned Sun Jinlong, former Party Secretary of the XPCC, and Peng Jiarui, Deputy Party Secretary and Commander of the XPCC.[90]

Similarly, in March 2021, the then Foreign Secretary Dominic Raab announced first UK sanctions against Chinese Government officials.[91] These sanctions, including asset freezes and travel bans, were imposed against four Chinese Government officials Zhu Hailun, Wang Junzheng, Deputy Secretary of the Party Committee of Xinjiang Uyghur Autonomous Region and previously Secretary of the Political and Legal Affairs Committee of the Xinjiang Uyghur Autonomous Region, Wang Mingshan, and Chen Mingguo, Vice Chairman of the Government of the XUAR, and Director of the XUAR Public Security Department, as well as a Xinjiang security body (the Public Security Bureau of the Xinjiang Production and Construction Corps), for their role in systemic violations against Uyghurs and other minorities.

In each case, the Chinese Government imposed retaliation sanctions against the most vocal critics of their alleged atrocities.

4.2   Investigating and Prosecuting the Crimes

At the time of writing this book, little has been done to investigate and prosecute the crimes.

4.2.1   Prosecutions by International Tribunals
On 6 July 2020, lawyers for the East Turkistan Government in Exile (ETGE) and the East Turkistan National Awakening Movement

---

[89] US State Department, 'The United States Imposes Sanctions and Visa Restrictions in Response to the Ongoing Human Rights Violations and Abuses in Xinjiang' (9 July 2020). Available at: https://2017-2021.state.gov/the-united-states-imposes-sanctions-and-visa-restrictions-in-response-to-the-ongoing-human-rights-violations-and-abuses-in-xin jiang/index.html.

[90] US State Department, 'On Sanctioning Human Rights Abusers in Xinjiang, China' (31 July 2020). Available at: https://2017-2021.state.gov/on-sanctioning-human-rights-abusers-in-xinjiang-china/index.html.

[91] FCDO, 'UK Sanctions Perpetrators of Gross Human Rights Violations in Xinjiang, Alongside EU, Canada and US' (22 March 2021). Available at: https://www.gov.uk/government/news/uk-sanctions-perpetrators-of-gross-human-rig hts-violations-in-xinjiang-alongside-eu-canada-and-us.

(ETNAM) have submitted a communication to the Office of the Prosecutor (OTP) at the ICC asking for an investigation to be opened against senior Chinese leaders for genocide and crimes against humanity allegedly committed against the Uyghur and other communities. As China is not a party to the Rome Statute, preventing the ICC from exercising territorial jurisdiction over any crimes committed there, the communication advanced the argument, used previously in the case of Myanmar/Bangladesh, that part of the criminal conduct had occurred within the territory of a state party to the Rome Statute. In the case of Myanmar/Bangladesh, Pre-Trial Chamber I of the ICC held that 'the Court may assert jurisdiction pursuant to article 12(2)(a) of the Statute if at least one element of a crime within the jurisdiction of the Court or part of such a crime is committed on the territory of a state party to the Statute.'[92] In the case of Myanmar/Bangladesh, the argument enabled the ICC to engage and investigate the atrocities against the Rohingya in Myanmar.

The communication argued that as part of the criminal conduct occurred in Tajikistan and Cambodia, it could technically open the door for the ICC to engage on the Uyghur case. The communication incorporated evidence of 'brutal torture through electrocution, humiliation in the form of being forced to eat pork and drink alcohol, mandatory insertion of IUD birth control for Uyghur women of child-bearing age– of which there is recent evidence of a major increase, and an estimated 500,000 Uyghur children being separated from their families and sent to "orphanage camps" where there have been credible reports of attempted suicide by the children.'

On 14 December 2020, OTP to the ICC confirmed that it could not take the case of the Uyghurs any further. In its report, OTP stated that there was no basis to proceed at this time.[93] The OTP examined the cases and stated that the precondition for the exercise of the ICC's territorial jurisdiction did not appear to be met with respect to the majority of the crimes alleged, including genocide, crimes against humanity of murder, imprisonment or other severe deprivation of liberty, torture, enforced

---

[92] ICC, 'Decision on the Prosecution's Request for a Ruling on Jurisdiction under Article 19(3) of the Statute', ICC-RoC46(3)-01/18-37, 6 September 2018. Available at: https://www.icc-cpi.int/Pages/record.aspx?docNo=ICC-RoC46(3)-01/18-37.

[93] ICC, 'Report on Preliminary Examination Activities' (2020). Available at: https://www.icc-cpi.int/itemsDocuments/2020-PE/2020-pe-report-eng.pdf.

sterilisation, and other inhumane acts. The OTP further assessed the alleged crimes perpetrated in Cambodia and Tajikistan, and observed that 'while the transfers of persons from Cambodia and Tajikistan to China appear to raise concerns with respect to their conformity with national and international law, including international human rights law and international refugee law, it does not appear that such conduct would amount to the crime against humanity of deportation under article 7(1)(d) of the Statute.'[94]

The OTP concluded that:

> In the present situation, from the information available, it does not appear that the Chinese officials involved in these forcible repatriations fulfilled the required elements described above. While the conduct of such officials may have served as a precursor to the subsequent alleged commission of crimes on the territory of China, over which the Court lacks jurisdiction, the conduct occurring on the territory of States Parties does not appear, on the information available, to fulfil material elements of the crime of deportation under article 7(1)(d) of the Statute.[95]

The OTP confirmed that it has received a request for reconsideration pursuant article 15(6) on the basis of new facts or evidence. The OTP is yet to consider the new evidence and make a further determination.

4.2.2   Other Inquiries

On 3 September 2020, Sir Geoffrey Nice QC, a prominent British lawyer, announced the launch of a new independent inquiry, the Uyghur Tribunal, to assess the evidence of the alleged atrocities perpetrated against Uyghurs and other Turkic Muslims in the Uyghur Region of Northwest China. The launch of the Uyghur Tribunal followed a request from the World Uyghur Congress for an independent review of the allegations of international crimes being perpetrated against the minority communities. There are encouraging precedents for this initiative. In 1966, the British philosopher, Bertrand Russell, and the French philosopher, Jean Paul Sartre, created a People's Tribunal to investigate war crimes committed in Vietnam.[96] The Russell model has been applied

---

[94] Ibid.

[95] Ibid.

[96] Russell Tribunal on Vietnam (1966–1967).

in other situations—including a Tribunal into the military dictatorships in Argentina, Brazil, and Chile.[97] Subsequently, a Permanent Peoples' Tribunal (PPT) was established in Bologna in 1979.[98] In 1984, the PPT retrospectively considered the motives of the Ottoman Turks in the 1915 Armenian massacre and concluded that if the Genocide Convention had been enacted, all of the Ottomans Empire's actions met the criteria of genocide—through deportation and massacre.[99]

In the case of the Uyghur, where we see grave and serious allegations that point towards mass atrocities, as genocide or crimes against humanity, the international community has done little to nothing to ensure that the alleged atrocities are investigated and those responsible brought to justice. International bodies, such as the United Nations, have been silent, apart from a few meaningless statements never followed by decisive action to provide justice for the targeted communities. The undisclosed report and the UN visit to China raise more questions than can provide solutions. In this context the independent inquiry initiated by Sir Geoffrey has been greatly welcome.

Although the Uyghur Tribunal was unable to fully investigate crimes and prosecute perpetrators, it was able to shed light on the atrocities and trigger action by the international community. It is the first independent body to collect and analyse the evidence. As international actors, including the UN, shy away from undertaking such investigations, this is a much-appreciated initiative. Of course, further steps will need to be taken, including the establishment of a UN mechanism to collect and preserve the evidence of the atrocities against the Uyghurs and to prosecute the perpetrators.

On 9 December 2021, as the UN was marking the International Day of Commemoration and Dignity of the Victims of the Crime of Genocide and of the Prevention of this Crime, the Uyghur Tribunal published its findings stating that the PRC has committed genocide, crimes against humanity, and torture against Uyghur, Kazakh, and other ethnic minority citizens in the Northwest region of China. The Uyghur Tribunal found that: 'Torture of Uyghurs attributable to the PRC is established beyond

[97] Russell Tribunal on Latin America (1973–1976).

[98] Permanent Peoples' Tribunal (1979-now). See more at: http://permanentpeoplestribunal.org/?lang=en.

[99] Permanent Peoples' Tribunal, Verdict of the Tribunal (16 April 1984). See: https://www.armenian-genocide.org/Affirmation.66/current_category.5/affirmation_detail.html.

reasonable doubt. Crimes against humanity attributable to the PRC is established beyond reasonable doubt by acts of: deportation or forcible transfer; imprisonment or other severe deprivation of physical liberty; torture; rape and other sexual violence; enforced sterilisation; persecution; enforced disappearance; and other inhumane acts.'[100] The Uyghur Tribunal further added that it 'is satisfied beyond reasonable doubt that the PRC, by the imposition of measures to prevent births intended to destroy a significant part of the Uyghurs in Xinjiang as such, has committed genocide.' Commenting further on the issue of measures to prevent births within a group, the Uyghur Tribunal identified that the PRC has 'put in place a comprehensive system of measures to "optimise" the population in Xinjiang' including by way of mandatory sterilisation and forced abortions, including sterilisation by removal of wombs, widespread forced insertion of effectively removable IUDs. In May 2022, Michelle Bachelet, who, since 2018, has served as United Nations High Commissioner for Human Rights, visited China. She said the visit was 'not an investigation' and faced considerable criticism for failing to hold the Chinese Government to account or to pursue the findings of the Uyghur Tribunal that a genocide is underway.

[100] See: https://uyghurtribunal.com/wp-content/uploads/2021/12/Uyghur-Tribunal-Summary-Judgment-9th-Dec-21.pdf.

CHAPTER 4

The Burmese Military's Genocide

1   INTRODUCTION

Lord Alton first travelled, illegally, into Burma/Myanmar in 1998 to visit the Karen State. The Karen people were still in active combat in what had become the world's longest running civil war. In the course of the past seventy years, there have been over twenty wars in Burma/Myanmar resulting in thousands of deaths and the displacement of millions.

And, as we write, the killing continues, following the *coup d'état* which began on the morning of 1 February 2021, when the Tatmadaw (the Burmese military) deposed the elected government of Daw Aung San Suu Kyi and the National League for Democracy. Among their recent depredations was the killing, on Christmas Eve 2021, of 38 people, many of them women and children, after the Tatmadaw attacked an ethnic minority village in the eastern state of Kayah. The bodies of victims were found in eight burnt vehicles close to the village of Mo So near Hpruso Township. Witnesses said that government soldiers had forced people from their cars, arrested some, and killed others and burnt their bodies. Simultaneously, the Tatmadaw launched airstrikes and fired heavy artillery on Lay Kay Kaw, a small town controlled by ethnic Karen resistance fighters. Western embassies condemned these attacks and serious human rights violations committed by the regime and '*indiscriminate attacks on Karen state*.'

© The Author(s), under exclusive license to Springer Nature Switzerland AG 2022
E. U. Ochab and D. Alton, *State Responses to Crimes of Genocide*, Rethinking Political Violence, https://doi.org/10.1007/978-3-030-99162-3_4

99

Lady Mountbatten of Burma once told Lord Alton that her father regarded the Karen people '*as the bravest of our allies: now our forgotten allies.*' During his visits to the region, Lord Alton met Karen leaders who had been awarded the Burma Star in recognition of their courage and bravery in action against the Japanese during World War II. He also taken evidence in refugee camps, met representatives of other ethnic minorities, including the Rohingya, and has frequently raised concerns about the targeting of Burma's many ethnic minorities. He serves as Vice Chair of the All-Party Parliamentary Groups on Burma and the Rohingya—who have faced serious discrimination, and persecution, including the denial of citizenship.

In Parliament, on 17 July 2006, he first raised the question of Rohingya citizenship, and the conditions faced by displaced Rohingya refugees—and, since then, in speeches and questions, on over 70 further occasions. In 2006, he urged the UK Government to coordinate an approach to the United Nations, especially by involving Islamic countries, in raising the plight of the Rohingya and the deplorable conditions in the camps in which they had taken refuge, warning that the camps would become the '*perfect breeding ground for nurturing a generation of alienated and hostile jihadists.*'[1]

Rohingya are the people indigenous to the western Rakhine State of Burma/Myanmar. They are predominantly Muslims. Of the 135 officially recognised ethnicities in Burma/Myanmar (40% of the population inhabiting 60% of the land), the Rohingya are not included. Despite their indigenous status, the Burmese Government refuses to recognise their identity as Rohingya, labelling them as illegal immigrants from Bangladesh.[2] The denial of citizenship has had a profound impact on the 'othering' and ostracism of Rohingya.

2   The Atrocities Against Rohingya Muslims

For many years, the Rohingya have faced significant hostility. In 1952, Normal Lewis, a British journalist and author, writing in '*Golden Earth:*

---

[1] See: House of Lords Deb, 5 June 2013, c1232.

[2] David Dapice, 'A Fatal Distraction from Federalism Religious Conflict in Rakhine' (2015) Harvard Kennedy School, Ash Centre for Democratic Governance and Innovation. Available at: https://ash.harvard.edu/files/a_fatal_distraction_from_federalism_religious_conflict_in_rakhine_10-20-2014_rev_6-26-15.pdf.

Travels in Burma,' recorded his shock at the way in which Burmese people expressed their hatred for the Rohingya. They told Lewis it was too dangerous to travel to their region, describing them as gypsies.[3] Over the past fifteen years (and from earlier exchanges concerning the Karen and other ethnic minorities in Burma/Myanmar who have been the subject of terrible atrocities), we have identified a number of issues which we will now try to address.

2.1   From No Citizenship to Genocide

The first is the right to citizenship: the right to belong. It hardly needs to be said that by denying the Rohingya the citizenship status it has had a profound effect on their ability to enjoy the rights which accompany citizenship.[4] Erin Rosenberg, lawyer and expert on genocide, wrote that:

> in the 1960s, following the military coup and the government becoming a military dictatorship, led by General Ne Win, hostility toward the Rohingya increased along with efforts to erase their connection and history in Myanmar. These efforts culminated in the passage of the 1982 Citizenship Law.[5]

Article 4 of the 1982 Citizenship Law states that: '*The Council of State may decide whether any ethnic group is a national or not*' and so equipping Ne Win and members of the Tatmadaw to make the decision on who was and was not to be granted citizenship. As a result, while 135 ethnic groups have been recognised as national groups under Article 4, the Rohingya were not included.[6]

On five occasions in 2010, Lord Alton pressed Ministers to engage with the UN and the governments of Burma/Myanmar and Bangladesh, about the humanitarian crisis, harassment, arrests, and deportation faced

---

[3] Normal Lewis, *Golden Earth: Travels in Burma* (Eland Publishing Ltd., 2003).

[4] Erin Rosenberg, 'Practical Prevention. How the Genocide Convention's Obligation to Prevent Applies to Myanmar. Report 2: The Denial of the Right to Citizenship and the Right to Participate in Public Affairs' (USHMM, 2020).

[5] Erin Rosenberg, 'Practical Prevention. How the Genocide Convention's Obligation to Prevent Applies to Myanmar. Report 2: The Denial of the Right to Citizenship and the Right to Participate in Public Affairs' (USHMM, 2020) 8.

[6] Ibid.

by increasing numbers of Rohingya refugees and displaced people—many of them undocumented.[7] The lack of documentation and status was an issue to which he returned in 2011 and 2013 when he asked Ministers to '*confirm that since 2012, around 5000 Rohingya Muslim people have been murdered and that many thousands have disappeared… they are living in a system of 21st century apartheid, their citizenship rights having been formally stripped from the constitution.*'[8]

In 2013, he asked the UK Government to press the '*authorities in Burma/Myanmar to revisit this question and inquire of the UN Special Rapporteur on Religious Liberty whether he would be willing to make a visit to the Rohingya people in Arakan state?*'[9] Two months later, he asked what steps the UK was '*taking to support reconciliation efforts between the Arakan and Rohingya populations in Arakan State; and what representations they had made to the Government of Burma regarding (1) the reform of the 1982 Citizenship Law to bring it into line with international standards, and (2) discrimination against that country's ethnic minorities.*'[10]

In a debate which he initiated, he said that:

> the Rohingya are living in a system of 21st century apartheid with their citizenship rights having been formally stripped from the constitution. The years, the months and the weeks have passed by, but there has been very little sense of urgency among or a coherent, determined response from the international community. Six weeks ago, through five further Parliamentary Questions, I again raised the conditions in the camps. I asked about the core issue, the question of the Rohingya claim to citizenship. The Government of Burma need to repeal the 1982 citizenship laws which stripped the Rohingya of their citizenship, rendering them stateless. They need to introduce a new citizenship law in line with international norms.[11]

In addition to citizenship rights, Parliament was urged to take note of restrictions on Rohingya births: '*They should also be challenged for trying to impose a two-child policy on the Rohingya, which in the past seven days Daw*

---

[7] For more information, see Hansard entries.

[8] House of Lords Deb, 28 February 2013, c1157.

[9] Ibid.

[10] WPQ UIN HL6811, tabled on 23 April 2013.

[11] House of Lords Deb, 5 June 2013, c1232.

Suu has described as, "illegal and against human rights".'[12] The House was told that there was a need for two independent inquiries:

> ... one through the United Nations to investigate the violence in Arakan state last year and to assess whether crimes against humanity have been committed; (...) and the other perhaps consisting of independent academics and other experts to assess the historical basis for the claims of the Rohingya in order fully and conclusively to address the claims of the Government of Burma and many in Burmese society that the Rohingya are, as they put it, illegal Bengali immigrants. Years of misinformation about the Rohingya in Burma need to be countered with a full, comprehensive and independent assessment of the history and the facts, if the suffering of the Rohingya is ever to end.[13]

Following a fact-finding visit to Burma in 2013, during which the plight of the Rohingya was on the agenda when he and the human rights campaigner, Benedict Rogers, met with Aung San Suu Kyi, Lord Alton warned of the consequences of not addressing the fundamental issue of the denial of citizenship and the need to bring the perpetrators of violence against Rohingya to justice. He later told Parliament:

> having seen for myself quite recently the spread of violence against the Rohingya to other parts of Burma and following last week's violence in Lashio, in Shan state, and this week's reports of the escalating exodus of people from the Rakhine state into neighbouring countries, what pressure is being put on the authorities in Burma to prevent such violence, to bring the perpetrators of crimes against humanity to justice, to ensure the rule of law and to resolve the Rohingya's demands for full citizenship and constitutional rights, which after all lie at the heart of the problem?[14]

Investigations and reports of human rights violations in Burma, published in 2013, had clearly concluded that ethnic cleansing and crimes against humanity had taken place against the Rohingya.

Despite the previously revered status of Daw Aung San Suu Kyi, and her own experiences as a political prisoner, she, along with the political leadership of the National League for Democracy, the institutions of

[12] Ibid.

[13] Ibid.

[14] House of Lords Deb, 5 June 2013, c1171.

government, and the security and armed forces, had simply not come to terms with the idea of Burma/Myanmar as a multilingual, multireligious, and multi-ethnic state. Nor, given the horrific crimes committed in the previous decades, had they done anything like enough work on reconciliation or the need for a South African-style Justice and Truth Commission (notwithstanding a welcome visit by Burmese Ministers to Northern Ireland, where they expressed interest in its model of power sharing and the resetting of civil society after conflict).

During the 2013 Parliamentary debate, Lord Alton reflected on the address which Daw Aung San Suu Kyi had given to both Houses of Parliament in June 2012 (during which the then Prime Minister, David Cameron, and Foreign Secretary, William Hague, privately raised the status of the Rohingya with Daw Suu) and said: '*There was an understandable sense of euphoria and a sense of "problem solved" (...) During a recent visit to Burma it became clear to me that the euphoria is premature, misplaced and profoundly dangerous.*'[15]
He said there had been:

> a change of atmosphere rather than a change of system' in Burma and that the focus needed to shift to 'ethnic tensions and the limitations of recent developments' which included 'anti-Muslim violence last week'... 'attacks on journalists trying to document what occurred. Mosques, schools and shops had been burnt down, and violence took place in more than 18 townships hundreds of kilometres apart from one another.[16]

Lord Alton also warned that:

> ... if the challenges posed by ethnic violence are not addressed, they have the capacity to derail Burma's evolution from military dictatorship into a plural, federal democracy. I met representatives of the Rohingya and the Kachin, whose home states are the two of the bloodiest theatres of ethnic violence. Over the past year, some 192 people have been killed and 140,000 displaced in Arakan state.[17]

[15] House of Lords Deb, 5 June 2013, c1232.
[16] Ibid.
[17] Ibid.

Around that time, a 150-page Report published by Human Rights Watch (HRW), entitled *'All You Can Do Is Pray,'* detailed *'mass graves from violence that swept Arakan state in June and October last year' – and raised the question of genocide.*[18] The report further:

> categorised what is happening to the Rohingya people as genocide, and said that what is happening in Kachin state amounts to war crimes in the perfectly technical sense, not just in the rhetorical sense? Given those allegations, can she tell us what the Government are doing about raising that issue, particularly in the Security Council? Does she accept the underlying point that the ethnic minorities in Burma are in grave danger?[19]

A Foreign Office Minister replied that: *'at this stage we feel that rather than an UN-mandated inquiry, it would be better and probably more likely to be effective if it were done internally by the Burmese.'*[20] This seemed comparable to asking a serial offender whether he would like to be judge, jury, prosecution, and defence, in determining the evidence and the verdict in his own case.[21] When pressed to say whether it believed a genocide was underway, the Foreign Office declined to do so saying such determinations were a matter for the courts to decide.

Lord Alton told Parliament that:

> The Rohingya are among the most persecuted and marginalised people in the world, and they are now facing an intensified campaign of ethnic cleansing... thousands of displaced Rohingya who have been forced to flee.[22]

Describing the burning of Ayela, a village near the capital, Naypyidaw, which he had visited, Lord Alton said that for 200 years Muslims and Buddhists had lived peacefully together.[23] Three days earlier, the village's

---

[18] Human Rights Watch, 'All You Can Do Is Pray. Crimes Against Humanity and Ethnic Cleansing of Rohingya Muslims in Burma's Arakan State' (2013). Available at: https://www.hrw.org/reports/burma0413_FullForWeb.pdf.

[19] House of Lords Deb, 9 December 2013, c582.

[20] House of Lords Deb, 9 December 2013, c582–583.

[21] It is noteworthy that a few years later, the Burmese Government initiated such an inquiry, but it has been challenged for not being independent and as self-serving.

[22] House of Lords Deb, 5 June 2013, c1232.

[23] Ibid.

Muslims had been forced to flee as their homes and village mosque had been set alight in an orgy of hatred, intolerance, and violence.

The killings and violence continued unabated.

The question of genocide was raised in 2015, with the UK government asked '*to support calls for the establishment of a full, international, independent investigation by the UN into claims of genocide against the Rohingya in Burma.*'[24] This came on the back of reports by Yale Law School and Queen Mary University of London, an investigation by Al-Jazeera, and the human rights group, Fortify Rights, which provided evidence that genocide was being committed against the Rohingya people in Burma. The time-honoured Foreign Office reply was: '*...any judgement on whether genocide has occurred is a matter for international judicial decision, rather than for governments or non-judicial bodies. A UN investigation would require high level international support for which we assess there is little prospect of agreement at this stage.*'[25]

2.2   2016 and Subsequent Developments

The situation further deteriorated over subsequent years and particularly rapidly after the events on 9 October 2016, when nine Burmese police officers were killed by armed militia.[26] The response to the killings of the Burmese police officers was reportedly violent, leading to widespread and systematic indiscriminate attacks against Rohingya Muslims.[27] The response to the events of October 2016 cannot be seen as proportionate and has led to atrocities that have reached the level of international crimes.

In response, British Parliamentarians called for a '*full and transparent international inquiry into the plight of Burma's Rohingya people*'[28]; for full access to humanitarian agencies and the restoration of humanitarian aid to the Rohingya; and for the Burmese Government to show restraint.

---

[24] WPQ UIN HL3170, tabled on 2 November 2015.

[25] Ibid.

[26] Reuters, 'Myanmar Says Nine Police Killed by Insurgents on Bangladesh Border' *Reuters* (10 October 2016), Available at: https://www.theguardian.com/world/2016/oct/10/myanmar-nine-police-killed-insurgents-bangladesh-border.

[27] UN News, 'Devastating Cruelty Against Rohingya Children, Women and Men Detailed in UN Human Rights Report' (3 February 2017). Available at: www.ohchr.org/EN/NewsEvents/Pages/DisplayNews.aspx?NewsID=21142.

[28] WPQ UIN HL3641, tabled on 29 November 2016.

The UK Government agreed that violence against the Rohingya was a matter of deep concern. However, this was not followed up by action. In January 2017, the attention of Parliament was drawn to the Amnesty International report '*We Are at Breaking Point*'[29] and its findings which pointed to '*mass rape, mass displacement and the murder of men, women and children; the burning of houses; and crucially, the denial of access to the affected areas for humanitarian aid.*'[30]

In a letter to *The Guardian* on 28 November 2016, Lord Alton, Baroness Cox, and Baroness Kinnock had called for an international inquiry: '*The international community cannot stand idly by while peaceful civilians are mown down by helicopter guns, women are raped and tens of thousands left without homes.*'[31]

Government Ministers continued to refer Lord Alton to the Rakhine Investigation Commission. That Commission's interim report said that there were, '*no cases of malnutrition, due to the area's favourable fishing and farming conditions … and … no cases of religious persecution.*'[32] In Parliament, this response from Burma's investigation into itself was described as '*palpably risible*'[33] concurring with the view of Human Rights Watch that the investigation was little more than a '*Myanmar government whitewash mechanism.*'[34] Similarly, twenty-three of the world's most prominent human rights voices, including a dozen Nobel Laureates, had called on the UN Security Council to end 'ethnic

[29] Amnesty International, 'We Are At Breaking Point. Rohingya: Persecuted in Myanmar. Neglected in Bangladesh' (2016). Available at: https://www.amnesty.org/en/documents/asa16/5362/2016/en/.

[30] House of Lords Deb, 12 January 2017, c2116.

[31] Lord Alton of Liverpool, Jonathan Ashworth MP, David Burrowes MP, Baroness Nye of Lambeth, Baroness Cox of Queensbury, Baroness Kinnock of Holyhead, Paul Scully MP, Valerie Vaz MP, Fiona Bruce MP, Myanmar must react to humanitarian crisis. Letters. The Guardian (28 November 2016). Available at: https://www.theguardian.com/world/2016/nov/28/myanmar-must-react-to-humanitarian-crisis.

[32] Interim Report of the Investigation Commission on Maungtaw, 3 January 2017. Available at: http://www.statecounsellor.gov.mm/en/node/581.

[33] House of Lords Deb, 12 January 2017, c2116.

[34] Human Rights Watch, 'Burma Events of 2017.' Available at: https://www.hrw.org/world-report/2018/country-chapters/myanmar-burma#.

cleansing against humanity' in the Rakhine State,[35] and in February 2017, the UN Special Adviser on the Prevention of Genocide said that:

> the scale of violence alleged to have been perpetrated by the Burmese security forces against the Rohingya community amounts to 'dehumanisation', and the existing government of Burma commission is not a credible option to undertake a new investigation into allegations of human rights abuses in Rakhine State.[36]

Ultimately, on 3 February 2017, the UN Office of the High Commissioner for Human Rights (OHCHR) Mission to Bangladesh released a report based on interviews with Rohingya who fled Burma/Myanmar following the 2016 attacks.[37] The OHCHR Mission to Bangladesh interviewed 240 people whose accounts informed the preparation of the report, including 204 in-depth interviews. This led the OHCHR Mission to Bangladesh to conclude that the Burmese military was responsible for:

> Extrajudicial executions or other killings, including by random shooting; enforced disappearance and arbitrary detention; rape, including gang rape, and other forms of sexual violence; physical assault including beatings; torture, cruel, inhuman or degrading treatment or punishment; looting and occupation of the property; destruction of property; and ethnic and religious discrimination and persecution.[38]

The OHCHR Mission to Bangladesh raised concerns that the atrocities perpetrated against the Rohingya Muslims amounted to 'persecution against a particular ethnic and religious group.'[39] The report went on to

---

[35] Oliver Holmes, 'Nobel Laureates Warn Aung San Suu Kyi Over "Ethnic Cleansing" of Rohingya' *The Guardian* (30 December 2016. Available at: https://www.theguardian.com/world/2016/dec/30/nobel-laureates-aung-san-suu-kyi-ethnic-cleansing-rohingya.

[36] UN News, 'Violence in Myanmar's Rakhine State Could Amount to Crimes Against Humanity—UN Special Adviser' UN News (6 February 2017). Available at: https://news.un.org/en/story/2017/02/550942-violence-myanmars-rakhine-state-could-amount-crimes-against-humanity-un-special.

[37] Report of OHCHR Mission to Bangladesh, 'Interviews with Rohingya fleeing from Myanmar Since 9 October 2016' (3 February 2017). Available at: www.ohchr.org/Documents/Countries/MM/FlashReport3Feb2017.pdf (Later cited as the OHCHR Report 2017).

[38] Ibid.

[39] Ibid.

say that as of 20 January 2017, over 22,000 Rohingya remained internally displaced in Burma/Myanmar. It suggested that crimes against humanity or even ethnic cleansing was under way.

In response to that report, and as a result of the deteriorating situation, in March 2017, the UN Human Rights Council passed a resolution establishing the Independent International Fact-Finding Mission on Myanmar (the IIFFMM) to collect information about alleged human rights violations, focusing mainly on the Rakhine State.[40] The resolution condemned the violence in Myanmar and called for peaceful solutions. In the same month, the ethno-religious character of the conflict in Myanmar was also recognised in a resolution of the UN Human Rights Council, which:

> Strongly encourage[d] the Government of Myanmar to take the measures necessary to address discrimination and prejudice against women, children and members of ethnic, religious and linguistic minorities across the country, and to take further action to publicly condemn and speak out against any advocacy of national, racial or religious hatred that constitutes incitement to discrimination, hostility or violence, and to adopt measures to criminalize incitement to imminent violence based on nationality, race or religion or belief...[41]

In May, following the passage of this resolution, the UN Human Rights Council appointed Ms Radhika Coomaraswamy and Mr Christopher Dominic Sidoti as two of the members of the fact-finding mission.[42] The Chair, Mr Marzuki Darusman, was appointment in July 2017. The fact-finding mission was ready to fulfil its mandate to explore the human rights violations in Myanmar, but the Burmese Government refused to cooperate and allow it into the country.[43] As such, despite the establishment of the fact-finding mission, the team was prevented from conducting its work in the field and from investigating the situation in Burma/Myanmar, being forced to continue its work remotely.

[40] UN Human Rights Council, Resolution 34/22 on Situation of human rights in Myanmar, 3 April 2017, A/HRC/RES/34/22.

[41] Ibid.

[42] See: The OHCHR Report 2017.

[43] Reuters, 'Myanmar Refuses Visas to UN Team Investigating Abuse of Rohingya Muslims' *Reuters* (30 June 2017). Available at: https://www.theguardian.com/world/2017/jun/30/myanmar-refuses-visas-un-abuse-rohingya-muslims.

Although, over the next few months, Burma/Myanmar was subjected to increased scrutiny by the United Nations, the plight of the Rohingya Muslims deteriorated further, sparking international condemnation and criticism. Media reports confirmed that hundreds of people were slaughtered in clashes between Burmese forces and Rohingya insurgents.[44] The fatalities reportedly included many civilians, while many buildings were destroyed, and thousands of Rohingya Muslims were forced to flee to Bangladesh. The Burmese Government blamed Rohingya insurgents for the killings and property destruction.[45] However, increasing numbers of reports suggested that the Burmese army was responsible for the burning down of villages and the shooting of civilians.[46] On 29 August 2017, in response to the ever-growing crisis, Zeid Ra'ad Al Hussein, the then UN High Commissioner for Human Rights, made a statement condemning the dire situation of Rohingya Muslims in Myanmar.[47] However, these numerous condemnations have done little to engage the Burmese Government or to bring a change in its appalling treatment of the Rohingya people.

In September 2017, the UK Government was again pressed to rest the case for Rohingya citizenship rights, and in a parliamentary debate, attention was drawn to attacks on the Rohingya which:

amount to crimes against humanity and ethnic cleansing. As one journalist put it, "the Burmese army, wants to destroy an ethnicity, not end an insurgency." When more than 600,000 Rohingya—over half the population—have fled to Bangladesh, and harrowing accounts of the most

---

[44] Samuel Osbornes, 'Clashes in Burma Leave Scores Dead as Thousands of Rohingya Muslims Flee Ongoing Violence' (27 August 2017). Available at: www.independent.co.uk/news/world/asia/burma-rohingya-muslim-myanmar-clashes-attack-dead-thousands-flee-violence-bangladesh-a7915496.html.

[45] Amnesty International, 'Myanmar: Military Land Grab as Security Forces Build Bases on Torched Rohingya Villages'; Human Rights Watch, 'Burma: Scores of Rohingya Villages Bulldozed', 23 February 2018. Available at: https://www.hrw.org/news/2018/02/23/ burma-scores-rohingya-villages-bulldozed.

[46] Samuel Osbornes, 'Rohingya Muslim villages "burned by Burmese army"' (29 August 2017). Available at: www.independent.co.uk/news/world/asia/rohingya-muslims-burma-army-burn-villages-persecute-minority-rakhine-state-a7917926.html.

[47] UN News, 'Alarming Deterioration in Northern Rakhine Was Preventable, Zeid Says, Urging Restraint' (29 August 2017). Available at: www.ohchr.org/EN/NewsEvents/Pages/DisplayNews.aspx?NewsID=22004&LangID=E.

extreme barbaric human rights violations are consistently repeated by survivors, it is impossible to reach any other conclusion.[48]

During the debate, Lord Alton referred to a statement from the former President of East Timor, Nobel Peace Prize Laureate José Ramos-Horta: '*A human tragedy approaching ethnic cleansing is unfolding in Burma, and the world is chillingly silent… If we fail to act, Rohingya may starve to death if they aren't killed by bullets first.*'[49]

It was remarked that '*so often we say "never again"*', only to watch it happen all over again, from Rwanda, Kosovo, Bosnia, Darfur to the genocide—it was named as such by the House of Commons—of Christians, Yazidis and other minorities in Syria and Iraq.'[50] Indeed, the UN Secretary General described the humanitarian crisis facing the Rohingya as '*catastrophic*' stressing the need to address impunity and to gain urgent unhindered access for international aid organisations and human rights monitors. Burma/Myanmar's commander-in-chief, General Min Aung Hlaing, was named as '*the person with the power to order the troops to stop the carnage… If the violence is to end, the decision to immediately cease their operations in Rakhine state lies squarely with him.*'[51] The UK Government was asked whether it would lead the initiative at the UN and make a referral to the ICC.[52] However, an affirmative response did not follow.

Two months later, in November 2017, calls were renewed for those responsible for the atrocities against the Rohingya to be brought to justice and that '*at the root cause of this was the denial of citizenship to the Rohingya people and called for the imposition of sanctions on members of the military who have been responsible for the depredations against the Rohingya.*'[53] In answer to further questions in 2018, the UK Government confirmed that '*more than 655,000 refugees have arrived in Bangladesh since August 2017, and approximately 100 Rohingya are still crossing*

---

[48] House of Lords Deb, 26 October 2017, c1032.

[49] José Ramos-Horta and Benedict Rogers, 'Burma Edges Closer to Ethnic Cleansing' *Wall Street Journal* (30 November 2016). Available at: https://www.wsj.com/articles/burma-edges-closer-to-ethnic-cleansing-1480528807.

[50] House of Lords Deb, 26 October 2017, c1032.

[51] Ibid.

[52] Ibid.

[53] House of Lords Deb, 23 November 2017, c287.

per day.'[54] Lord Alton raised reports from the Burma Human Rights Network of the discovery of mass graves of Rohingya in Inn Din village, southern Maungdaw Township, and of BBC Burma reports that witness in Kanyin Tan village, southern Maungdaw Township, who reported that 28 bodies of Rohingya civilians had been discovered in a local cemetery; reports that refugees faced refoulement from Bangladesh to Burmese camps where they would be held indefinitely (which the government said had to be done *'voluntarily and with dignity'*); and asked about measures the UK was taking to support birth registration activities in relation to Rohingya children born in Bangladesh to ensure that their rights would be protected while they are refugees and when, or if, they return to Burma/Myanmar.

In 2018, the UK Parliament was told that: *'Those responsible have been emboldened by the ethnic cleansing of 750,000 Rohingya Muslims, the destruction of villages and killings, torture and rape'*[55] and pointed to the United Nations estimate that fighting in Kachin and Shan States had driven a further 120,000 people into 167 inaccessible displacement camps. Lord Alton urged the government to respond positively to the request of the prosecutor of ICC that *'these unconscionable war crimes and crimes against humanity be referred to her court'* saying it was *'high time that senior members of the Burmese military such as General Min Aung Hlaing are targeted with sanctions and brought to justice.'*[56] The Foreign Office Minister, Lord Ahmad of Wimbledon replied by saying that Burma/Myanmar had signed a Memorandum of Understanding:

> Not only has the Rohingya community suffered immensely following its displacement—with almost 1 million in Bangladesh, if you take it over a longer period—but so too have specific communities in Kachin, predominantly Christian minority communities. There has been internal displacement, and quite often the full extent of that displacement has not been revealed because of lack of access. There is a glimmer of hope from the civilian Administration in that, for the first time, we have seen Burma sign an MoU with the UN agencies concerned—the UNHCR and the UNDP which took place on 7 June.[57]

---

[54] WPQ, UIN HL4874, tabled on 18 January 2018.

[55] House of Lords Deb, 12 June 2018, c1581.

[56] House of Lords Deb, 12 June 2018, c1581.

[57] House of Lords Deb, 12 June 2018, c1581.

Later, in June 2018, the UK Government was asked a specific question on the issue of genocide and what consideration the UK Government had given to evidence suggesting genocidal techniques being used against Rohingya Muslims in Rakhine, Christian minorities in Kachin, and other protected groups.[58] It responded in the usual way side-stepping the question about genocidal techniques—and saying, leave it to the Burmese suggesting that the newly established Commission of Inquiry in Burma/Myanmar was the right response, ignoring concerns of experts about transparency and impartiality.[59]

On 27 August 2018, the IIFFMM published its report on Burma/Myanmar that shed more light on the scope and nature of the atrocities.[60] According to the report, the Burmese military has used a wide range of methods to bring about this genocide—as we believe it to be—including mass killings (10,000 deaths being a conservative estimate), rape and sexual violence, sexual slavery, abductions, and much more. The report mentions some of the barbaric atrocities, for example,

In both Min Gyi and Maung Nu, villagers were gathered together, before men and boys were separated and killed. In Min Gyi, women and girls were taken to nearby houses, gang-raped, then killed or severely injured. Houses were locked and set on fire. Few survived. In numerous other villages, the number of casualties was also markedly high. Bodies were transported in military vehicles, burned and disposed of in mass graves.[61]

According to the IIFFMM, the methods used by the Burmese military 'disproportionately affected the elderly, persons with disabilities and young children, unable to escape.'[62] The Burmese military had used rape and sexual violence against women and girls on a mass scale, including a large-scale gang rape in at least ten villages, with up to 40 women and girls

[58] WPQ UIN HL8755, tabled on 19 June 2018. Available at: https://questions-sta tements.parliament.uk/written-questions/detail/2018-06-19/HL8755.

[59] Ibid.

[60] Human Rights Council, 'Report of the Independent International Fact-Finding Mission on Myanmar' (12 September 2018), A/HRC/39/64. Available at: https://www.ohchr.org/Documents/HRBodies/HRCouncil/FFM-Myanmar/A_HRC_39_64.pdf.

[61] Ibid., para. 36.

[62] Ibid., para. 37.

being raped together, in front of their families and local communities. The IIFFMM Report also found that as a result of this violence,

> Victims were severely injured before and during rape, often marked by deep bites. They suffered serious injuries to reproductive organs, including from rape with knives and sticks. Many victims were killed or died from injuries. Survivors displayed signs of deep trauma and face immense stigma in their community. There are credible reports of men and boys also being subjected to rape, genital mutilation and sexualised torture.[63]

Many victims of the atrocities committed by the Burmese military were children. They were both subjected to and witnessed mass atrocities that will inevitably stay with them for the rest of their lives. Many of the approximately 500,000 Rohingya children in Bangladesh had visible injuries caused by shootings, stabbings, or from being burnt.[64] Boys (and also men) were rounded up and taken away and are feared dead.

The report went on to identify the challenges faced by those who fled the atrocities. Many died on their way to safe havens, some due to their injuries; some died when their boats capsised or when crossing rivers. The Burmese military also killed many Rohingya who were trying to escape Myanmar, including, at border crossings.[65] In September 2017, they planted landmines in border areas to prevent Rohingya from returning to Myanmar. Even though the Burmese Government disputes the events identified in the report and in other overviews, the report indicates that '*satellite imagery and first-hand accounts corroborate widespread, systematic, deliberate and targeted destruction, mainly by fire, of Rohingya-populated areas across the three townships.*'[66]

As a result of this campaign, at least 392 villages were totally or partially destroyed. This amounts to 40% of all villages in northern Rakhine.

> Approximately 80% were burned in the initial three weeks of the operations; a significant portion of which after the Government's official end date of the "clearance operations." Over 70% of the destroyed villages were in Maungdaw, where the majority of Rohingya lived. Most destroyed

---

[63] Ibid., para. 38.

[64] Ibid., 39.

[65] Ibid., 41.

[66] Ibid., 42.

structures were homes. Schools, marketplaces and mosques were also burned. Rohingya-populated areas were specifically targeted, with adjacent or nearby Rakhine settlements left unscathed.[67]

When asked whether the Minister believed that the violence against Rohingya constituted a genocide, the House of Lords was treated to the standard Foreign Office response that it was a matter for the courts: '*The Foreign Secretary has made clear that the military operations conducted in Rakhine in August and September 2017 constitute ethnic cleansing, and may even be genocide, though that should be a determination for an international court to make.*'[68]

It was issue that led in September 2018 to a question for short debate on the inadequate response to genocide and crimes against humanity.[69] Parliament heard that earlier that day a letter signed by Rushanara Ali MP and supported by more than 160 British parliamentarians from both Houses was sent to the Prime Minister calling on the government to take a lead on seeking a referral of the Burmese military to the ICC. The letter repeated the concerns identified by the UN fact-finding mission that the new inquiry established by the Burmese Government will not be able to deliver on the promises to provide independent and transparent processes, and: 'Expecting justice and truth from any Myanmar domestic process is simply naïve.'[70]

This led to a further exchange on the floor of the House of Lords in December when Lord Alton reported that:

> 700,000 Rohingya have now fled to Bangladesh and there are reports of villages being burned and horrific human rights violations including the burning of homes, schools and mosques; the deliberate burning of people to death inside their homes; mass rape; torture; execution without trial;

---

[67] Ibid., 42.

[68] WPQ UIN HL8679, tabled on 18 June 2018. Available at: https://questions-sta tements.parliament.uk/written-questions/detail/2018-06-18/HL8679.

[69] House of Lords Deb, 13 September 2018, c2451.

[70] See: Statement of Christopher Sidoti, Fact Finding Mission to Myanmar, as reported in Euan McKirdy, 'Myanmar Military Leaders Should Face Genocide Charges, UN says' *CNN* (28 August 2018). Available at: https://edition.cnn.com/2018/08/27/asia/un-myanmar-genocide-investigation-intl/index.html.

the blocking of aid; and similar offences being conducted against the Shan and the Kachin as well.[71]

In a debate in May 2019, Lord Alton told the House that the Rohingya were facing:

> untold misery, whether for those who take to the sea or for those who try to cross the borders into Bangladesh and have now been displaced for what is approaching years, with very little progress made to establish their rights to citizenship or to deal with the fundamental issues that led to them fleeing in the first place.[72]

In response to the government assertion that an arms embargo and selective sanctions were an appropriate response, Lord Alton said that the sanctions:

> only amount to a ban on some 14 military and security personnel in Burma going on holiday to European Union member states. When we think of that as a response to crimes against humanity and what may even be approaching genocide—it is, to coin a phrase used in a note I received only this morning from Burma Campaign UK, "pretty pathetic."[73]

In a foretaste of the controversial question raised in the Genocide Amendment to the Trade Bill 2020/21, Ministers were asked whether it was legitimate to trade—business as usual—with a state credibly accused of genocide,

> I pressed the same issue with his noble friend Lady Fairhead (the Trade Minister), given that trade is central to the question of sanctions. I had asked [the Foreign Office Minister], whether the Government planned to issue official guidance to companies not to engage in any form of business with companies owned by the Burmese military. The reply from the noble Baroness simply did not accord with the sort of words used by both the Foreign Secretary and the noble Lord speaking for the Foreign Office.[74]

---

[71] House of Lords Deb, 17 December 2018, c1583.
[72] House of Lords Deb, 1 May 2019, c1027.
[73] Ibid., c1028.
[74] Ibid.

The Foreign Office declined to support a call for trade sanctions or to press for a UN Security Council resolution for a global arms embargo on Burma/Myanmar saying that '*The Government continues to assess that there is insufficient support at present.*'[75]

Lord Alton responded:

> even if you know you are going to be defeated there are moments when it is right to take a stand and to put people on the spot. If we are saying that representatives of the People's Republic of China are the ones who would veto such a resolution, let them do so and let us demonstrate the difference between their values and ours.
>
> Sometimes, I get frustrated that we use this argument as the first line of defence in places like North Korea, which has been described by the UN as a state without parallel when it comes to human rights violations, and in the case of Myanmar. We are saying that we will not take this forward because we think that others will oppose or veto it. Well, let them do so.[76]

In October 2019, the All-Party Parliamentary Group on the Rights of the Rohingya published a report: '*A New Shape of Catastrophe: two years on from the 2017 Rohingya Crisis*'—which drew attention to the continuing plight of the displaced people.[77] The report concluded that:

> Rohingya face continued gross human rights abuses and are denied citizenship, basic rights and justice. Restrictions on freedom of movement, an ongoing humanitarian crisis, the escalation of conflict in northern Rakhine, and the continued denial of citizenship, basic rights and justice mean the Rohingya living in Myanmar are unable to live in safety and with dignity. In the words of a Rohingya student living in an internal displacement camp in Rakhine state, the Myanmar Government is 'trying to create a new shape of catastrophe'. Without significant progress in Myanmar, safe and dignified return for the displaced and an end to the crisis will remain out of reach. This means the longer-term needs of the refugee population and

[75] Ibid.

[76] Ibid.

[77] APPG on Rohingya, 'A New Shape of Catastrophe: Two Years on From the 2017 Rohingya Crisis' (2019). Available at: https://reliefweb.int/report/myanmar/new-shape-catastrophe-two-years-2017-rohingya-crisis.

their host communities must be addressed, including through international responsibility-sharing initiatives.[78]

Meanwhile, the government confirmed that, since 2017, it had provided £256 million in aid to the refugees in Bangladesh. Beyond this human misery—and the sticking plasters—a hearing into the committing of war crimes was held in the International Court of Justice—and which we explore later.

At the time of writing, Myanmar became a bloodbath yet again after a military coup turned against civilians in February 2021. In early April 2021, Assistance Association for Political Prisoners (AAPP), total number of people killed stood at 550 since 1 February 2021, with at least 46 children.[79] The youngest victim is a seven-year-old girl, Khin Myo Chit. In addition, more than 2750 people have been detained, including 38 sentenced. The AAPP further reports attacks and looting in villages and central Gant Gaw town in Magwe Region. '*The perpetrators looted kitchen knives, money, mobile phones and jewellery. Over ten thousand residents hence fled into the forest. Number of villagers fleeing homes across Burma is rapidly increasing.*' The number continued to increase over the following months.

2.3   *The Situation of Christian Minorities in Myanmar*

Even though the Rohingya Muslims are arguably the most persecuted religious and ethnic minority group in Burma/Myanmar, the situation of other religious and ethnic minority groups is also dire. One group who have been under particularly severe pressure are the Christian Kachin.

A 2018 Sky News investigation into the situation in the predominantly Christian Kachin State revealed that they are being subjected to mass atrocities at the hands of the Burmese military.[80] In addition to acts of violence against Kachin, the Sky News investigation reported that the Burmese Government has been deliberately inflicting conditions of life

---

[78] Ibid., 5.

[79] Regular updates are available at: https://aappb.org/?p=14034.

[80] Alex Crawford, 'Uncovered: "Worrying Evidence" of New Genocidal Campaign on Kachin Christian Minority in Myanmar' *Sky News* (5 June 2018). Available at: https://news.sky.com/story/uncovered-worrying-evidence-of-new-genocidal-campaign-in-myanmar-11395173.

calculated to bring about the physical destruction in whole or in part. The investigation found that the Burmese Government has been denying '*aid agencies, international observers, foreign diplomats and politicians' access to the state*,' all of whom could have brought greatly needed assistance to the Kachin.[81]

This dire treatment of minorities is not a recent development. The fighting between the Kachin Independence Army and the Burmese Army began in 2011 and has led to over 100,000 people becoming internally displaced. There have been reports of the use of rape and sexual violence as a weapon of war, none of which have been adequately investigated or prosecuted.

Comparably, acts of discrimination, or persecution, against Christians in Burma/Myanmar are also common in other states, including Chin and Karen. Despite being predominantly Christian—Chin State population is over 90% Christian—there have been forced conversions to Buddhism; disruptions of religious gatherings and services; denial of building permits for places of worship; destruction and removal of crosses; burdensome bureaucracy for religious gatherings; and much more besides. Similarly, Christians in Karen State have been targeted by the Burmese army and have been subjected to forced labour, abuse, and killings.[82] While these examples of discrimination and persecution may not have reached the level of the atrocities experienced by the Rohingya Muslims in Rakhine, they must not be overlooked and are a harbinger of worse which can follow. The increase in the level of crimes has led to international condemnation and to call for the ending of the violence.

3   Do the Atrocities Amount to Genocide?

The UN High Commissioner for Human Rights described the atrocities committed against the Rohingya as '*a textbook example of ethnic cleansing*'[83] and the UN Special Envoy for human rights in

---

[81] Ibid.

[82] Ibid.

[83] UN News, UN High Commissioner for Human Rights Zeid Ra'ad Al Hussein highlights human rights concerns around the world in an address to the 36th session of the Human Rights Council in Geneva, 11 September 2017. Available at: https://www.ohchr.org/EN/NewsEvents/Pages/DisplayNews.aspx?NewsID=22044&LangID=E.

Burma/Myanmar identified '*hallmarks of a genocide.*'[84] Nonetheless, the word '*genocide*' concerning the persecution of the Rohingya Muslims in Burma/Myanmar has not yet been formally used by any international institution.

In part, this reluctance is due to the sheer number of other mass atrocities that, in recent years, have been deemed to be genocide. Despite this omnipresent reluctance to formally name and determine cases of genocide—and without diluting or diminishing the word by using it for polemical or rhetorical purposes—it is nevertheless always incumbent on us to examine whether specific atrocities meet the legal definition of genocide. This enables us to adequately address the atrocities and to assist communities on the verge of annihilation.

At the outbreak of mass atrocities in October 2016, the Rohingya population was assessed at 1 million. Systematic atrocities have seen between 700,000 and 1 million Rohingya flee to Bangladesh, while approximately 520,000–600,000 remain in Rakhine State.[85] Recall, too, that the religious demographics in Myanmar frequently but not always overlap with ethnic demographics. Theravada Buddhism is predominately practised by the majority Bamar, Shan, Rakhine, Mon, and numerous other ethnic groups.[86] Christianity is the dominant religion among the ethnic groups like Kachin, Chin, and Naga. Karen and Karenni ethnic groups have adherents to Christianity and Buddhism. Islam is practised in Karen, Rakhine, Rangoon, Irrawaddy, Magwe, and Mandalay. Despite this overlap between religious and ethnic characteristics, the persecution in Myanmar is often characterised as ethnic. However, the religious nature of this persecution should not be understated. The persecution has a strong religious component. To forestall such atrocities, it is crucial to address all aspects of the crimes, including the religious nature of the atrocities.

It was also made very clear in the Report of the OHCHR Mission to Bangladesh that the conflict has an ethno-religious character. Rohingya

---

[84] UN News, Statement by Ms. Yanghee Lee, Special Rapporteur on the situation of human rights in Myanmar at the 37th session of the Human Rights Council. Available at: https://www.ohchr.org/EN/NewsEvents/Pages/DisplayNews.aspx?NewsID=22806&LangID=E.

[85] *Burma 2019. International Religious Freedom Report* (US Department of State, 2019) 2. Available at: https://www.state.gov/reports/2019-report-on-international-religious-freedom/burma/.

[86] Ibid., 3.

Muslims, as a religious and an ethnic minority in Burma/Myanmar, are a protected group under Article II. Because their ethnicity and religion are closely linked, it is not always clear whether the atrocities are perpetrated because of the ethnicity or because of their religious identity, or a mixture of both. For example, the atrocities perpetrated against the Rohingya Muslims appear to lean more towards ethnic cleaning while, for example, the atrocities against Christian minorities lean more in the direction of religious persecution. Consideration of the nature and motivation of the persecution do matter because it helps to identify what needs to be done.

The atrocities perpetrated against the Rohingya Muslims, as mentioned in the preceding section, and which still require a full judicial investigation, clearly fall within the acts listed in Article II as methods designated to bring about genocide.

The question which then arises is whether it is possible to establish the specific intent to destroy the group in whole or in part. The report of the IIFFMM suggests that this specific intent is established. Among others, the report emphasises that some of the statements made by top military officials may be read as a direct incitement to genocide:

> the nature, scale and organization of the operations suggests a level of preplanning and design on the part of the Tatmadaw (the military) leadership consistent with the vision of the Commander-in-Chief, Senior-General Min Aung Hlaing, who stated at the height of the operations, *"The Bengali problem was a long-standing one which has become an unfinished job despite the efforts of the previous governments to solve it. The government in office is taking great care in solving the problem."*[87]

'*Solving a problem*' in this case means nothing less than annihilating the targeted communities. In addition to state propaganda stirring up ethnic and religious hatred,[88] anti-Muslim attitudes and propaganda have been in evidence for many years. This is an example from an interview with

---

[87] Ibid., 35 (emphasis added).

[88] Penny Green, Thomas MacManus, Alicia de la Cour Venning, *Genocide Achieved, Genocide Continues: Myanmar's Annihilation of the Rohingya* (with Penny Green and Alicia de la Cour Venning) (International State Crime Initiative: London, 2018) 40.

U Wirathu, a leading 969 and MaBaTha monk, cited by Iselin Frydenlund, a Postdoctoral Fellow at the MF Norwegian School of Theology
and Research Fellow at the University of Oslo:

> There are lots of difficulties due to the Muslims, they cause problems.
> They rape Burmese Buddhist women in many towns and cities. They
> rape teenagers and children underage... The women are very vulnerable
> (in marriage). The man pretends to be Buddhist, and then she is allured
> into Islam and she is forced to wear burqa. Some women are tortured if
> she continues the practices of her religion. If she is pregnant, she will be
> mistreated until miscarriage. In one case, a woman was even killed. If a
> woman of another religion marries a Muslim man, she loses all her reli-
> gious freedom and all her human rights... Then they are forced to commit
> sacrilege, for example, to step on Buddha images. They force Buddhist
> women to sin... When we as monks give sermons, we inform laypeople
> about these stories so that they can shy away from Muslim males.[89]

There is overwhelming evidence to suggest that the atrocities perpetrated
by the Burmese army against Rohingya Muslims meet the legal definition
of genocide. Further evidence about the extent and intention behind the
atrocities perpetrated against other religious minorities may also meet the
threshold of international crimes, for example, crimes against humanity.
In April 2022, the US State Department formally recognised the atrocities perpetrated by the Burmese military as genocide—the only such a
determination made by a government.

4   Responses to the Atrocities

Despite the perpetrator here being a state actor, the responses from the
international community were proactive and diverse—and, as we note in
the case of The Gambia, provide a role for countries often excluded from
top table UN Security Council or G7 discussions.

---

[89] I. Frydenlund, 'Religious Liberty for Whom? The Buddhist Politics of Religious
Freedom during Myanmar's Transition to Democracy' (2017) 35 Nordic Journal of
Human Rights 55, 63.

4.1 Attempts to Prevent and Suppress the Atrocities

Attempts to prevent and suppress Burma/Myanmar's mass atrocities have predominately been focused on diplomatic engagement. However, there was a sea change when on 11 November 2019, The Gambia, in a brave and unexpected move by a small country, initiated proceedings against Myanmar at the ICJ.[90]

The application filed by The Gambia alleged that the Government of Burma/Myanmar has been involved in atrocities against the Rohingya Muslims, including *'killing, causing serious bodily and mental harm, inflicting conditions that are calculated to bring about physical destruction, imposing measures to prevent births, and forcible transfers, are genocidal in character because they are intended to destroy the Rohingya group in whole or in part'* in violation of the Genocide Convention.[91] The Gambia's application further alleged that:

> from around October 2016, the Myanmar military (the "Tatmadaw") and other Myanmar security forces began widespread and systematic "clearance operations" – the term that Myanmar itself uses – against the Rohingya group. The genocidal acts committed during these operations were intended to destroy the Rohingya as a group, in whole or in part, by the use of mass murder, rape and other forms of sexual violence, as well as the systematic destruction by fire of their villages, often with inhabitants locked inside burning houses. From August 2017 onwards, such genocidal acts continued with Myanmar's resumption of "clearance operations" on a more massive and wider geographical scale.[92]

The document discusses various evidential sources, said to show the atrocities perpetrated against the Rohingya Muslims, including evidence obtained by the UN. Aside from an adjudication, The Gambia has also requested the implementation of several provisional measures to take effect as a matter of urgency, including:

---

[90] ICJ, Application instituting proceedings and Request for the indication of provisional measures, 11 November 2019. Available at: https://www.icj-cij.org/files/case-related/178/178-20191111-APP-01-00-EN.pdf.

[91] Ibid., 2.

[92] Ibid., 6.

(a) Myanmar shall immediately, in pursuance of its undertaking in the [Genocide Convention], take all measures within its power to prevent all acts that amount to or contribute to the crime of genocide...

(b) Myanmar shall, in particular, ensure that any military, paramilitary, or irregular armed units which may be directed or supported by it, as well as any organizations and persons which may be subject to its control, direction, or influence, do not commit any act of genocide, of conspiracy to commit genocide, or direct and public incitement to commit genocide, or of complicity in genocide, against the Rohingya group...

(c) Myanmar shall not destroy or render inaccessible any evidence related to the events described in the Application...[93]

The Gambia justified the need for such provisional measures by asserting that there is a risk of irreparable harm. According to the application, members of the Rohingya Muslim group are in *'grave danger of further genocidal acts because of Burma/Myanmar's deliberate and intentional efforts to destroy them as a group, and the remaining Rohingya communities and individuals in Burma/Myanmar continue to face daily threats of death, torture, rape, starvation and other deliberate actions aimed at their collective destruction, in whole or in part.'*[94]

On 23 January 2020, the ICJ ordered Burma/Myanmar to initiate several provisional measures to protect the Rohingya Muslim minority in the country, including:

(1) ... in accordance with its obligations under the [Genocide Convention], in relation to the members of the Rohingya group in its territory, take all measures within its power to prevent the commission of all acts within the scope of Article II of [the Genocide Convention], in particular:

(a) killing members of the group;

(b) causing serious bodily or mental harm to the members of the group;

(c) deliberately inflicting on the group conditions of life calculated to bring about its physical destruction in whole or in part; and

(d) imposing measures intended to prevent births within the group;

(2) ... in relation to the members of the Rohingya group in its territory, ensure that its military, as well as any irregular armed units which may be directed or supported by it and any organizations and persons which may be subject to its control, direction or influence, do not commit any

[93] Ibid., 132.
[94] Ibid., 131.

acts described in point (1) above, or of conspiracy to commit genocide, of direct and public incitement to commit genocide, of an attempt to commit genocide, or of complicity in genocide;

(3) … take effective measures to prevent the destruction and ensure the preservation of evidence related to allegations of acts within the scope of Article II of the [Genocide Convention];

(4) … submit a report to the [ICJ] on all measures taken to give effect to this Order within four months, as from the date of this Order, and thereafter every six months, until a final decision on the case is rendered by the [ICJ].[95]

The measures ordered by the ICJ were to enforce Burma/Myanmar's duties under the Genocide Convention, that is to prevent, suppress, and punish the crime of genocide. This historic ruling sent a strong and welcome message that those responsible for such crimes will not always be able to evade and escape justice and that the pledges made by states in legally binding international documents are to be enforced. The ICJ ruling is an important step towards justice for the Rohingya. The ICJ is yet to consider the case fully and whether Burma/Myanmar is in breach of the Genocide Convention obligations.

4.2   Investigating and Prosecuting the Crimes

4.2.1   UN Monitoring

As indicated above, the IIFFMM has been established to collect the evidence of atrocities in the country even without access to the territory of the country. This demonstrates—to China for instance—that refusing admission to an affected territory—does not close down an investigation into atrocity crimes.

Although the IIFFMM was prevented by the Burmese Government from entering the country, it did collect evidence from Rohingya Muslims who had managed to escape to Bangladesh—even though, without access to the areas in which the crimes are alleged to have been committed, much evidence was inevitably lost. The IIFFMM made several recommendations on how to address the situation and included the need to,

---

[95] ICJ, Decision on Provisional Measures, 23 January 2020. Available at: https://www.icj-cij.org/files/case-related/178/178-20200123-ORD-01-00-EN.pdf.

ensure accountability for crimes under international law committed in Myanmar, preferably by referring the situation to the International Criminal Court or alternatively by creating an *ad-hoc* international criminal tribunal. Further, the Security Council should adopt targeted individual sanctions, including travel bans and asset freezes, against those who appear most responsible for serious crimes under international law. It should also impose an arms embargo on Myanmar.[96]

Some countries, such as the UK, have imposed limited, targeted '*Magnitsky*' sanctions on several army officers.

The UN Security Council has not yet taken any steps to impose sanctions, and there appears to be no consensus—with countries such as China providing encouragement to the leaders of the 2021 military coup and who have been responsible for Aung San Suu Kyi's imprisonment. Publicly, China and Russia argue that whatever occurs in Myanmar is an internal matter—while privately embracing their new authoritarian compatriots in the Tatmadaw.

Although the UN Charter provides the UN Security Council with the power to impose sanctions and oblige compliance, the failure to do so is yet another demonstration of the subversion of multilateral institutions and powers designed to uphold the rule of law and international norms.

Notwithstanding calls by Western democracies for sanctions, in October 2019, the writing was clearly on the wall when Yanghee Lee, the Special Rapporteur on Human Rights in Myanmar, called on the UN not to '*hesitate to impose targeted sanctions against the Tatmadaw's companies and its commanders most responsible for serious violations, refer the entire situation to the ICC or establish an international tribunal, and work with civil society to develop transformative processes in accordance with the pillars of justice, truth, reparations and guarantees of non-recurrence*'[97]—and when neither of these steps were taken.

---

[96] UN Human Rights Council, 'Report of the Independent International Fact-Finding Mission on Myanmar' (12 September 2018), A/HRC/39/64. Available at: https://www.ohchr.org/Documents/HRBodies/HRCouncil/FFM-Myanmar/A_HRC_39_64.pdf.

[97] UN, Statement by Ms. Yanghee Lee Special Rapporteur on the situation of human rights in Myanmar, 22 October 2019. Available at: https://reliefweb.int/report/myanmar/statement-ms-yanghee-lee-special-rapporteur-situation-human-rights-myanmar.

4.2.2   Proceedings before International Tribunals

The ICC does not have territorial jurisdiction over the situation in Burma/Myanmar as it is not a signatory to the Rome Statute. However, in April 2018, the then Chief Prosecutor of the ICC, Ms Fatou Bensouda, sought a ruling from the President of the Pre-Trial Division on the status of ICC jurisdiction in Burma/Myanmar. The question she submitted asked *'whether the Court may exercise jurisdiction over the alleged deportation of the Rohingya people from Myanmar to Bangladesh'*[98] which is a signatory to the Rome Statute.

The ICC Chief Prosecutor's submission sought to clarify whether the ICC can exercise jurisdiction *'when persons are deported from the territory of a state which is* not *a party to the Statute directly into the territory of a state which* is *a party to the Statute'* to be able to investigate the crime and prosecute the perpetrators. The focus of the question was limited to the forcible deportation (which is a crime against humanity under Article 7(1)(d) of the Rome Statute) of the Rohingya Muslims and not on any other crimes that are believed to have been committed within the territory of Burma/Myanmar. Nonetheless, this question of cross-border deportation was a proactive step seeking to engage the ICC with the dire situation in the country. Such creativity was especially welcome as the other options to engage the ICC, whether by way of Burma/Myanmar voluntarily accepting the jurisdiction of the ICC or referral of the situation in Burma/Myanmar to the ICC by the UN Security Council were highly unlikely.

The ICC Chief Prosecutor's submission contained information of consistent and credible public reports to suggest that since at least August 2017, *'more than 670,000 Rohingya, lawfully present in Burma/Myanmar, have been intentionally deported across the international border into Bangladesh.'*[99] She relied on evidence presented by UN organisations and agencies, including the OHCHR, the IIFFMM, the UN Special Rapporteur on the Situation of Human Rights in Myanmar, the UN Office

---

[98] ICC, Prosecution's Request for a Ruling on Jurisdiction under Article 19(3) of the Statute, 9 April 2018, ICC-RoC46(3)-01/18-1. Available at: https://www.icc-cpi.int/Pages/record.aspx?docNo=ICC-RoC46(3)-01/18-1.

[99] ICC, Prosecution's Request for a Ruling on Jurisdiction under Article 19(3) of the Statute, 9 April 2018, ICC-RoC46(3)-01/18-1. Available at: https://www.icc-cpi.int/Pages/record.aspx?docNo=ICC-RoC46(3)-01/18-1.

of the High Commissioner for Refugees, the International Organisation for Migration Inter Sector Coordination Group, the UN Children's Fund, and international non-governmental organisations, including the Human Rights Watch, Amnesty International, Fortify Rights, *Médecins Sans Frontières*, and the International Rescue Committee, corroborative video footage and reports, and 42 individual communications received by the Office of the Prosecutor.

In 2018, the Burmese Government was asked by the ICC to respond on specific issues so that the ICC could decide if it could have jurisdiction in the case of the deportations of over 700,000 Rohingya Muslims from Burma/Myanmar to Bangladesh.

In a statement dated 9 August 2018, the Burmese Government declined to engage with the ICC by way of a formal reply stating that such a request for engagement may be *'interpreted as an indirect attempt to acquire jurisdiction over Myanmar which is not a state party to the Rome Statute.'*[100] The Burmese Government accused the ICC of lacking fairness and transparency, castigating the ICC for allowing organisations filing *amicus curiae* submissions which the Burmese Government branded as containing *'allegations consisting of mostly charged narratives of harrowing personal tragedies calculated to place emotional pressure on the Court.'*

The Burmese Government concluded that the *'prosecution's request for a ruling on jurisdiction under Article 19(3) of the (Rome) Statute is meritless and should be dismissed.'*[101] The Burmese Government confirmed that, in July 2018, it had established an Independent Commission of Enquiry (ICE) to investigate the *'allegations of human rights violations and related issues following the terror attacks by the Arakan Rohingya Salvation Army.'* (Arakan Rohingya Salvation Army is an insurgency group which the Burmese Government blamed for the atrocities in Myanmar and for the forced displacement of the 700,000). The ICE consisted of four members: two international and two national members. It is a moot point as to whether the ICE, a government-established body, could ever deliver an independent and transparent inquiry, especially as the government was

---

[100] Government of the Republic of the Union of Myanmar Ministry of the Office of the State Counsellor, Press Release, 9 August 2018. Available at: http://www.president-office.gov.mm/en/sites/default/files/Government%20of%20the%20Republic%20of%20the%20Union%20of%20Myanmar.pdf.

[101] Ibid.

itself accused of having been complicit (whether by authorising or not stopping) the mass atrocities perpetrated against the Rohingya Muslims by the Burmese military. In January 2020, ICE concluded that:

> war crimes, serious human rights violations, and violations of domestic law took place during the security operations between 25 August and 5 September 2017... there are reasonable grounds to believe that members of Myanmar's security forces were involved.[102]

The report further added that:

> The ICE has not found any evidence suggesting that these killings or acts of displacement were committed pursuant to intent or plan to destroy the Muslim or any other community in northern Rakhine State. There is insufficient evidence to argue, much less conclude, that the crimes committed were undertaken with the intent to destroy, in whole or in part, a national, ethnical, racial or religious group, or with any other requisite mental state for the international crime of genocide.'[103]

While the report found that mass atrocities had been perpetrated in Burma/Myanmar, the findings on genocide are still at odds with the evidence collected by other international and independent bodies.

Ultimately, in November 2019, the Pre-Trial III authorised the ICC Prosecutor to proceed with an investigation into,

> any crime within the jurisdiction of the Court committed at least in part on the territory of Bangladesh, or the territory of any other State Party or State making a declaration under Article 12(3) of the Statute, if the alleged crime is sufficiently linked to the situation as described in this decision...
>
> crimes allegedly committed on or after 1 June 2010, the date of entry into force of the Statute for Bangladesh. Further, the Prosecutor may extend the investigation into crimes allegedly committed at least in part on the territory of other States Parties after the date of entry into force

---

[102] Independent Commission of Enquiry. Available at: https://www.icoe-myanmar.org/.

[103] Ibid.

of the Statute for those States Parties, insofar as the alleged crimes are sufficiently linked to the situation as described in this decision.[104]

These proceedings are still at early stages.

4.2.3   Steps Taken by Individual States

To date, not many states have taken steps to prosecute the perpetrators, for example, by way of relying on universal jurisdiction. Notably, in Argentina, Tomás Quintana, who served as the Special Rapporteur on the situation of human rights in Myanmar from 2008 to 2014, is leading a universal jurisdiction case with Tun Khin as lead plaintiff. As Quintana commented, '*this complaint seeks the criminal sanction of the perpetrators, accomplices and cover-ups of the genocide. We are doing it through Argentina because they have no other possibility of filing the criminal complaint anywhere else.*'[105]

Over the years, using other means, some states have taken steps to address the situation in Myanmar. For example, just before the IIFFMM published its findings of genocide in its September 2018 Report, the US State Department imposed sanctions on several members of the Burmese military, Border Guard Police commanders, and two Burmese military units for their involvement in mass atrocities.[106] In announcing this decision, Sigal Mandelker, the Treasury's Acting Undersecretary for Terrorism and Financial Intelligence, justified it by stating that '*Burmese security forces have engaged in violent campaigns against ethnic minority communities across Myanmar, including ethnic cleansing, massacres, sexual assault, extrajudicial killings, and other serious human rights abuses.*'[107]

---

[104] ICC, Pre-Trial Chamber III, 'Decision Pursuant to Article 15 of the Rome Statute on the Authorisation of an Investigation into the Situation in the People's Republic of Bangladesh/Republic of the Union of Myanmar', 4 November 2019, No.ICC-01/19, 126, 131. Available at: https://www.icc-cpi.int/CourtRecords/CR2019_06955.PDF.

[105] Agence France-Presse, 'Myanmar's Aung San Suu Kyi Faces First Legal Action Over Rohingya Crisis' *The Guardian* (14 November 2019). Available at: https://www.theguardian.com/world/2019/nov/14/myanmars-aung-san-suu-kyi-faces-first-legal-action-over-rohingya-crisis.

[106] US Department of the Treasury, Treasury Sanctions Commanders and Units of the Burmese Security Forces for Serious Human Rights Abuses, 17 August 2018. Available: https://home.treasury.gov/news/press-releases/sm460.

[107] Ibid.

The UK has made a similar decision to impose sanctions (asset freezes) against several individuals involved in the atrocities,[108] and the Council of the European Union imposed an asset freeze and a travel ban.[109] In April 2018, the Council of the European Union also extended and strengthened the EU arms embargo on Myanmar and prohibited the provision of military training to and military cooperation with the Burmese army.[110]

In Burma/Myanmar, sanctions must be accompanied by the preparation of the case for the prosecution. Such steps include conducting independent investigations, never accepting assurances that those accused of such crimes will investigate the crimes and sit in judgement on themselves. The clear objective must be that perpetrators will be held accountable for their crimes. As we suggested earlier, the most proactive and commendable steps in this direction have been taken at the ICJ by the Gambia, in ensuring that the UN finally addresses the issue of the genocide against the Rohingya Muslims in Burma/Myanmar.

The Gambia's actions throws into sharp relief the too frequent failure of states to engage the ICJ on the question of genocide.

In only a few rare circumstances has the ICJ considered and determined the question, as in the cases *of Pakistan v India, Bosnia and Herzegovina v Yugoslavia, Yugoslavia v NATO and Croatia v Yugoslavia.* Many states have shied away from making referrals to the ICJ, through fear of upsetting their diplomatic or economic relationships (a very real consideration for countries which have become indebted to powerful nations such as China). They have to weigh these considerations against speaking up for a group of people facing annihilation. They may also be

---

[108] UK, Consolidated List of Financial Sanctions Targets in the UK. Available at: https://assets.publishing.service.gov.uk/government/uploads/system/uploads/attach ment_data/file/733494/Burma.pdf.

[109] European Council, Myanmar/Burma: EU sanctions 7 senior military, border guard and police officials responsible for or associated with serious human rights violations against Rohingya population. Available at: https://www.consilium.europa.eu/en/press/press-releases/2018/06/25/myanmar-burma-eu-sanctions-7-senior-military-bor der-guard-and-police-officials-responsible-for-or-associated-with-serious-human-rights-vio lations-against-rohingya-population/.

[110] European Council, Myanmar/Burma: EU extends and strengthens its arms embargo and adopts a framework for targeted measures against officials responsible for serious human rights violations. Available at: https://www.consilium.europa.eu/en/press/press-releases/2018/04/26/myanmar-burma-eu-extends-and-strengthens-its-arms-embargo-and-adopts-a-framework-for-targeted-measures-against-officials-responsible-for-serious-human-rights-violations/.

conscious of their own record on human rights and treatment of minorities. We hope that The Gambia's rather brave decision may in the future encourage other states to maximise the use of the existing UN mechanisms, mechanisms which could accommodate a more forceful discussion with states which allow, enable, or participate in genocide and other such mass atrocities.

None of this is history. The consequences of Burma/Myanmar's 2021 *coup d'état* for the country's ethnic and religious minorities—especially the plight of Rohingya Muslims—is contemporary.

What is happening in Burma/Myanmar on a day-by-day basis demands an urgent and comprehensive response: to stop the continuing violence and to help the victims with all their needs and ensure rights. It demands an adequate investigation of the crimes against the minorities, and it demands that they have a future in Burma/Myanmar. This persecution needs to be addressed with strong protections of the right to freedom of religion or belief and other basic human rights.

Paradoxically, the *coup d'état* may have produced some very unintended consequences in Burma/Myanmar. Through their violent and illegal actions, the Tatmadaw have united majority and minority communities in a brave common defence of democracy. This has been regardless of religious and ethnic differences—the very opposite of what the Tatmadaw wanted when it illegally seized power.

Through a united struggle for the restoration of a civil society and the overthrow of authoritarian, corrupt, military dictatorship, we must ardently hope that the value and place, the dignity, and rights, of everyone in Burma/Myanmar will finally be recognised and become part of that wonderful country's DNA.

CHAPTER 5

The Daesh Genocide Against Religious or Belief Minorities in Syria and Iraq

1 INTRODUCTION

Since the removal of Saddam Hussain, in 2003, and with the exception of the area governed by the Kurdish Regional Government, Iraq has largely remained an unstable and unsafe country. However, the atrocities did not start then. Atrocity crimes were also common during Saddam's dictatorship.

In March 1988, Saddam's depredations were brought into sharp focus when, as part of the Anfal campaign against the Kurds, he used chemical weapons to attack Kurdish residential areas in Halabja. At the time, Lord Alton described the attack as a crime against humanity, when between 3200 and 5000, mainly Kurdish civilians, were killed.[1] Most died within minutes of the bombing; survivors trying to leave Halabja the following day sustained injuries when passing contaminated roads.[2] On 23 December 2005, a Dutch Court sentenced Franz van Anraat—a businessman who sold chemicals to Saddam to 15 years imprisonment.[3]

---

[1] Human Rights Watch, Genocide in Iraq: The Anfal Campaign Against the Kurds (1993). Available at: https://www.refworld.org/docid/47fdfb1d0.html.

[2] See more at: Jonathan C. Randal, *After Such Knowledge, What Forgiveness? My Encounters with Kurdistan* (Westview Press, 1998).

[3] *Public Prosecutor v. Frans Cornelis Adrianus van Anraat*, 09/751003-04, 23 December 2005. See more at: https://www.asser.nl/upload/documents/DomCLIC/Docs/NLP/Netherlands/vanAnraat_Judgment_23-12-2005_EN.pdf.

© The Author(s), under exclusive license to Springer Nature Switzerland AG 2022
E. U. Ochab and D. Alton, *State Responses to Crimes of Genocide*, Rethinking Political Violence, https://doi.org/10.1007/978-3-030-99162-3_5

The Court ruled that the chemical attack on Halabja constituted genocide, but van Anraat was found guilty of the lesser offence of complicity
in war crimes. The massacre was defined by the Supreme Iraqi Criminal
Tribunal as '*a genocidal massacre*' and in 2010 the Iraqi High Criminal
Court recognised the Halabja massacre as an act of genocide.[4]

Having considered these events, and having seen two million Kurds
flee to the mountains, the UK's Prime Minister, John Major, was in no
doubt about Saddam Hussain's intentions. With the authority of UN
Security Council Resolution 68, the UK imposed a no-fly zone which
then protected the Kurds for twelve years from Saddam Hussein's air
force—enabling the Kurds to return to their homes and to create the
autonomous Kurdish region of Iraq.[5]

During a visit in late 2019, Lord Alton met the Speaker, Rewaz Faye
Hussein and her Deputy, Mr. Hawarmi, and other senior officials of the
Kurdish Regional Parliament. They repeatedly said that UK intervention
had saved lives, forestalled monstrous crimes, and enabled the creation
of an oasis amidst the region's many conflicts. Iraq's Kurds survived
Saddam's genocidal campaign and returned home to establish today's
flourishing democracy. Its capital, Erbil, has today become a rare place of
relative safety for Yazidis, Christians, and other minorities fleeing Daesh.
Madam Speaker Rewaz Faye Hussein told us that unlike the monochrome
ideology of Daesh, they welcome diversity:

> Our diversity shows the beauty of our region and our Parliament, with
> members from the Turkmen, Christian and Armenian minorities reflect
> this welcome of difference. We have enshrined the rights and culture of
> minorities in law.

Deputy Speaker Hawarmi, who comes from Halabja, re-enforced this
message stating that tolerance and mutual respect had to '*become deep
rooted, part of genes.*'

---

[4] See: Iraqi High Tribunal (Second Criminal Court), Iraq, 1/ (C) Second/ 2006,
Special Verdict, 24 July 2007. Available at: http://www.internationalcrimesdatabase.org/
Case/1233/Al-Anfal/.

[5] UN Security Council Resolution 688 (1991) [Iraq], 5 April 1991, S/RES/688
(1991).

Taking evidence in that region left us in no doubt about the scale of that challenge—especially amongst the minority ethnic and religious communities—Assyrians, Syriacs, Chaldeans, Yazidis, and many more, all of whom have suffered grievously—and all of whom have been subjected to repeated cycles of appalling violence, including genocide. For centuries, these ancient peoples have been decimated in systematic campaigns to eradicate and eliminate them, to eradicate their culture, and their way of life. Their crime is simply to live differently from the majority.

Their suffering is symbolised in the Kurdish town of Simele, where in 1933, a genocide was carried out against the Assyrians (adherents of the Church of the East, sometimes called Nestorians)—a massacre in which around 3000 men, women, and children from 63 villages in areas around Dohuk and Mosul had their throats cut.[6] In considering the nature of mass atrocities, Raphael Lemkin, carefully studied Simele and the Armenian Genocide. No memorial has ever been erected to these Assyrian Christians and the site of their bloody end is shamefully littered with garbage and rubbish—a failure to memorialise, which Lord Alton raised directly with the Kurdish authorities.

Historians are uncertain whether corpses were taken away to a mass-grave, but evidence can still be seen at the site of fragments of bone protruding from broken walls of what was once a police station.[7] In 2019, Dindar William of the Assyrian Democratic Movement accompanied Lord Alton on his visit to Simele and said that '*the desecration of the site is deliberate adding insult to injury.*'

In 1933, the British authorities rejected calls for an international inquiry into the killings, cravenly arguing that it might lead to further massacres against Christians.[8] They did not support calls to punish the offenders as they had become national heroes. The Simele Genocide had been preceded by demonstrations in the city of Mosul where frenzied mobs decorated the city with melons pierced with daggers, symbolising the heads of murdered Assyrians. Even Iraq's Crown Prince came

[6] S. Zubaida, 'Contested nations: Iraq and the Assyrians' (2000) 6 Nations and Nationalism 3, 363–382; Reeva S. Simon, *Iraq Between the Two World Wars: The Militarist Origins of Tyranny* (Columbia University Press, 2004).

[7] See for example: R. Stafford, *The Tragedy of the Assyrians* (Gorgias Press LLC, 2006).

[8] Max J. Joseph, *The Simele Massacre in Iraq: A Legacy of Trauma and British Neglect* (2018). Available at: https://deadmanmax.medium.com/the-simele-massacre-in-iraq-a-legacy-of-trauma-and-british-neglect-ae21d96afe4d.

to encourage the bloodletting—the atrocities and hateful *'othering'*[9] of difference which followed would, as we shall see, be repeated in 2014.

Over decades, even centuries, Assyrians, Syriacs, Chaldeans, Yazidis, and other minorities have been systematically targeted, caught in an existential struggle—and these minorities still live in fear. The seeds of genocide are invariably planted in a climate of indifference and impunity, and many descendants point to a continuing indifference, with one Assyrian reminding us that:

> Pre-2003 our intellectuals, elites and scholars had been exiled, imprisoned, tortured and some martyred. Since then, (...) persecution has become institutionalised... we feel abandoned by the international community... we feel unsafe, politically disempowered, and excluded.

Simele happened just 18 years after the deaths of anything between 75,000 and 150,000 Assyrian Christians, during the Assyrian Genocide of 1915—at the hands of the Ottoman Turks.[10] Whether, standing in the ruins of Simele, or listening to the heirs of those silenced victims, it is a challenging rebuke to our generation to do better than the British authorities of 1933 in defending minorities and remaining alert to the signs of impending mass atrocities.

Ironically, it is often said that in the 1980s and 90s, while murdering Kurds—along with political opponents—Saddam Hussein's regime provided a degree of protection to some of Iraq's religious minorities.[11] Some, maybe, but certainly not all. Under Saddam's regime, millions of Shiaa Arabs, Sunni Kurds, and Assyrian Christians suffered widespread military operations which caused the displacement of millions and the death of tens of thousands in Ahwar, Halbja, and Barwar. And, following the fall of Saddam, a combination of revenge, Iranian influence, and sectarian politics which marginalised and discriminated against the Sunni Arabs, contributed to the emergence of extremist organisations

---

[9] R. Stafford, *The Tragedy of the Assyrians* (Gorgias Press LLC, 2006).

[10] See for example: K. Husry, The Assyrian Affair of 1933. Volumes I and II (Cambridge University Press, 1974).

[11] Elizabeth Ferris and Abbie Taylor, 'The Past and Future of Iraq's Minorities' Brooking (8 September 2014). Available at: https://www.brookings.edu/opinions/the-past-and-future-of-iraqs-minorities/.

such as Qaeda and Daesh which caused death and havoc and which have affected everybody.[12]

2 DAESH'S ATROCITIES AGAINST RELIGIOUS OR BELIEF COMMUNITIES

Iraq

In 2003, with Saddam's removal, the security apparatus that he commanded fell apart and, in a poorly planned aftermath, there was little to replace it other than warlords and militias. As a consequence, minority groups, including Christians and Yazidis, became subjected to ever-growing persecution from these insurgency groups which filled the void left by Saddam Hussain's removal.[13] Even during the Saddam Hussain era the Yazidi minorities were undoubtedly subjected to discrimination or persecution.[14] However, Saddam Hussain's fall accelerated the deterioration of their situation. Despite the growing discrimination, harassment, and persecution of religious minorities, the new Government of Iraq failed to address rank persecution or to protect its minority population. Extortion, kidnappings for ransom, forced displacement, and violence became a frequent occurrence in the lives of Iraq's minority groups.[15] However, it did not stop there.

This internal instability was an easy target for a new threat that quickly emerged on the back of the insurgency: Daesh, also known as ISIS, ISIL and Islamic State.

Daesh gained power through instability caused by the Syrian Civil War and swept across the Iraqi border to quickly gain control over many

---

[12] Ian Tuttle, 'Iraq's Christian Martyrs,' *National Review* (8 September 2014). Available at: https://www.nationalreview.com/magazine/2014/09/08/iraqs-christian-martyrs/.

[13] 'Iraqi Christians' long history,' *BBC News* (1 November 2010). Available at: https://www.bbc.co.uk/news/world-middle-east-11669994.

[14] Unrepresented Nations and Peoples Organization, *Iraq: The Situation of Ethnic and Religious Minorities* (20 June 2013). Available at: http://www.europarl.europa.eu/mee tdocs/2009_2014/documents/d-iq/dv/05unpodiqbriefingnote_/05unpodiqbriefingn ote_en.pdf.

[15] Frances Harrison, 'Christians besieged in Iraq,' *BBC News* (13 March 2008). Available at: http://news.bbc.co.uk/1/hi/world/middle_east/7295145.stm.

regions. The disbanding of the Iraqi security forces was a major factor contributing to the growth and power of Daesh.[16] When militias backed by Iran began attacking the Sunni population, some former army officers joined Daesh, believing it was their only option to defend their Sunni communities (a judgment they would soon regret). In this way, a relatively small group of Islamist fundamentalists almost managed to take over a country.

Daesh imposed even stricter Islamist rule than the post-Saddam Hussain insurgency. For example, Daesh gave some Christians an ultimatum to convert to Islam, pay a religious tax, flee, or be killed.[17] Others have not been given this 'choice.' In Mosul, Daesh fighters marked Christian homes with the Arabic letter 'N' for Nazarene to distinguish Christian homes from homes of their Sunni Muslim neighbours.[18] The letter 'N' would then signify to Daesh fighters which homes to target. The homes of Shia Muslims were similarly daubed, with R (Rafidah–Reject).

The Syrian Orthodox Bishop of Mosul, Bishop Nicodemus, told us *'Daesh destroyed our homes, our churches, our monasteries, our dignity. They destroyed everything.'* Refusal to convert or to yield to extortion led to confiscation, forced conversion, exile, or death. Gathering evidence from survivors did not reveal a determined international effort to bring perpetrators to justice. Two men whose families fled from Mosul and another whose home was burnt down in Sinjar told us that no one from the international community, or the governments in Baghdad or Erbil, had ever asked to meet them or to take their statements. Yet the claim is repeatedly made that *'we are collecting evidence'* and that perpetrators will *'be brought to justice.'*

We also collected evidence from Yazidi survivors and met their spiritual leader, the late Baba Sheikh. Yazidis described how throughout 2014, Daesh established self-proclaimed *'caliphate'* in many regions of Iraq,

[16] Coalition Provisional Authority, Order Number 2: Dissolution if Entities (23 May 2003).

[17] Chris Mitchell, 'ISIS Swallowing Iraq: 'They're Killing Children,' *CBN News* (9 September 2014). Available at: http://www1.cbn.com/cbnnews/world/2014/August/ISIS-Swallowing-Iraq-Theyre-Beheading-Children.

[18] 'Nearly All Gone. The conquering jihadists are evicting or killing Mosul's last Christians,' *The Economist* (26 July 2014). Available at: https://www.economist.com/news/middle-east-and-africa/21608804-conquering-jihadists-are-evicting-or-killing-mosuls-last-christians-nearly-all.

most notably, in the predominately Christian Nineveh Plains and Sinjar, populated by the Yazidi minorities.

On 3 August 2014, Daesh launched a violent attack against Yazidis in Sinjar. Daesh fighters killed hundreds, if not thousands of men. The victims' mass graves continue to be discovered to this day. On becoming British Foreign Secretary, Boris Johnson said that Daesh *'are engaged in what can only be called genocide of the poor Yazidis'*—and yet, to this day his government has still not recognised it as a genocide.[19] As part of the same campaign, Daesh fighters abducted boys to turn them into child soldiers and women and girls for sex slavery. More than 3000 women and girls are still missing, and their fate is unknown.[20] In February 2021, 104 bodies of Yazidis, which have been thrown into mass graves and were exhumed in 2020, were taken for a respectful reburial.

On 6 August 2014, after an attack on Yazidis in Sinjar, Daesh came after Christians in Nineveh Plains—which Dr Ewelina Ochab and Lord Alton visited in 2016 and 2019 respectively.

Overnight, Daesh captured 13 villages and forced approximately 120,000 Iraqi Christians to flee their homes leaving their lives behind and walking towards an uncertain future in Kurdistan. They did not take much with them as they hoped that they would be able to return after a few days. This hope began to perish when days turned into weeks, months, and years. Thousands of Iraqi Christians found themselves in Kurdistan, mostly Ankawa, a Christian friendly district of Erbil. Kurdistan was not adequately prepared for wave after wave of IDPs arriving at once.

The IDPs turned to churches for help. They found refuge in churches, church courtyards, parks, and streets—homeless but safer than in the hands of Daesh. As the situation progressed and Daesh continued to rule over Nineveh Plains, tents and temporary accommodations were provided for some IDPs. Some people were also moved from the churches to a construction site of a shopping mall before IDPs camps were up and running.

For over two years Daesh managed to exert its power and control over the region, destroying the villages and towns, and removing all signs of Christianity or other religious groups having ever being present in the

---

[19] Boris Johnson, 'Bravo for Assad—He Is A Vile Tyrant But He Has Saved Palmyra' *The Daily Telegraph* (27 March 2016).

[20] UN Human Rights Council, the Independent International Commission of Inquiry on the Syrian Arab Republic, *'They Came to Destroy': ISIS Crimes Against the Yazidis*, UN Doc A/HRC/32/CRP.2 (15 June 2016).

area.[21] During the second half of 2016, the Global Coalition against Daesh[22] steadfastly won back territory and by December 2017 succeeded in liberating many towns in the Nineveh Plains.[23]

While curbing the shocking atrocities of Daesh, the ideology which led to these genocidal atrocities against religious minorities, is far from defeated. The Yazidis, Assyrians, Syriacs, Chaldeans, and Kurds have all suffered grievously. They have an indomitable spirit and with international support it is not unrealistic to believe that a respectful and diverse society can be created—the antidote to the visceral hatred offered by the ideology of Daesh.

Healing the history of the region and coming to terms with multiple acts of genocide will be an enormous challenge—incapable of being progressed without a much clearer understanding of the monstrous crimes which have occurred, truthfully telling the stories of genocide, and ensuring that, however long it takes, perpetrators are brought to justice. These terrible events challenge our generation to break the unremitting cycle of hatred and brutality.

Syria

Daesh used the long-standing conflict in Syria to expand its power in the region and establish a caliphate in many parts of Syria. Its growth in power and the specific targeting of religious minorities has resulted in a significant decline of the country's religious minorities. In 2011, the population of Syrian Christians was assessed at over 2 million (10% of the population): by early 2015 it had fallen to less than 1 million.

In 2015, the UN Commission of Inquiry on the Syrian Arab Republic (the UN Commission of Inquiry) reported that:

---

[21] Aid to the Church in Need, *Persecuted and Forgotten? A Report on Christians Oppressed for their Faith 2013–2015* (2015). Available at: http://www.acnuk.org/persec uted#countries.

[22] The Global Coalition Against Daesh, *Partners*. Available at: http://theglobalcoalit ion.org/en/partners.

[23] Maher Chmaytelli and Ahmed Aboulenein, 'Iraq declares final victory over Islamic State,' *Reuters* (online), 9 December 2017. Available at: https://uk.reuters.com/article/ uk-iraq-is-liberated/iraq-declares-final-victory-over-islamic-state-idUKKBN1E30B7.

Some communities have been specifically targeted, with discriminatory intent, on the grounds of their actual or perceived religious and/or ethnic background, by [Daesh] and Jabhat Al-Nusra...

Hundreds of Yazidi women abducted during the [Daesh] August 2014 attack on the Sinjar region of northern Iraq were forced over the border into the Syrian Arab Republic. One of the earliest [Daesh] convoys of women and children crossed on 17 August 2014...

Yazidi women were specifically targeted because of their community's religious identity, which [Daesh] believes to be pagan. [Daesh] has subjected Yazidi women and children to horrific abuse. Women and girls have been sold or gifted (and resold and regifted) to [Daesh] fighters and tribal leaders in [Daesh]-controlled Syrian Arab Republic. Others are imprisoned in houses in towns and villages across the Syrian Arab Republic, where they are held in sexual slavery. One young woman described [Daesh] fighters arriving late at night and surveying the girls as though they were 'in a sheep market.' Without exception, all interviewees described multiple rapes by several men, including incidents of gang rape...

In mid-February, [Daesh] fighters entered Assyrian Christian villages, including Tel Hermes, along the Khabour River in Hasakah. They forced villagers to remove all Christian imagery from their churches, homes and cemeteries. Fighters threatened to impose jizya—a tax imposed on non-Muslims living in an Islamic caliphate—and to kill the local priest if residents did not comply.[24]

On 16 June 2016, the UN Commission of Inquiry released a report recognising Daesh atrocities against the Yazidis as genocide.[25] It is believed that close to 3000 of women and children abducted by Daesh in Sinjar are currently held in Syria.

The threat of Daesh has not gone away and because incipient genocide is once more possible the international community must remain engaged with the security situation in the region.

Having shaved their beards, many Daesh militants have melted back into the Arab Sunni population but, in Iraq, regularly emerge to intimidate government officials and members of the security forces. Frequently,

[24] UN Human Rights Council, Report of the Independent International Commission of Inquiry on the Syrian Arab Republic, (13 August 2015) UN Doc A/HRC/30/48. 110–119.

[25] UN Human Rights Council, Report of the Independent International Commission of Inquiry on the Syrian Arab Republic, 'They Came to Destroy': ISIS Crimes Against the Yazidis (15 June 2016) UN Doc A/HRC/32/CRP.2.

they face attacks and explosions particularly around the oil fields in Kirkuk. Daesh has been burning farmers' fields to intimidate local people. It is estimated that Daesh still earns $100,000 a week from its smuggling and other illicit activities. In other words, it would be foolish to believe that the Daesh rule of terror is just a thing of the past. Hence our need for vigilance and engagement, not treating this as a regrettable historical event.

3   Do the Atrocities Amount to Genocide?

Daesh specifically targeted for destruction the region's Christians, Yazidis, and other religious minorities, including Muslim minorities. This was an attempt to annihilate religious pluralism. This aim is well documented in its official videos and newspapers, including *Dabiq*, the official Daesh propaganda magazine. For example, in August 2016, in the 15th issue of *Dabiq*, Daesh declared its intention to, '*Break the Cross*,' Christians and Christianity. The statements in the newsletter specify their intent to destroy these groups in whole or in part, clearly meeting the definition of genocide enunciated in the Genocide Convention. Further evidence of the specific intent to destroy can be inferred from the atrocities perpetrated against the communities.

Throughout their brutal theocratic dictatorship, Daesh fighters committed murder, extermination, enslavement, deportation and forcible transfer of population, imprisonment, torture, abductions of women and children, exploitation, abuse, rape, sexual violence, forced marriage, and enforced disappearance, and much more. These atrocities clearly match the technical criteria listed as genocidal methods in Article II of the Genocide Convention.

Because of the overwhelming evidence of the atrocities meeting the definition of genocide, the atrocities committed by Daesh against religious minorities have been recognised as such by the Council of Europe, the European Parliament, and a number of governments and parliaments.[26] These determinations were made close to two years after the

[26] Council of Europe Resolution 2091 (2016), (27 January 2016), 2; European Parliament Resolution 2015/2599(RSP) on recent attacks and abductions by ISIS/Daesh in the Middle East, notably of Assyrians, (4 February 2016), 2; John Kerry, 'Remarks on Daesh and Genocide' (speech, US Department of State, Washington DC, 17 March 2016); UK House of Commons, Daesh Genocide of Minorities Debate, Hansard, April

atrocities were perpetrated. However, the risk of genocide was clearly visible in the years prior to the August 2014 attacks.[27]

Further attention should also be given to the crimes which Daesh committed against groups not covered by the Genocide Convention, and among others, these include gay men. Daesh declared homosexuality to be punishable by execution.[28] There are shocking reports of gay men being tortured and killed. In July 2016, it was reported that in Kirkuk, Daesh executed a young Iraqi man by throwing him from the top of a building on charges of being gay.[29] His corpse was later stoned by the crowd. In August 2016, Daesh issued a video showing '*hisbah*,' their religious police throwing another gay man off a building in Mosul and in the same month the execution of four gay men was reported in Nineveh province.[30]

The BBC published the testimony of a gay Iraqi man, using the pseudonym, Taim.[31] He had fled an area overrun by Daesh. He explained that many in the community in which he was raised cheered Daesh's

---

2016, Volume 608; 'Australia Recognizes Crimes Committed By ISIS Against Assyrians As Genocide' *AINA*, 2 May 2016; Canadian House of Commons, 42nd Parliament, 1st Session, Number 74, 16 June 2016; Assemblee Nationale, Resolution N° 3779.

[27] After the fall of the former regime in 2003, individuals and armed groups used the power vacuum this created to further their own agenda. Over the ensuing years, sporadic incidents of violence turned into organized and systematic attacks. Slowly but surely the plight of religious minorities in Iraq began its journey from single attacks to organized mass atrocities, then to the ultimate crime of crimes; genocide.

In 2011, the UK Border Agency published a report on the situation in Iraq. The report identified deadly attacks on religious minorities, especially during religious gatherings. This included kidnapping and murder, both crimes were carried out with impunity. Armed groups attacked Christian, Yazidi, and Shabak communities, labeling them crusaders, devil-worshipers, and infidels. Such labeling of groups with names like crusaders, devil-worshipers, and infidels is a clearly identifiable stage of genocide; dehumanization. In the same way, the Nazis labeled the Jews as vermin and the Hutu labeled Tutsi as cockroaches.

[28] Corey Charlton, 'Inside ISIS Sharia courts: Gay man sentenced to be thrown to his death was asked if he was happy with the verdict. 'I'd prefer you shoot me' he replied... then they threw him anyway' *Daily Mail* (2 December 2015).

[29] ARA News, 'Radical ISIS group executes Iraqi man for being gay' *ARA News* (23 July 2016). Available at: https://web.archive.org/web/20170805055631/, http://ara news.net/2016/07/radical-isis-group-executes-iraqi-man-for-being-gay/.

[30] S. J. Prince, *New ISIS Execution Compilation Video Shows Gay Man Thrown from Roof* (10 August 2016).

[31] BBC, 'Why my own father would have let IS kill me' *BBC* (22 July 2015). Available at: https://www.bbc.co.uk/news/magazine-33565055.

persecution of homosexuals. He described how systematic Daesh was *'when it comes to tracking gay people. They hunt them down one by one. When they capture people, they go through his phone and his contacts and Facebook friends. They are trying to track down every gay man. And it's like dominoes. If one goes, the others will be taken down too.'*[32] As he added:

> It has been devastating to see the public reaction to the killings. Usually, when Daesh posts pictures online, people sympathise with the victims — but not if they're gay. You should see the Facebook comments after they post video of the killings. It's devastating. 'We hate [Daesh] but when they do things like this, we love them. God bless you [Daesh].'[33]

While the atrocities against gay man cannot be classified as genocide as the definition of genocide does not include specific targeting because of sexual orientation, such atrocities certainly constitute crimes against humanity, with sexual identity captured within the definition of 'gender' as a protected identity for the crime against humanity of persecution or included in *'other grounds'* catch-all of the persecution provision.

4   Responses to the Atrocities

Despite Daesh being a non-state actor and, as such, responding to the atrocities should not pose diplomatic challenges, the responses in Syria and Iraq were relatively slow and different.

4.1   *Attempts to Prevent and Suppress the Atrocities*

In many parts of Syria and Iraq, the Daesh dictatorship wreaked havoc requiring a broad range of responses. These included military action, reconstruction of the destroyed villages, assistance to the survivors, and steps to ensure the future of the persecuted groups in the region. In reacting to the significant international security threat posed by Daesh, over 80 partners came together, establishing the Global Coalition against Daesh. It conducted military attacks on the growing caliphate established

---

[32] Ibid.
[33] Ibid.

by Daesh in significant areas of Syria and Iraq.[34] During the second half of 2016 and throughout 2017 this well organised and focused cooperation led to the liberation of many parts of Iraq.[35]

However, Daesh ideology and Jihadists persisted in hotspots, with estimates that these numbered more than 10,000 in Syria and Iraq combined. Subsequent reports have suggested that as state resources in Iraq have been redirected to fight COVID-19 Daesh has been regrouping under the cover of the pandemic. A UN report states that:

> groups are using the outbreak to advance propaganda and fundraising and, in some regions, are seeking to take advantage of perceptions that the attention of security forces is diverted elsewhere... It has exploited security gaps caused by the pandemic and by political turbulence in Iraq to relaunch a sustained rural insurgency, as well as sporadic operations in Baghdad and other large cities.[36]

As the world continues to battle the COVID-19 pandemic, there is a grave danger that combatting Daesh may slip from global priorities, thus enabling Daesh to re-emerge.

Meanwhile, Daesh genocide against the targeted communities continues while, with wholly inadequate resources to support them, the targeted communities continue to try and deal with the consequences of the atrocities which they have already experienced.

Nevertheless, we are able to report that in Iraq, in early 2021, a positive step towards comprehensive assistance was taken.

On 1 March 2021, the Iraqi parliament passed the Yazidi [Female] Survivors Bill (the Bill), a law which aims to aid survivors of the Daesh atrocities. The Bill seeks to assist:

---

[34] See: Global Coalition against Daesh. Available at: https://theglobalcoalition.org/en/.

[35] See for example: Reuters, 'Iraqi PM Declares 'End of War against Daesh' in Iraq' *Reuters* (9 December 2017). Available at: https://www.geo.tv/latest/171492-iraq-is-totally-liberated-from-islamic-state-iraqi-armed-forces.

[36] UN Security Council, Twenty-sixth Report of the Analytical Support and Sanctions Monitoring Team Submitted Pursuant to Resolution 2368 (2017) Concerning ISIL (Da'esh), Al-Qaida and Associated Individuals and Entities, S/2020/717, 23 July 2020.

1. Every Yazidi [female] survivor kidnapped by Daesh and who was freed afterwards.
2. Women and girls from the (Turkmen, Christian, Shabak) communities who were subjected to the same crimes mentioned in Article 1 [namely, every woman or girl who has been subjected to crimes of sexual violence from her kidnapping, sexual slavery, selling her in slavery markets, separating her from her family, forcing her to change her religion, forced marriage, pregnancy and forced abortion or inflicting physical and psychological harm to her by [Daesh] since the date [August 3, 2014] and was freed afterward].
3. Yazidi child survivors who were under the age of eighteen at the time of their kidnapping.
4. Yazidi, Turkmen, Christian and Shabak survivors from the mass killings and mass elimination carried out by [Daesh] in their areas.

This Bill aims to provide survivors with compensation to secure '*a decent life for them*.' It aims to ensure that survivors are provided with rehabilitation; any other assistance needed to help with their integration into society; and to prevent the recurrence of the violations.

In addition to prescribing assistance for survivors of the Daesh atrocities, the Bill determines that the atrocities perpetrated by Daesh against the Yazidis, Turkmen, Christians, and Shabaks constitute genocide and crimes against humanity. The Bill designates 3 August as a national day of remembrance of victims and survivors of the atrocities.

Iraq's legislators also emphasised the need to prosecute the perpetrators of the atrocities.

In concluding this appraisal, we return to the Kurdish Regional Government (KRG) and commend the positive steps it has taken to embrace minorities.

The KRG has introduced a Minority Rights Law (to protect the freedom of religion and prohibit religious discrimination), appointed diverse religious representatives, and has attempted to diversify the Peshmerga.[37]

---

[37] It must also be considered that Peshmerga were the only security force in the region in August 2014. They maintained bases and checkpoints throughout Sinjar and have been defending the area for many months if not years. However, the events of early August 2014, have shown a different side of Peshmerga. In its report 'They came to destroy,' The IICoISAR summarised the abandonment by the Peshmerga fighters as follows:

Religious and ethnic pluralism is demonstrated in their Parliament, with Members from the Yazidi, Turkmen, Christian, and Armenian minorities underlining the emphasis and importance which they are placing on respect for difference. Their officials reassured us that they will continue to modernise and enforce these laws to ensure fair participation and equality of citizenship. Like the Assyrians, Syriacs, Chaldeans, and Yazidis, the Kurds have also experienced considerable suffering, pain, and betrayal—and have a chequered history themselves. Kurds have experienced genocide, crimes against humanity, and the barbarism of war lords and militias—and still do.

Following his 2019 visit to Northern Iraq Lord Alton, in a joint letter with Baroness D'Souza, to *The Times* of 12 October 2019, described the heavy aerial bombardment by Turkey of 181 targets in Kurdish areas of north-east Syria. The use of white phosphorous—which is not listed as a chemical weapon in the Convention on the Use of Chemical Weapons—led to appalling disfiguration of civilians, including badly mutilated children.

Lord Alton visited the newly established refugee camps at Bardarash, in northern Iraq, to which 2520 Kurdish families from Syria had fled. He asked Bardarash refugees what message they would send to those who forced them from their homes in Hassaka, Qamishli, Kobane, and Rass Alein. A mother of four told him that *'the war planes came at 4.00 pm. As they dropped their bombs and chemicals many children were burnt. Some were killed. We all started to run. One of my children fell and concussed his skull. We kept running and were eventually offered places in a car. We had to give them $250 to bring us here to safety. I just want to go home with my children- but everything was destroyed and we would be slaughtered.'*

24. As they moved into Sinjar, ISIS fighters faced little or no resistance. Many of the Peshmerga reportedly withdrew in the face of the ISIS advance, leaving much of the Sinjar region defenceless. The decision to withdraw was not effectively communicated to the local population. No evacuation orders were issued and most villages were initially unaware of the collapse of the security situation.

25. As word spread that the Peshmerga had left their checkpoints, a few *ad-hoc* groups of lightly armed, local Yazidi men mounted a very limited defence of some villages, such as Girzerik and Siba Sheikh Khedir, in an attempt to give their families and neighbours more time to escape. By daybreak, Yazidi families from hundreds of villages across Sinjar were fleeing their homes in fear and panic. They took little with them. Others were advised by Arab neighbours to stay in the villages and raise white flags over their houses.

Asked what message she would send to Turkey's President Erdogan, she said: '*I would ask him how he can sleep in his bed knowing that he has made us suffer like this. May God punish him.*'

Another Bardarash refugee, Hamid, described how he saw people choking as their homes were burnt: '*children were throwing up and we had to leave the injured behind as we fled.*' Hamza, whose wife and mother of their 3-year-old daughter—was killed—told Lord Alton he would like to send a message to President Trump: '*Ask him where is the justice in letting Erdogan force Kurdish families to flee their homes and for them to be given to families from Aleppo, Idlib, or Homs.*'

Challenging an illegal invasion and ethnic cleansing, carried out by a NATO power, Hamza said '*It was Trump who opened the door to the attacks and allowed Erdogan to commit this massacre. And the international community did nothing about it.*'

Salem Farhim Mohammed—whose family are no strangers to massacres, ethnic cleansing and being forced to flee for their lives, says '*Erdogan thinks he is God.*' Salem is from Teltama and has a family of five. His grandfather was an Armenian who fled from Mardin, a Christian enclave in south-east Turkey when the Armenian Genocide began in 1914.

The Kurds in Teltama provided food and shelter and he settled there. Two months previously his grandson and great grandchildren were forced from their home '*we were told that we are infidels.*' One of his cousins was killed in a mortar attack. Their generators, tools, and possessions were seized. They fled.

Salem told Lord Alton: '*Mr. Trump says we Kurds are "not angels." No. But,*' he said, '*we are human beings.*'

All this begs the question, what outrage does a NATO country have to commit—just what does it have to do to innocent civilians—before other NATO members declare it to be unfit for membership?

And when did it become acceptable to break the Geneva Conventions—and potentially the Chemical Weapons Convention—and illegally occupy territory and ethnically cleanse a population, and face no investigation, little censure, no Security Council resolution, and no consequences?

And in the context of a global refugee crisis—with more than 80 million people displaced—can't statesmen and stateswomen—if they are to be worthy of the name—see that ignoring atrocity crimes merely exacerbates the most serious crisis facing the human race? Do they not also understand that, as they fail to tackle the root causes of displacement, far from offering a solution, refugee camps are perfect recruiting grounds for extremist organisations able to exploit despair and hopelessness.

Bardarash and places like it are a symbol of the breakdown of global leadership. Millions who are displaced experience the direct consequences of atrocity crimes. They are the ones paying the price of our abysmal failure to hold to account those responsible.

Despite all of this—and maybe because of it—within the area of Iraq controlled by the Kurdish Regional Government a genuine attempt is being made to try and create a respectful, diverse society. That, and initiatives like it, remain the antidote to the visceral hatred offered by the ideologies of racism, sectarianism, and religious extremism. Learning to live together in respect for one another's traditions and beliefs is the great challenge of our times.

Genocide need not be the final word.

4.2   *Investigating and Prosecuting the Crimes*

Where genocide has occurred, there is a clear duty to bring those responsible to justice. Some investigations and prosecutions of the Daesh perpetrators have been conducted in domestic courts. However, two main problems have emerged. First, those prosecutions conducted to date have been for lower offences, specifically for terrorism-related offences (and not for other offences, such as '*murder, kidnapping, (…), sale into or otherwise forced marriage, trafficking in persons, rape, sexual slavery and other forms of sexual violence, recruitment and use of children*',[38] forced transfer of population, destruction of cultural heritage and much more, or for international crimes such as genocide, crimes against humanity or war crimes). Second, due process surrounding such trials, especially in Syria and Iraq, has been problematic.

4.2.1   *Prosecuting Daesh in Iraq*
Reports from Iraq suggest that Daesh fighters are prosecuted for terror-related offences only.[39] Shortcomings with the Iraqi Penal Code prevent prosecutions for the more serious crimes we have cited above. For

---

[38] UN Security Council Resolution 2379 (21 September 2017) UN Doc S/RES/2379.

[39] Margaret Coker and Falih Hassan, 'A 10-min Trial, a Death Sentence: Iraqi Justice for ISIS Suspects' *New York Times* (17 April 2018). Available at: https://www.nytimes.com/2018/04/17/world/middleeast/iraq-isis-trials.html.

example, the Iraqi Penal Code does not criminalise genocide and other international crimes.[40] Iraq has been working with the UN Investigative Team for Accountability of Daesh/ISIL (UNITAD) with the intention of introducing such law. However, at the time of writing, such legislation has not yet been introduced. Even if enacted, the question then arises about whether it could retrospectively be used to prosecute Daesh.

Furthermore, the Iraqi Penal Code does not address a number of shocking crimes perpetrated against women and girls, thus preventing the prosecution of Daesh fighters. For example, marital rape is not criminalised in Iraq. Similarly, the law does not criminalise domestic violence, and it is clear from Paragraph 41(1) of the Iraqi Penal Code, that '*punishment*' of a wife can be justified. This is clearly a central issue when considering the rise of Daesh, its use of rape, sexual violence, and forced marriage against women and girls, and impunity for these crimes.

Paragraph 41(1) of the Iraqi Penal Code states that '*(1) The punishment of a wife by her husband, the disciplining by parents and teachers of children under their authority is within certain limits, prescribed by law or by custom.*' If the '*marriages*' between Daesh fighters and the abducted and enslaved women and girls are accepted, it may be argued that the provisions in Paragraph 41(1) of the Iraqi Penal Code will ultimately prevent women and girls from ever seeing perpetrators brought to justice for the abhorrent violence they suffered at the hands of Daesh. As things stand, the Daesh fighters who forcibly married Yazidi women and girls and abused them are unlikely to face criminal sanction for those crimes as they can, legally, be justified under the Iraqi Penal Code.

This provision was not amended when, in 1986, Iraq first agreed to accept the UN Convention on the Elimination of Discrimination Against Women (CEDAW). In fact, when acceding to CEDAW, Iraq made several reservations that significantly weakened the protections demanded by CEDAW, most notably to Articles 2(f) and (g) and 16.[41] Article 2(f) of CEDAW places an obligation on states '*to take all appropriate measures, including legislation, to modify or abolish existing laws, regulations, customs and practices which constitute discrimination against*

---

[40] See: Iraq: Penal Code [Iraq], No. 111 of 1969, July 1969. Available at: https://www.refworld.org/docid/452524304.html.

[41] See: https://indicators.ohchr.org/.

women.' Article 2(g) requires states '*to repeal all national penal provisions which constitute discrimination against women.*' As Iraq made a reservation concerning the provisions, it preserved the discriminatory provisions contained within the Iraqi Penal Code (including Paragraph 41[1]). Article 16 of CEDAW places an obligation on states to 'take all appropriate measures to eliminate discrimination against women in all matters relating to marriage and family relations and, in particular, shall ensure, on a basis of equality of men and women.' By virtue of the reservation to Article 16, Iraq preserved the inequality between men and women concerning marriage—and it remains in place to this day.

In the case of women and girls forcibly married to Daesh fighters, the question is whether these marriages could be seen as legal under Iraqi law. Article 9 of Iraq's Personal Status Law No. 188 of 1959 criminalises forced marriage. Article 9(1) states that 'No relative or non-relative has the right to force marriage on any person, whether male or female, without their consent. The contract of forced marriage is considered void if the marriage is not yet consummated.' As the provision suggests, once the marriage is consummated, the forced marriage is not considered to be void. This despite the fact that, in case of forced marriage, consummating marriage most likely means rape.

In response to the mass atrocities perpetrated by Daesh in Iraq, states must ensure that all Daesh fighters are prosecuted for rape and sexual and gender-based violence which they perpetrated against women and girls. The crimes should not be set aside under the cover of Paragraph 41(1) of the Iraqi Penal Code or any other provisions. The Iraqi Government should introduce changes to its Penal Code, and ensure that any provisions of the Iraqi Penal Code stop discriminating against women. They could do this by repealing Paragraph 41(1) of the Iraqi Penal Code. Furthermore, the provisions on forced marriage should also be revised. 'Consummating' a forced marriage should never make it lawful.

When considering the reform of Iraqi law, legislators should also address the abhorrent hatred directed at men with same sex attraction. Murder motivated by a hatred of another's orientation, along with rape and sexual and gender-based violence, should all be considered as part of the crime of genocide and other international crimes. Legal reform in Iraq could begin to address this by introducing the crime of genocide and other international crimes into the Iraqi Penal Code in accordance with international standards (notably the Genocide Convention).[42]

Advocates from Nadia's Initiative have rightfully expressed concern about reported practices within Iraq's domestic courts that '*Daesh members held in Syria have been released and that fighters transferred to Iraq have been sentenced to death following rushed trials that exclude victims and do not comply with international fair-trial standards*.'[43] Reports of Daesh fighters being sentenced to death in trials failing to meet minimum international standards on fair trials and without the involvement of the victims are not new allegations.[44] Such procedures mean it is simply not possible to ensure justice for victims deprived of their day in court and desired the right to tell their stories,[45] nor are perpetrators forced to face those whom they have so cruelly abused. Nor are there visible traces of justice for future generations who will bear the weight of the missed opportunity for truth and justice to shine through the Daesh trials in response to the Daesh atrocities and leaving legacy for future generations.

Iraq's domestic courts are simply not equipped to prosecute Daesh fighters for their atrocities.[46] Radical steps are needed to ensure that Iraqi courts are able to fulfil their duties.

4.2.2   Prosecuting Daesh in Syria

According to news reports, there have been some prosecutions of Daesh fighters in Syria. However, the continuing war impedes an adequate judicial response. The atrocities and the nature of the Syrian regime, and its compromised institutions, hardly inspire confidence in the possibility of due process and the fair and proper administration of justice.

---

[42] *Prosecutor v Akayesu*, Caso No. ICTR-96–4-T (Judgment, September 2, 1998) 496. See also: Sherrie L. Russell-Brown, 'Rape as an Act of Genocide' (2003) 21 *Berkeley Journal of International Law* 350; Reid-Cunningham, Alllison Ruby, 'Rape as a Weapon of Genocide' (2008) 3 *Genocide Studies and Prevention: An International Journal*.

[43] See: Nadia's Imitative, Press Release.

[44] See for example: Margaret Coker and Falih Hassan, 'A 10-min Trial, a Death Sentence: Iraqi Justice for ISIS Suspects' *New York Times* (17 April 2018). Available at: https://www.nytimes.com/2018/04/17/world/middleeast/iraq-isis-trials.html.

[45] Eric Stover, *The Witness. War Crimes and the Promise of Justice in The Hague* (University of Pennsylvania Press: Philadelphia, 2007).

[46] Physicians for Human Rights, Building Forensic Capacity to Document, Collect, Identify, Analyse, and Preserve Evidence of War Crimes and Crimes against Humanity in Northern Iraq, Capacity Assessment Report (July 2017).

4.2.3 Prosecutions of Daesh Outside of Syria and Iraq

Outside of Iraq and Syria, the number of prosecutions against Daesh fighters and complicit actors continues to be very low.[47] This is the case in every country from which Daesh foreign fighters originate. In June 2017, the Parliamentary Assembly of the Council of Europe collected data on the prosecutions of Daesh from all member states to the Council of Europe.[48] This data was gathered for a report by Pieter Omtzigt MP, Special Rapporteur on Brining Daesh to Justice. The data revealed a large discrepancy between the numbers of Daesh foreign fighters returning to their home countries and the number who have been prosecuted.

For example, while the UK Government confirmed that approximately 425 British Daesh fighters have now returned to the UK,[49] in its response to the inquiry, the UK identified that, as of June 2017, there have been 101 successful convictions directly related to the atrocities committed by Daesh.[50] This number includes Daesh foreign fighter returnees but also individuals from the UK who have facilitated the atrocities (and are not included in the number of the returnees). Furthermore, in response to Lord Alton's question asking how many individuals accused of participation or complicity in the Daesh's atrocities have been prosecuted in the UK, to date, Baroness Williams of Trafford, the Home Office Minister indicated that '*as of June 2018, there had been around 40 convictions of individuals who had been prosecuted following their return from Syria, for a range of offences connected to their activities overseas or subsequent counter-terrorism investigations.*'[51] Baroness Williams added '*The majority of those who have returned did so in the earlier stages of the conflict and have been investigated. A significant proportion of these individuals are assessed as*

---

[47] See for example: Committee on Legal Affairs and Human Rights, Prosecuting and punishing the crimes against humanity or even possible genocide committed by Daesh. Replies to questionnaire. Available at: http://website-pace.net/documents/19838/311 5026/AS-JUR-2017-30-EN.pdf/2def016d-fc77-4bb7-823b-a57e113687ce.

[48] Ibid.

[49] Committee on Legal Affairs and Human Rights, Prosecuting and punishing the crimes against humanity or even possible genocide committed by Daesh. Replies to questionnaire. 56. See also: A. Schmid, *Foreign (Terrorist) Fighter Estimates* (ICCT: The Hague, 2015) 11.

[50] Ibid.

[51] UK House of Lords, Islamic State: Crimes against Humanity: Written question— HL14768. Available at: https://www.parliament.uk/business/publications/written-questi ons-answers-statements/written-question/Lords/2019-03-25/HL14768/.

no longer being of national security concern.'[52] This statement appears to conflate the need to punish with the need to rehabilitate the returnees. Even if they no longer pose a threat, surely, they should be prosecuted for atrocity crimes committed while they were with Daesh?

Other countries have been more proactive. Some have used universal jurisdiction to prosecute Daesh perpetrators for genocide. In October 2019, Germany began its first genocide trial involving a Daesh fighter,[53] relying on the principle of universal jurisdiction.[54] The accused was an Iraqi national, Taha A.-J., who was transferred from Greece to Germany to stand trial for a litany of crimes. The 27-year-old man stood accused of the crime of genocide and crimes against humanity. He was also facing accusations of war crimes and human trafficking for the purpose of forced labour.

Taha A.-J. is the husband of Jennifer W., a 28-year-old German citizen who was also on trial before the Higher Regional Court of Munich for war crimes and crimes against humanity committed against members of the Yazidi community.[55] Although Taha A.-J. is not a German national, his victims are not German and his crimes have not been committed on Germany territory, under the principle of universal jurisdiction German courts have jurisdiction over his crimes where they amount to the crime of genocide, war crimes and crimes against humanity. The accused faced life sentence if convicted. According to press reports, Taha A.-J. joined Daesh before March 2013. The allegations state that in the summer of 2015, Taha A.-J. and Jennifer W. 'purchased' and enslaved a five-year-old Yazidi girl and her mother. The couple kept the woman and girl enslaved in Fallujah, Iraq, and subjected them to forced conversion and physical abuse including battery and starvation. Allegedly, Taha A.-J. chained the girl outside and left her there to die of thirst.

---

[52] Ibid.

[53] Der Generalbundesanwalt, Festnahme eines mutmaßlichen Mitglieds der ausländischen terroristischen Vereinigung Islamischer Staat (IS) wegen des Verdachts des Völkermords u. a. (11 October 2019). Available at: https://www.generalbundesanwalt.de/de/showpress.php?newsid=856.

[54] See for example: Mary Robinson, 'Foreword,' in *The Princeton Principles on Universal Jurisdiction* (Princeton University Press: Princeton, 2001) 16.

[55] Ibid.

On 30 November 2021, a court in Frankfurt imposed a life sentence on Taha A.-J. for genocide against the Yazidi minority—the first genocide conviction of a Daesh fighter in the world. Taha A.-J. was convicted of genocide, crimes against humanity, war crimes, aiding and abetting war crimes and bodily harm resulting in death. At the time of writing this manuscript, this convictions was being appealed. Also, at the time of writing this manuscript, this is the only judicial convictions for the Daesh genocide anywhere in the world.

With Iraqi courts unable to ensure justice, the proactive approach taken by German courts is commendable. Other states should extend a helping hand and also exercise universal jurisdiction to prosecute some of the worst atrocities that we have witnessed in recent times. There is no reason not to do so in the case of Daesh atrocities.

4.2.4   Prosecutions by International Tribunals

In 2021, more than six years after Daesh unleashed its genocidal atrocities in Syria and Iraq, there have been no prosecutions of Daesh fighters by international tribunals, and scandalously, there is still no international tribunal with the jurisdiction to carry out such prosecutions.

The ICC, the only permanent criminal tribunal, does not have territorial jurisdiction over the situation in Syria or Iraq as the states are not parties to the Rome Statute.[56] The ICC could exercise its personal jurisdiction over the Daesh foreign fighters from states that are parties to the Rome Statute, but has not yet done so. The UN Security Council could refer the situation to the ICC or establish *ad-hoc* tribunals for situations in both states.[57] After an attempt in 2014 was vetoed by Russia and China, a UN Security Council referral of the genocide and crimes against humanity in Syria to the ICC is very unlikely.[58] Such a referral in relation to Iraq might be more plausible. However, states have instead expressed more willingness to establish an *ad-hoc* tribunal to prosecute Daesh.

Apart from the ICC, there is currently no other international tribunal which could prosecute the Daesh perpetrators. But, be clear, such a tribunal could be established by the UN Security Council. It is the only

[56] Article 12(1) of the Rome Statute.

[57] Article 13(b) of the Rome Statute.

[58] UN News, Referral of Syria to International Criminal Court Fails as Negative Votes Prevent Security Council from Adopting Draft Resolution, (22 May 2014). Available at: https://www.un.org/press/en/2014/sc11407.doc.htm.

UN body with the power to do so.[59] If it chose to, the UN Security Council could follow the approach taken in response to the atrocities in Rwanda[60] or Bosnia.[61] In both cases, the UN Security Council took a two-stage approach in (1) establishing a group of experts to collect and analyse the evidence of the atrocities and (2) establishing *ad-hoc* tribunals to prosecute the perpetrators.

4.2.5   Ad-Hoc Tribunal for Daesh in Iraq?

The UN Security Council has at least taken one step which could lead to the tried and tested approach used in Rwanda or Bosnia. In September 2017, in Resolution 2379,[62] the UN Security Council established an Investigative Team (also referred to as UNITAD) to collect and preserve the evidence of the Daesh atrocities in Iraq and prepare the evidence for future prosecution.

The Investigative Team is to support the Iraqi domestic courts by *'collecting, preserving, and storing evidence in Iraq of acts that may amount to war crimes, crimes against humanity and genocide committed by [Daesh] in Iraq.'*[63] The evidence obtained is to be used *'before national courts, and complementing investigations being carried out by the Iraqi authorities, or investigations carried out by authorities in third countries at their request.'*[64] The Resolution also raises the possibility that the newly established team could collect evidence of Daesh atrocities in countries other than Iraq. Nevertheless, any such request would first need to be approved by the UN Security Council.

In one respect, Resolution 2379 is very clear in its purpose. It envisages that Daesh fighters will be prosecuted by *'competent national-level courts'*[65] and not international or hybrid tribunals. Any other use of the

---

[59] See: Article 41 of the UN Chapter,

[60] UN Security Council Resolution 955 (8 November 1994) UN Doc S/RES/955.

[61] UN Security Council Resolution 827 (25 May 1993) UN Doc S/RES/827.

[62] UN Security Council Resolution 2379 (21 September 2017) UN Doc. S/RES/2379 (2017).

[63] Ibid., 2.

[64] Ibid., 2.

[65] UN Security Council Resolution 2379 (2017) 5.

evidence obtained by the Investigative Team is to be '*determined in agreement with the Government of Iraq on a case by case basis.*'[66] That Daesh fighters are to be prosecuted by Iraqi national courts raises concerns not satisfactorily addressed by the operative paragraph encouraging '*Member States, and regional and intergovernmental organisations, to provide appropriate legal assistance and capacity building to the Government of Iraq in order to strengthen its courts and judicial system.*'[67]

In June 2020, the Investigative Team presented a progress report and said that it is helping to address fundamental challenges faced by domestic authorities in prosecuting Daesh members. It said its work has been facilitated '*thanks to the collection and exploitation of call data and related records, the forensic digital extraction of evidence from devices formerly used by Daesh and the digitisation of documentary records held by Iraqi authorities, the Team can significantly broaden the basis on which accountability processes can be built.*'[68] This had led the Investigative Team to identify 344 alleged Daesh operatives involved in the atrocities unleashed against religious minorities in 2014. This number will increase as the Investigative Team continues its work.

While the Investigative Team collects and preserves evidence, it is attempting to introduce a new way of reaching larger groups of people able to provide evidence of the Daesh atrocities.

The Investigative Team has been developing a secure and structured mobile reporting application (app) to allow members of targeted communities and others, to submit information about the atrocities and the perpetrators. The app was developed in response to travel limitations imposed by the COVID-19 pandemic but should enable the Investigative Team to continue with their mandate.

The Investigative Team reports that '*the [app] contains a series of survey questions and fields, enabling individuals to provide leads and information to the Team, including photographs, document scans and other materials. It is hoped that the application will serve as an effective pre-screening tool,*

---

[66] Ibid., 5.

[67] UN Security Council, 'Fourth report of the Special Adviser and Head of the United Nations Investigative Team to Promote Accountability for Crimes Committed by Da'esh/Islamic State in Iraq and the Levant' (2020) S/2020/386.

[68] Ibid., 113.

reducing the need for in-person meetings with survivors and witnesses.'[69] It is hoped that this will improve the efficiency of data protection.

Once the evidence of Daesh atrocities has been collected and preserved it will be crucial for a tribunal to engage with the evidence and secure prosecutions.

The Investigative Team is similar to the commission of experts established for the International Criminal Tribunal for the former Yugoslavia (ICTY) and International Criminal Tribunal for Rwanda (ICTR). But, despite this, and the very welcome establishment of the Investigative Team, the UN Security Council has failed to come forward with a resolution to establish an *ad-hoc* tribunal.

In accordance with Resolution 2379, evidence is being collated to assist with prosecutions by domestic courts in Iraq. Logically and crucially, as happened in Rwanda and the former Yugoslavia, the UN Security Council should now establish an *ad-hoc* tribunal to prosecute Daesh fighters for their crimes in Iraq. Until that happens, Resolution 2379 simply proposes that Iraqi domestic courts should prosecute Daesh fighters. Even though domestic courts could play an important role in the prosecution of Daesh fighters, this flawed arrangement neglects several important issues which we discuss below. But the real problem is that the national courts may simply be incapable of prosecuting Daesh fighters for genocide, crimes against humanity and war crimes.

First, the Iraqi legal framework does not contain provisions criminalising genocide, crimes against humanity and war crimes. Even if changes were made to domestic law to introduce amendments to the penal code, such laws would be ex-post facto and any future prosecution could be in breach of prohibitions on applying retrospective law. However, before and during World War II, such retrospective law was applied to Nazi crimes and might be acceptable if the atrocities, while not prohibited under domestic law, were clearly in breach of a set of common values that was regarded by international community as paramount and required protection on international level.[70] The set of common values was rooted

---

[69] Ibid., 54.

[70] Stefan Glaser, 'The Charter of the Nuremberg Tribunal and New Principles of International Law' in Guenael Mettraux (eds.) *Perspectives on the Nuremberg Trial* (Oxford University Press: New York, 2010) 69; Guenael Mettraux, 'Judicial Inheritance: The Value and Significance of the Nuremberg Trial to Contemporary War Crimes Tribunals' in Guenael Mettraux (eds.) *Perspectives on the Nuremberg Trial* (Oxford University Press:

in the broad concept of upholding humanity, which may be perceived as an equivalent of the basic human rights.[71] Nevertheless, the complete absence of these crimes in the Iraqi penal code is hardly a trivial omission. They simply do not exist. So how would the Iraqi judiciary have the necessary competence—or expertise—to deal with such cases in domestic courts?

Second, while evidence of Daesh atrocities has been collected by a number of actors, the evidence may not meet the standards required for criminal prosecution. This failure may be addressed by the new Investigative Team. However, evidence obtained to date will need to be reviewed to ensure that it meets the required standard. This is a massive endeavour and it remains unclear whether the Investigative Team will have the capacity to undertake this task.

Third, the current care routinely provided to the victims of Daesh atrocities is provided by state and non-state actors. The care provided is not standardised. The medical and medico-legal evidence obtained during the provision of such care is not being adequately recorded or at all. There is an urgent need to create specialised training and to build capacity in accordance with local needs.

Fourth, the nature of the crimes committed by Daesh requires strong cooperation and collaboration between professionals across several sectors. This collaboration had yet to emerge.

These four challenges faced by the judicial system in Iraq suggest that its judicial system is not in a position to prosecute Daesh operatives. Considerable work needs to be undertaken to reform Iraqi courts to be competent to undertake the job required of them by the UN Security Council. Indirectly, Resolution 2379 does encourage 'Member States and regional and intergovernmental organisations, to provide appropriate legal assistance and capacity building to the Government of Iraq in order to strengthen its courts and judicial system.'[72] But the failings in the Iraqi judicial system, and the essential changes needed to the penal code, must be urgently addressed first. Such initiatives must be coordinated to ensure

New York, 2010) 602, Joseph B. Keenan and Brendan F. Brown, *Crimes Against International Law* (Public Affairs Press: Washington, 1950) 122.

[71] 78th Congress, 1st Session, S. Con. Res., House Calendar No. 53, [Report No. 2521], In the House of Representatives, 11 March 1943, Referred to the Committee on Foreign Affairs, 16 March 1943.

[72] UN Security Council 2379 (2017) 9.

their effectiveness—and there is little evidence that this is happening. Considering these challenges faced in Iraq and the wide-ranging reforms that would be needed, serious thought must be given to whether, instead of focusing on the use of domestic courts, Daesh fighters should be prosecuted instead by a specialised hybrid tribunal. Such a step could circumvent the challenges associated with introducing new provisions into the Iraqi penal code to criminalise genocide, crimes against humanity and war crimes.

A few years ago, many states were in support of an initiative to establish an *ad-hoc* tribunal. Some of the available options have been discussed at the Council of Europe. In September 2017, Pieter Omtzigt MP, Rapporteur on 'prosecuting and punishing crimes against humanity or possible genocide by Daesh' presented his report on bringing Daesh to justice. In it, Omtzigt scrutinised the international and regional options to bring Daesh to justice, moving away from the Iraqi domestic prosecutions. The report was unanimously adopted. Following his report, Omtzigt tabled a resolution on 'Prosecuting and punishing the crimes against humanity or even possible genocide committed by Daesh.'[73] On 12 October 2017, the resolution was debated and taken to a vote. It passed with 67 votes in favour, 4 abstentions, and no votes against. Some of the noteworthy provisions of the resolution include calling upon members of the Council of Europe to:

> 6.2.1. providing for universal jurisdiction over crimes covered by the Rome Statute of the ICC, where this is not already the case, and, following the example set by Sweden and Germany, investigating and, where justified, prosecuting any suspected Daesh members who come within their jurisdiction or control;
> 6.2.2. prosecuting all offences committed within their jurisdiction relating to Daesh activities abroad, and in this connection, ratifying and fully implementing the 2005 Council of Europe Convention on the Prevention of Terrorism (CETS No. 196) and its 2015 Additional Protocol (CETS No. 217) (...)

---

[73] Resolution 2190 (2017), 'Prosecuting and punishing the crimes against humanity or even possible genocide committed by Daesh' PACE (12 October 2017).

6.2.8. not obstructing any possible future United Nations Security Council resolution that may contribute to the prosecution of Daesh members before an international, hybrid or national tribunal.[74]

In 2018, Pieter Omtzigt convened a working group to explore what other options might be available to bring Daesh fighters to justice for genocide, crimes against humanity, or other related crimes and to ensure that the survivors of the atrocities would be fully engaged in the process. During the discussions, the Iraqi representatives agreed that they needed support in prosecuting Daesh fighters and said that they would be willing to consider proposals. In April 2019, the US Department of State's Office of Global Criminal Justice (J/GCJ), in cooperation with the Bureau of Near Eastern Affairs and Office of Assistance Coordination (NEA/AC), announced their new initiative and significant funding to promote criminal accountability for abuses and violations in Iraq and Syria, including war crimes, crimes against humanity, and genocide. This initiative was to consider funding programmes which include components designed to 'develop local investigative and judicial skills; to collect and preserve evidence and maintain the chain of custody of evidence; provide information to national authorities with jurisdiction over crimes, and to conduct other activities that directly support investigations and prosecutions of perpetrators of atrocities in Iraq and Syria.'[75] In May 2019, Sweden's Interior Minister Mikael Damberg proposed the creation of an international tribunal to prosecute Daesh fighters for crimes committed in Iraq and Syria and organised a European summit to discuss the proposal.[76] Despite these initiatives, there has been no progress in establishing such a tribunal. The absence of justice is matched by the absence of restitution.

The objective of enabling all who were forced out of their homes and deprived of their homes and livelihoods, to be able to return and to be assured of safety has only been falteringly realised. With the realisation of justice, it will be easier to build a respectful and decent society based on social and political equality, in where religious freedom and human rights

---

[74] Ibid., 6.

[75] See: https://www.grants.gov/web/grants/search-grants.html?keywords=SFOP0005764.

[76] Ministry of Justice, 'Sweden to host expert meeting on ISIS tribunal' (3 June 2019). Available at: https://www.government.se/press-releases/2019/06/sweden-to-host-expert-meeting-on-isis-tribunal/

are safeguarded along with new investment to restore the communities so aggressively targeted.

Resolution 2379 should, however, be welcomed for expanding the scope of the investigation into atrocities to incorporate '*murder, kidnapping, hostage-taking, suicide bombings, enslavement, sale into or otherwise forced marriage, trafficking in persons, rape, sexual slavery and other forms of sexual violence, recruitment and use of children, attacks on critical infrastructure, as well as its destruction of cultural heritage, including archaeological sites, and trafficking of cultural property.*'[77]

This destruction of cultural heritage and trafficking of cultural property are an aspect of the Daesh atrocities which has gained insufficient attention. Daesh atrocities have aimed to destroy and eliminate evidence of the very existence of religious minorities. These atrocities cannot be neglected or downgraded in their importance. They contribute to the establishment of the specific intent to destroy the protected groups—and specific intent is required for the atrocities to be classified as genocide.

Attacks on cultural artefacts have a long history.

When, in the thirteenth century, Tamerlane (Timur) and his Mongols embarked on their '*pilgrimage of destruction*,' they invaded thirteenth-century Baghdad, intent on destroying thousands of that city's books.[78] It is said that the River Tigris flowed black from the ink which was spilt. Others said that '*they formed a bridge that would support a man on horseback.*'[79] One thousand years ago the '*mad caliph*' of Cairo, Hakim, decreed that all churches, including the Holy Sepulchre in Jerusalem, the burial site of Jesus, should be torn down, razed to the ground.[80] And long ago, Nineveh had been laid waste by the Babylonians.[81] Today, UNESCO lists 22 of the world's 38 endangered cultural-heritage sites as being in the Middle East.

---

[77] Ibid., Preamble.

[78] Alice Barnes-Brown, 'Tamerlane's Reign of Terror' History of Wars (5 July 2018). Available at: https://www.historyanswers.co.uk/people-politics/tamerlanes-reign-of-terror/.

[79] Michael H. Harris, *History of Libraries in the Western World* (Scarecrow Press, 1999) 85.

[80] Ruth Schuster, '1009: The 'Mad Caliph' Destroys Jewish, Christian Sites in Fatimid Empire' *Haaretz* (18 October 2016). Available at: https://www.haaretz.com/jewish/.premium-1009-the-mad-caliph-attacks-christian-sites-in-fatimid-empire-1.5450335.

[81] Will Durant, *Our Oriental Heritage* (MJF Books, 1997) 283.

Genocidal assaults on a people are often intertwined with attempts to wear down their confidence and sense of belonging and to obliterate the sacred places and collections that embody their beliefs and identity. Sacred places represent a crucial part of identity and psyche. Their obliteration was part of the attempt by Daesh to eradicate identity and history.

In Churches and holy sites, in religious cultural artefacts and the beauty of written and printed words memory and the present meet, lived lives and hopes for the future, days of joy and moments of sorrow, immense aesthetic beauty and the genius of great architecture, not to mention the physical ability to bring people together beyond bureaucracy and what many would see as a spiritual skill to provide a joining point between the earth and heaven itself.

In June 2014, it was reported that Daesh had issued instructions to destroy all churches in Mosul.[82] The orgy of violence began in July when the Church of the Virgin Mary was destroyed with several improvised devices. Most other churches in the city suffered a similar fate.[83]

Christian roots in Mosul date back 1800 years or more. Before 2014, 15,000 Christians lived in Mosul but after what has occurred many Christians find it hard to believe that they have a future there and are reluctant to return. In addition to destroying churches and evidence of Christianity, in 2014, in Mosul, Daesh also destroyed the Tomb of Jonah—a site dating from the eighth century BC—and of great importance to Christians, Jews, and many Muslims—but like the Sufi memorials in many other parts of the world unacceptable to the Daesh ideologues.[84]

On 23 July 2014, in an opinion piece in *The Times*, Lord Alton warned: *'The last Christian has been expelled from Mosul... The light of religious freedom, along with the entire Christian presence, has been extinguished in the Bible's "great city of Nineveh" (...) This follows the*

---

[82] See for example: RASHID, 'The Intentional Destruction of Cultural Heritage in Iraq as a Violation of Human Rights.' Available at: https://www.ohchr.org/Documents/Issues/CulturalRights/DestructionHeritage/NGOS/RASHID.pdf.

[83] Ibid.

[84] Sigal Samuel, Sara Farhan, and Atoor Lawandow, 'ISIS Destroyed Jonah's Tomb, but Not Its Message' *The Atlantic* (27 July 2017). Available at: https://www.theatlantic.com/international/archive/2017/07/tomb-of-jonah-mosul-isis/534414/.

uncompromising ultimatum by the jihadists of Isis to convert or die.[85] He said that, '*the world must wake up urgently to the plight of the ancient churches throughout the region who are faced with the threat of mass murder and mass displacement.*'[86] The world chose not to wake up and for those caught up in these barbaric events, the stakes have proved to be utterly existential, catastrophic.

Destruction and displacement went hand in hand. The list of holy sites which have been desecrated and destroyed as part of the cultural genocide is shocking.

In 2014, Dair Mar Elia, the oldest monastery in Iraq, was demolished[87] while, in 2015, St Markourkas Church, a tenth-century Chaldean Catholic church, was destroyed and a nearby cemetery bulldozed.[88] In 2016, Mosul's Sa'a Qadima Church was blown up.[89] Daesh also blew up or demolished other churches elsewhere in Iraq and Syria, including the Armenian Genocide Memorial Church in Deir-ez-Zor, in Syria—built to memorialise and remember the 1.5 million Armenians killed in the Genocide of 1915 to 1923.[90]

The Deir Ez-zor had become an annual destination for pilgrims from around the world.

Destroyed, too, was the seventh-century Green Church (also known as St Ahoadamah Church) in Tikrit belonging to the Assyrian Church of

---

[85] Lord David Alton, 'The world must respond to the cry of Iraq's Christians' *The Times* (23 July 2014). Available at: https://www.thetimes.co.uk/article/the-world-must-respond-to-the-cry-of-iraqs-christians-3jbpknm3g2s.

[86] Ibid.

[87] Steven Lee Myers, 'ISIS Has Destroyed One of Iraq's Oldest Christian Sites' *The New York Times* (20 January 2016). Available at: https://www.nytimes.com/2016/01/21/world/middleeast/isis-iraq-st-elijahs-monastery.html#:~:text=via%20Associated%20Press-,The%20monastery%20of%20St.,Iraqi%20forces%20in%20June%202014.

[88] Anadolu Agency, 'Iraq: Daesh "destroys historical church" in Mosul' *Anadolu Agency* (10 March 2015). Available at: https://www.aa.com.tr/en/politics/iraq-daesh-destroys-historical-church-in-mosul/68300.

[89] Anugrak Humar, 'ISIS Destroys Iraq's Iconic 'Clock Church' in Ongoing Attacks to Annihilate Church History' *The Christian Post* (28 April 2016). Available at: https://www.christianpost.com/news/isis-destroys-iraqs-iconic-clock-church-attacks-annihilate-church-history.html.

[90] Asbarez, 'Armenian Genocide Memorial Church in Deir ez-Zor Liberated' *Azbarez* (6 November 2017). Available at: https://asbarez.com/168519/armenian-genocide-memorial-church-in-deir-ez-zor-liberated/.

the East[91]; the Mar Benham Monastery in Khidr Ilyas near Bakhdida in Iraq[92]; the Assyrian Christian church of the Virgin Mary in the Syrian town of Tel Nasri,[93] and the historic monastery of St. Elian near Al-Qaryatayn in the Homs Governorate.[94]

Daesh also set fire to, or stole, important collections of books and papers.

Some destroyed or stolen works date back to 5000 BC and at Palmyra—a classical oasis in the Syrian desert—they detonated and destroyed anything that might recall beliefs other than their own.[95] This is not just collateral damage from 'war.' The stated goal was to destroy all non-Islamic books. The UN reported that half of the old city of Mosul, in Iraq, and a third of the old city of Aleppo, in Syria, were reduced to rubble.

This all bears comparison with the charred husk of desecrated sacred buildings like the Fasanenstrasse Synagogue in Berlin, part of the orgy of violence which erupted in 1938 when, during Kristallnacht, Jewish synagogues, homes, hospitals, and schools were ransacked, and pillaged. The sledgehammers and petrol left more than 1000 synagogues burnt and over 7000 Jewish shops and businesses ruined as the streets were left covered in shards of smashed glass from broken windows. It was an attempt to eradicate the memory of Jewish people—a prelude to the Holocaust.

Benchmark the terror of 1938 with the more recent fear of Egypt's Copts, who constitute more than half of all Christians in the Middle East.

---

[91] The Telegraph, 'Destruction of Middle East's heritage is "cultural genocide"' *The Telegraph* (23 July 2015). Available at: https://www.telegraph.co.uk/travel/destinations/middle-east/articles/Destruction-of-Middle-Easts-heritage-is-cultural-genocide/.

[92] John Hall, 'Another blow to Christianity and civilisation: ISIS destroy 4th Century Mar Benham monastery in Iraq' *Daily Mail* (19 March 2015). Available at: https://www.dailymail.co.uk/news/article-3002530/Another-blow-Christianity-civilisation-ISIS-destroy-4th-Century-Mar-Benham-monastery-Iraq.html.

[93] Reuters, 'Christmas Revived in a Village Devastated by Daesh' *Gulf News* (26 December 2018). Available at: https://gulfnews.com/world/mena/christmas-revived-in-a-village-devastated-by-daesh-1.61121053#.

[94] The Guardian, 'Islamic State Destroys Fifth-Century Monastery in Central Syria' *The Guardian* (21 August 2015).

[95] Helga Turku, *The Destruction of Cultural Property as a Weapon of War. ISIS in Syria and Iraq* (Palgrave Macmillan, Cham, 2018).

They have seen members of their community left dead, others assaulted, and their 118th Pope, Tawadros II, put under protection having had death threats made against him.

In 1938, *The Times* commented that: '*No foreign propagandist bent upon blackening Germany before the world could outdo the tale of burnings and beatings, of blackguardly assaults on defenceless and innocent people, which disgraced that country yesterday.*'

In August 2013, in an almost identical vein, *The Times* reported how '*Dozens of churches, homes and businesses have been set alight and looted in Egypt, forcing millions of Christians into hiding amid the worst bout of sectarian violence in the country's modern history. Some Coptic Christian communities are being made to pay bribes as local Islamists exploit the turmoil by seeking to revive a seventh-century tax, called jizya, levied on non-Muslims.*'

The newspaper reported that more than 90 churches, monasteries, and church buildings had been attacked across the country and that Imams had urged supporters to go out and attack churches and Christians. Islamist Jihadists said that Egypt's Copts were their '*favourite prey.*' Joe Stork, of Human Rights Watch reported that '*Dozens of churches are smouldering ruins, and Christians throughout the country are hiding in their homes, afraid for their very lives.*'

In Cairo, Franciscan nuns saw the cross over their school gate torn down and replaced by an al-Qaeda flag while the school was burnt down. Three nuns were frog-marched through the streets while mobs showered them with abuse. One nun said, '*They paraded us like prisoners of war.*'

The late Jonathan (Lord) Sacks said that what the Copts were suffering was '*a tragedy going almost unremarked*' and the '*religious equivalent of ethnic cleansing.*' And this was before, on 12 February 2015, Daesh beheaded and released a video of 20 Egyptian Coptic Christian construction workers, and a Ghanaian co-worker, murdered on a beach in Libya. A caption in the video called the captives the '*People of the Cross, followers of the hostile Egyptian Church.*' This was not genocide but it was laying the foundations for genocide. Ignore such visceral hatred and violence at your peril. Unchecked, it invariably morphs into something even worse.

The way in which the destruction of churches, monuments, and artefacts paves the way to the destruction of whole peoples was a theme addressed at a meeting hosted by Lord Alton in the British House of Lords, in 2017. The Melkite Greek Catholic Archbishop of Aleppo, Jean-Clément Jeanbart, asked '*What are the great nations waiting for before they put a halt to these monstrosities? Let me cry with my people, violated and murdered… they have lost so many loved ones, fathers, mothers, brothers and sisters and cherished children.*[96]

In a similar vein, the Iraqi Archbishop of Erbil, the Rt. Revd. Basha Warda, asked us '*Will a peaceful and innocent people be allowed to be persecuted and eliminated because of their faith? Will the world be complicit in our elimination?*'[97] They were right.

And, in many respects, UN Security Resolution 2379—which created the independent investigative team—still fails to answer Archbishop Warda's question. We see little evidence that the forced displacement of communities, clearly the main genocidal crime perpetrated against these religious and ethnic minorities—is being addressed. These living stones included 120,000 Iraqi Christians from Nineveh Plains who were forcibly displaced in August 2014, and who fled to other regions. Similarly, thousands of Yazidis were forcibly displaced from Sinjar. The failure to include forced displacement in the Resolution 2379 raises serious concerns. Is it specifically aimed at excluding cases of forcibly displaced Christians or Yazidis from the investigation or is it 'merely' gross negligence on the part of the drafters who managed to forget about this crime? It seems an extraordinarily misplaced sense of priorities to give cultural heritage— important though this is—a *greater* significance and attention than the forcible displacement and suffering of thousands of people fleeing for their lives. Forced displacement should be brought within the scope of the inquiry and the Investigative Team must consider all atrocities, even if they are not expressly included in the Resolution 2379 (and especially as the list of atrocities is included in the preambular and not operative paragraphs of the resolution). Restitution and restoration are hardly likely to be successfully addressed if the cause of their loss—displacement—is not recognised from the outset as a major injustice.

---

[96] ICN, 'Syria: Bishop Makes Desperate Appeal for Intervention from West' *ICN* (1 June 2015).

[97] Frank Gardner, 'Iraq's Christians "close to extinction"' *BBC* (23 May 2019).

CHAPTER 6

The Genocide in Nigeria—A Mirror Image of Darfur

1 INTRODUCTION

In 2020, World Watch Monitor reported that Boko Haram had killed more people than Daesh in Iraq and Syria combined.[1] Whether the deadly assault on Nigeria's Christians should be described as a genocide is something to which the co-authors have given significant attention and which we will now explore.

In Nigeria, there has been no shortage of evidence of systematic, organised, and targeted violence. It has been the subject of numerous interventions by Lord Alton and Baroness Cox of Queensbury who, between them, on hundreds of occasions, have flagged up parliamentary questions and debates, and instigated an inquiry by the All-Party Parliamentary Group on Freedom of Religion or Belief, which Lady Cox and Jim Shannon MP co-chair and which, with colleagues, they founded.

---

[1] Julia Bicknell, 'Boko Haram has Killed More than Islamic State in Iraq and Syria combined' *World Watch Monitor* (29 July 2020). Available at: https://www.worldwatchmonitor.org/2020/07/boko-haram-has-killed-more-than-islamic-state-in-iraq-and-syria-combined/.

© The Author(s), under exclusive license to Springer Nature Switzerland AG 2022
E. U. Ochab and D. Alton, *State Responses to Crimes of Genocide*, Rethinking Political Violence,
https://doi.org/10.1007/978-3-030-99162-3_6

The inquiry's report, published in 2020, was entitled '*Nigeria: An Unfolding Genocide?*' and we refer to in greater detail later in this chapter.[2]

The views of Lady Cox and Lord Alton, concerning atrocity crimes in Nigeria have been heavily influenced by their first-hand experiences in Sudan—where, in the south of what was then one country, more than 2 million people died during a civil war driven by Khartoum's Jihadist agenda. They both visited the south during the War and Lord Alton, who travelled to Sudan's Darfur region at the outset of the genocide there, served as Chairman of the All-Party Parliamentary Group on Sudan.

In contextualising the continuing violence in Nigeria (and the targeting of minority communities in neighbouring countries across Sub-Saharan Africa), along with atrocity crimes in countries such as Ethiopia (in Tigray), Cameroon, Mali, and Mozambique, we should recall the destruction and partition of Sudan in July 2011, the 1994 genocide in Rwanda and the 2003 (and continuing) genocide in Darfur.

Undoubtedly, what occurred in South Sudan and Darfur was a precursor of what is happening in Northern Nigeria. They all face issues connected to scarcity of land and resources, but murder's signature has been written across both regions by a distorted religious ideology. Khartoum and the Janjaweed have exported this poisonous ideology across and through Sub-Saharan Africa with appalling, lethal consequences.

In July 2019, the Bishop of Truro's Independent Report to the UK Foreign Secretary was in no doubt about the ferocity of the attacks against Christians in Sub-Saharan Africa:

> Some of the most egregious persecution of Christians has taken place in Sub-Saharan Africa, where reports showed a surge in attacks during the period under review. Evidence from across the region points to the systematic violation of the rights of Christians both by state and non-state actors… the most widespread and violent threat came from societal groups, including many with a militant Islamist agenda. The most serious threat to Christian communities came from the militant Islamist group Boko Haram

---

[2] APPG on IFoRB, 'Nigeria: An Unfolding Genocide' (2020). Available at: https://appgfreedomofreligionorbelief.org/nigeria-unfolding-genocide-new-appg-report-launched/.

in Nigeria, where direct targeting of Christian believers on a comprehensive scale set out to eliminate Christianity and pave the way for the total Islamisation of the country.[3]

Extremist Muslim militancy was also present in other countries in the region, including Tanzania and Kenya, where Al Shabaab carried out violent attacks on Christian communities. Elsewhere, extremist groups exploited domestic conflicts and unrest in countries such as Somalia where violence against Christians took place against a backdrop of popular uprisings, economic breakdown and endemic poverty. The threat to Christians from Islamist militancy was by no means confined to societal groups. Sudan continued to rank as one of the most dangerous countries for Christians; destruction of church property, harassment, arbitrary arrest initiated by state actors remained a problem and non-Muslims were punished for breaking Islamic Shari'a law.

Reports consistently showed that in Nigeria, month after month, on average hundreds of Christians were being killed for reasons connected with their faith. Whilst the reasons for this are complex there is no doubt that Christian faith was an integral, and sometimes central, component. An investigation showed that in 2018 far more Christians in Nigeria were killed in violence in which religious faith was a critical factor than anywhere else in the world; Nigeria accounted for 3731 of the 4136 fatalities: 90% of the total. The single-greatest threat to Christians over the period under review came from Islamist militant group Boko Haram, with US intelligence reports in 2015 suggesting that 200,000 Christians were at risk of being killed.

The extremist movement's campaign was not just directed against Christians but towards all 'political or social activity associated with Western society', with attacks on government buildings, markets and 190 schools. That said, Christians continued to be a prominent target. Those worst affected included Christian women and girls 'abducted, and forced to convert, enter forced marriages, sexual abuse and torture.' In 2014, Boko Haram 191 kidnapped 276 schoolgirls from Chibok, a mainly Christian village. A video released later purported to show the girls wearing Muslim dress and chanting Islamic verses, amid reports that a number of them had been "indoctrinated" into Islam. In the video Boko Haram leader Abubakar Shekau warns of retribution for those who refuse to convert, adding: 'we will treat them… the way the prophet treated the 31 infidels

---

[3] Bishop of Truro Review, 'Independent Review for the UK Foreign Secretary of Foreign and Commonwealth Office Support for Persecuted Christians' (2019). Available at: https://christianpersecutionreview.org.uk/.

he seized.' In its 2018 report on Nigeria, the United States Commission on International Religious Freedom described how Boko Haram had 'inflicted mass terror on civilians', adding: 'The group has killed and harmed people for being "nonbelievers".'

In Maiduguri city, north-east Nigeria, Catholic Church research reported that massacres by the Islamists had created 5000 widows and 15,000 orphans and resulted in attacks on 200 churches and chapels, 35 presbyteries and parish centres. A Boko Haram spokesman publicly warned of an impending campaign of violence to eradicate the presence of Christians, declaring them 'enemies' in their struggle to establish 'an Islamic state in place of the secular state.' Evidence of intent of this nature combined with such egregious violence means that Boko Haram activity in the region meets the tests for it to be considered as genocide against Christians according to the definition adopted by the UN.

The precise motives behind a growing wave of attacks by nomadic Fulani herdsmen in Nigeria's Middle Belt has been widely debated, but targeted violence against Christian communities in the context of worship suggests that religion plays a key part, alongside other factors such as a clash of lifestyles exacerbated by climate change. On 24 April 2018, a dawn raid, reportedly by Fulani herders, saw gunmen enter a church in Benue State, during early morning Mass and kill 19 people, including two priests. On 18 April 2019, in a detailed account it was reported that on Sunday April 14th Fulani herdsmen killed 17 Christians, including the mother of the child, who had gathered after a baby's dedication at a church in an attack in Konshu-Numa village, in Nasarawa state's Akwanga County in central Nigeria.

Attacks on Christians by Muslim extremist groups took place on a lesser scale in other parts of Sub-Saharan Africa...(where) long-term widespread internal conflict and endemic poverty had incubated a form of religious extremism specifically intolerant of Christians...

Elsewhere in Sub-Saharan Africa, responsibility for the persecution of Christians lay with the state. In Sudan, 'the Sudanese government continued to arrest, detain and prosecute Christian leaders, interfere in church leadership matters and destroy churches.' Evidence suggests that since the secession of the south to form South Sudan in 2011, the Khartoum government has increased its clampdown on Christians. Over the next six years, 24 churches and church-run schools, 211 libraries and cultural centres were reportedly '"systematically closed", demolished or confiscated on government orders.' Other countries with an explicitly

Islamic constitution and government also denied Christians their basic rights.[4]

This extraordinarily powerful description of the genocidal ideology—which continues to disfigure countless lives and communities—is an unwelcome narrative in the UK Foreign, Commonwealth and Development Office and, on and off, depending on who is in power, in the US State Department. It is a narrative which has been knowingly ignored by government officials in their briefings to Ministers—preferring to offer, instead, a critique which is based on religious illiteracy and the self-serving agenda that all the region's problems can be resolved by allocating extra resources for combating climate change. We are not climate change deniers but challenge those who are Jihadist ideology deniers.

They should learn the lessons of the despoliation of Darfur and also recall how ideologically driven hatred led to the partition of Sudan into two greatly weakened states following the deaths of more than 2 million people in a civil war. It is key to understanding the trauma of Northern Nigeria, to what it is leading in Nigeria and right across sub-Saharan Africa.

1.1   The Lessons of Darfur

In 2004, Lord Alton travelled to Darfur. He had just visited Rwanda—where in 1994 up to 800,000 Tutsis had been killed in horrific atrocities.[5] He went to genocide sites, met survivors, and political leaders, including President Paul Kagame. Before returning to the UK, together with Rebecca Tinsley, founder of Waging Peace, he travelled to Darfur. An appalling assault was underway on the ethnic tribes of Darfur by the Sudanese regime led by Field Marshall Omar Al Bahir. Having taken evidence from tribal leaders and victims—especially accounts from women who had been subjected to rape and sexual violence, they compiled a report for Jubilee Campaign and which *The Independent* newspaper

---

[4] Bishop of Truro Review, 'Independent Review for the UK Foreign Secretary of Foreign and Commonwealth Office Support for Persecuted Christians' (2019). Available at: https://christianpersecutionreview.org.uk/.

[5] André Guichaoua, 'Counting the Rwandan Victims of War and Genocide: Concluding Reflections' (2020) 22 *Journal of Genocide Research* 125–141.

published on its front page under the headline '*If this isn't genocide, what is?*'.[6]

In the same year—2004—Colin Powell, the US Secretary of State, arrived at the same conclusion.

In testimony to the US Senate's Foreign Affair Committee, for the first time in US Government history, a continuing crisis was referred to as '*genocide*' when he stated that events in Darfur could be labelled as such. Powell said, '*We concluded—I concluded—that genocide has been committed in Darfur and that the Government of Sudan and the Janjaweed bear responsibility—and that genocide may still be occurring.*'[7]

Meanwhile, commenting on the complicity of the state in resourcing the killing, the UN High Commissioner for Human Rights concluded that '*the Janjaweed have operated with total impunity and in close coordination with the forces of the government of Sudan.*'[8] In 2005, Kofi Annan, then Secretary General of the United Nations, told the world that Darfur is '*little short of hell on earth.*'[9]

Yet, in January 2005, the United Nations' International Commission of Inquiry on Darfur concluded that the Government of Sudan had not pursued a policy of genocide—but did conclude that there had been crimes against humanity.[10]

---

[6] Lord Alton of Liverpool, 'If This Isn't Genocide, then What on Earth is?' *The Independent* (17 September 2011). Available at: https://www.independent.co.uk/news/world/africa/if-isn-t-genocide-then-what-earth-5351315.html.

[7] Colin Powell, Senate Foreign Relations Committee, 9 September 2004.

[8] UN, 'Violations in Darfur, Sudan May Constitute War Crimes, Crimes Against Humanity, UN Human Rights Office Report Says' UN Press Release (7 May 2004). Available at: https://www.un.org/press/en/2004/afr921.doc.htm.

[9] UN, 'International Community Must Immediately Find Way to Halt Killing in Darfur, Sudan, Secretary General Tells Security Council' UN Press Release (16 February 2005). Available at: https://www.un.org/press/en/2005/sgsm9722.doc.htm.

[10] International Commission of Inquiry on Darfur, 'Report to the United Nations Secretary-General' (25 January 2005). It further stated that: 'Arguably, two elements of genocide might be deduced from the gross violations of human rights perpetrated by Government forces and the militias under their control. These two elements are, first, the actus reus consisting of killing, or causing serious bodily or mental harm, or deliberately inflicting conditions of life likely to bring about physical destruction; and, second, on the basis of a subjective standard, the existence of a protected group being targeted by the authors of criminal conduct. However, the crucial element of genocidal intent appears to be missing, at least as far as the central Government authorities are concerned. Generally speaking the policy of attacking, killing and forcibly displacing members of some tribes

The Commission was heavily criticised, not least by the scholar, Eric Reeves.[11] Their finding did not prevent dissenting voices from being raised. Among those who declared a genocide were the International Association of Genocide Scholars, Genocide Watch, the Committee on Conscience at the US Holocaust Memorial Museum, the US Congress, President George W Bush, Jewish World Watch, the Armenian Assembly of America, the Anti-Defamation League, Senators Barack Obama and Hillary Clinton, The Portuguese National Assembly, Physicians for Human Rights, Africa Confidential, Yad Vashem, and many more.

By 2008, the categorisation of Darfur as genocide began to be more widely accepted after prosecutors at the ICC filed three counts of genocide, ten charges of war crimes, five of crimes against humanity and two of murder against Sudan's President Omar Al-Bashir.[12] The ICC's prosecutors said Al-Bashir *'masterminded and implemented a plan to destroy in substantial part three tribal groups.'*[13]

Marlise Simons, writing, in the *New York Times* believed that the decision to prosecute would cynically allow the international community to do nothing further—and certainly not to provide protection for those subjected to the genocide. She quoted UN diplomats as saying, the decision *'would allow the UN Security Council to postpone direct intervention and nonetheless appear to be taking action.'*[14] And, for the next decade, Bashir did indeed evade justice while Darfur—a region the size of France—was simply sent a few peacekeepers.

does not evince a specific intent to annihilate, in whole or in part, a group distinguished on racial, ethnic, national, or religious grounds. Rather, it would seem that those who planned and organised attacks on villages pursued the intent to drive the victims from their homes, primarily for purposes of counter-insurgency warfare.' Ibid., 4.

[11] Eric Reeves, 'Report of the International Commission of Inquiry on Darfur: A Critical Analysis (Part II)' (11 February 2005). Available at: https://sudanreeves.org/2005/02/11/report-of-the-international-commission-of-inquiry-on-darfur-a-critical-analysis-part-ii-february-6-2005/.

[12] ICC, 'ICC Prosecutor Presents Case Against Sudanese President, Hassan Ahmad Al-Bashir, for Genocide, Crimes Against Humanity and War Crimes in Darfur' ICC Press Release (14 July 2008). Available at: https://www.icc-cpi.int/Pages/item.aspx?name=a.

[13] Ibid.

[14] Marlise Simons, 'Sudan Poses First Big Trial for World Criminal Court' *The New York Times* (29 April 2005). Available at: https://www.nytimes.com/2005/04/29/world/africa/sudan-poses-first-big-trial-for-world-criminal-court.html?auth=login-google.

Finally, in April 2019, with the overthrow of Bashir's regime, on 11 February 2020, the Government of Sudan agreed that Bashir would be tried by the ICC.[15] The commitment came during peace talks with rebel groups from Darfur but on 25 October 2021, the Sudanese military led by General Abdel Fattah al-Burhan, took control of the government in a military coup.

Senior government figures were initially detained and the civilian Prime Minister, Abdalla Hamdok refused to endorse the coup and called for popular resistance. He was arrested but later released, leading to Hamdok and al-Burhan to sign a 14-point deal which reinstated Hamdok as Prime Minister and announced that all political prisoners would be freed. It remains a very uneasy arrangement.

Some commentators have suggested that supporters of Bashir helped to instigate the coup to prevent his removal to trial by the ICC and, thereby, to prevent their own role in the genocide from being exposed.

At the time of writing no trial date has been announced, nor has Bashir been transferred to The Hague pursuant to the outstanding arrest warrant. Bashir has appeared in a Sudanese Court on the charge of being involved in the 1989 *coup d'état* in Sudan (a far less serious charge but one which carries the death sentence—raising the possibility of execution before being tried for genocide).

In 2006, two years after he visited Darfur, Lord Alton wrote about the consequences of the failure to understand the nature of what was underway in Darfur:

> It has been two years since I visited the wretched refugee camps of Darfur. The bewildered people there had fled from the Janjaweed militias who destroyed their villages, stole their cattle and killed as many locals as they could find. Many of the women who survived had been raped and tortured by their attackers. At the time of my visit, it seemed Darfur's suffering was so terrible that the world would respond promptly by sending peacekeeping troops to protect the civilians.
>
> Two years later, it shames me to say that women are still being raped by the Janjaweed, and the black African civilians of Darfur are still being ethnically cleansed by their own government. Incredible as it seems, the situation in Darfur is even worse than it was when I was there. The

---

[15] France 24, 'Sudan agrees to transfer 'those indicted by the ICC' to the Hague' *France 24* (11 February 2020). Available at: https://www.france24.com/en/20200211-sudan-agrees-to-transfer-ex-president-bashir-to-icc-for-war-crimes.

Janjaweed horsemen, armed and paid by the Sudanese government, are now attacking and killing refugees who have found shelter in neighbouring Chad.

It is thought that as many as 400,000 people may have died, and there is cholera in the camps, threatening to increase the daily death rate massively. Militias have made the whole area so dangerous that emergency relief agencies are withdrawing to the main towns. An unprecedented number of humanitarian workers have been murdered this summer.

As a result, the United Nations has warned that it cannot reach many of those who rely on the outside world for food. Ominously, we have no idea what is happening to displaced people in large sections of this vast and inhospitable region. As I saw for myself, there are virtually no roads, and the Sudanese authorities make sure the media has no access to the unspeakable suffering of millions of uprooted people.

When I asked the Darfur refugees, whom I met, what message they wanted me to take away, they were clear: "We must return to our land so we can plant our crops," one of their white-robed elders told me. "We are farmers. Please take the guns away from the men who are trying to kill us."

Since then, the UN Security Council has passed resolutions that specifically called for sanctions to be targeted at the architects of this genocide, and a no-fly zone to stop the Sudanese bombing their own civilians. Neither of these measures has been implemented. We are still waiting for the international community to stand up to the Khartoum regime and look as if it means what it says.

Meanwhile the world's attention has been drawn to the Tsunami and more recently the war in Lebanon, where television cameras were on hand to record the suffering of ordinary families.[16]

As the media outlets moved on, leaving them without even television cameras to witness the terror, the Sudan regime flatly refused to accept UN peacekeepers in Darfur. The international community failed to set aside their vested interests by taking decisive action. Lord Alton went on to describe how:

For three members of the Security Council, China, France and Russia, their business relationships with Khartoum are their priority. The other two permanent members, Britain and America, wish to stay friendly with Sudan

[16] Lord Alton, 'Darfur's Violent Tragedy—Two Years on' (23 December 2010). Available at: https://www.davidalton.net/2010/12/23/darfurs-violent-tragedy-two-years-on/.

in case they are given intelligence on Khartoum's former good friend and fellow Islamist, Osama bin Laden. Sadly, our officials and politicians have forgotten that for twenty years the same skilled leaders in Khartoum led them a merry diplomatic dance while they waged war on the Christians and animists in the south of Sudan, resulting in two million deaths.

This weekend (September 17th) Christians and Jews, Muslims and Sikhs will come together to demonstrate their unity in opposing the genocide in Darfur. They are also asking the Prime Minister to make sure Britain uses its role on the UN Security Council to enforce the resolutions against the Khartoum junta. Our priority must be getting UN peacekeepers into Darfur with a mandate to protect the long-suffering civilians we have neglected all this time.[17]

The US Special Envoy to Darfur said that the world's response to the crisis in western Sudan had been '*anaemic.*'[18] But in July 2008, the decision by the ICC had at least named the atrocities for what they were. When Luis Moreno Ocampo, the ICC prosecutor, announced the indictment of Bashir and issued a warrant for his arrest, it created history as the first ever warrant to be issued against a sitting head of state.[19] The ICC spokeswoman, Laurence Blairon, said that Bashir was suspected of being criminally responsible for, '*intentionally directing attacks against an important part of the civilian population of Darfur, murdering... raping, torturing and forcibly transferring large numbers of civilians and pillaging their property.*'[20] She said that the violence in Darfur was the result of a common plan organised at the highest levels of the Sudanese Government.

The following year, in 2009, Lord Alton commented that, in addition to hundreds of thousands of deaths, Darfur '*has seen 2.7 million people displaced, and 90% of the homes razed to the ground. These millions of lost*

---

[17] Lord Alton, 'Darfur's Violent Tragedy—Two Years On' (23 December 2010). Available at: https://www.davidalton.net/2010/12/23/darfurs-violent-tragedy-two-years-on/.

[18] Louis Charbonneau, 'World Response to Darfur is "Anemic": US envoy' *Reuters* (3 April 2008). Available at: https://www.reuters.com/article/us-sudan-darfur-usa-idUSN0 330618520080403.

[19] ICC, The Prosecutor v. Omar Hassan Ahmad Al-Bashir, Warrant of Arrest for Omar Hassan Ahmad Al-Bashir, ICC-02/05–01/09, 4 March 2009. Available at: https://www.icc-cpi.int/Pages/record.aspx?docNo=ICC-02/05-01/09-1.

[20] ICC, 'ICC Issues a Warrant of Arrest for Omar Al-Bashir, President of Sudan' ICC Press Release (4 March 2009). Available at: https://www.icc-cpi.int/pages/item.aspx? name=icc+issues+a+warrant+of+arrest+for+omar+al+bashir_+president+of+sudan.

lives represent a human catastrophe, and it is an indictment of our failure to protect rather than the duty to protect[21] in what was described by Dr Mukesh Kapila, a former high-ranking British and United Nations official as *'the first genocide of the twenty first century.'*[22] The UK Government still declined to use the word genocide and continued to say that it was *'monitoring the situation.'*

In 2010, in Parliament, Lord Alton referred to *'the description used by the United Nations of Darfur being the world's worst humanitarian crisis, and the Swedish Government's description of what is happening in Darfur—where there are mass executions, the burning of villages and the destruction of food supplies—as genocide'* and asked *'when will the Government raise this issue by way of resolution in the United Nations Security Council in an endeavour to bring together an international campaign to hold the Sudanese Government to account? What has to happen to change the passive role we have taken so far of merely monitoring the situation? Are we not in grave danger of making the same mistakes that we made at the time of the genocide in Rwanda?'*[23]

In 2013, he told the House of Lords that:

> While the world looked on, 90% of Darfur's villages were razed to the ground... Those who unleashed this torrent of unconscionable violence on their own people are undoubtedly mass murderers and fugitives from justice, having been indicted by the International Criminal Court for crimes against humanity. In South Kordofan and Blue Nile, more than 1 million are now displaced, and the perpetrators are attempting to repeat what happened in Darfur, but this time by closing borders and refusing access, a genocide without witnesses.[24]

During the Parliamentary proceedings horrific personal accounts were cited, including one from Colonel Samir Jaja, a deserter from the Sudanese army, who described how he had abandoned the army after taking part in an attack on the villages of Korma, Ber Tawila, and Sanj Koro in Southern Darfur in April 2003. The soldiers had been ordered

---

[21] House of Lords Deb, 5 March 2009, c897.

[22] Dr. Mukesh Kapila, *No Stranger to Kindness* (Sharpe Books, 2019).

[23] House of Lords Deb, 20 May 2004, c876.

[24] House of Lords Deb, 7 November 2013, c162.

to, '*rape the women, kill the children, leave nothing.*'[25] Jala described how they killed the villagers as well as their livestock and the wells were poisoned. Oumba Daoud Abdelrasoul, one of 17,000 refugees in Djabal refugee camp in eastern Chad, about 90 miles from the village in Darfur from which he fled, told the UK Parliament about the horrific atrocities suffered by his family: '*My younger brother and my two uncles had their throats slit in front of me. I had to watch as others were thrown alive into fires.*'[26]

This evidence, and much more besides, was provided to the ICC Prosecutor who attended a meeting at Westminster, of the APPG for Sudan, chaired by Lord Alton at which Mr. Ocampo discussed the indictment of Bashir and the role of the ICC. He made it clear that his mandate was to examine the evidence and to act accordingly, not to make calculations about politics or diplomacy. Some of those present at the meeting, and others commenting on the indictment, criticised the Prosecutor and the ICC because of potential political repercussions, particularly on the 2005 comprehensive peace agreement between warring factions in Sudan. This argument exposes a fundamental problem when political and diplomatic considerations are allowed to interfere with a declaration of genocide. Either we have a court that is capable of holding those who kill, plunder and rape to account, or we do not. Similarly, despots cannot be permitted to offer the pretext of state sovereignty or immunity, or a trade off with a diplomatic initiative, to cover up the extermination of their own citizens.

Bashir's own response to the ICC was instructive. He contemptuously told the ICC it could eat its arrest warrant[27]; and Salah Abdallah 'Gosh,' head of Sudanese security and intelligence, said that he would amputate the arms and cut of the heads of anyone co-operating with

---

[25] Mark Tran, 'Rape the Women. Kill the Children. Leave Nothing' *The Guardian* (5 March 2009). Available at: https://www.theguardian.com/world/2009/mar/05/sudanese-army-deserter-darfur-account.

[26] House of Lords Deb, 5 March 2009, c897; Angelique Chrisafis, 'An Accord is Not Possible. Bashir Must be Judged First' *The Guardian* (5 March 2009). Available at: https://www.theguardian.com/world/2009/mar/05/president-omar-al-bashir-sudan.

[27] Mike Pflanz, 'Sudan's Omar al-Bashir says ICC can 'Eat' his Arrest Warrant' *The Telegraph* (4 March 2009). Available at: https://www.telegraph.co.uk/news/worldnews/africaandindianocean/sudan/4933329/Sudans-Omar-al-Bashir-says-ICC-can-eat-his-arrest-warrant.html.

the ICC.[28] Yet, it was argued by people who should have known better that these were people whom we should accommodate. Bashir, the man then defended, responded to the warrants by demonising and expelling humanitarian and aid agencies,[29] which were a lifeline to his beleaguered people. The charity, Save the Children, pointed to the implications for the 50,000 children it supported. It said a lot about the indicted President that he would vindictively retaliate against children and refugees and threaten aid workers and charities, seeking to intimidate and blackmail the international community. As for trading a genocide determination for diplomatic progress, it should be noted that Bashir's regime broke every peace deal it had signed in the previous six years of violence in Darfur, often within 24 hours of making commitments to honour its pledges and responsibilities under international law.

The appeasement of war criminals fails to stand up to moral scrutiny, suggests that, whatever your crimes, law abiding countries are prepared to overlook atrocities and strike deals with the perpetrators—demonstrating extraordinary naivety in believing that those who stand accused of heinous crimes are likely to be trustworthy. We have also heard the same argument about war crimes in Ukraine. The co-authors have met many who have suffered at the hands of regimes responsible for atrocity crimes. They see no conflict in pursuing both peace and justice. The exiled Sudanese bishop, Macram Max Gassis once told Lord Alton that '*Peace without justice is like building a house without foundations; it is a pseudo-peace doomed to collapse at the very first storm.*'

Leaders the world over—such as Slobodan Milosevic, Charles Taylor, and Omar al-Bashir—must learn that when they collaborate in the killing of their own citizens it will not be met with appeasement or impunity and that one day they will be held to account. The mills of the gods grind slowly as do the wheels of justice, but malefactors must know that impunity does not reign. The process may be grindingly slow but as Thomas Paine once said '*Tyranny, like hell, is not easily conquered; yet we*

---

[28] James Smith, 'Despots Cannot Hide, Despite their Threats' *Independent* (5 March 2009). Available at: https://www.independent.co.uk/voices/commentators/james-smith-despots-cannot-hide-despite-their-threats-1637732.html.

[29] Xan Rice, 'Sudanese President Expels Aid Agencies' *The Guardian* (5 March 2009). Available at: https://www.theguardian.com/world/2009/mar/05/sudan-aid-agencies-expelled.

have this consolation with us, that the harder the conflict, the more glorious the triumph.'[30]

At the height of the hellish genocide in Darfur some 500 people were dying every day and millions have never been able to return to their homes or destroyed villages. Justice and restitution have both been in short supply. The consequences for individuals have been horrendous— whether the killing of loved ones, the rape of women, or the millions displaced living in camps. Again, impunity will beget further crime. And even in 2020 there were three mass shootings. On 1 January 2021, after 13 years in Darfur, the last members of the joint United Nations and African Union peacekeeping mission (UNAMID) left with many Darfuris fearful that its withdrawal will leave them even more vulnerable.[31]

The easy explanation, usually advanced by officials and politicians, that Darfur was just a clash between *'herders and farmers,'* driven by scarce resources, is an insult to those who have endured appalling suffering, justified by a religious ideology. That ideology tried to impose itself on Muslims with different beliefs about how to follow their religion— in addition to targeting Christians and people with traditional beliefs. Not only did this vicious ideology inflict terrible suffering, hardship on millions it ultimately led to the destruction of their country and to its partition into the Republic of Sudan and South Sudan. Darfur's story is instructive and contextual in considering the lethal game of grandmother's footsteps being played out across Sub-Saharan Africa—and especially as it is threatening to break the unity of Africa's most populous country: Nigeria.

1.2   Ignore the Atrocities in Nigeria at Your Peril

There are many striking parallels between the fool's paradise argument used in Darfur and the argument used now to explain many atrocity crimes in Northern Nigeria—and increasingly in its Middle Belt—as being entirely attributable to climate change and scarcity of resources.

---

[30] Thomas Paine, *The American Crisis* (1776).

[31] UN News, 'UN Confirms Closure of Darfur Peacekeeping Mission' UN News (30 December 2020). Available at: https://news.un.org/en/story/2020/12/1081122.

As Rabbi Abraham Cooper and Johnnie Moore, insist in '*The Coming Jihad*,' the world can't pretend it didn't see this coming.[32] Undoubtedly there are many contributory factors which contribute to the violence—and they can certainly include tribal enmities, control of resources, bitter resentments, historical grievances, power, and domination. But religion, too, has often been used to justify violence.

We know how in Northern Ireland, the Thirty Years War, the Crusades—fought under the sign of the Cross—and the Ottoman conquests—fought under the banner of the Prophet—have all had a distorted religious dimension. Ignore that dimension in Sub-Saharan Africa at your peril. The Parliamentary record provides ample evidence of indifference in the face of shocking persecution in Nigeria with repeated warnings that it does not take long for discrimination and persecution, which has been ignored, to morph into something far worse.

2   THE ATROCITIES AGAINST CHRISTIANS

A cursory examination of Hansard over the past twenty years reveals that Lord Alton and his colleague, Baroness Cox, have, on over 300 occasions, made parliamentary interventions concerning Nigeria and repeatedly called out indifference in the face of shocking persecution—warning, again and again, that it doesn't take long for discrimination and persecution, which has been ignored to lead to something far worse.

What follows highlights some of these interventions, in which they raised the atrocities by Boko Haram and Fulani militias, and in which they questioned the total failure of UK officials to recognise the warning signs or to consider whether the £2 billion of aid which the UK had poured into the country over the last decade was addressing any of the root causes of potential genocide.

2.1   Boko Haram

Boko Haram is a Sunni Islamist terrorist group principally active in north-east Nigeria. It was formed in 2002 to reject the secular aspects of Nigerian society, in particular Western education. Its first leader was Mohammed Yusuf. Boko Haram carried out its first attack in 2003.

---

[32] Rabbi Abraham Cooper and Johnnie Moore, *The Coming Jihad* (Thomas Nelson, 2020).

Its murderous activity increased significantly following a violent clash between Boko Haram militants and the Nigerian police in 2009. A subsequent uprising was quashed by Nigerian security forces and Yusuf was killed. Under the leadership of Abubakar Shekau, Boko Haram carried out attacks between 2010 and 2014, including targeting the inauguration of Nigerian President Goodluck Jonathan and the UN office in Abuja. In 2012, Boko Haram attacked twelve villages targeting Christians in Plateau State. Fleeing from the violence, local Christians took refuge in the house of Pastor Ayo Oritsejafor. The house was bombed, and more than 50 people were burned alive, including the pastor's wife and children.[33] Pastor Oritsejafor, the President of the Christian Association of Nigeria, is seen by many of the country's Christians as their symbolic leader. He had also denounced a previous bomb attack by Boko Haram on a church. He had been targeted in this incident. Boko Haram made clear that their objective is to establish an Islamic State and that Christians will not be welcome there, issuing an ultimatum for them to leave and threatening to eradicate them from the region.[34] Reports highlighted the extension of Boko Haram's campaign into the Middle Belt, where the population is more evenly mixed between Muslims and Christians. On 10 June 2012, a bomber killed around 10 people in a church in Jos, capital of Plateau state.[35]

In 2014, Boko Haram came to greater international prominence following its kidnapping of 276 girls from a secular school in Chibok. While many of the girls have since been rescued, several remain missing years after their abduction. The abduction of the Chibok girls was not the first and nor the last of such crimes. 2021 saw repeated copy-cat abductions of school children—leading Lord Alton, in November 2021, to join with Mervyn Thomas, Founding President of CSW, and others to lead a protest outside the Nigerian High Commission in London. Movingly,

---

[33] Christian Today, 'Nigeria Pastor, Wife, Children Burned Alive Along with 50 Church Members' *Christian Today*. Available at: https://christiantoday.com.au/news/nigeria-pastor-wife-children-burned-alive-along-with-50-church-members.html.

[34] See for example: BBC, 'Islamic State in Nigeria 'Beheads Christian Hostages'' *BBC News* (27 December 2019). Available at: https://www.bbc.co.uk/news/world-africa-509 24266.

[35] The Telegraph, 'Several Dead in Nigeria Church Attacks' *The Telegraph* (10 June 2012). Available at: https://www.telegraph.co.uk/news/worldnews/africaandindian ocean/nigeria/9322742/Several-dead-in-Nigeria-church-attacks.html.

abandoned children's shoes were left on the pavement to represent the children abandoned by the Buhari Government and its international supporters.

The platitudes trotted out by a succession of spokesmen and women have been risible.

When, in March 2014, Boko Haram attacked a boarding school in Yobe state, and students at St. Joseph's Seminary, Shuwa and at St. Paul's Catholic Church in Waga Chakawa, Madagali, Ministers admitted to Lord Alton that a *'series of horrific attacks on civilians in northern Nigeria that have taken place over recent months'*.[36] They claimed to have raised the attacks with the Nigerian Government and that the UK had reaffirmed *'its commitment to assist Nigeria in its fight against terrorism.'*[37] But three months later nothing had been done and in the debate on the Queens Speech Lord Alton challenged the apparent impunity which enabled Boko Haram to *'abduct 276 schoolgirls in April in north-east Nigeria, along with 20 more women abducted this week.'*[38]

Subsequently, he raised the case of Mubarak Bala, a Nigerian, who was confined to a mental institution for denying the existence of God; in October the burning of churches and forced religious conversion of Christian women in north-east Nigeria.[39] The UK Government replied that they condemned *'the destruction of churches and all other atrocities conducted by Boko Haram They have caused great suffering across all communities, deliberately targeting the weak and vulnerable with no respect for gender, ethnicity, religion or age. The UK, alongside other international partners, is committed to helping Nigeria end this violence and tackle the threat posed by Boko Haram.'*[40]

In 2015, Boko Haram declared its allegiance to Islamic State.[41] The same year, the AU-endorsed Multinational Joint Task Force (MNJTF), including troops from Chad, Nigeria, Cameroon, Niger, and Benin, was deployed. The atrocities by Boko Haram continued, nonetheless.

---

[36] House of Lords Deb, 27 March 2014, c146W.

[37] Ibid.

[38] House of Lords Deb, 11 June 2014, c418.

[39] WPQ UIN HL1867, tabled on 26 September 2014.

[40] Ibid.

[41] BBC, 'Nigeria's Boko Haram Pledges Allegiance to Islamic State' *BBC News* (7 March 2015). Available at: https://www.bbc.co.uk/news/world-africa-31784538.

Throughout 2018, Ministers were pressed about abductions by Boko Haram and the increasing role of the Fulani militias, the culture of impunity spreading terror across the region with Ministers urged to engage with their Nigerian counterparts, and to:

> address two of the causes of the growth of the Fulani militias and Boko Haram…, in defiance of the Nigerian constitution and Article 18 obligations, sharia law has been imposed in 12 states, providing impunity during the displacement of hundreds of thousands of people, abductions, land seizures, murders and violence such as the shooting in the mouth of a female choir singer.[42]

Secondly, Ministers were asked how they would persuade:

> The Nigerian Government [to] address the fertile breeding ground for recruiting sergeants [and] the kleptomania of corrupt leaders that has led the Nigerian Economic and Financial Crimes Commission to state that some $360 billion has been stolen, while in the impoverished north where these groups have been growing some 70% of children never go to school.[43]

Replying for the UK Government, the ever courteous and genuinely diligent Lord Ahmad of Wimbledon said that corruption was '*very prevalent*' in parts of Nigerian and was one of the drivers resulting in '*groups such as Boko Haram and the Islamic State of West Africa coming to the fore. Those vacuums exist and need to be filled. On the issue of sharia law being imposed on communities that do not adhere to sharia, it is against all principles, it is against the Nigerian constitution and—and against Islam itself. They need to wake up and smell the coffee, because they are perpetrating heinous crimes against humanity and are nothing to do with any constitution or religion.*'[44]

Tariq Ahmad's own background, from the persecuted Ahmadis of Pakistan, makes him one of the few Ministers who has personal experience of hatred and persecution but he has faced a constant battle to convince

---

[42] House of Lords Deb, 26 March 2018, c615.
[43] House of Lords Deb, 26 March 2018, c615.
[44] Ibid.

officials that being a Foreign Office official is not about pursuing politically correct causes or playing a shallow imitation of the Great Game. It's not only in Nigeria that they '*need to smell the coffee.*'

On 28 June 2018, Lord Alton secured a full parliamentary debate on Nigeria, which he opened by saying that:

> the tragic topicality of today's debate was underlined last weekend when more than 200 people were reported to have died in co-ordinated attacks on around 50 communities in Plateau state in Barkin Ladi. These attacks began on 22 June and lasted until 24 June. The majority of the victims were women and children. At one location, 120 were killed as they returned from the funeral of an elderly member of the Church of Christ in Nations. A dawn to dusk curfew was established and, as I heard first-hand yesterday from the honourable Rimamnde Shawulu Kwewum, a member of the Nigerian Federal House of Representatives, the area remains tense. This most recent episode is shocking, but it is also the latest in an extended pattern of violence that has become all too common across Nigeria, particularly in the Middle Belt and increasingly in some of the more southern states.[45]

The debate was held a week after Sam Brownback, the then admirable US Ambassador-at-Large for International Religious Freedom, had been in Nigeria. On a single day during his visit, Boko Haram carried out six suicide bombings—the largest number ever on any single day, attacks which have become systematic and unabated. Parliament was told that human rights groups such as CSW have catalogued every reported attack. While that may not be a definitive list, it will be invaluable evidence as the ICC is now to carry out the formal investigation which it announced at the end of 2020.

Aid to the Church in Need, a charity, also documented appalling acts of violence. They described how, during early morning Mass, militants attacked the parish of Makurdi, killing two priests and 17 members of the congregation. ACN also highlighted the 15,000 orphans and 5000 widows in the north-east—an area that has come under repeated attack from Boko Haram.[46]

[45] House of Lords Deb, 28 June 2018, c283.

[46] ACN, '$101,500 in Emergency Aid for Nigeria.' Available at: https://acn-canada.org/emergencynigeria/.

In 2019, together with the breakaway group, the Islamic State in West Africa, Boko Haram was responsible for 765 violent events in the Lake Chad Basin region including Nigeria, Niger, Chad, and Cameroon. This represented a 35% increase in the number of attacks from 2018. The combined fatalities—3225 people—represented a 4% increase from 2018.[47]

2.1.1   The Shocking Story of Lea Sharibu—And the Other Abducted Girls and Women of Nigeria

Leah, a teenage Nigerian girl, was one of the 110 schoolgirls abducted by Boko Haram from the girl's school in Dapchi in February 2018. On every anniversary of Leah's captivity, her case has been raised with Ministers who have been asked what representations they had made on her behalf. The usual reply is given every year—that they were *'very concerned'* etc.

Leah continues to be enslaved even though all of the other girls have now been released. According to one of them, Leah declined to renounce her Christian faith, and it was for this reason that Boko Haram has kept her in captivity.

But UK officials seem sufficiently satisfied to merely repeat that standard line that *'The Government of Nigeria have assured us that they are making all efforts to secure her return.'*[48] In shorthand their response sounded like: *'Now, please just go away and don't ask us to upset the Government of Nigeria or the Islamists. But do read our well-publicised policy statement about our priority being to stop sexual violence against women and girls,* etc.ete.etc. *Don't ask us to apply it in Leah's case or that of other Nigerian girls and women. After all, we are all adults and understand the rules of the Game. And please don't remind us about what has happened in Afghanistan at the hands of the Taliban.'*

---

[47] Center for International Security and Cooperation, 'Boko Haram.' Available at: https://cisac.fsi.stanford.edu/mappingmilitants/profiles/boko-haram. Africa Center for Strategic Studies, 'Threat from African Militant Islamist Groups Expanding, Diversifying' (18 January 2020). Available at: https://africacenter.org/spotlight/threat-from-african-militant-islamist-groups-expanding-diversifying/.

[48] WPQ UIN HL13965, tabled on 25 February 2019.

And then there is the perennial question about the sort of regimes which we prop up, believing it to be in the UK's 'interests.'

Following reports that Nigeria's Presidential and National Assembly elections had been marred by violence with allegations of electoral fraud, UK Ministers were asked what representations they would be making to the Government of Nigeria about ensuring free, fair, and peaceful gubernatorial elections to be held on 9 May.

The UK Government said that the Africa Minister had telephoned his counterpart to address the concerns raised by the Nigerian Independent National Elections Commission.[49] Parliamentarians also heard about the cases of Sambo Dasuki, Sheikh Ibrahim Zakzaky, and Zeenah Ibrahim, who had all been detained since 2015 despite court orders for their release[50] And they heard about killings and attacks in Nassarawa State, Benue State, Kaduna State, and Gombe.[51] Ministers gave their usual disingenuous replies that: '*Tension between farming and herding communities, exacerbated by population growth and climate change has disrupted traditional grazing routes.*'[52]

In May 2019, reports suggested that 900 churches in Nigeria had have been destroyed by Boko Haram what could be seen as a part of a campaign to eradicate Christianity in the north of that country.[53] In reply the UK claimed that Boko Haram '*attacks civilians, both Christian and Muslim*' and that '*the majority of Boko Haram's victims have been Muslims.*' The then Foreign Secretary had used a visit to Nigeria, during the previous month, to meet religious leaders '*to discuss how the UK can support their work to promote interfaith dialogue and long-term peace.*'[54]

Yet, despite this apparent recognition of the role of a radical religious ideology, on 24 July, the UK again emphasised climate change without referencing the role of religious ideology: '*80% of people are dependent on pastoral and subsistent agriculture, so we are looking carefully at how we can support people to thrive in a region that is so affected by climate change and using our expertise in the UK in technology and scientific innovations,*

---

[49] WPQ UIN HL14238, tabled on 5 March 2019.

[50] WPQ UIN HL14239, tabled on 5 March 2019.

[51] WPQ UIN HL15290, tabled on 24 April 2019.

[52] Ibid.

[53] WPQ UIN HL15824, tabled on 20 May 2019.

[54] Ibid.

such as early warning systems for shocks. If we are to see an end to conflict, we need to ensure that we address the issues of climate change.[55]

Climate change must be addressed but climate change doesn't march into student dormitories and murder sleeping students or behead Christians.

In the Queen's Speech debate, following the election of Boris Johnson's Government, on 7 January 2020, Lord Alton told Parliament that:

> the parallel re-emergence of [Daesh] in northern Iraq's Hamrin and Qara Chokh mountains led, in December, to the deaths or injury of more than 30 brave Kurdish Peshmega soldiers, while its ISIS affiliate in Nigeria beheaded 11 Christians in retaliation for the demise of Abu Bakr al-Baghdadi.
>
> The signal failure of the international community to bring genocidaires such as Baghdadi or men such as Qasem Soleimani to justice or to challenge countries that arm proxies or bomb civilians creates a culture of impunity and erodes a rules-based international order... There can be no lasting peace and reconciliation without justice and the rule of law..., to try those responsible for war crimes, crimes against humanity or genocide. Until we do, lawless militias and proxies will go on behaving with impunity and retaliatory assassinations and killings will be the order of the day, with unpredictable consequences for people who have already experienced appalling suffering and persecution.[56]

The situation has only deteriorated during the COVID-19 pandemic.

On 18 May 2020, Lord Alton told the House that in Nigeria, under the cover of COVID-19, terror groups such as Boko Haram have intensified the frequency of attacks. He questioned whether the UK Government was getting help to victims, seeking to end the violence, and seeking to bring perpetrators to justice.[57]

On 16 December 2020, the UK Government was asked what steps it had taken to establish what had happened to students kidnapped by Boko Haram on 11 December in Katsina; what assistance they were giving to the government of Nigeria in securing their release; what assessment they had made of the statement by Abubakar Shekau claiming responsibility

---

[55] House of Lords Deb, 24 July 2019, c748.

[56] House of Lords Deb, 7 January 2020, c104.

[57] House of Lords Deb, 18 May 2020, c945.

for the kidnappings, and the impact of jihadist ideology on violence in northern Nigeria.[58]

In their final response of 2020, the UK Government replied that it was '*deeply concerned about the abduction of Nigerian schoolboys from their school in Kankara, Katsina State, North West Nigeria on 11 December.*'[59] They welcomed the news that some had been released and that the UK Deputy National Security Advisor had discussed the kidnap with the President's Chief of Staff, Ibrahim Gambari.[60]

At the beginning of December 2020, a conference was organised by the Nigerian human rights advocates which included contributions from H.E. Olusegun Obasanjo, the former President of Nigeria, Dr. Gloria Puldo, Executive Director of the Leah Foundation, James Duddridge MP, then UK Minister for Africa, Professor Zachary Anger Gundu of Benue State University, the Reverend Gideon Para-Mallam, CEO of the Para Mallam Peace Foundation, and Lord Alton.

He told the conference that '*the word genocide should never be used lightly but that it was irresponsible to ignore signs of genocide and to challenge the dangerous and self-serving suggestion that by remaining silent it would contribute to the resolution of conflict and that by attributing the massacres and killings to other motives was wilful blindness.*' He said:

> President Buhari appears to have belatedly woken up to the seriousness of the SARS protests and the outrage felt by many of the country's citizens about the abject failure to uphold the rule of law or to bring to account those who corrupt it. He needs to show a similar belated understanding of the same anger felt by beleaguered communities subjected to the most terrible violence and depredations, and why many of them believe the country's government has failed to read the signs of an emerging genocide and prevent it.
>
> President Buhari needs to understand that a failure to protect pluralism and diversity in Nigeria risks turning his wonderful country into another Sudan.
>
> The 1948 Convention on the Prevention of Genocide lays duties on all signatories to prevent, protect, and punish those responsible for genocide.

---

[58] WPQ UIN HL11516, tabled on 16 December 2020.

[59] Ibid.

[60] WPQ UIN HL11516, tabled on 16 December 2020.

The dismal threefold failure to do any of these 3 things – prevent, protect or punish - results in repeated mass atrocities.

Recall that the same failure - in Rwanda - led to one million deaths during 100 days of slaughter. Between 250,00 and 500,000 women were subjected to systematic rape and sexual violence – just like the crimes being committed by Boko Haram and others in Nigeria today.

I visited the genocide sites in Rwanda and saw the shocking mass graves and I was the first parliamentarian to go into Darfur during Bashir's genocide – which led to 300,000 deaths and 2 million displacements.

All the evidence shows that Boko Haram fighters have committed sex and gender-based violence, including sexual slavery, rape, forced marriage, and forced pregnancies. The atrocities are widespread. Think of young Leah Sharibu – sadly one among many.

Boko Haram's use of sexual violence against women and girls first gained international attention when on April 14, 2014, the terrorist group abducted 276 girls, mostly between 16 and 18 years of age, from a secondary school in Chibok in Borno State, Nigeria.

International attention to Chibok faded as the juggernaut of media and celebrities move on. Be clear, the Boko Haram atrocities have affected much greater numbers than those kidnapped at Chibok.

Boko Haram chooses its targets for a variety of reasons, including on the basis of the religion of its targets, for tactical reasons including land control and it often targets schools especially those which are attended by women and girls.

The impact of these crimes on women and girls is devastating. Even if they survive the attacks and abuse, they will probably struggle with mental or physical injuries requiring medical assistance, therapy and counselling, not easily accessed. They are traumatised and also stigmatised.

Boko Haram has specifically targeted Christian minorities and others they considered as 'non-believers' on account of their faith. Indeed, as Boko Haram's leader Abubakar Shekau justified such acts of violence against Christians stating that: "All those clerics are to be killed for following democracy, all of them are infidels. I will tell Muslims what Allah wants them to do. We are anti-Christians, and those that deviated from Islam, they are forming basis with prayers but infidels. (...) To the people of the world, everybody should know his status, it is either you are with us Mujahedeen or you are with the Christians. We know what is happening in this world, it is a Jihad war against Christians and Christianity. It is a war against western education, democracy and constitution. (...) This is a war against Christians and democracy and their constitution, Allah says we should finish them when we get them.

In addition to Boko Haram, in their thirst for blood curdling headlines, we have seen shocking reports emanating from the Middle Belt where farmers are under attack from Fulani militia and from Northern Nigeria where, in January of this year, Daesh-affiliated terror groups intensified their attacks.

They have been reported to have killed Christians with a promise to continue to spill more blood without mercy.

The merging of Boko Haram, Fulani militias, and Nigerian's [Daesh] – who between them have already taken thousands of lives – endangers the future cohesion of Nigeria and creates the conditions for genocide.

In addressing the conference Lord Alton remarked that he had met Rebecca Sharibu, Leah's mother: '*She implored us not to ignore the ignore ideological motives behind executions, abductions, and genocide - with a misplaced self-serving narrative which reduces the ills of the world to climate change or competition for resources (which may indeed be a contributory but less significant factor). Global warming didn't abduct Leah Sharibu or behead 11 Nigerian Christians on Christmas Day.*'

Referring to '*The Next Jihad*,' by the Reverend Johnny Moore and Rabbi Abraham Cooper, he said that anyone who wondered about the title on the parliamentary report published by the APPG on Freedom of Religion or Belief, '*Nigeria: An Unfolding Genocide?*,' should read the book.

As Nina Shea of the Hudson Institute says about the book, it records the relentless, unspeakable death and torment of countless Nigerian Christians in Jos, Kano, Plateau State, and Nigeria's many other slaughterhouses while the courageous witness of these, African Christians is met by silence as their own government and the international community respond with cold indifference.

Johnny Moore and Rabbi Cooper write with clarity, insight, and urgency about what doesn't' any longer need a question mark. This is clearly an unfolding genocide, driven by Jihadist ideology and hatred of difference. They detail the hacking to death and beheading of Christians; the destruction of homes, livelihoods, and places of worship; and the abduction and rape of young women— personified by the story of Leah Sharibu— and they ask, why are we so indifferent?

They argue that this next jihad may not only jeopardise the security of all of western Africa but take much of the world with it, especially an already weakened Europe. Think of France and other European countries too.

Nigeria has the largest Christian population in Africa. If nothing is done, Christians will not be the last victims, for no person of any faith (Christian, Muslim, Hindu, Jew, or no faith at all) will be spared the ravages of terrorists who believe that their profane mission of death is in service to God.

Their fifteen recommendations in their book should be a call to action for politicians the world over.

Lord Alton quoted Winston Churchill who once issued a solemn warning to people who were indifferent and silent in the face of the rise of Nazism. He said: '*Each one hopes that if he feeds the crocodile enough, the crocodile will eat him last. All of them hope that the storm will pass before their turn comes to be devoured. But I fear greatly that the storm will not pass. It will rage and it will roar ever more loudly, ever more widely.*'

He concluded by saying: 'President Buhari and the Nigerian authorities must stop feeding the crocodiles and before this storm destroys Nigeria – and is further exported to the streets of Europe and Australia, India, and the United States we must do far more to raise our voices and speak for those in mortal danger.'

Before the year ended CSW reported on the shocking attacks in the few days preceding Christmas 2020. These reports are a glimpse of life and death, over just a few days, in some of Nigeria's beleaguered Christian communities. CSW reported that:

> on 24 December, that Mrs Jumai Luka, the wife of the Reveren Luka Shaho of Assemblies of God Church in Ungwan Waziri, in Chikun Local Government (LGA), central Kaduna state, was abducted by armed men who had beaten her husband "mercilessly." On 21 December, Reverend Thomas James of Godiya Baptist Church Gwazunu was abducted following an attack by over 100 well-armed men on the Gwazunu community in Gwagwada, Chikun LGA.
>
> The militia went on to attack the Gbaja Katarma community, where eight people were killed and four reportedly sustained gunshot injuries. According to information received by the media house WarDesk, villagers subsequently fled to the Sarkin Pawa community in neighbouring Niger state as attacks continued and assistance was not forthcoming. On 19 December, the Reverend Luka Dani of the Evangelical Church Winning All (ECWA) was abducted following at attack on the Galumi community in Gwagwada, Chikun LGA. Several villagers had reportedly been abducted from Kugosi and surrounding communities a week prior to this attack. Rev Dani was eventually released on 23 December and has now left the area.

On 17 December, 10 people were killed, and 18 homes burnt down during an attack by armed men of Fulani ethnicity on Gora Gan village in Zangon Kataf LGA in the Atyap Chiefdom in southern Kaduna state. Five of the victims were from the same family. The attack constitutes the latest violation of a much-vaunted peace accord, the most infamous breach being the murders on 15 November of the District Head of Ma'Zaki, Mr Haruna Kuye and his son Destiny, 9. Mr Kuye's wife and daughter survived the attack despite suffering severe injuries.

In a letter addressed to the Chief Executive of Zagon Kataf Local Government Council, dated 21 December, the Ikulu Traditional Council warned that the Government Secondary School in Unwan Gimba was being used as a base by unidentified armed men. These men, who were suspected of being responsible for the attack on Gora Gan, had killed a local youth and "forced the inhabitants to flee the area to nearby villages for their safety.

Elsewhere, on 17 December, armed men riding in pairs on motorcycles attacked Kujeni Tudu in Kajuru LGA, southern Kaduna, killing Bala Umaru, 75, and looting the village. According to the Southern Kaduna Peoples Union (SOKAPU), four people went missing after the attack. They were named as Dada Bulus, 55; Peter Tanko, 43; Buba Yakubu, 51; and Emma Dauda, 38. (...)

Reports emerged on 23 December of the death of Pastor Kabiru Babangida, a convert to Christianity who worked in remote villages in the north western states of Kebbi and Niger. The pastor was abducted and hacked to death by assailants who had initially demanded N4 million in ransom, before raising the amount to N10 million, then switching off their phones. Villagers subsequently decided to search for the pastor and eventually found his bound and mutilated corpse.

Mervyn Thomas, the Founding President of CSW said in response to these attacks: "*The urgent and deteriorating situation in Kaduna must not be forgotten, nor must the religious element to these attacks be brushed aside. The authorities must develop a comprehensive security plan that considers the different dimensions to this security crisis, amid signs that the violence is not only continuing but has also spread to other areas.*[61]

While this extract shows clear targeting of Christians by Boko Haram, it has to be emphasised that Boko Haram also targets those who do not align with their precise interpretation of Islam, including Muslims.

---

[61] CSW, 'Church Leaders Abducted Amid Renewed Violence in Kaduna State' (24 December 2020). Available at: https://www.csw.org.uk/2020/12/24/press/4934/article.htm.

Furthermore, Boko Haram—like Daesh in Iraq and Syria—has been targeting homosexuals.

In 2014, Lord Alton asked the UK Government for their assessment of reports that homosexuals in Nigeria had been tortured by the authorities to obtain the names of other homosexuals following the enactment of laws criminalising homosexuality in that country—to which the UK Government replied by stating it *'infringes on the human rights of the Nigerian LGBT community and on the rights of expression and association which are guaranteed by the Nigerian Constitution and by Nigeria's international treaty obligations.'*[62] After attacks on villages in Adamawa and Borno state, Ministers told him: *'We are appalled by these attacks which resulted in the deaths of innocent Nigerians. There can be no justification for attacks which target ordinary people going about their daily business. The UK will continue to support the Nigerian authorities in their efforts to counter the terrorist threat and to help bring those responsible to justice.'*[63]

2.2   Fulani Militia

The Fulani militia are a semi-nomadic, pastoralist ethnic group living in the central regions of Nigeria, predominately in the Middle Belt. The regions most affected by the violence include the areas of Jama'a, Kachia, Kagarko, Kaura, and Sanga in southern Kaduna. The majority of the Fulani herdsmen are Muslim.

The atrocities perpetrated by the Fulani militia show clear signs of targeting Christians, including the destruction of churches, the seizure of land and properties belonging to Christian farmers. Reports have also emerged of the Fulani militia kidnapping *'Christian schoolgirls to marry them to Muslim men.'*[64]

In its 2015 report, *Open Doors* lists detailed examples of such targeted attacks. The report rebuts the argument that the clashes were caused by environmental degradation and result from migration. The report presents a more comprehensive picture incorporating some elements

---

[62] House of Lords Deb, 27 January 2014, c200W.

[63] Ibid.

[64] Open Doors, 'Crushed But Not Defeated. The Impact of Persistent Violence on the Church in Northern Nigeria.' Available at: https://www.opendoorsuk.org/about/how-we-help/advocacy/nigeria-report-12.

of religious persecution.[65] Indeed, the conflict is extremely complex. However, the religious element of the atrocities cannot be swept under the carpet.

The atrocities perpetrated by the Fulani herdsmen include the destruction of houses, churches, and places of worship, as well as the seizure of land and properties belonging to Christian owners. Reports have also emerged of the Fulani herdsmen '*kidnapping Christian schoolgirls to marry them to Muslim men.*'

Indeed, *Open Doors'* 2015 report lists detailed examples of such targeted attacks. The report rebuts the argument that the clashes were caused by environmental degradation and resulting migration. The report presents a more comprehensive picture incorporating some elements of religious persecution. The conflict is indeed extremely complex and by 2017, it was becoming clear that Boko Haram were not the only threat in Nigeria.

Fulani militia had emerged as a new and significant threat spreading death, destroying homes, and seizing land.[66] In what would become the UK Government's standard response Fulani attacks were described as '*recurrent clashes involving pastoralists and local farmers over land, farming rights, grazing routes and access to water in Nigeria. These conflicts, which are exacerbated by climate change and population growth, cause immense suffering to both the pastoralist and farming communities in Central and Northern Nigeria*'[67]—with no reference whatsoever to the ideology motivating many of the attacks and attackers.

CSW reported that in the first quarter of 2018, Fulani militia perpetrated at least 106 attacks in central Nigeria. The death toll over four months, attributed entirely to herder militia violence, stood at 1061. An additional 11 attacks recorded on communities in the south of the country claimed a further 21 lives.[68] One spokesman said: '*It is purely a religious jihad in disguise.*'[69] During the debate reference was made to the

---

[65] World Watch Research, 'Migration and Violent Conflict in Divided Societies' (2015). Available at: https://www.worldwatchmonitor.org/wp-content/uploads/2015/07/Migration-and-Violent-Conflict-in-Divided-Societies-March-2015-1.pdf.

[66] WPQ, HL215, 27 June 2017.

[67] Ibid.

[68] CSW, 'Nigeria sees 106 Attacks by Herder Militia in Central States' *CSW* (25 June 2018). Available at: https://www.csw.org.uk/2018/06/25/press/4011/article.htm.

[69] Ibid.

long history of disputes between nomadic herders and farming communities right across the Sahel, over land, grazing and scarce resources: leading to attacks by herder militia which have, on occasion, led to retaliatory violence, as communities conclude that they can no longer rely on the Government for protection or justice. Between 1 January and 1 May 2018, there were 60 such attacks.[70]

Parliamentarians pointed out that compared with an escalation in attacks by well-armed Fulani herders upon predominately Christian farming communities, the asymmetry had become stark, challenging the UK Government's characterisation and narrative of this violence.

It was suggested that the escalation, frequency, organisation, and asymmetry of Fulani attacks, meant that references to *'farmer-herder clashes' no longer sufficed and moral equivalence suggesting that both are 'as bad as one another'* was a crude and unsustainable piece of convenient shorthand. Parliament was told that some local observers had described the rising attacks as a campaign of ethno-religious cleansing.[71] Armed with sophisticated weaponry, including AK47s and, in at least one case, a rocket launcher and rocket-propelled grenades, the Fulani militia had murdered more men, women, and children in 2015, 2016, and 2017 than even Boko Haram, destroying, overrunning and seizing property and land, and displacing tens of thousands of people.[72] It had become organised and systematic.

Parliamentarians asked from where a group of nomadic herdsmen were getting such sophisticated weaponry and criticised the UK Government: *'while recognising the complex, underlying causes of this violence, we must also acknowledge a growing degree of religious motivation behind the violence.'*[73] Parliament was told that the local chapter of the Christian Association of Nigeria had revealed that since 2001 militias had destroyed over 500 churches in Benue State alone; that there had been, reports that during many well-planned attacks by Fulani militia, their cattle had been nowhere in sight, and that survivors frequently reported that their attackers shouted 'Allahu Akbar' during attacks.[74]

---

[70] House of Lords Deb, 28 June 2018, c284.

[71] House of Lords Deb, 28 June 2018, c283.

[72] Ibid.

[73] Ibid.

[74] Ibid.

Lord Alton complained that:

Beyond intermittent verbal condemnations, I cannot see much practical action that has been taken to end the violence, which has emboldened perpetrators even further. Moreover, in the light of such an inadequate response thus far, communities will begin—and indeed already are beginning—to feel that they can no longer rely on government for protection or justice, and a few take matters into their own hands. In the words of an Anglican canon in the Middle Belt, "Why do so many security service personnel spend their time guarding our politicians, rather than protecting our people?"[75]

This was a view echoed by the Catholic Bishops' Conference of Nigeria in a robust statement to President Buhari, in which they said:

Since the President who appointed the Heads of the nation's Security Agencies has refused to call them to order, even in the face of the chaos and barbarity into which our country has been plunged, we are left with no choice but to conclude that they are acting on a script that he approves of. If the President cannot keep our country safe, then he automatically loses the trust of the citizens. He should no longer continue to preside over the killing fields and mass graveyard that our country has become.[76]

On 18 June 2018, the Archbishop of Abuja described 'territorial conquest' and 'ethnic cleansing' and said that 'The very survival of our nation is... at stake.'[77] The highly respected former army chief of staff and Defence Minister, Lieutenant General Theophilus Y Danjuma, raised concerns about the partiality of the armed forces. He insisted that the armed forces were, 'not neutral; they collude' (with Fulani militia) in the, 'ethnic cleansing in ... riverine states.'[78] He warned that villagers must defend themselves because, 'depending on the armed forces,' will lead to

[75] Ibid.

[76] Eno Adeogun, 'Step Aside to Save the Nation: Bishop's Message to Nigerian President Buhari' *Premier News* (28 April 2018). Available at: https://premierchristian. news/en/news/article/step-aside-to-save-the-nation-bishop-s-message-to-nigerian-presid ent-buhari.

[77] House of Lords Deb, 28 June 2018, c283.

[78] Ibid.

them dying, *'one by one. The ethnic cleansing must stop... in all the states of Nigeria; otherwise, Somalia will be a child's play.'* [79]

Parliamentarians urged the Government of Nigeria to develop effective solutions to bring an end to this escalating violence; to put in place a strategic plan; to recalibrate security arrangements; and to resource their forces as a matter of urgency, in order to offer sufficient protection to vulnerable communities.

In closing remarks to the 2018 House of Lords debate Parliament was asked: *'Are we to watch one of Africa's greatest countries go the way of Sudan? Will we be indifferent as radical forces sweep across the Sahel seeking to replace diversity and difference with a monochrome ideology that will be imposed with violence on those who refuse to comply? We must not wait for a genocide to happen, as it did in Rwanda. Ominously, history could very easily be repeated.'*[80]

On 15 June 2020, following the publication of the report of the APPG on Freedom of Religion or Belief, *'Nigeria: An Unfolding Genocide?'*[81] Lord Alton said that the most important part about the report was the question mark: *'it's a question which requires the gravest consideration – and yet there is no Court in the UK and no other body capable of giving a definitive answer.'*

The Westminster launch of the report—dedicated to Leah Sharibu—featured speeches from the Chair of the APPG, Jim Shannon MP, Co-Chairs Baroness Cox, Lord Alton, Fiona Bruce MP, and Rebecca Sharibu, the mother of the kidnapped and grossly violated Leah.

Jim Shannon MP said that APPG members had become *'alarmed by the dramatic and escalating violence in Nigeria characterised as "the farmer-herder conflict".'* This led to the decision to hold an Inquiry which involved witness statements and the taking evidence at hearings held throughout the previous year.

The report contested the proposition that the atrocities in the north were solely about availability of land and water and were an extension of age-old disputes between predominantly ethnic Fulani Muslim herders and predominantly Christian farmers. In launching its Inquiry, the APPG

[79] Ibid.

[80] Ibid.

[81] All-Party Parliamentary Group on Freedom of Religion or Belief, 'Nigeria: An Unfolding Genocide?' (2020). Available at: https://appgfreedomofreligionorbelief.org/media/200615-Nigeria-Unfolding-Genocide-Report-of-the-APPG-for-FoRB.pdf.

said its motive was to develop an understanding of the drivers of violence and increase parliamentary, public, and governmental interest in the issue.

The APPG Inquiry found that Nigerian Christians were experiencing devastating violence, with attacks by armed groups of Islamist Fulani militia resulting in the killing, maiming, dispossession, and eviction of thousands. The exact death toll is unknown. However, Humanitarian Aid Relief Trust (HART) quotes reliable reports that over 1000 Christians were killed between January-November 2019, in addition to the estimated 6000 + deaths since 2015.[82] International Crisis Group estimated that over 300,000 people have been displaced and that the violence has claimed the lives of six times more people than the conflict with Boko Haram.[83] Violence by herders, and periodic retaliatory violence, is costing the Nigerian economy £10.5 billion per year.[84]

The report found that a key factor driving this violence is the impact of the growing power and influence of Islamist extremism across the Sahel, which drives some militant Fulani militia to target Christians and symbols of Christian identity, such as churches. Hundreds of churches have been destroyed, including over 500 in Benue State alone.[85]

In addition to the major factor of religious ideology, the APPG said that other contributory factors include climate change, desertification, resource competition, the influence of politics, criminality, the ready availability of firearms, and the spread of misinformation. It found that attacks by armed groups of Islamist Fulani militia had resulted in the killing, maiming, dispossession, and eviction of thousands of Christians.[86]

These factors have been compounded by the Nigerian Government's failure to respond adequately to the violence, to protect communities, or to bring perpetrators of violence to justice. The APPG's report concluded that, if lives are to be saved and violence prevented, all of these issues need

[82] Humanitarian Aid Relief Trust, 'Your Land or Your Blood: The Escalating Persecution of Christian in Northern and Central Nigeria' (November 2019).

[83] International Crisis Group, 'Stopping Nigeria's Spiraling Farmer-Herder Violence. Africa Report No. 262' (ICG, 2018). Available at: https://d2071andvip0wj.cloudfront.net/262-stopping-nigerias-spiralling-farmer-herder-violence.pdf.

[84] All-Party Parliamentary Group on Freedom of Religion or Belief, 'Nigeria: An Unfolding Genocide?' (2020) 4.

[85] Ibid., 5.

[86] Ibid., 6.

to be addressed urgently and report makes a series of recommendations about how this can be achieved.

In the Foreword to the report, Jim Shannon MP, said:

> Over my ten years as a Member of the UK Parliament, the COVID-19 crisis has surely been one of the most difficult and surreal challenges I have experienced. Constituents have told me of their physical suffering, of job losses, and the pain of not being able to visit their loved ones. This widespread and tremendous difficulty is a somewhat novel experience for many of us in the UK but for countless Christians living in Nigeria, extreme challenges are nothing new.
>
> Shockingly for a Commonwealth country, Nigeria ranks twelfth on Open Doors World Watch List 2020 of the countries in which Christians are most persecuted. By comparison, Syria ranks eleventh and Saudi Arabia ranks thirteenth, with Iraq fifteenth and Egypt sixteenth.
>
> One of the main drivers of this persecution in Nigeria is the militant group Boko Haram who frequently abduct and kill those who refuse to conform to their extremist brand of Islam.
>
> Unfortunately, Boko Haram are not the only threat that Nigerian Christians face. Attacks by armed groups of Islamist Fulani herdsmen have resulted in the killing, maiming, dispossession, and eviction of thousands of Christians.
>
> As Parliamentarians, I believe it is our responsibility to speak out on behalf of all the survivors and victims of violence, and all those who are suffering but who cannot speak out for themselves. One such survivor is Leah Sharibu, whose mother I was honoured to meet on a recent London visit. Two years ago, 14-year-old Leah Sharibu was abducted by Islamist extremists from her school in Dapchi, north-east Nigeria. There are reports that she was enslaved, raped and impregnated, giving birth to a child, and that she has been denied her freedom for refusing to convert to Islam as a precondition for her release. There are thousands of Leahs held all over Nigeria, and across the world. This report is dedicated to her and the millions of others who suffer so unspeakably. Its purpose is to explore the drivers of conflict and to highlight the seriousness of the situation and the level of injustice that Nigerian Christians face.
>
> Among all the injustices for the UK to help correct in the near future, the widespread and growing persecution of Christians should be top of the list. Thus, as the UK faces the challenge of lockdown and mass quarantine for the first time in living memory, I ask you to please spare a thought for

those Christians who face not only a pandemic but also threats of violence and persecution that we can't imagine.[87]

The report urged the Government of Nigeria and the international community to implement its recommendations. Leah Sharibu's mother, Rebecca, told Parliamentarians, *'don't grow weary or tired of helping us – the captivity and killing continues – hold President Buhari to account.'*

Writing about the report in *The Independent* newspaper, the greatly respected Dr. Rowan Williams, the former Archbishop of Canterbury, said that if the unremitting attacks weren't tackled urgently, *'The violence in Nigeria could end in genocide – both Christian and Muslim populations need help now.'*[88] Baroness Cox told *The Daily Telegraph*: *'We cannot ignore the chilling signs of a new genocide in Africa.'*[89]

In response, the UK Government said they would *'consider the report and its recommendations in detail.'* The then Africa Minister, James Duddridge MP said he would provide a full response *'in due course.'* The UK Government gave the same reply when asked what financial, technical, and capacity building support they intended to offer to the Government of Nigeria to implement the recommendations of the report.

Ministers were also urged to press for the implementation of the National Livestock Transformation Plan to help reduce the conflict involving farmers and herders in Nigeria. This was followed by a call to introduce mandatory training for FCDO staff in Nigeria to enable them to better on identify patterns of discrimination and conflict with religious characteristics, and to identify and contextualise the interaction of religion and religious actors with specific questions concerning society and conflict.

Ministers were then asked whether discussions had been held with the Government of Nigeria about the investigation of cases of reported military complicity in violence against Christians and other human rights

[87] Ibid., 1–2.

[88] Rowan Williams, 'The Violence in Nigeria Could End in Genocide—Both Christian and Muslim Populations Need Help Now' *The Independent* (15 June 2020). Available at: https://www.independent.co.uk/voices/nigeria-boko-haram-isis-violence-christian-muslim-coronavirus-a9566451.html.

[89] Baroness Cox, 'We Cannot Ignore the Chilling Signs of a New Genocide in Africa' *The Daily Telegraph* (15 June 2020). Available at: https://www.telegraph.co.uk/news/2020/06/15/cannot-ignore-chilling-signs-new-genocide-africa/.

abuses. Back came the reply that they were aware that such allegations had been made by '*communities of all faiths*.'[90] They were also aware of allegations of human rights abuses made against Nigerian military detention facilities in the Amnesty International report, '*We Dried our Tears*,' and said that had called for a full investigation into the allegations and prosecution of any individuals found to have committed abuses.[91]

The FCDO then briefed against the report and the parliamentarians who had produced it and told Lord Alton that the report had adopted the wrong tone.

Lord Farmer chided Ministers for referring to attacks by Fulani militia as '*a consequence of population growth*' and as a consequence of '*land and water disputes*.' He said that this did not reflect the reality on the ground, identified by local observers as a campaign of ethno-religious cleansing.

He went on to urge the UK Government to revisit the characterisation of this violence to acknowledge the significance of the perpetrators' ferocious ideology, while Lord (Donald) Anderson of Swansea—a former chair of the House of Commons Foreign Affairs Select Committee—suggested it was '*clearly beyond the capacity, or perhaps the will, of the Government of Nigeria to end the conflict and ethnic cleansing*.'[92]

Bishop Matthew Hassan Kukah of Sokoto, and many others, have concluded that these crimes are genocidal in nature. Although stressing that Muslims also fall foul of violence, he has said that systematic violence against Nigerian Christians by Fulani militia constitutes genocide. His intervention came followed the execution of five aid workers by Islamic State West African Province (ISWAP). When asked whether he agreed that Fulani killings of Christians can be categorised as genocide according to international law, Bishop Kukah said: '*I believe so*.'[93]

In November 2020, Jubilee Campaign submitted a devastating 89-page report on Nigeria to the ICC.[94] It proposed that:

---

[90] WPQ UIN HL5823, tabled on 17 June 2020.

[91] Ibid.

[92] Ibid.

[93] Fionn Shiner, 'Bishop Kukah—'Genocide is Happening in Nigeria' (6 August 2020). Available at: https://acnuk.org/news/nigeria-bishop-kukah-genocide-is-happening-in-nig eria/.

[94] Jubilee Campaign, 'Jubilee Campaign Submits Report to the ICC Describing How Genocide is Loading in Nigeria' (18 November 2020). Available at: http://jubileecampa ign.org/jubilee-campaign-submits-report-to-the-icc-describing-how-genocide-is-loading-in-nigeria/.

An ICC investigation and prosecution of the Fulani militant in Nigeria serves the best interests of justice. Since the Office of the Prosecutor at the ICC opened its preliminary assessment of the situation in 2010, the Fulani militant violence has increasingly grown both deadly and systematic, and there is increasing evidence that the attacks are genocidal.

The alleged crimes are grave, and local authorities have time and time again proven unwilling to end the violence or hold the perpetrators to account.[95]

The Jubilee report cited Agnes Callamard, the then UN Special Rapporteur for Extrajudicial, Summary or Arbitrary Executions, as stating the threat to security posed by impunity in Nigeria had resulted in: '*the absence today of accountability functionality is on such a scale that pretending this is anything short of a crisis is a major mistake. It is a tragedy for the people of Nigeria. Unchecked, its ripple effects will spread throughout the sub-region if not the continent, given the country's central economic, political and cultural leadership role.*'[96]

In November 2020, in an important article, '*Secular Myopia Warps the West's View of Nigeria,*' Professor Paul Marshall suggested that our failure to understand what drives Jihadism in Nigeria hampers our ability to find solutions.[97] He wrote:

Ethnic Fulani, Muslim herdsmen, who have been targeting Christians, are largely responsible for the killings, which total in the thousands and probably tens of thousands—the largest-scale butchery in the world today. Since many of the attackers explicitly and repeatedly announce that they are engaged in a religiously determined jihad, they also target Muslims who do not go along with their extremist agenda.... there is still widespread resistance among many Western elites to recognize the religious element of the Fulani attacks on predominantly Christian villages, people, and churches.[98]

---

[95] Ibid.

[96] Ibid.

[97] Paul Marshall, 'Secular Myopia Warps the West's View of Nigeria' (23 November 2020). Available at: https://providencemag.com/2020/11/secular-myopia-warps-wests-view-nigeria-conflict/?fbclid=IwAR317gSezkWfvrpfYjHHTg_JyCqYbixfZr2PsEtIiYulUdU VJfMlq2aQzH0.

[98] Ibid.

In his analysis, he included details of a meeting with the US Ambassador to Nigeria, Mary Beth Leonard, who insisted, in a script which could have been choreographed by the FCDO, that Nigeria's conflicts were '*fundamentally a resource issue*' and minimised the role of religion.

In an excoriating appraisal Professor Marshall says this represents '*an introverted, parochial inability even to see, much less understand, the role of religion in human life.*'[99] He concluded that this is:

> a self-declared jihad that employs sophisticated tactics and uses advanced weapons on a large scale while burning churches amid cries of "Allahu Akbar." No person facing drought decides automatically to behead local pastors and bishops, or raze churches using chemical weapons.
>
> Religion is, and increasingly so, a major factor in human affairs, including very violent affairs. It is also often necessarily intertwined with political and economic factors... Westerners who don't understand religion miss this. What people believe about the fundamental realities of existence will shape their view of politics, and their politics will shape their views of what is fundamental in human life.
>
> Any failure to recognize these religious dimensions in general and, particularly, in the present conflicts in Nigeria's Middle Belt and elsewhere in West Africa, divorces us from the complex realities of concrete human life. It restricts our view of human motivation in favour of a truncated pseudo-materialist interpretation of human action. Hence, it distorts our analysis of conflict and can cripple any search for political and religious solutions to conflict. We need to recognize and diagnose secular myopia and realize that its effects can be deadly.[100]

At the end of 2020, during a Congressional Hearing of the Tom Lantos Commission on Human Rights, Congressman Christopher Smith (New Jersey, R), the Commission's co-chair, said that genocide in Nigeria is '*happening before our eyes.*'

Similar statements emanated from the Knights of Columbus and the Bishop of Ghoko.

The Hearing was held in the aftermath of the decision of the US, under the provisions of the 1998 Religious Freedom Act, to designate Nigeria a

---

[99] Ibid.
[100] Ibid.

'country of particular concern,' noting the abduction of the 300 school-boys at Kankara and the shooting of 51 peaceful protestors in Lagos on 20 October.

Bishop William Anvenya told the Hearing:

> our Middle Belt region has truly become a vale of tears, a region where mass burials are very common. Since the consistent attacks began some five years ago, there has hardly been a single day without killing in one part of the region or the other. No one has ever been arrested of questioned, or prosecuted, or convicted of any charge…yet these killers are not invisible, neither are they unknown. Instead, these atrocities are made to look as though they were ethnic or communal clashes.[101]

Mr. Carl Anderson, the Supreme Knight of the Knights of Columbus, gave evidence to the Hearing, stating that: *'Nigeria's Christians have suffered grievously at the hands of Boko Haram and other groups. The Christians of Nigeria, both Catholic and Protestant, deserve attention, recognition, and relief right now.'*

Miss Ann Buwalda, Director of Jubilee Campaign USA, told the Hearing that genocide had *'become virtually a daily threat.'*[102] She pointed to *'the rising frequency of deadly midnight attacks on predominantly Christian farming communities which are carried out by groups of heavily armed radical Islamist Fulani militants.'*[103]

Professor Robert Destro of the US State Department added that Nigerian officials are in denial with one telling him that it was *'impossible'* that religion was even a factor in the killings. He said there needed to be more *'early warning networks'* to detect further mass atrocities before they occur.

2.3 Similar Attacks Across Sub-Saharan Africa

This spread of a brutal radical ideology across Sub-Saharan Africa, from Darfur, Sudan, and Somalia, through the Sahel and into West and Central Africa was how we began this exploration of the situation in Nigeria.

---

[101] Congressional Hearing, Tom Lantos Commission on Human Rights (2020).

[102] Ibid.

[103] Ibid.

It was an issue which was examined by the International Relations and Defence Select Committee of the House of Lords, of which Lord Alton is a member, and which published a report on Sub-Saharan Africa in July 2020.[104] Subsequently there have been recurrent reports of further mass atrocities. For example, in early 2021, horrific carnage including mass beheadings and mutilation in Mozambique.[105]

Witnesses told the House of Lords Inquiry that in the last five to 10 years conflict in the region had become *'more transnational'*; *'conflicts bleed into one another'*; that when thinking about security in the region, *'the unit of analysis'* was *'no longer the nation state'* that *'many of the challenges to stability and prosperity'* do *'not respect borders'*; that the change in the nature of conflict has had profound consequences for traditional approaches to conflict management, including peacekeeping; that there was an *'increasing threat'* from terrorist groups that were *'embedding'* into civilian communities and *'linking with... local and global agendas'* of *jihad*.[106]

The Committee heard that terrorists who had fought with jihadist groups in Yemen, Iraq, and Syria were *'relocating'* to Africa. New involvement from regional and international actors had encouraged or created proxy wars. While not all existing conflicts involving non-state armed groups were caused by international networks, they were often *'seen and tackled as part of the global terrorism narrative.'*[107]

The Inquiry reported that *'several witnesses considered the role of identity issues in Nigerian conflicts.'* The Coalition for Genocide Response said that the settler/herder conflict was *'presented as a clash over grazing land,'* but had an *'underlying religious and ideological nature.'* In her evidence, Ms Mathews said there was a *'strong religious dimension'* to some of the insecurity, and the International Organisation for Peace and

[104] House of Lords International Relations and Defence Select Committee, 'The UK and Sub-Saharan Africa: Prosperity, Peace and Development Cooperation' (2020). Available at: https://committees.parliament.uk/publications/1830/documents/17881/default/.

[105] BBC, 'Mozambique Insurgency: Children Beheaded, Aid Agency Reports' BBC (16 March 2021). Available at: https://www.bbc.co.uk/news/world-africa-56411157.

[106] House of Lords International Relations and Defence Select Committee, 'The UK and Sub-Saharan Africa: Prosperity, Peace and Development Cooperation' (2020) 483.

[107] Ibid., 484.

Social Justice said that north-east Nigeria was '*increasingly uninhabitable for Christians.*'[108]

The Inquiry took evidence from the then Africa Minister, James Duddridge MP, who said that the Prime Minister, at the UK-Africa Investment Summit in January 2020, had '*discussed UK support for fighting terrorism in Nigeria with President Buhari.*'[109] The Government was 'committed to upholding human rights for all' and condemned '*the appalling abduction and continued captivity of Leah Sharibu and other Christian and Muslim school children by Boko Haram and Islamic State West Africa.*'[110] The UK had '*offered assistance and expertise to help the Nigerian Government in their efforts to recover the missing girls.*'[111]

The Committee said that:

> women and girls play multiple roles in conflicts across the region, including as victims, participants, and in governmental responses to insecurity and that women and girls are central to the prevention and resolution of conflict. The Government should continue to champion their rights in its work on peace and security in Sub-Saharan Africa.[112]

The House of Lords Inquiry concluded that: '*the UK and its international partners have too often focused on addressing the immediate consequences of conflict, to the detriment of efforts to tackle the underlying conditions that allow conflict to emerge.*'[113]

It added that: '*The Government should, in its Integrated Review, consider how the UK can best use its resources and influence to develop longer-term strategies to prevent conflict, and above all to prevent genocide, and support regional partners.*'[114]

The international community should acknowledge the long-term, far-reaching issues in the Sahel region where uneducated, unemployed young men are being mobilised by Islamist fundamentalists who offer them a

---

[108] Ibid., 538.
[109] Ibid., 541.
[110] Ibid., 541.
[111] Ibid.
[112] Ibid., 569.
[113] Ibid., 619.
[114] Ibid.

more attractive life than herding goats in the baking hot sun. Climate disruption is exacerbating the likelihood they will not find meaningful occupation in their traditional homes and through their lifestyles.

Nigeria (after Pakistan) is the UK's second largest recipient of billions of pounds of aid. It is also the source of many migrants arriving in the UK—which will increase if the security situation persists. The UK has a huge Nigerian diaspora, and many have expressed their concern to us that the UK has failed to recognise the nature and scale of the atrocities in Nigeria, or to deploy the UK's massive aid programme to bring about change. Delta oil and significant commercial links also suggest that it is in Britain's own interests to combat instability born out of ideology. For these and many other reasons the UK should pay much closer attention to the situation in Nigeria and engage accordingly.

3   Do Nigeria's Atrocities Amount to Genocide?

Although the violence which we have catalogued has been affecting northern Nigeria's Christian minority for some time, in December 2019, news filtered out of Nigeria that Islamic State in West Africa, a Daesh-affiliated terror group, had been responsible for the new wave of brutal murders of Christians. That new wave of killings did not come as a surprise but was illustrative of a further disturbing new dimension, merely adding to the terror unleashed by Boko Haram (which, in the past, had previously pledged allegiance to Daesh) and by the Fulani militia. Neither should its ability to grow fast have come as a surprise either.

The growing and unaddressed impunity in Nigeria is an open invitation to such groups to make this their new killing ground and for such atrocities to continue and to grow. Simultaneously, as we have described, the issue of violence based on religion or belief in Nigeria is greatly neglected. Boko Haram has largely targeted Northern Nigeria's Christians—which they publicly celebrate.

At the very minimum, such persecution is undoubtedly a crime against humanity. Boko Haram's abduction of Christian women and girls and forcibly converting and marrying them is crime of a high order. And far from being an isolated case, Leah Sharibu's abduction, rape, impregnation, and forced conversion graphically and poignantly illustrate what can happen to many young Nigerian women.

Both, Boko Haram and Fulani militia, terrorise and perpetrate atrocities that affect the whole community and can most certainly be classified as crimes against humanity. However, both groups also specifically target religious minorities. This specific targeting of religious minorities may bring the crimes within the purview of the crime of genocide as per Article II of the Genocide Convention. A report from *Genocide Watch* estimated that, during 2020, 2200 Christians were hacked to death in Nigeria. *Genocide Watch* said that in two months alone over 350 Christians were killed and according to their data that '*over 11,500 Christians have been murdered since June 2015.*'[115] The International Committee on Nigeria said, in 2020, that since 2015 Fulani militant attacks had '*increased exponentially.*'[116] The latest risk assessment of the Holocaust Memorial Museum's Simon Skjodt Centre for the Prevention of Genocide calculated that Nigeria faced a 7.3% risk of experiencing a new mass killing by the end of 2021, the sixth highest in the world. It had climbed up the rankings from 17th to 6th place since 2019.[117]

Boko Haram leaders have been very clear about their targeting of Christians, infidels, non-believers. Its leader, Abubakar Shekau declared:

> University is forbidden, girls you should return to your homes. In Islam, it is allowed to take infidel women as slaves and in due course we will start taking women away and sell them in the market.[118]

> The people of Bama, who we have killed, now may call themselves Muslims, but we see them under the category of infidels,' highlighting the gap in perception between Boko Haram and the local populace.[119]

Analysis of such statements may help to identify the specific intention to destroy the religious groups in whole or in part.

---

[115] See: Genocide Watch. Available at: https://www.genocidewatch.com/single-post/2020/04/13/nigeria-is-a-killing-field-of-defenseless-christians.

[116] Ibid.

[117] See: Holocaust Memorial Museum's Simon Skjodt Centre for the Prevention of Genocide. Available at: https://earlywarningproject.ushmm.org/countries/nigeria.

[118] Ola' Audu, 'Boko Haram: Shekau Claims Responsibility for Attack on Giwa Barracks, Threatens to Attack Universities, Civilian-JTF' *Premium Times* (24 March 2014). Available at: http://www.premiumtimesng.com/news/157374-bokoharam-shekau-claims-responsibility-attack-giwa-barracks-threatensattack-universities-civilian-jtf.html.

[119] Omar S. Mahmood, 'More than Propaganda. A Review of Boko Haram's Public Messages' (2017) Institute for Security Studies. Available at: https://www.ecoi.net/en/file/local/1426834/1226_1521122538_war20.pdf.

In the case of the Fulani militia, in the absence of any official statements or documents concerning their targeting of religious groups, this specific intent may be deduced from their acts. The atrocities perpetrated by the Fulani militia also show clear signs of the targeting of Christians, including the destruction of churches, and the seizure of land and properties belonging to Christian farmers.

Reports have also emerged of the Fulani militia kidnapping '*Christian schoolgirls to marry them to Muslim men.*' In its 2015 report, *Open Doors* detailed examples of such targeted attacks. Their report rebuts the argument that the clashes were caused by environmental degradation and migration. Although there are undoubtedly many factors at work it is palpably absurd and intellectually bankrupt to lazily (or possibly deliberately) suggest that a distorted religious ideology is not the major factor at work in justifying the horrific violence in the minds of those who carry out these barbaric attacks. That, too, was the ultimate conclusion of the June 2020 APPG report '*Nigeria: An Unfolding Genocide?*' described earlier.

4   Responses to the Atrocities

The atrocities in Nigeria referred to in this chapter are atrocities perpetrated by non-state actors and in particular by Boko Haram and Fulani militia. Despite this, the responses to the atrocities have been negligent, both by the Nigerian Government and by international bodies.

4.1   Attempts to Prevent and Suppress the Nigerian Atrocities

The predominant focus of UK engagement in seeking to prevent and suppress the Nigerian atrocities has been on diplomatic engagement. It was also reported that the Royal Air Force and UK armed forces offered assistance to the Nigerian Government to help recover the schoolgirls abducted by Boko Haram. It is said that the Nigerian Government refused the offer claiming it was a national issue requiring a national response.[120]

Lord Alton and Baroness Cox have frequently told the UK Government that insufficient is being done to prevent further bloodshed and loss

---

[120] Oliver Harvey, 'Inside Boko Haram Leader Abubakar Shekau's Rule of Terror Forcing Children into Sexual Slavery and Suicide Bombings' *The Sun* (21 December 2020).

of life. The purpose of their many interventions is not simply to ensure government accountability—the first duty of parliamentarians—but also to demonstrate that the indicators of a creeping, rising genocide have been there for a sustained period. Those signs of an emerging genocide have been wilfully ignored by the Government of Nigeria, which has failed in its triple duties to prevent, protect, and punish. But the Government of the United Kingdom and every other state which is a signatory to the Genocide Convention have also failed in their duty to look for the harbingers of genocide.

Legislators can also use their positions to exert pressure on international bodies—political, diplomatic and judicial, challenging them not to avert their eyes to the crime on genocide. And it does have an effect.

Having written to the International Criminal Court on 14 February, 25 June, and 23 July, and having held a meeting in July 2020 with Phakiso Mochochoko and other officials at the ICC, on 6 August 2020, Lord Alton and Lady Cox decided to place their concerns on the record with Fatou Bensouda, the then Prosecutor of the ICC, and, to draw her attention to the genocidal acts and the culture of impunity, in which the Nigerian courts had failed to bring perpetrators to justice.[121]

4.2   Investigating and Prosecuting the Crimes

Having ratified the Rome Statute, the ICC has territorial jurisdiction in Nigeria to investigate alleged crimes amounting to international crimes such as genocide, crimes against humanity, or war crimes. On 18 November 2010, the Prosecutor of the ICC opened a preliminary examination of the situation in Nigeria. This followed several communications received by the OTP to the ICC, as early as 2005. As we remarked earlier, it took until 2020 for the Prosecutor to produce a formal statement identifying Boko Haram and elements of the Security Forces as responsible for crimes against humanity.

The Prosecutor's preliminary examination focused on the crimes committed in the regions of central and northern Nigeria and the Niger Delta, and the crimes committed by Boko Haram across Nigeria. It examined political and sectarian violence since approximately 1999, including clashes between Berom groups and Hausa-Fulani, Gamai and Jarawa,

---

[121] See: Appendix C.

and between Hausa-Fulani Muslims and Igbo. In its 2015 report on the progress of the preliminary examination, the OTP identified six potential cases of Boko Haram committing crimes against humanity and two cases of such crimes being committed by the Nigerian security forces.

The OTP confirmed that there is a reasonable basis to believe that since 2009, Boko Haram has committed crimes against humanity in Nigeria. These include *(i) murder pursuant to article 7(1)(a), and (ii) persecution pursuant to article 7(1)(h) of the Statute; and war crimes including 'murder pursuant to article 8(2)(c)(i); cruel treatment pursuant to article 8(2)(c)(i) and outrages upon personal dignity pursuant to article 8(2)(c)(ii); intentionally directing attacks against the civilian population or against individual civilians pursuant to article 8(2)(e)(i); intentionally directing attacks against buildings dedicated to education and to places of worship and similar institutions pursuant to article 8(2)(e)(iv); pillaging a town or place pursuant to article 8(2)(e)(v); rape, sexual slavery and sexual violence pursuant to article 8(2)(e)(vi); conscripting and enlisting children under the age of fifteen years into armed groups and using them to participate actively in hostilities pursuant to article 8(2)(e)(vii) of the Statute.'*

Over the years, the OTP expanded its focus. In its 2018 report, it confirmed that it has been considering the *'attacks allegedly carried out by Fulani herders and Christian settlers in the context of the violence in Nigeria's North Central and North East geographical zones.'* It went on to state that *'this violence, which has been observed by the [OTP] since 2016, is often referred to as a conflict between Fulani herders and Christian farmers, stemming from limited access to water, land and other resources.'*

All this culminated, on 11 December 2020, in a powerful statement from Fatou Bensouda who accused Boko Haram and the Nigerian security forces of crimes against humanity and war crimes including murder, rape, torture, and cruel treatment; enforced disappearances; forcible transfer of population and outrages on personal dignity.

The statement from the ICC said:

> Boko Haram and the Nigerian State's Security forces are accused of crimes against humanity and war crimes: murder, rape, torture, and cruel treatment; enforced disappearance; forcible transfer of population; outrages upon personal dignity; intentionally directing attacks against the civilian population as such and against individual civilians not taking direct part in hostilities; unlawful imprisonment; conscripting and enlisting children

under the age of fifteen years into armed forces and using them to participate actively in hostilities; persecution on gender and political grounds;
and other inhumane acts.

While my Office recognises that the vast majority of criminality within
the situation is attributable to non-state actors, we have also found a
reasonable basis to believe that members of the Nigerian Security Forces
("NSF") have committed the following acts constituting crimes against
humanity and war crimes: murder, rape, torture, and cruel treatment;
enforced disappearance; forcible transfer of population; outrages upon
personal dignity; intentionally directing attacks against the civilian population as such and against individual civilians not taking direct part
in hostilities; unlawful imprisonment; conscripting and enlisting children
under the age of fifteen years into armed forces and using them to participate actively in hostilities; persecution on gender and political grounds;
and other inhumane acts.

These allegations are also sufficiently grave to warrant investigation by
my Office, both in quantitative and qualitative terms.[122]

The ICC investigation covers the years since 2013. The Prosecutor made
clear that she had given the Nigerian authorities repeated opportunities
to investigate and prosecute the crimes in their domestic courts:

We have engaged in multiple missions to Nigeria to support national
efforts, shared our own assessments, and invited the authorities to act.
However, despite being told that some low-level offenders had been appre-
hended our assessment is that none of these proceedings relate, even
indirectly, to the forms of conduct or categories of persons that would
likely form the focus of my investigations.[123]

The next step will now be for Mr. Karim A.A. Khan QC, who has replaced
Fatou Bensouda as Chief Prosecutor, to request authorisation from the
Judges of the Pre-Trial Chamber of the Court to open investigations.
However, as the ICC is chronically underfunded with zero net growth,

---

[122] ICC, 'Statement of the Prosecutor, Fatou Bensouda, on the Conclusion of the
Preliminary Examination of the Situation in Nigeria' (11 December 2020). Available at:
https://www.icc-cpi.int/Pages/item.aspx?name=201211-prosecutor-statement.

[123] Ibid.

while at the same time, becoming overwhelmed by cases, this may affect the handling of the next stage. The international community will need to ensure that the ICC has all the resources it requires to be able to do the important job of investigating atrocities and prosecuting those responsible.

As things stand, this long and grinding process, spanning more than ten years, has yet to consider the issue of possible genocide. It remains unclear whether this issue will be explored as the investigation proceeds. However, when the ICC considered Bashir's crimes in Darfur the initial allegations of crimes against humanity were later expanded to include genocide.

We will consider the role of the ICC in further detail in the next section of the book.

4.2.1   Domestic Prosecutions

According to the Nigerian Government, Nigerian courts have been engaging with the prosecution of Boko Haram members. However, as the previous Prosecutor of the ICC confirmed, such prosecutions have been inadequate:

> We have engaged in multiple missions to Nigeria to support national efforts, shared our own assessments, and invited the authorities to act. We have seen some efforts made by the prosecuting authorities in Nigeria to hold members of Boko Haram to account in recent years, primarily against low-level captured fighters for membership in a terrorist organisation. The military authorities have also informed me that they have examined, and dismissed, allegations against their own troops.
>
> I have given ample time for these proceedings to progress, bearing in mind the overarching requirements of partnership and vigilance that must guide our approach to complementarity. However, our assessment is that none of these proceedings relate, even indirectly, to the forms of conduct or categories of persons that would likely form the focus of my investigations. And while this does not foreclose the possibility for the authorities to conduct relevant and genuine proceedings, it does mean that, as things stand, the requirements under the Statute are met for my Office to proceed.[124]

---

[124] ICC, 'Statement of the Prosecutor, Fatou Bensouda, on the Conclusion of the Preliminary Examination of the Situation in Nigeria' (11 December 2020). Available at: https://www.icc-cpi.int/Pages/item.aspx?name=201211-prosecutor-statement.

Because of the failures of domestic courts to prosecute the perpetrators, the OTP was able to conclude the preliminary examination and take the next step towards investigation. Meanwhile, while investigations proceed at a snail's pace, Nigeria's massacres, pillage, and abductions continue unabetted. There are no known prosecutions of Boko Haram or Fulani militia based on the universal jurisdiction.

The situation requires urgent attention. Nigeria is a member of the Commonwealth—which seems to have nothing to say about these atrocities. It is a member of the African Union—which also seems to have nothing to say about these atrocities. It is a member of the United Nations—which has largely choosen to look the other way. It is a country with deep and close connections to the UK, which seems content to provide Nigeria with staggering amounts of taxpayers' money with insufficient thought as to how that money is used and into whose pockets it goes—certainly not reaching those about whom we have written.[125]

---

[125] 2009—121,277 (in thousands £); 2010—171,335; 2011—186,428; 2012—197,313; 2013—248,734; 2014—236,639; 2015—262,685; 2016—319,583; 2017—327,199; 2018—296,819.

Other Situations of Concern

1   WHAT ABOUT THE ARMENIANS?

Low Hill is a neighbourhood in inner city Liverpool. While still a student, Lord Alton was elected to represent it as a City Councillor and for 25 years continued to do so as a City Councillor or Member of Parliament.

Low Hill is not far from Rodney Street, where William Ewart Gladstone was born.

On 24 September 1896, at the age of 86, and having been elected Prime Minster four times, it was to Low Hill's Hengler's Circus that Mr. Gladstone returned to give his last public speech. To the thousands who had gathered to hear him he said they might wonder what had brought an old man out of his quiet retirement at Hawarden Castle in North Wales. He then provided the answer: *'two Armenian gentlemen.'*[1]

In 1876, Gladstone had published his *'Bulgarian Horrors and the Question of the East.'* In a tirade against the tyranny of the Ottoman Turks in the Balkans Gladstone used all his powers of rhetoric:

[1] The Times, 'Mr. Gladstone on the Armenian question' *The Times* (25 September 1896).

© The Author(s), under exclusive license to Springer Nature Switzerland AG 2022

E. U. Ochab and D. Alton, *State Responses to Crimes of Genocide*, Rethinking Political Violence, https://doi.org/10.1007/978-3-030-99162-3_7

Let the Turks now carry away their abuses, in the only possible manner, namely, by carrying off themselves... from the province that they have desolated and profaned. This... is the only reparation we can make to those heaps and heaps of dead, the violated purity alike of matron and of maiden and of child; to the civilization which has been affronted and shamed; to the laws of God, or, if you like, of Allah to the moral sense of mankind at large. (...) That such things should be done once is a damning disgrace to the portion of our race which did them; that the door should be left open to their ever so barely possible repetition would spread that shame over the world![2]

By 1879, he had taken his arguments to the country, giving 30 substantial speeches, heard by an estimated 87,000 people. In turning his moral indignation into a nationwide clarion call, his Midlothian Campaigns of 1879, 1880, and 1884, called on civilised nations to stand together; for Britain to assert a doctrine of 'equal rights of all nations'[3]; and, in particular, for Britain to condemn the brutality of the Ottoman Empire against its Christian subjects and to defend their right to believe and worship freely.

The Midlothian Campaigns were a barnstorming nationwide assault on the indifference of the British Government and the great powers lambasting them for their limp response to extraordinary cruelties which the people in the Turkish-occupied Balkans were experiencing because of their ethnicity and religion. So, Mr. Gladstone was well aware of the nature and motivation of such crimes—especially those of the Ottoman Turks—when, twenty years later, those two Armenian gentlemen came to see him at Hawarden to describe the persecution of their people and to appeal for his help.

The Hengler's Circus speech came after a minor uprising in 1894, in Sasun, in Turkish Armenia.[4] Throughout 1895, a series of pogroms had occurred throughout Turkey's Armenian provinces—and even in the capital, Istanbul. The Armenians—and other Christian minorities—were

[2] William E. Gladstone, *Bulgarian Horrors and the Question of the East* (John Murray: London, 1876) 31.

[3] Speech in West Calder, Scotland (27 November 1879), quoted in William E. Gladstone, *Midlothian Speeches 1879* (Leicester University Press, 1971) 116–117.

[4] F. W. Hirst, 'Gladstone's Fourth Premiership and Final Retirement 1892–1897' in Wemys Reid (ed.), *the Life of William Ewar Gladstone* (Cassell and Company Limited: London, 1899) 734.

forced to pay *'double taxes'* and were denied many civil rights.[5] Their protests against this discrimination led to their wholesale slaughter.[6]

At Hawarden, Gladstone had carefully taken first-hand accounts from his two visitors, and he began his remarks by saying *'the powers of language hardly suffice to describe what has been and is being done, and exaggeration, if we were ever so much disposed to it, is in such a case really beyond our power.'*[7] Gladstone reflected that only the enormity of the *'sickening horrors'* perpetrated against the Armenians, and *'a strong sense of duty'* could have induced *'a man of my age'* to abandon what he called *'the repose and quietude'* of his retirement.[8] But, he declared, '*We are not dealing with a common and ordinary question of abuses of government. We are dealing with something that goes far deeper (...) four awful words – plunder, murder, rape, and torture.'*[9]

6000 people gathered to hear Gladstone and *The Times* reported that even more people thronged outside Hengler's Circus while *The Liverpool Daily Post* recorded that *'the entire city turned out for him'* and had greeted him with *'a tornado of applause.'*[10] He knew that it was his duty to rouse the conscience of the nation.

In describing the *'horribly accumulated outrages,'* he demanded a non-sectarian and non-partisan approach; and he also emphasised that *'this is no crusade against Mohammedanism'*; that, whatever faith had been held by the Armenians, *'it would have been incumbent upon us with the same force and the same sacredness'* to speak out on their behalf.[11] With precision, Gladstone identified and named the Ottoman Turkish Sultan Abdul Hamid II—*'the assassin'*—as responsible for the order to massacre the Armenians; and he roundly condemned the European powers for

[5] Facing History and Ourselves, *Crimes Against Humanity and Civilization. The Genocide of the Armenians* (History and Ourselves National Foundation, Inc.: Brookline, MA, 2004) 35.

[6] Ibid.

[7] Ibid.

[8] William E. Gladstone, Speech on 6 August 1895 cited in Richard B. Cook, *The Grand Old Man* (Publishers' Union, 1898).

[9] Ibid.

[10] Liverpool Daily Post, 24/25 September 1896.

[11] William E. Gladstone, Speech of 24 September 1896.

giving the Sultan *'the assurance of impunity.'*[12] While believing that ideally Europe should act together, he bitterly criticised their failure to do so: *'Collectively, the powers have under-gone miserable disgrace.'*[13] But, when Europe failed to act, Gladstone said Britain had the right to act alone and not *'make herself a slave to be dragged at the chariot wheel of other powers of Europe.'*[14]

A German newspaper, *The Hamburger Nachrichten*, took Mr. Gladstone to task and responded: *'For us [Germans] the sound bones of a single Pomeranian [German] grenadier are worth more than the lives of 10,000 Armenians.'*[15]

Many of these same arguments have relevance and application in our own times but so does the challenge which comes at the culmination of his Hengler's Circus address. He demands no ambiguity, no neutrality but condemnation of crimes against humanity: *'which have already come to such a magnitude and to such a depth of atrocity that they constitute the most terrible, most monstrous series of proceedings that have ever been recorded in the dismal and deplorable history of human crime.'*[16]

Gladstone was right to prophesy that indifference would lead to catastrophic consequences.

He told his audience that if they were indifferent when people in faraway provinces were slaughtered it would only be a matter of time before the same horrors were visited upon them.

Seventeen years after Gladstone's death, the Armenian genocide of 1915–16 would become the second genocide of the twentieth century (after the Herero and Nama genocide).

Over one million men, women, and children were killed as the Ottoman Turks sought to entirely erase the Armenian identity from eastern Turkey.[17]

---

[12] Ibid.

[13] Ibid.

[14] Ibid.

[15] Ibid.

[16] William E. Gladstone, Speech of 24 September 1896.

[17] Jakub Bijak and Sarah Lubman, *The Disputed Numbers: In Search of the Demographic Basis for Studies of Armenian Population Losses, 1915–1923* (Palgrave Macmillan, 2016) 26–43.

The land was dyed red with Armenian blood. Hundreds of thousands of other Armenians were the subject of mass deportations and they form the basis of today's worldwide diaspora. Others—perhaps as many as a million in the area bordering the Black Sea—were forced to convert to Islam, and, to this very day, many families are said to hold on to their hidden Christian faith.

In 1965, Leonid Brezhnev gave permission for a genocide memorial to be erected in Yerevan, the capital of what was then the Soviet Republic of Armenia (part of the Soviet Union).[18] The towering obelisk, forty metres high, is said to symbolise both the genocide and the renaissance of the Armenian people. During a visit in September 2001, Pope John Paul II planted a tree at the memorial and composed a blessing for Armenia which begins with the plea: *'Remember O Lord how the sons and daughters of this land have suffered.'*[19] The museum adjacent to the memorial has collated the memories, photographs, and records into a damning indictment of both the objectives of the Ottoman Turks and the abject failure of the international community to act on the information which its own diplomats had assembled.

The Director of the Armenian Genocide Museum-Institute, Hayk Demoyan, uncovered graphic material and poignant letters.

When Lord Alton met him in Yerevan in 2007, he had just obtained letters written by three women who had been deported to Brazil. One had been pregnant but had miscarried her baby. In a letter, she wrote: *'These eyes saw things the world should never see.'*[20] Mr. Demoyan says that collating the records and assembling numerical evidence of the genocide is numbing but that the personal stories cut to the quick: *'The killing of millions is statistics but the killing of one person is a tragedy.'*[21] Mr. Demoyan and his colleagues have unearthed photographs in the St. Petersburg Photographic Archives, and hundreds of photographs held in the Royal Archive of Norway. Among the material which has been

---

[18] Maike Lehmann, 'Apricot Socialism: The National Past, the Soviet Project, and the Imagining of Community in Late Soviet Armenia' (2015) 74 Slavic Review 9–31.

[19] Armenpress, 'Glance back at Pope John Paul's 2001 visit to Armenia' *Armenpress* (24 June 2016). Available at: https://armenpress.am/eng/news/852045/glance-back-at-pope-john-paulE28099s-2001-visit-to-armenia.html.

[20] See: www.davidalton.net. Discussion with Lord Alton in 2007.

[21] Ibid.

assembled are the first-hand accounts of Christian relief workers and missionaries working with the Armenians at the time of the genocide.

Maria Jacobsen who was a Danish missionary based at Harpoot from 1907 until 1919 wrote in her diary that the atrocities had their beginning in June 1915:

> It was proclaimed from all mosques today that all Armenians are to be sent into exile. They are to be given four days in which to dispose of their possessions, to be ready for their journey to an unknown destination for an indefinite period. It is said that they will be sent to the desert south of Ourfa. If this is true, then it is obvious that the whole meaning behind this movement of the Armenian people is their extermination.[22]

On 24 July, she noted *'Any Turk who hides an Armenian will be hanged and his house burnt. All houses from the poorest to the richest are to be searched.'*[23] By 14 August, she was writing *'Poor, poor Armenians, what you have had to endure.'*[24]

The historian, Arnold Toynbee, meanwhile, wrote of the premeditated and systematic nature of the genocide: *'The attempt to exterminate the Armenians during world War One was carried out under the cloak of legality by cold-blooded government action. These are not mass murders committed spontaneously by mobs and private people.'*[25] Winston Churchill commented that *'There is no reasonable doubt that this crime was planned and executed for political reasons.'*[26] Despite the overwhelming evidence and contemporary accounts—and Sultan Abdul Hamid II's own assertion

---

[22] Maria Jaconsen, *Diaries of a Danish Missionary: Harpoot, 1907–1919* (Gomidas Institute: Princeton, 2001).

[23] Ibid.

[24] Ibid.

[25] Arnold Toynbee, *Experiences* (1969) 241.

[26] Winston S. Churchill, *The World Crisis. Volume 5. The Aftermath* (Charles Scribner's Sons: New York, 1929). 'The opportunity presented itself for clearing Turkish soil of a Christian race opposed to all Turkish ambitions, cherishing national ambitions that could only be satisfied at the expense of Turkey, and planted geographically between Turkish and Caucasian Moslems. It may well be that the British attack on the Gallipoli Peninsula stimulated the merciless fury of the Turkish Government. Even, thought the Pan-Turks, if Constantinople were to fall and Turkey lost the war, the clearance would have been effected and a permanent advantage for the future of the Turkish race would be granted.'

that *'the best way to finish the Armenian question is to finish the Armenians.'*[27] To this day, Turkey has persisted in denying that the genocide ever took place. They have also refused to open their borders and to normalise relations with Armenia until all talk of genocide is stopped.

In 1991, during the dissolution of the Soviet Union, Armenia became an independent country. But there are still those who wish to see its destruction.

Unlike modern Germany, Turkey has failed to come to terms with her past. Denying the truth helps no one; it becomes impossible to heal the past and to move on. But it also contains within it the cypher that you can do these things and from generation to generation you can get away with what your forbearers did.

As Recap Tayyip Erdogan's Turkey absorbs that message it emboldens Turkey to use its proxies to continue genocide by extension—against Armenians in Nagorno-Karabakh, Kurds in Northern Syria and to eliminate what remains of the tiny religious minorities in Turkey. Erdogan does not hide his indifference towards the lives of religious minorities and with little regard to history or contemporary events he merely states that: *'It is not possible for a Muslim to commit genocide.'*[28] The evidence does not bear him out.

In the late 1990s, Lord Alton led a fact-finding mission to south-east Turkey on behalf of the human rights group, the Jubilee Campaign.

He subsequently published a report warning that the ancient churches of that region faced systematic destruction, detailing examples of individual atrocities and what he described as *'cultural genocide.'*

In the intervening period, little has changed. Turkey's tiny Christian minority—probably fewer than 100,000 people—Armenians, Syrian Orthodox, Roman Catholic, Chaldean, Greek and Syrian Catholic, Bulgarian Orthodox, Assyrians, and Protestants—still face systematic persecution.[29] Many are double minorities, coming from ethnic minority

---

[27] Ibid.

[28] Asbarez, 'Erdogan Defends al-Bashir, Says Muslims Incapable of Genocide' *Asbarez* (9 November 2009). Available at: http://asbarez.com/73093/erdogan-defends-al-bashir-says-muslims-incapable-of-genocide/.

[29] Demetrios Ioannou, "Bad news' for Turkey's marginalized Christians' *Politico* (5 August 2020). Available at: https://www.politico.com/news/2020/08/05/turkey-christians-hagia-sophia-392125.

groups as well as holding a different faith from the Muslim majority—
double minorities, doubly vulnerable and doubly endangered.

Lord Alton travelled through the militarised Kurdish areas in south-
east Turkey to visit the Tur Abdin region, the spiritual centre of the Syrian
Orthodox Church and stayed at the Mor Gabriel monastery established
some 1600 years ago. Until the turn of the twentieth century, there had
been some 200,000 Syriannis living in Tur Abdin. Today, the figure is
nearer 2000. Many Syrian Orthodox and Chaldean Catholic villages—
such as Hassana, Arbo, Habab, and Sedei—have been destroyed and
emptied of people. Many Christians have been beaten, injured, or killed.
At one time, the village of Kerburan had a population of some 1500
Christians, but even their graves have been desecrated.

The rise of Turkish nationalism and Islamist extremism has been exacerbated as Erdogan seeks to exclude ethnic and religious minorities,
inflaming what was already a fragile situation. Erdogan's gratuitous decisions to turn Istanbul's Hagia Sophia into a mosque is indicative of this
unwillingness to live with difference or to respect one another's traditions
or history.[30]

The Greek Orthodox Patriarch of Jerusalem, Theophilus III, was right
to recall that in previous epochs of history the seizure or destruction of
one another's sacred places and holy sites has led to centuries of bitterness
and hostility. He said:

> Our experience in Jerusalem is that to attempt to treat contested holy
> sites in an exclusive manner is simply a recipe for bitterness and suffering.
> When our holy sites are open to all, there is peace and mutual respect. (...)
> Turkey is a country with great potential to show the world the benefits of
> our common humanity and our common human destiny. The Orthodox
> world appeals to the Turkish government: We urge Turkey to live up to
> that potential, and show the world the value of coexistence between its
> various communities.[31]

---

[30] Dorian Jones, 'Turkey Battles Criticism Over Decision to Turn Hagia Sophia Into
Mosque' *VOA* (22 July 2020). Available at: https://www.voanews.com/europe/turkey-
battles-criticism-over-decision-turn-hagia-sophia-mosque.

[31] Greek Orthodox Patriarch of Jerusalem Theophilus III cited in ICN, 'Christian
responses to conversion of Hagia Sophia into mosque' ICN (27 July 2020). Available at:
https://www.indcatholicnews.com/news/40116.

Erdogan's agenda is a very different one. He sees himself as heir to the Ottoman Empire and staged the reopening of Hagia Sophia, as a mosque, to take place on the anniversary of the capture of Constantinople by Mehmet II—celebrating an act of conquest. This sequestration and usurping of buildings and artefacts is done with clinical precision and a purpose—it is to create the fiction, the lie, that these people no longer exist, that they are non-persons, and that no one much cares.

Erdogan's determination to change the status quo on the ground can also be seen in his invasion of North East Syria which we described in chapter five; the alleged use of chemical weapons against that population; the absorption of supporters of Daesh to fight alongside Turkey's army, and in the further displacement of 160,000 people—many from the religious minorities—and the ethnic cleansing and repopulation of the areas from which the minorities have been driven.[32] Thanks to Erdogan's military action, in one detention camp alone, where there had been 68,000 Daesh families, whom the Kurds had been holding prisoner, the Daesh flag has been flying again. And, once more along with Kurds, among those being hunted down by mercenaries and militias, enslaved, or killed, are a few surviving Armenians, Assyrian Christians, and Yazidis.[33]

When such a death warrant can be issued against a whole race—as happened with the Armenians—when outrageous brutality, mutilation, and violence are left to haunt a country's landscape, when despots can plan the ethnic cleansing or the annihilation of an entire people, it should be the subject of careful study—not least in our schools and universities. If you don't want history to repeat itself, you must at least be told truthfully about historical events and the role of your country in those events. The belief that no one really cares is what always encourages the tyrant.

Hitler believed he could invade Poland and do so with impunity. His *'final solution'* of the Jews was preceded by his notorious question: *'who after all, speaks today of the annihilation of the Armenians?'*[34] The same

---

[32] Patrick Cockburn, 'Erdogan's ethnic cleansing of the Kurds is still happening now—and we have Trump to thank' *The Independent* (15 November 2019). Available at: https://www.independent.co.uk/voices/erdogan-turkey-kurds-border-syria-war-trump-ethnic-cleansing-a9204581.html.

[33] See for example: https://www.securitycouncilreport.org/atf/cf/%7B65BFCF9B-6D27-4E9C-8CD3-CF6E4FF96FF9%7D/s_pv_8645.pdf.

[34] Adolf Hitler, Speech, 22 August 1939. Cited in Louis P. Lochner, *What About Germany?* (Dodd, Mead & Co.: New York, 1942) 1–4.

rationale—a culture of impunity—led to the industrialised murders of the concentration camps. The folly of forgetting—collective amnesia about what has gone before—led to Hitler's ideology of a purified Master-Race—directly inspired by the biological vision of a purified pan-Turkism, based on racial origins and racial superiority; even Hitler's corruption of medicine and science drew inspiration from the deliberate infecting of Armenians with typhus in a sequence of medical experiments.[35] To this day, the UK's Foreign Office has never been prepared to recognise the reality of Armenian genocide and defends Turkey as a potential ally in the *'fight against terror'* and as a *'NATO ally'*[36] and as a post-Brexit target trading partner.

Although the United States has taken much the same position as the UK, in 2019, the US House of Representatives decided that truth mattered more than pandering to Erdogan. Anna Eshoo, a Democrat Congresswoman from California, the only Armenian-Assyrian member of Congress said:

> I've been waiting for this moment since I first came to Congress 27 years ago… Members of my own family were among those murdered, and my parents fled with my grandparents to America. What all of the persecuted had in common was that they were Christians.[37]

In 2021, the US Administration recognised the atrocities in Armenia as genocide. The facts on the ground throughout the region bear out the scale of what has been allowed to occur. In 1914, Christians made up a quarter of the Middle East's population. Now they are less than 5%. Syria's Christian population has declined from 1.7 million in 2011 to below 450,000; in Iraq ethnic cleansing and genocide has reduced the ancient Christian population from 1.5 million in 2003 to below 120,000 today.[38] Archbishop Bashar Warda of Erbil has remarked: *'The world*

---

[35] Mustafa Karatepe, 'The role of Turkish physicians in the vaccination against typhus during the years of World War I' (2008) 42 Mikrobiyol Bul.

[36] House of Commons Deb, 24 May 2016, c411.

[37] Lindsay Wise, 'House Passes Resolution Commemorating Armenian Genocide' *WSJ* (29 October 2019). Available at: https://www.wsj.com/articles/house-passes-resolution-commemorating-armenian-genocide-11572385514.

[38] Bishop of Truro Review, 'Independent Review for the UK Foreign Secretary of Foreign and Commonwealth Office Support for Persecuted Christians' (2019). Available at: https://christianpersecutionreview.org.uk/.

should understand that on our path to extinction we will not go quietly any longer... so that, if some day we are gone, no one will be able to ask: how did this happen?'.[39]

This slow burn genocide began with the Armenians in 1915 and it hasn't ended yet. In 1942, Stefan Zweig (whose books were burnt by the Nazis) published *'The World of Yesterday – Memoirs of a European.'*[40] In it he describes how quickly a relatively civilised and humane society, and a seemingly permanent golden age, can be ruthlessly and swiftly destroyed. His masterful autobiography charts the rise of visceral hatred; how scapegoating and xenophobia, cultivated by populist leaders, can rapidly morph into genocide, and culminate in the hecatombs of the concentration camps.[41]

A fatal chain of events stretches from the Turkish genocide of the Armenians to Hitler's concentration camps and to the depredations of Stalin's gulags and Mao's Cultural Revolution; from the pestilential nature of persecution, demonisation, scapegoating, and hateful prejudice, to the recent genocides against Christians and other minorities in Iraq and Syria and to the razed villages of Rohingya in Burma/Myanmar to the horrific atrocities in Northern Nigeria to the concentration camps of Xinjiang. When innocent human beings are murdered because of their identify, whether religious, ethnic, or other, it is inexpressibly tragic and hauntingly cruel. It is a moral outrage that whole swathes of humanity are murdered, terrorised, victimised, intimidated, deprived of their belongings and driven from their homes, simply because of the way they worship or practise their faith.

When a regime tries to control what you believe, it will generally seek to control every other aspect of your life. Where Christians are persecuted, other human rights are often brutally abused. But as the story of the Armenians demonstrates, the failure to hear and respond to the alert of danger sounded by the canary in the mine has far reaching and lethal consequences. It is hard not to conjecture that if, in 1896 or 1915, the world had saved the Armenians—or after World War I had held those

[39] Cited in ACN, 'The future of Christians in Iraq, five years after ISIS invasion' (12 August 2019). Available at: https://www.churchinneed.org/the-future-of-christians-in-iraq-five-years-after-isis-invasion/.

[40] Stefan Zweig, 'The World of Yesterday—Memoirs of a European' (Pushkin Press, 2011).

[41] Ibid.

responsible to account—Hitler might not have so cavalierly believed he could strike against the Jews with impunity.

1.1   A Slow Burn Genocide: Nagorno-Karabakh and the 'Leftover of the Sword'

The size of Belgium, Armenia is a landlocked country. Iran is to the south of Armenia and Georgia to the north. To the west it has a closed border with Turkey and to the east a closed border with Azerbaijan—with whom it remains at war over the disputed territory of Nagorno-Karabakh. In 2020, that unresolved conflict erupted once more when Azerbaijan, with the support and encouragement of Turkey, launched a major military offensive on Nagorno-Karabakh. It has been described as being a part of a 'slow burn' genocide.[42]

In 2007, Lord Alton visited Nagorno-Karabakh with his parliamentary colleague, Baroness Cox. Armenia's capital, Yerevan, looks longingly westward to the snow-capped Armenian holy mountain of Ararat where Noah's ark is said to have had its final resting place. Armenians believe that they are descended from Haik, one of Noah's sons. Today, the mountain, along with the ruins of the ancient capital, Ani, is, as Armenians say, 'trapped behind enemy lines'—part of eastern Turkey.

After the genocide of 1915–16, and the culmination of World War I, what remained of ancient Armenia—the first nation to embrace Christianity, some 1700 years ago—was subsumed into the Soviet Union. Stalin and his successors kept it firmly within the Soviet empire until Communism collapsed in 1991.[43] Stalin's ruthless policy of 'divide and rule' accompanied by mass deportations and the horrors of the Gulags led him to encourage ethnic tensions in the southern Caucuses between the Azeris and Armenians. Throughout the 1920s, Stalin created boundaries that placed Armenian villages deep inside Azerbaijan and vice-versa and, in particular, he placed Nagorno-Karabakh (mountainous black garden),

[42] More on the issue, see: Melanie O'Brien and Suren Manukyan, 'Genocide Risk in Nagorno-Karabakh' (2021) International Law under Construction. Available at: https://grojil.org/2021/01/04/genocide-risk-in-nagorno-karabakh/.

[43] The Guardian, 'Post-soviet world: what you need to know about Armenia' The Guardian (9 June 2014). Available at: https://www.theguardian.com/world/2014/jun/09/-sp-post-soviet-world-need-to-know-armenia.

whose population was largely Armenian, and had initially been promised autonomy, inside Azerbaijan.

Throughout the 1930s and 1940s, Stalin tried to systematically destroy Armenian culture and national identity. During the 1930s, at least 100,000 Armenians were victims of his purges and all the churches, except Ejmiatsin, the seat of the Catholicos (the senior ecclesiastical leader of the Apostolic Armenian Church), were closed.[44] In 1938, even Ejmiatsin was suppressed[45] and the Catholicos Khoren I was murdered.[46] Every church in Nagorno-Karabakh was shut and Archbishop Pargev Martirosyan, the Primate of Shushi, the fortress city of Karabakh, told Lord Alton how one wave of horror was followed by another. One of his Episcopal predecessors had been decapitated by the Turks at the time of the genocide, his great-uncle, a priest, was murdered, all the churches and monasteries were closed by Stalin, and as recently as the 1990s *'Armenian soldiers were literally crucified'* during the war with Azerbaijan.

In 1985, after the ascent to power of Mikhail Gorbachev, Armenians began to reclaim their national identity. In Nagorno-Karabakh, there were demonstrations demanding its transfer from Azerbaijan to Armenia. In 1988, it seceded, and Moscow imposed direct rule. A rebellion erupted. Armenia declared Nagorno-Karabakh to be part of Armenia. Azerbaijan and Turkey responded by closing their borders and imposing a blockade. The collapse of the Soviet Union led to a referendum in which the people of Armenia voted for independence. Azerbaijan followed suit and a war erupted between them over Karabakh. 25,000 died before an uneasy ceasefire was agreed in 1994.[47] Despite the technical halt of hostilities, every few months new lives continued to be claimed by snipers and Karabakh remained scarred and pock-marked by the ravages of war, not least by the presence of deadly land mines.

---

[44] Elisabeth Bauer-Manndorff, *Armenia: Past and Present* (Armenian Prelacy: New York, 1981) 178.

[45] George Bournoutian, *A Concise History of the Armenian People* (Mazda Publishers: Costa Mesa, California, 2006) 323.

[46] Christopher J. Walker, *Armenia: The Survival of a Nation* (St. Martin's Pres: New York, 1990) 368.

[47] The Guardian, 'Nagorno-Karabakh: Azeri-Armenian ceasefire agreed in disputed region' *The Guardian* (5 April 2016). Available at: https://www.theguardian.com/world/2016/apr/05/nagorno-karabakh-azeri-armenian-ceasefire-agreed.

In 2007, Lord Alton, who also visited Azerbaijan—including its refugee camps—warned that failure to find a long-term settlement meant that *'the war could erupt again at any time.'* In 2007, the President of Karabakh, Bako Sahakian, told Lord Alton that *'step by step, we are working to build a fully-fledged civil society,'* and he said he was committed to solving the conflict *'by peaceful means'* and was emphatic that he was *'ready to initiate direct negotiations with Azerbaijan.'*

The failure to broker a long-term solution meant that the conditions continued to exist for the conflict to erupt once more—as they did in 2020. Furthermore, the decision by Azerbaijan not to resettle people who had been displaced from Karabakh and to leave them in festering refugee camps created a propaganda narrative rather than a reason to find solutions for everyone who has suffered from this painful conflict.

As long ago as 1992, the international community established the Minsk Group—co-chaired by Russia, the United States, and France—to find a solution.[48]

In considering its failure to achieve progress, it would be worth drawing some parallels with the UK's own troubled enclave of Northern Ireland; and the role which a mediator was able to play. But it is a given that for a mediator to make progress in peace building there has to be a renunciation of violence and end to the demonising of the other party. There has to be a willingness to allow people themselves to decide their future and a referendum of all those who lived there before the hostilities began. The democratic decision determines the future of the territory must then be given internationally recognised and guaranteed status. But a referendum would be worthless if one or other party is determined to annihilate the other. Karabakh is not the only disputed area in the Caucuses. Chechnya, Ossetia, and Abkhazia are three of the better known—and if a peaceful solution could be found in Karabakh it would have a positive effect on them all—but, in the case of Nagorno-Karabakh, there remains both the haunting memory of the Armenian genocide, the continuing refusal to recognise it for what it was, and the spectre of a slow burn genocide hovering over its future. The simple choice is between peaceful co-existence and the ever-present threat of extinction.

In 2007, Lord Alton noted that after Armenians re-established control over their enclave *'the churches and monasteries of Karabakh have reopened*

---

[48] OSCE, The Minsk Group. Available at: https://www.osce.org/minsk-group/108306.

and its towns and stunning countryside have gradually returned to normality but political leaders and diplomats need to match those endeavours by building relationships based on co-existence and by finding a lasting and just settlement for Armenians and Azeri alike.'

In 2020, the choice which Azerbaijan decided to make was based on conquest rather than co-existence, and it instigated a full-scale military assault on Nagorno-Karabakh. It did this with the encouragement and support of Turkey's President Erdogan. And he made no secret of his objectives or motivations. For Erdogan this is the unfinished business of the Armenian genocide—fulfilling the mission of the grandfathers. On a number of occasions, he has referred to the Armenians as '*Leftover of the sword*' (*kılıç artığı* in Turkish)—a commonly used insult in Turkey that refers to the survivors of the Christian massacres which targeted Armenians, Greeks, and Assyrians in the Ottoman Empire—and an explicit and overt threat to complete what had been begun in the Armenian genocide.[49]

The '*softening up*' which invariably occurs before the unleashing of such ferocious actions can often be seen in foreshadowing propaganda and controlled media outlets. Before the attacks in Nagorno-Karabakh, those who had been monitoring mass media and social media networks reported examples of incitement to hatred encouraging violence, including calls for killings, spread from both Turkish and Azerbaijani sources.

On 27 September 2020, those incitements culminated in Azerbaijan's launch of a large-scale military attack on Nagorno-Karabakh—endangering the lives of the 150,000 Armenians who live there—and unilaterally ending the 1994 cease fire.[50] Turkey has made no secret of its involvement in the attacks, *New York Times* journalists identified Turkish F-16 fire jets in a satellite image from Azerbaijan and a Turkish military jet shot down an Armenian plane on the territory of the Republic

---

[49] Genocide Watch, 'Turkey: Erdogan uses "Leftovers of the Sword" anti-Christian hate speech' Genocide Watch (11 May 2020). Available at: https://www.genocidewatch.com/single-post/2020/05/11/turkey-erdogan-uses-leftovers-of-the-sword-anti-christian-hate-speech.

[50] BBC, 'Armenia and Azerbaijan fight over disputed Nagorno-Karabakh' *BBC News* (27 September 2020). Available at: https://www.bbc.co.uk/news/world-europe-543 14341.

of Armenia. The assault was pre-planned and closely coordinated by Azerbaijan and Turkey.[51]

Within the conflict zone journalists have been targeted and Azerbaijan has banned access to foreign media other than Turkish Government-controlled media, who were embedded with the assault force. Reports broadcast to home audiences in Azerbaijan have frequently been inflammatory, propagandistic, and intended to caricature their Armenian opponents. Azerbaijan has also been accused of deploying foreign mercenaries transferred from Syria by Turkey—and accused of war crimes. President Emmanuel Macron said '*We now have information which indicates that Syrian fighters from jihadist groups have (transited) through Gaziantep (south eastern Turkey) to reach the Nagorno-Karabakh theatre of operations. It is a very serious new fact, which changes the situation.*'[52]

During their assault on Karabakh, Azerbaijan's armed forces attacked more than 150 civilian settlements, including densely populated ones (including the capital, Stepanakert, the towns of Shushi, Hadrut, Martuni, Martakert, Askeran, Karvajar, Berdzor, villages of Taghaser, Vardashat, Spitakshen, Maghavus, Nerkin Horatagh, Alashan, and Mataghis) with aerial, artillery, rocket and tank fire strikes, most of which were targeted or indiscriminate killing and injuring civilians—displacing an estimated 70,000 people, half of Nagorno-Karabakh's population. Reports also suggested that Azerbaijan has used white phosphorus—not covered by the Chemical Weapons Convention—but the use of which is a war crime. It has been used by Russia in Ukraine. Turkey has also been accused of using white phosphorous against civilian populations in northern Syria,[53] an issue which Lord Alton has raised with the UK Government and with international organisations.

Azerbaijan twice shelled Shushi's Holy Saviour Cathedral, causing substantial damage to a sacred religious site or immense significance

---

[51] Andrew E. Kramer, 'Armenia and Azerbaijan: What Sparked War and Will Peace Prevail?' *New York Times* (21 January 2021). Available at: https://www.nytimes.com/article/armenian-azerbaijan-conflict.html.

[52] John Irish and Michal Rose, 'France accuses Turkey of sending Syrian jihadists to Nagorno-Karabakh' *Reuters* (1 October 2020). Available at: https://www.reuters.com/article/us-armenia-azerbaijan-putin-macron-idUSKBN26L3SB.

[53] HART, 'Update on the Conflict in Nagorno-Karabakh (Artsakh)' (2 November 2020). Available at: https://www.hart-uk.org/news/update-on-the-conflict-in-nagorno-karabakh-artsakh/.

to Armenians. Armenian cross stones and other cultural monuments were also destroyed by Azerbaijani fire in different parts of Karabakh.[54] Attacks have also been made on the territory of Armenia—resulting in civilian casualties and the destruction of critical infrastructure. Amnesty International confirmed that residential areas of Nagorno-Karabakh were bombed by cluster munitions, the use of which is banned under international humanitarian law, general rules of governing the conduct of hostilities.[55]

Attention has also been drawn to Azeri media reports which appear to show extensively abused bodies of local combatants from the Karabakh defence force. Both Armenia and Nagorno-Karabakh have supported the calls of the Minsk Group, and the international community for negotiations. By contrast, Azerbaijan and Turkey initially made bellicose statements that negotiations would only be possible after they had changed '*the status quo on the ground*' and conquered Nagorno-Karabakh.[56]

Then, on 10 November 2020, Armenia, Azerbaijan, and Russia signed an agreement to end military conflict. However, as Baroness Cox, who travelled to the region during the 2020 invasion reported:

Serious concerns nevertheless remain, with reports emerging of brutality inflicted on military and civilian prisoners, including torture and beheadings, with claims that equivalent brutalities have been perpetrated by jihadists who receive payment for every Armenian beheaded.[57]

In the light of the Azerbaijan's actions and emerging evidence, *Genocide Watch*, a non-governmental organisation led by Gregory Stanton, a

[54] BBC, 'Nagorno-Karabakh: Armenia accuses Azerbaijan of targeting cathedral' *BBC News* (8 October 2020). Available at: https://www.bbc.co.uk/news/world-europe-544 65172.

[55] Amnesty International, 'Armenia/Azerbaijan: Civilians must be protected from use of banned cluster bombs' (5 October 2020). Available at: https://www.amnesty.org/en/latest/news/2020/10/armenia-azerbaijan-civilians-must-be-protected-from-use-of-banned-cluster-bombs/.

[56] Alexander Gabuev, 'Viewpoint: Russia and Turkey—unlikely victors of Karabakh conflict' *BBC* (12 November 2020) Available at: https://www.bbc.co.uk/news/world-europe-54903869.

[57] Baroness Cox, Statement of 10 November 2020. See: https://www.politicshome.com/thehouse/article/the-uk-government-must-change-tack-and-urgently-bring-to-justice-those-responsible-for-war-crimes-against-the-armenian-people.

world-renowned genocide expert, issued a Genocide Emergency Alert. According to *Genocide Watch*:

> Although a paper ceasefire was signed on October 15, 2020, Azerbaijani forces are still attempting to capture new territory. Azerbaijan uses laser-guided drones from Turkey, Russia, and Israel to attack Artsakh's defenders, who are mostly Artsakh civilian volunteers. Azerbaijan is using Syrian mercenaries. Azerbaijan's political ally, Turkey, provides air support for Azerbaijani forces, sparking fears that Turkey will resume the Armenian Genocide of 1915–1922.[58]

Genocide Watch goes on to say:

> Azerbaijan denies displaced Armenians the right to return to Azerbaijan and forbids a person of Armenian heritage from entering Azerbaijan's territory. If Azerbaijan retakes control of Artsakh (Nagorno-Karabakh), it could forcibly deport all Armenians in Artsakh to Armenia. Forced displacement is a crime against humanity. The Azerbaijani government under Ilham Aliyev denies its past and current violence against Armenians. Aliyev is also a denier of the 1915 Armenian Genocide committed by the Ottoman Empire. The Azerbaijani government promotes hate speech and encourages violence against Armenians.[59]

Genocide Watch identified several early warnings of genocide and issued a statement that it considers Azerbaijan to be engaging in '*Stage 8: Persecution*' and '*Stage 10: Denial*' of the Ten Stages of Genocide. However, shortly afterwards, *Genocide Watch* updated this to '*Stage 9: Extermination*' and '*Stage 10: Denial*.' The warning of genocide was followed by several recommendations to address the unfolding atrocities. A similar genocide warning was issued by several experts and members of the *International Association of Genocide Scholars*. They emphasised that:

> history, from the Armenian genocide to the last three decades of conflict, as well as current political statements, economic policies, sentiments of the societies and military actions by the Azerbaijani and Turkish leadership

---

[58] Genocide Watch, 'Genocide Emergency Alert on the War in Artsakh' (6 November 2020). Available at: https://www.genocidewatch.com/single-post/genocide-emergency-alert-on-the-war-in-artsakh-nagorno-karabakh.

[59] Ibid.

should warn us that genocide of the Armenians in Nagorno-Karabakh, and perhaps even Armenia, is a very real possibility. All of this proves that Armenians can face slaughter if any Armenian territory is occupied, consequently recognizing of the independence of the Republic of Artsakh is the way to save Armenians of Artsakh from extermination now or in the near future.[60]

Despite the ceasefire, we would be wrong to disregard or to set aside the warnings and findings of these experts. 100 years ago, Armenians were betrayed. What a double tragedy if we allowed further atrocities of a genocidal nature to occur on our watch.

1.2   Is It Too Late to Describe Atrocities Against the Armenians as a Genocide?

The atrocities against the Armenians were perpetrated three decades before the Genocide Convention came into being. Nevertheless, this does not preclude the naming of these atrocities as a genocide. Indeed, the Preamble of the Genocide Convention recognised the existence of previous genocides, even if without a name at the time, stating that '*at all periods of history genocide has inflicted great losses on humanity.*'

The Armenian genocide took place between 1915 and 1923 when 1.5 million ethnic Armenians were arrested, deported, or murdered by the Ottoman Empire. When discussing the atrocities, Geoffrey Robertson QC, a renowned barrister, concluded that:

> the evidence is compelling that the Ottoman State is responsible, on the legal principles discussed…, for what would now be described as genocide. Those running that state in 1915 must have known what was apparent to unbiased foreign observers, and their racist intention may be inferred, not just from their reported statements, but from their knowledge of racial and religious pogroms in 1894-96 and 1909; their deliberate fanning of racial superiority theories in the Turkification programme; the deportation orders and their foresight of the consequences; their failure to protect the deportees or to punish their attackers, some of whom were state agents. They instigated, or at very least acquiesced in, the killing of a significant

---

[60] Genocide Museum, 'Statement from a group of Genocide scholars on the Imminent Genocidal Threat deriving from Azerbaijan and Turkey against Artsakh (Nagorno-Karabakh).' Available at: http://www.genocide-museum.am/eng/23.10.2020.php.

part of the Armenian race-probably about half of those who were alive in Eastern Turkey at the beginning of 1915... if these same events occurred today, in a country with a history similar to Turkey's in 1915, there can be no doubt that prosecutions for genocide would be warranted and indeed required by the Genocide Convention.[61]

Despite the overwhelming evidence, just 33 countries currently recognise the crimes to which the Armenian people were subjected as a genocide. This failure to recognise past genocides and to name them for what they are is not insignificant. Such denialism, and associated impunity for the crimes committed, inevitably results in further atrocities. But Turkey should note that despite its threats to countries which recognise the Armenian genocide, the issue never goes away and will not do so until Turkey itself honestly recognises this chapter in its history for the infamy which it was.

Unhealed history can never and should never be suppressed. As a child, Lord Alton's grandfather gave him pictures of Armenians, executed by the Ottomans, during their retreat, after the capture of Jerusalem, in December 1917, by General Edmund Allenby's Egyptian Expeditionary Force, in which his grandfather served. Whether through the oral, or written word, history finds its voice in the future generations.

In 1933, Franz Werfel published his novel, *'The Forty Days of Musa Dagh,'* set during the Armenian genocide. Werfel tells the story of several thousand Christians who took refuge on the mountain of Musa Dagh (the mountain of Moses). The intervention of the French navy led to their dramatic rescue. His books were burnt by the Nazis, no doubt to give effect to Hitler's determination that the Armenians would not be remembered.[62] Despite numerous attempts by Armenians to have Werfel's novel made into a movie, Turkish pressure has prevented it from reaching a mass audience. Not only should we recall and give new definitions to those terrible events, giving the lie to Hitler's question *'who now remembers the Armenians?'*—insisting that we will never forget—but also because that deadly phenomenon of deportations, concentration camps, rape and killings did not end in 1915 with the Ottomans. Hitler simply believed

---

[61] Geoffrey Robertson, 'Was There an Armenian Genocide?' (2010) 4 University of St. Thomas Journal of Law and Public Policy 106.

[62] Adolf Hitler, Speech, 22 August 1939. Cited in Louis P. Lochner, *What About Germany?* (Dodd, Mead & Co.: New York, 1942) 1–4.

that people's indifference meant that he too could mass murder with impunity. He correctly assumed that people would murmur but take little action as he began his campaign of Jewish annihilation.

There is an old Armenian saying, echoed in Musa Dagh, that *'to be an Armenian is an impossibility'*[63]—a saying which had equal applicability to the Jews of Hitler's Germany. That impossibility of being able to be who you are is a wretched experience shared today by minorities the world over, including persecuted Christians—from North Korea to Pakistan, from China to Sudan—where an orgy of crimes are directed against them, leading Prince Charles to describe it as *'an indescribable tragedy.'*[64] In that remark he was referring specifically to what has happened to Christians in the Middle East.[65] The numbers starkly illustrate the scale of that tragedy. Just as the Armenian genocide was beginning, the last census of the Ottoman era, was being conducted and as we documented earlier, just a fraction of the people of the ancient Christians still live in their ancestral homeland.

This indescribable tragedy happened because we did not listen to the Armenians when they sought our help. It happened because we chose to forget the Armenians. It happened because we allowed the perpetrators to believe that we didn't care; that their crimes would carry no consequences. Unless we urgently recalibrate our response to the remaining besieged communities of the Middle East what began with the Armenians will prove fatal for the rest. Even today's Armenians, living in their homeland and in the enclave of Nagorno-Karabakh, face the ever-present danger of constant unspeakable acts, motivated by the same hatred which ignited the genocide of 1915.

2   WHAT ABOUT THE NORTH KOREAN POLITICIDE?

Other situations from which news of mass atrocities has emerged include North Korea (DPRK). These reports have been emerging for many years.

---

[63] Cited in Yair Auron, *Banality of Indifference: Zionism and the Armenian Genocide* (Transaction Publishers: New Brunswick, N.J., 2000) 296–300.

[64] Cited in BBC, 'Prince Charles says Christian persecution in Middle East "a tragedy"' *BBC* (4 November 2014). Available at: https://www.bbc.co.uk/news/uk-29899571.

[65] Ibid.

For example, in 2003, David Hawk produced a chilling report entitled 'The Hidden Gulag,'[66] first of the series, shedding light on:

> multifaceted network of large-scale political prison camps… Hidden Gulag sought to expose North Korea's prison camp system to a much larger international public by providing descriptions of the prisons and labour camps based on the interview testimonies of 30 former prisoners who fled North Korea and resettled in South Korea. And, for the first time in a human rights report, satellite photographs of the prison camps, in which the former prisoners identified their residence units, work sites, and other landmarks, buttressed the prisoners' testimony.[67]

In 2004, a BBC documentary documented examples of lethal chemical weapons tests against civilians, and particularly, on women and children, the families of dissidents and political prisoners held in secret jails.[68] The UK Government agreed that there was *'cruel and inhuman treatment in those kinds of facilities'* but that *'on wider issues of human rights, the North Koreans are finding it hard to engage with us, we shall persist.'* In later remarks, the Minister said *'There can be no possible excuse for such experimentation involving whole families being herded into rooms and subjected to lethal conditions. It was disgusting and appalling to see.'*[69]

Subsequently, at a conference in Warsaw, Professor Leon Kieres explained that *'hundreds of thousands of people have lost their lives in the camps,'* and estimated that, 'about 150–200,000 prisoners are still being held in them.'[70] One defector and prison inmate, Lee Young-Kuk, graphically described the degrading situation in prison:

> From the very first day, the guards with their rifles beat me. I was trampled on mercilessly until my legs became swollen, my eardrums were shattered, and my teeth were all broken. They wouldn't allow us to sleep from 4 am till 10 pm and once while I was sleeping, they poured water over my head.

---

[66] David Hawk, 'The Hidden Gulag' (2003).

[67] David Hawk, 'The Hidden Gulag IV' (2015) 3.

[68] BBC, 'Access to Evil' *BBC* (1 February 2004). Available at: http://www.bbc.co.uk/pressoffice/pressreleases/stories/2004/02_february/01/korea.shtml.

[69] House of Lords Deb, 3 February 2004, c547.

[70] House of Lords Deb, 21 April 2004, c292.

Since the conditions within the prison were poor, my head became frost-bitten from the bitter cold. As I was trying to recuperate from the previous mistreatment, they ordered me to stick out my shackled feet, through a hole on my cell door, and then tortured them in almost every possible way. Not a single day passed without receiving some form of torture and agonizing experience.

Forced repatriation to these prisons, in breach of China's obligations under the UN Convention Relating to the Status of Refugees, has led to cruel treatment and even execution of repatriated refugees. The UNHCR is denied unimpaired access, both in the DPRK and in China. Only last week, the Jubilee Campaign reported that the Chinese shot dead a North Korean attempting to enter Mongolia. Seventeen others were arrested. At the Warsaw Conference organised by the Citizens' Alliance for North Korean Human Rights, Byyn Nanee described to me her treatment in China and how her brother was executed after repatriation.[71]

At the end of 2006, in a parliamentary debate on modern day slavery, Lord Alton returned to the human rights violations affecting North Korea's people:

During the famine of the 1990s, around 50,000 North Koreans fled to China's Jilin province. The exodus was spurred by a mixture of starvation, political oppression, and economic necessity. Leaving North Korea without permission is a criminal offence that can carry the death penalty. Once deported, people will spend between one and three months in a prison labour camp in which they are likely to become malnourished, live in unsanitary conditions and be subjected to forced labour. From those who have escaped, there are testimonies of beatings, torture, degrading treatment, and even forced abortions and infanticide.

The workday in a prison camp begins at five in the morning and ends at seven or eight in the evening. Pregnant, elderly, and sick women are not exempt from the work. Types of labour include farming, construction, collecting heavy logs and brick making. For meals they are given a meagre quantity of corn and soup. The hard-labour leads to a high number of fatalities. There are many first-hand accounts which attest to malnourishment, appalling hygiene, and an absence of medical care to treat illness or injury. However, you choose to define it, this is slavery.[72]

---

[71] David Alton and Rob Chidley, *Building Bridges: Is There Hope for North Korea?* (Lion Hudson, 2013) 118.

[72] House of Lord Deb, 19 December 2006, c1963.

In 2010, Lord Alton and Baroness Cox of Queensbury published their report *'Building Bridges, Not Walls: The Case for Constructive, Critical Engagement with North Korea'* in which they raised *'a number of serious concerns over the grave, systematic and widespread violation of human rights, including reported executions, abuses in prison camps, torture, violations of religious freedom, women's rights, child rights, disabled rights, and humanitarian concerns including malnutrition.'*[73]

The report states that:

> It is almost impossible to obtain accurate figures for the number of North Korean refugees in China, but it is estimated that as many as 300,000 have fled over the years, and are mostly in hiding in Jilin province along the border with the DPRK. At least 50,000 are believed to be in China currently, while an estimated 20,000 are in South Korea, having endured an epic journey through China and South-East Asia or Mongolia to reach Seoul. A few thousand are now in Europe and the United States.[74]

In 2013, international outrage led to the UN Human Rights Council finally establishing the Commission of Inquiry on Human Rights in the Democratic People's Republic of Korea (UN Commission of Inquiry)[75] to investigate the systematic, widespread and grave violations of human rights in the DPRK, and to ensure *'full accountability, in particular where these violations may amount to crimes against humanity.'*[76] In 2014, the UN Commission of Inquiry, led by the Australian jurist, Justice Michael Kirby published its findings. It found that crimes against humanity have been perpetrated in the DPRK and concluded that:

> 1160. (...) crimes against humanity have been committed in the Democratic People's Republic of Korea, pursuant to policies established at the highest level of the state. These crimes against humanity are on-going,

---

[73] Lord Alton and Baroness Cox of Queensbury, 'Building Bridges, Not Walls: The Case for Constructive, Critical Engagement with North Korea' (2010). Available at: http://www.jubileecampaign.org/BuildBridgesNotWalls.pdf.

[74] Ibid., 29.

[75] UN Human Rights Council, 'Situation of human rights in the Democratic People's Republic of Korea', 9 April 2013, A/HRC/RES/22/13. Available at: https://www.sec uritycouncilreport.org/atf/cf/%7B65BFCF9B-6D27-4E9C-8CD3-CF6E4FF96FF9%7D/ a_hrc_res_22_13.pdf.

[76] Ibid., 5.

because the policies, institutions and patterns of impunity that lie at their root remain in place.

1161. Persons detained in political prison camps (*kwanliso*) and other prison camps, those who try to flee the country, adherents to the Christian religion and others considered to introduce subversive influences are subjected to crimes against humanity. This occurs as part of a systematic and widespread attack of the state against anyone who is considered to pose a threat to the political system and leadership of the Democratic People's Republic of Korea. The foregoing attack is embedded in the larger patterns of politically motivated human rights violations experienced by the general population, including the discriminatory system of classification based on *songbun*.

1162. In addition, crimes against humanity have been committed against starving populations. These crimes are sourced in decisions and policies violating the universal human right to food. They were taken for purposes of sustaining the present political system, in full awareness that they would exacerbate starvation and contribute to related deaths. Many of the policies that gave rise to crimes against humanity continue to be in place, including the deliberate failure to provide reliable data on the humanitarian situation in the Democratic People's Republic of Korea, denial of free and unimpeded international humanitarian access to populations in need, and discriminatory spending and food distribution.

1163. Finally, crimes against humanity have been, and are still being, committed against persons from the Republic of Korea, Japan and other countries who were systematically abducted or denied repatriation to gain labour and other skills for the Democratic People's Republic of Korea. These persons are victims of ongoing crimes of enforced disappearance. Officials who fail to acknowledge their deprivation of liberty or fail to provide available information about their fate and whereabouts may also incur criminal responsibility, even if they did not themselves participate in the original abduction or denial of repatriation.[77]

The UN Commission of Inquiry also made this damning statement:

1164. In the DPRK, international crimes appear to be intrinsic to the fabric of the state. The system is pitiless, pervasive and with few equivalents in modern international affairs. The fact that such enormous crimes could be going on for such a long time is an affront to universal human rights.

---

[77] UN Human Rights Council, Report of the detailed findings of the Commission of Inquiry on human rights in the Democratic People's Republic of Korea, 7 February 2014, A/HRC/25/CRP.1, 1164.

These crimes must cease immediately. It is the duty of the DPRK and, failing that, the responsibility of the international community to ensure that this is done without delay.[78]

Although the UN Commission of Inquiry found evidence of crimes against humanity, it emphasised that the atrocities fall short of the definition of genocide, set out in Article II of the Genocide Convention. This is as the targeted group, the political opposition, was not a recognised 'protected group' within the mandate of the Convention. The UN Commission of Inquiry emphasised that the atrocities including '*hundreds of thousands of inmates have [being] exterminated in political prison camps and other places over a span of more than five decades… in conformity with the intent to eliminate class enemies and factionalists over the course of three generations, entire groups of people, including families with their children, have perished in the prison camps because of who they were and not for what they had personally done (…) might be described as a "politicide".*' However, in a non-technical sense, some observers would question why the conduct detailed above was not also, by analogy, genocide.[79]

The UN Commission of Inquiry went on to consider whether the specific targeting of Christians in North Korea, and particularly during the 1950s and 1960s, might meet the legal definition of genocide. The UN Commission of Inquiry concluded that:

> based on the Democratic People's Republic of Korea's own figures, that the proportion of religious adherents among the DPRK's population, who were mainly Christians, Chondoists and Buddhists, dropped from close to 24 per cent in 1950 to 0.016 per cent in 2002. The Commission also received information about purges targeting religious believers in the 1950s and 1960s. However, the Commission was not in a position to gather enough information to make a determination as to whether the authorities at the time sought to repress organized religion by extremely violent means or whether they were driven by the intent to physically annihilate the followers of particular religions as a group. This is a subject that

[78] UN Human Rights Council, Report of the detailed findings of the Commission of Inquiry on human rights in the Democratic People's Republic of Korea, 7 February 2014, A/HRC/25/CRP.1, 1164.

[79] Ibid., 1158.

would require thorough historical research that is difficult or impossible to undertake without access to the relevant archives of the DPRK.[80]

In the eight years since the publication of the report, the international community has shamefully failed to demonstrate its resolve in bringing to justice—however long that may take—these responsible for what the UN Commission of Inquiry unequivocally said are *'crimes against humanity.'* In the intervening eight years further evidence has emerged of the targeting of specific groups—particularly religious believers—which may well take those crimes beyond the threshold of genocide.

In 2013, in *'Building Bridges: Is there hope for North Korea?'* Lord Alton records examples of mass atrocities—instances of which have been emerging from escapees for many years.

Among the witness statements are first-hand testimonies from North Korean Christians given during hearings in Westminster but deadly control of the population and tightly controlled access to the country have been used to impede the flow of information to the world beyond the so-called Hermit Kingdom.

Both China and North Korea use information blockades to conceal the extent, nature, and gravity of the appalling crimes for which they are responsible. They stop information from reaching their citizens (in defiance of Article 19 of the Universal Declaration of Human Rights) and do all in their power to stop information from getting out.

But the 30,000 brave people who have managed to escape from the North have circumvented the problem of not being able to enter the country to collect first-hand witness statements from within the jurisdiction.

Some of that evidence is referred to in more than 400 interventions in Parliament which Lord Alton has made in since 2002. These interventions are part of the compelling case that the UK Government—and the international community—cannot hide behind the fig leaf that it was somehow unaware of these egregious and monstrous crimes.

2.1 Genocide Against Religious Minorities?

While the Commission of Inquiry did not feel able to make a determination of genocide, the evidence in relation to targeted religious minorities

---

[80] Ibid., 1159.

suggests that the question is still on the table and should be re-examined. Some of the evidence is discussed here.

It begins with an edict for the first of the three Kims.

Kim Il-sung once declared that, *'religious people should die to cure their habit.'*[81] And for the past 70 years that is exactly what has happened.

In *'Building Bridges: Is there hope for North Korea?'* Lord Alton details the history of Christianity in North Korea, whose capital, Pyongyang, was known as *'the Jerusalem of the East.'*

Ten years before its publication he described, in 2003, evidence of the specific targeting of Christians in North Korea:

> Becoming a Christian in North Korea is a serious crime. Many are thrown into camps or prison, where they are kept in horrific conditions. There is evidence of water torture, severe beatings, sexual assault, and violation, as well as psychological and verbal abuse. Up to 1 million people are incarcerated in the gulags of North Korea. On 2nd March at the 4th International Conference on North Korean Human Rights and Refugees held in Prague, the catalogue of human rights abuses was systematically documented. Professor Man-ho Heo, Professor of Law at Kyungpook National University, listed the human rights abuses in the detention camps. According to the Sunday Times of 9th March, children of the elite, and, bizarrely, children born as triplets, are taken from their parents by the age of two. They are placed in special schools to break family bonds and to indoctrinate them with the ideology of the regime.
>
> The regime teaches its children to hate the outside world, especially the United States. Simultaneously, the late Kim Il-sung has been elevated and is revered as a god to be followed with unswerving devotion. In 1998, Médecins Sans Frontiers pulled out of North Korea because aid agencies were denied access to the so-called 9-27 camps in which sick and disabled children were dumped under a decree issued by Kim to "normalise" the country.
>
> This repressive and powerfully armed Communist regime has subjugated its own people and now threatens and blackmails the world's democracies. It does so by threatening nuclear war unless the free world accedes to its demands. In particular, it insists that the international community recognises the permanence of its borders and continues to pay Danegeld. In any agreements made with this regime, human rights practices must be established and subsequently monitored. This was the

[81] *The Selected Works of Kim Il-sung, Vol 5* (Publisher of Workers' Party of Korea, 1972) 154.

process which was used by the US Government in negotiations with the Soviet Union in 1972, and it should form an integral part of any political security negotiations with Kim Jong-il.[82]

In 2014, the UN Commission of Inquiry concluded that Christians have been singled out for especially brutal treatment and that this is, *'a state that does not have any parallel in the contemporary world.'*[83] It says that the regime *'considers the spread of Christianity a particularly severe threat'*, and that what is happening resembles, *'the horrors of camps that totalitarian states established during the twentieth century.'*

The UN Commission of Inquiry found *'there is an almost complete denial of the right to freedom of thought, conscience and religion, as well as of the rights to freedom of opinion, expression, information and association'*; *'Christians are prohibited from practising their religion and are persecuted'* and that *'Severe punishments are inflicted on "people caught practising Christianity".'*[84] It catalogued crimes against humanity, that included *'extermination, murder, enslavement, torture, imprisonment, rape, forced abortions,'* as well as severe religious persecution, enforced disappearances, and starvation, and that *'unspeakable atrocities'* are faced by up to 120,000 prisoners in the country's system of prison camps. In 2019, the UK's Independent Inquiry led by Bishop of Truro reported that North Korea *'has consistently registered for the past 18 years as the most dangerous country in the world for Christians.'*[85]

During the hearings held in Parliament, escapees provided first-hand accounts of the atrocities.

Jeon Young-Ok testified that: *'They tortured the Christians the most. They were denied food and sleep. They were forced to stick out their tongues and iron was pushed into it.'* Hea Woo added: *'The guards told us that we are not human beings, we are just prisoners...the dignity of human life counted for nothing.'* North Korean refugees told us that having a Bible can lead to execution. A former security agent interviewed by *Open Doors*

---

[82] House of Lords Deb, 13 March 2003, c1548.

[83] UN Commission of Inquiry, 'Report of the detailed findings of the Commission of Inquiry on human rights in the Democratic People's Republic of Korea' (2014) UN Doc. A/HRC/25/CRP.1.

[84] Ibid.

[85] Bishop of Truro Review, 'Independent Review for the UK Foreign Secretary of Foreign and Commonwealth Office Support for Persecuted Christians' (2019).

said that he was trained to recognise religious activity and to organise fake '*secret*' prayer meetings to identify Christians. When Christians are discovered, they experience intense interrogation which normally includes severe torture, incarceration, and slave labour.

The UN Commission of Inquiry concluded that no official or institution is held accountable, because '*impunity reigns.*' It urged a referral to the ICC. Several years later, through fear of vetoes, nothing has happened.[86]

Having escaped to China, some of North Korea's desperate secret Christians are then forcibly repatriated by China—in breach of their obligations under the 1951 Convention Relating to the Status of Refugees and its 1967 Protocol. Refoulement sometimes has lethal consequences. Anyone who crosses the border because of religious persecution will undoubtedly fit the definition of a refugee and China is derelict in its duty by refusing to allow escaping North Korean Christians to travel safely to South Korea where they will be given sanctuary and full citizenship. During a hearing in March 2021, the APPG on North Korea, co-chaired by Lord Alton and Fiona Bruce MP, was told that if a woman has become pregnant by a Chinese man before being returned to the DPRK, she will be forcibly aborted. This was because of racist ideology and belief that Chinese parentage would dilute their bloodline.

China is also bound by the UN Convention against Torture and Other Cruel, Inhuman or Degrading Treatment or Punishment, which it ratified in 1988. This prohibits the return of persons to states '*where there are substantial grounds for believing*' that they would be subjected to torture. David Hawk's Hidden Gulag records the harrowing testimony of scores of North Koreans severely punished after being returned to North Korea. And that is the reason why they are fleeing in the first place: because of a regime which has committed unspeakable crimes against its own suffering people. Throughout East Asia a combination of authoritarianism, Communism, and nationalism are all key drivers in the persecution of Christians and other religious believers. As China has retreated from the welcome transformative reforms of Deng Xiaoping his successor, Xi Jinping has been taking the country back to the Maoist

[86] UN Commission of Inquiry, 'Report of the detailed findings of the Commission of Inquiry on human rights in the Democratic People's Republic of Korea' (2014) UN Doc. A/HRC/25/CRP.1.

Communist system which presided over the brutal persecution of the Cultural Revolution.

Justice Kirby said evidence adduced by the UN Commission of Inquiry *'was very similar to the testimony one sees on visiting a Holocaust Museum by those who were the victims of Nazi oppression.'*[87]

Although the UN Commission of Inquiry did not consider the atrocities to amount to the legal definition of genocide, Hogan Lovells, an international law firm, examined North Korea's human rights record, and concluded that their targeting and extermination of religious groups could constitute genocide.[88] Their independent legal opinion states that:

> We consider that there may be good arguments that the targeting by DPRK state-controlled officials of groups classified by the DPRK as being in the hostile class, Christians, and children of Chinese heritage with the intent to destroy such groups could be found to amount to geno cide," the report states. It also recommends further investigation of the possibility genocide to include, "collecting as much testimony as possible from victims, refugees and defectors and ensuring that such testimony is collected to a court evidence standard.[89]

To this day North Korea's atrocities have not been recognised as genocide but NGOs such as Korea Future Initiative, set up to investigate, document and preserve evidence of human rights violations and the identities of victims, perpetrators, and state organisation, has begun a systematic evaluation of whether the threshold of genocide has been met.

3   WHAT ABOUT TIGRAY?

On 26 November 2021, in a letter to *The Guardian,* Lord Alton, Helen Clark (former Prime Minister of New Zealand) and Michael Lapsley (President of Healing Memories), emphasised that:

---

[87] UN Commission of Inquiry, 'Report of the detailed findings of the Commission of Inquiry on human rights in the Democratic People's Republic of Korea' (2014) UN Doc. A/HRC/25/CRP.1.

[88] Hogan Lovells, 'Independent Report Finds Evidence of Genocide in North Korea.' Available at: https://www.hoganlovells.com/en/news/independent-report-finds-evidence-of-genocide-in-north-korea.

[89] Ibid.

Genocide happens when warning signs are not heeded. The world looks away, refusing to believe that mass ethnic killing is possible…to prevent genocide, we must sound the alarm before we arrive at certainty. Rarely before has the danger of genocide been so clearly signalled in advance than in Ethiopia." The writers said that "no side to the conflict is angelic…but only one side has committed violations on a scale and nature that could credibly quality as genocide – and that, we regret to say, is the coalition of the Ethiopian government, under the prime minister, Abiy Ahmad; the Amhara regional government; and the state of Eritrea.[90]

The writers detailed the nature of the atrocities and insisted that '*five warning signs for mass, ethnically targeted violence are flashing red*'— these included the demonising of Tigrayans as '*cancer*,' '*weeds*,' '*rats*,' and '*terrorists*.'

The writers recalled the litany of *mea culpas* and the international community's repeated failure to heed warning signs and to prevent genocide: '*genocide is preventable—if the political will is there to act on warnings*.' The writers said that such will had not been exercised and that the failure to act immediately was leading to '*catastrophe*.'

The failure to act had led, by the end of 2021, to 4 million people in Tigray being left without enough to eat, hundreds of thousands displaced, and many subjected to massacres, which we detail below—including the use of artillery in attacks on refugee camps.

In November 2020, in a Private Notice Question, Lord Alton pointed to the consequences of Ethiopia's decision to unleash its armed forces. He followed up the question with an urgent letter to the Foreign Office, in which he said: '*Despite a communications blackout in the Tigray, there are concerning reports coming from the region suggesting mass atrocities*.'[91] He specifically drew their attention to the Ethiopian Human Rights Commission preliminary report on the atrocities in Mai-Kadra on 9 November 2020. The report concluded that:

- The perpetrators killed hundreds of people with full intent, a plan and preparation,

---

[90] See: https://www.theguardian.com/commentisfree/2021/nov/26/ethiopia-genocide-warning-signs-abiy-ahmed.

[91] PNQ, 24 November 2020, c135.

- The conduct was committed as part of a widespread or systematic attack directed against a civilian population,
- The perpetrators knew that the conduct was part of or intended the conduct to be part of a widespread or systematic attack directed against a civilian population,
- The conduct took place in the context of an armed conflict between the Federal Government's National Defence Forces and the Tigray Regional Government's security forces while the latter were retreating following a defeat; and perpetrators targeted civilian residents of Maikadra they profiled based on their ethnic origin.[92]

The UK Government was asked what assessment it had made of the report and its conclusions, and what actions it had taken to meet its obligations under the Genocide Convention, to look for early warning signs of genocide, and its obligations to prevent, protect, and punish the perpetrators. First in April 2022, the UK Government confirmed that it did not conduct any such assessment. In April, 2022, the UK Government promised to make a formal assessment.

Lord Alton referred Ministers and officials to the ICJ Judgment of 2007 in the case of Bosnia and asked how the UK Government was planning to fulfil its duty to prevent as set out in that judgement. On 2 December 2020, he secured an Oral Question in the House of Lords in which he asked what efforts the UK was making to secure access to the region and what it was doing to secure evidence of war crimes.[93]

Simultaneously, with others, Lord Alton wrote to UN Secretary General Antonio Guterres, that *'In the midst of this conflict, the situation of some 100,000 Eritrean refugees in Tigray, most of whom live in four UN-sponsored refugee camps and many of whom are unaccompanied minors, has deteriorated markedly.'*

Mr. Guterres was told that attacks and raids had taken place on at least three of the four main refugee camps in the region that *'reports are emerging that a significant number refugees may have been seized at gunpoint from Hitsats, Shimelba and Shire town, and either forced onto the front lines of the fighting, or forcibly returned to Eritrea, where they will*

---

[92] Ethiopian Human Rights Commission, 'Preliminary Report (November 2020). Available at: https://ethiopia.me.uk/grave-human-rights-violation-in-maikadra/.

[93] OQ, 2 December 2020, c735.

inevitably face indefinite detention, forced conscription, torture and other inhuman, cruel and degrading treatment, or death.'

Indeed, since 1991 Eritrean officials have been deemed to have committed crimes against humanity. Their cruelty and barbarism—which has led to tens of thousands of people fleeing the country—is well-documented and well-known. Mr. Guterres was urged to *'remind the Ethiopian authorities of their obligations under the African and UN Refugee Conventions'*, and to call on the Ethiopian government *'to prioritise the protection of this vulnerable community… to fully restore communications and other suspended services to Tigray, and to facilitate independent investigation and verification of the wellbeing of refugees and civilians by African Commission and UN special procedures.'*

On 16 March 2021, through the *Coalition for Genocide Response*, the authors hosted a webinar with distinguished commentators including Professor Alex de Waal, Martin Plaut, Lord Boateng, Baroness Chalker, Archbishop Angaelos, and representatives of *Amnesty International and Human Rights Watch*. The webinar was organised in response to appalling reports of shocking violations of human rights, war crimes, and crimes against humanity in Ethiopia's region of Tigray. But speakers said the atrocities could also amount to genocide. Among others, Professor de Waal spoke about how deliberate starvation can be used as an *'instrument of genocide'* and said *'starvation is being used as a weapon of war.'* He said that the issue of intent was what had to be established.

Lord Alton told the webinar that since the war had begun in November 2020, in more than 30 parliamentary interventions, in a series of questions and correspondence with the FCDO, he had alerted Ministers and officials to the nature of the appalling carnage and man-made famine in Tigray.

In the weeks which followed, Lord Alton—who co-chairs the APPG on Eritrea—tabled more questions and wrote further letters. He drew to the attention of Ministers the warning of the UN Special Adviser on the Prevention of Genocide that if urgent measures were not immediately taken to address the ongoing challenges facing the country, the risk of atrocity crimes in Ethiopia remains high and likely to get worse.

On 9 February 2021, he had sent Ministers details of an appalling video of a massacre, that was circulating and details of the reported widespread deployment of Eritrean conscripts in Tigray and their involvement in looting, defilement by rape, pillaging, and murder in what was named as genocide of the Tigrayan people—information which had been provided by John Stauffer President of *The America Team for Displaced Eritreans*.

Also, in February 2021, the *Ethiopian Red Cross* assessed that 80% of the Tigray region of Ethiopia has been cut off from humanitarian assistance and the warning that tens of thousands could starve to death.[94] Abera Tola, president of the *Ethiopian Red Cross*, said that without improvements the number of starvation deaths within two months *'will be tens of thousands.'*[95] The following week, the *Associated Press* reported on the massacre in Axum:

> Bodies with gunshot wounds lay in the streets for days in Ethiopia's holiest city. At night, residents listened in horror as hyenas fed on the corpses of people they knew. But they were forbidden from burying their dead by the invading Eritrean soldiers.[96]

Those responsible knew that by attacking Axum an attack was being mounted on the very identity of Orthodox Tigrayans and also all Ethiopian Orthodox Christians. A witness, a university lecturer, said that *'I saw a horse cart carrying around 20 bodies to the church, but Eritrean soldiers stopped them and told people to throw them back on the street.'*[97]

Escaping refugees—many in Sudan—have described vicious attacks including systematic use of rape as a weapon of war and even the disembowelment of a woman.[98] UNHCR spokesperson Andrej Mahecic confirmed that: *'Latest arrivals tell of being caught in the conflict and being victims of various armed groups, facing perilous situations including looting of their houses, forceful recruitment of men and boys, sexual violence against women and girls. Refugees are arriving with little more than the*

---

[94] AFP, 'Ethiopian Red Cross says 80 percent of Tigray cut off from aid' *Yahoo News* (10 February 2021). Available at: https://news.yahoo.com/ethiopian-red-cross-says-80-142529026.html?soc_src=social-sh&soc_trk=tw&tsrc=twtr.

[95] Ibid.

[96] Cara Anna, '"Horrible": Witnesses recall massacre in Ethiopian holy city' *Associated Press* (18 February 2021). Available at: https://apnews.com/article/witnesses-recall-massacre-axum-ethiopia-fa1b531fea069aed6768409bd1d20bfa.

[97] Ibid.

[98] UN News, 'UNHCR relocates victims of Ethiopia's Tigray conflict to new site in Sudan' *UN News* (5 January 2021). Available at: https://news.un.org/en/story/2021/01/1081422.

clothes on their backs, fatigued and in weak conditions… More than 30% of them are estimated to be under 18 and 5% over 60 years old.[99]

In early February 2021, the UN Adviser on the Prevention of Genocide, Ms. Alice Wairimu Nderitu, confirmed that multiple reports had been received of extrajudicial killings, mass executions, sexual violence, looting, and impeded humanitarian access.[100] The Special Adviser has also received:

> disturbing reports of attacks against civilians based on their religion and ethnicity as well as serious allegations of human rights violations and abuses including arbitrary arrests, killings, rape, displacement of populations and destruction of property in various parts of the country. These are in addition to reported acts of hate speech and stigmatization including, ethnic profiling against some ethnic communities, notably, the Tigray, Amhara, Somali, and Oromo.[101]

On 19 February 2021, *The Daily Telegraph* published further shocking evidence and said it had photographs too graphic to publish showing bodies of children and adolescents blown to pieces:

> The ground of the Tigrayan village is soaked with blood and dozens of bodies lie strewn in the grass. Groans can be heard from a seriously wounded man squirming on the floor between two corpses. Chatting as they wander through the aftermath of what appears to be a mass execution of civilians in the Tigray region, soldiers laugh and joke among themselves.[102]

On 27 February 2021, US Secretary of State, Anthony Blinken emphasised that *'The immediate withdrawal of Eritrean forces and Amhara*

---

[99] Ibid.

[100] UN News, 'Statement by the Special Adviser of the Secretary-General on the Prevention of Genocide, Alice Wairimu Nderitu, on the situation in Ethiopia' UN Press Release(5 February 2021). Available at: https://www.un.org/en/genocideprevention/doc uments/Statement%20on%20Ethiopia%205%20Feb%2021.pdf.

[101] Ibid.

[102] Zecharias Zelalem, '"You should have finished off the survivors": Ethiopian army implicated in brutal war crime video' *The Telegraph* (19 February 2021). Available at: https://www.telegraph.co.uk/news/2021/02/19/should-have-finished-survivors-ethiopian-army-implicated-brutal/.

regional forces from Tigray are essential first steps… They should be accompanied by unilateral declarations of cessation of hostilities by all parties to the conflict and a commitment to permit unhindered delivery of humanitarian aid.'[103]

The next day, Lord Alton wrote to Ministers drawing their attention to a CNN report of another massacre—at Dengalet church where Eritrean soldiers opened fire on a defenceless congregation.[104] As some fled, the troops followed, spraying the mountainside with bullets. Another CNN report shed light on the atrocities stating: *'The corpses, some dressed in white church robes drenched in blood, were scattered in arid fields, scrubby farmlands and a dry riverbed. Others had been shot on their doorsteps with their hands bound with belts. Among the dead were priests, old men, women, entire families and a group of more than 20 Sunday school children, some as young as 14, according to eyewitnesses, parents and their teacher.*'[105]

On 4 March 2021, UN High Commissioner for Human Rights Michelle Bachelet warned about *'Credible information also continues to emerge about serious violations of international human rights law and humanitarian law by all parties to the conflict in Tigray in November last year,*'[106] including of:

> ongoing fighting across the region, particularly in the centre of Tigray region, as well as incidents of looting by various armed actors. Reliable sources have shared information about the killing of eight protestors by security forces between 9 and 10 February in Adigrat, Mekelle, Shire and Wukro. More than 136 cases of rape have also been reported in hospitals in Mekelle, Ayder, Adigrat and Wukro in the east of Tigray region between December and January, with indications that there are many more such

---

[103] US State Department, 'Atrocities in Ethiopia's Tigray Region' (27 February 2021). Available at: https://www.state.gov/atrocities-in-ethiopias-tigray-region/.

[104] Barbara Arvanitidis, Nima Elbagir, Bethlehem Feleke, Eliza Mackintosh, Gianluca Mezzofiore and Katie Polglase, 'Massacre in the mountains They thought they'd be safe at a church. Then the soldiers arrived' *CNN* (26 February 2021). Available at: https://edition.cnn.com/2021/02/26/africa/ethiopia-tigray-dengelat-massacre-intl/index.html.

[105] Ibid.

[106] UN News, 'Ethiopia: Persistent, credible reports of grave violations in Tigray underscore urgent need for human rights access—Bachelet' *UN News* (4 March 2021). Available at: https://www.ohchr.org/EN/NewsEvents/Pages/DisplayNews.aspx?NewsID=26838&LangID=E.

unreported cases. The Government has said investigations are under way into the cases of sexual violence.

The Office has also managed to corroborate information about some of the incidents that occurred in November last year, indicating indiscriminate shelling in Mekelle, Humera and Adigrat towns in Tigray region, and reports of grave human rights violations and abuses including mass killings in Axum, and in Dengelat in central Tigray by Eritrean armed forces.[107]

On 9 March 2021, Lord Alton secured a further oral question and asked the government how it had responded to reports of a massacre at Axum in Tigray, which Amnesty International said may amount to crimes against humanity: *'With vast numbers of Tigrayans having been displaced and 4 million now facing a manmade famine, reports from Amnesty and Human Rights Watch underline the allegations of crimes against humanity at Axum and allegations of an unfolding genocide. What are we doing to hold those responsible for this to account, including Nobel laureates? Why did we not jointly table a resolution (proposed by Ireland) to the United Nations Security Council, despite China and Russia threatening to block it, along with supporting the international calls there for an immediate withdrawal of Eritrean troops from Tigray? Surely this is a prerequisite to ending the depredations in Tigray.'*[108] In response the UK Government said that they *'believe that the allegations about human rights violations in the Amnesty report are credible.'* It said there is a *'need for urgent independent investigations into the atrocities in Tigray in order to end impunity.'*[109]

In a letter to Ministers, of 8 March 2021, Lord Alton drew their attention to a briefing note which had been sent to him by a charity which works in Tigray:

Brutal fighting has been reported across the region, and gross human rights violations against civilians, including forced displacement, massacres, abductions, and sexual abuse have been reported.

Additionally, local and regional transportation has been restricted, with roadblocks, bank closures, and federal authorities shutting down electricity, internet, and phone services in the region. As a result of such widespread

[107] Ibid.
[108] House of Lords Deb, 9 March 2021, c1468.
[109] Ibid.

devastation and upheaval, more than 4.5 million people in the region are in urgent need of food aid.

They said that *'rarely have we witnessed a need so great or heard of such atrocities…urgent assistance is needed to provide vital support to avoid complete tragedy on a vast human scale.'*[110]

On 17 March 2021, *Sky News* reported that *'The breadth and depth of human suffering in the Ethiopian region of Tigray is perfectly clear to humanitarian workers, human rights groups and the international diplomatic community.'*[111] They reported that more than 500,000 Tigrayans had lost their homes. Almost 60,000 had sought refugee status in neighbouring Sudan. Two refugee camps in Tigray had been obliterated by military force. Nearly 70% of 106 health facilities had been looted. Only 13% were functioning normally. One senior UN Official speaking to *Sky* said: *'We don't know what the situation is in the rural parts of Tigray and what we don't know really worries us.'*[112]

What we do know is that gross human suffering has been caused by man-made events. What we do know is that much of it was planned and is systematic. What we do know is that particular groups have been targeted. What we do know is that in Eritrea people have been brutalised and taught to hate Tigrayans as their enemy. What we do know is that in this dirty war the greatest price is being paid by those who are defenceless—and the highest price of all is being paid by women, an estimated 10,000 of whom have been raped.

No one wielding the levers of power can plausibly say they didn't know. Let no one say they weren't warned. Let no one say there were no predictors of genocidal crimes.

And we need to be resolute in holding to account those who unleashed these catastrophic events and who have perpetrated atrocity crimes with total contempt for humanity, for international law, and for fundamental human rights. Once more, our wholly inadequate and negligent response

---

[110] Ibid.

[111] John Sparks, 'Ethiopia: Hundreds executed, thousands homeless - the human cost of fighting in Tigray' *Sky News* (17 March 2021). Available at: https://news.sky.com/story/ethiopia-hundreds-executed-thousands-homeless-the-human-cost-of-fighting-in-tigray-12247307.

[112] Ibid.

to genocide, crimes against humanity, and war crimes as been laid bare in the suffering of Tigray.

As the evidence of atrocities was mounting, Lord Alton asked when was the UK going to put this evidence of war crimes and potential genocide before the UN Security Council. As a permanent member of the UN Security Council, the UK has a duty to use its seat to acts, including by way of demanding an emergency meeting, exposing the threatened use of vetoes, insisting on access to the region, and prosecution of those responsible. Failure to act makes it culpable. Nations that have permanent seats at the high table of the UN Security Council have a greater responsibility than other UN member states to act. Where such nations know of atrocity crimes, including genocide, and fail to act, they deserve to be held to account for their inaction.

Meanwhile, the people of Tigray are starving. Ethiopian road blockades have stopped food and medicine from reaching them.

In October 2021, Lord Alton urged the Africa Minister, Vicky Ford MP, to do what Margaret Thatcher had done during the 1984 Ethiopian Famine and organise the air lift of food to the starving. Beginning in November 1984 two RAF Hercules airlifted well over 12,600 tonnes of grain and dropped a further 7000 tonnes to places inaccessible by any other means of transport.

In her December reply, Minister Ford said this was not possible but confirmed *'the risk of famine and the possibility of large-scale loss of life occurring without a drastic improvement in the ability of relief actors to deliver aid.'* She admitted that *'delivery has been virtually impossible due, to the (road) blockade in Tigray by the federal government... The de facto blockade of Tigray is likely to constitute a war crime'* and that *'The situation in Tigray is catastrophic.'*

This example and many others which we have examined and raised— including the forced repatriation of Eritrean refugees to Eritrea, the rounding up of Tigrayans in other parts of Ethiopia, and the public incitement (by an Ethiopian military figure who also has UK citizenship) to commit massacres against Tigrayans—have demand an urgent response. Instead of which there is a collective wringing of hands.

Tragedy was predicted, and tragedy was avoidable.

The UK has been sending large amount of aid Ethiopia for decades and, at the very minimum, the UK has a longstanding relationship through which it could have exercised greater leverage and influence. The UK Government, along with the international community, has merely expressed *pro forma* 'concern' whenever asked, thereby establishing their pattern of complacency. Concern without accompanying deeds is devoid of meaning. This needs to be addressed.

Belatedly—but nonetheless welcome—on 17 December 2021, the UN Human Rights Council finally adopted a long overdue resolution on the human rights situation in Ethiopia which includes the establishment of an international commission of human rights experts to investigate alleged violations of international law by all parties to the conflict in Tigray.

Commissions and committees have their place but like ritual expressions of *'concern'* they can all too easily also become yet another way of avoiding the duty of individual states to act.

The international opposition to even establishing the commission was in itself instructive—and reveals how the watchdog and the burglar have, in some cases, become one and the same thing.

The resolution was adopted at a Special Session convened in response to the deteriorating human rights situation in Ethiopia following a request of the Permanent Mission of Slovenia on behalf of the European Union which was supported by 17 Human Rights Council Member States and 38 Observer States.

The session concluded with the adoption of a resolution mandating an international commission of three human rights experts to thoroughly and impartially investigate alleged violations of international human rights, humanitarian, and refugee law committed since 3 November 2020 by all parties to the conflict.

The mechanism will preserve evidence of the atrocities and, where possible, identify those responsible—a crucial step towards justice and accountability—but we have been told that a lack of funding may delay its establishment and compromise its effectiveness.

The resolution was adopted by vote, with 21 in favour, 15 against, and 11 abstentions. Predictably enough among those countries which voted against the setting up of the commission were China, Pakistan, Cuba, Eritrea, Somalia, and Venezuela—which given their own records on the upholding of human rights tells us a great deal about the composition of the UN Human Rights Council.

PART III

Why Are They Getting Away with Genocide?

CHAPTER 8

Why Are They Getting Away with Genocide?

Whenever we hear an account by a survivor, we are faced with a new reality. As Elie Wiesel once remarked: '*Whoever listens to a witness becomes a witness.*'[1] We then no longer have the luxury of silence or indifference. Dietrich Bonhoeffer, the German theologian executed by the Nazis, put it well when he said: '*not to speak is to speak, not to act, is to act.*'[2] And it really is impossible to hear the stories and testimonies of witnesses and to believe that life can go on just as before.

It is the central proposition of this book that we must accept the responsibility placed upon us by the Genocide Convention—which the UK and many other states have signed—and we must then act. Certainly, when the atrocities in Xinjiang are weighed against the criteria listed in Article II of the Genocide Convention, for determining the crime of genocide, it is difficult not to see the elements of genocide being met.

For the sake of women, whose stories we have told, such as Rahima Mahmut, Gulzira Auelkhan, Sayragul Sauytbay, and Ruqiye Perhat—and

---

[1] 'I believe firmly and profoundly that whoever listens to a witness becomes a witness, so those who hear us, those who read us must continue to bear witness for us. Until now, they're doing it with us. At a certain point in time, they will do it for all of us.' Elie Wiesel.

[2] 'Silence in the face of evil is itself evil: God will not hold us guiltless. Not to speak is to speak. Not to act is to act.' Dietrich Bonhoeffer.

© The Author(s), under exclusive license to Springer Nature Switzerland AG 2022
E. U. Ochab and D. Alton, *State Responses to Crimes of Genocide*, Rethinking Political Violence,
https://doi.org/10.1007/978-3-030-99162-3_8

a million other Uyghur women, men, and children—the challenge will be whether our belief in the rule of law will be greater than the belief of those who think they can rule by law; whether our belief in justice and freedom is greater than their belief in force and dictatorship; whether we will place our moral and legal obligations above mercantile considerations.

Important as advocacy is, it must be backed by legislative initiatives that challenge the long standing, abject, failure of all governments to determine genocide and hold to account those responsible for such mass atrocities. It also requires a clear exposition of what it is to that we have committed ourselves to do. If we had no intention of honouring such commitments, we should never have added our nation's signature to the Genocide Convention.

The 2017 ICJ judgement leaves no doubt that the duty to prevent genocide is conduct-oriented, not result-oriented—and not a duty for some signatory countries, but not others. Although *'a state cannot be under an obligation to succeed, whatever the circumstances, in preventing the commission of genocide'*—nevertheless *'the obligation of states parties is rather to employ all means reasonably available to them, to prevent genocide so far as possible.'*[3] The mechanism for genocide determination which we have presented to the British Parliament, whether by way of the Genocide Determination Bill or the Genocide Amendment to the Trade Bill, would have equipped the UK with such a mechanism, one which would trigger a more comprehensive response to mass atrocities than anything that is currently available. The authors are not so naïve as to imagine that determination alone will be enough but what is abundantly clear is that without this determination, there will be no action to address the atrocities. Words and actions are linked.

This final chapter discusses what states must do to fundamentally change their approach to genocide response; how they might address current challenges; and how they might add some meaning to the tired old promise of *'never again.'*

We have outlined the failure of states to take predictive measures to prevent unfolding genocide, but states also need to be more effective in fulfilling their duties to punish. To change the travel of direction, and for states to fulfil their duties under the Genocide Convention, they must first agree to take ownership of genocide determination. This means that states

---

[3] *Application of the Convention on the Prevention and Punishment of the Crime of Genocide (Bosnia and Herzegovina v. Serbia and Montenegro)* Judgment 2007.

must have comprehensive monitoring mechanisms for genocide (and mass atrocities) that would provide analysis of risk factors and early warning signs and contribute to the making of a determination. The act of genocide determination does not by itself fulfil the duty to prevent and punish the crime of genocide, but it will help states to inform their response and guide them through their obligation to prevent and punish.

This work would be aided by strong domestic mechanisms of genocide response, for example, by designating an inter-departmental team for genocide and mass atrocities response; by establishing a Ministerial role or a Special Envoy on Genocide (and mass atrocities) Response who would lead and be accountable for the state's response to genocide and mass atrocities, and ensure that a comprehensive action plan for genocide response is in place and functioning. Commendable though such mechanisms are they are doomed to fail if the state does not monitor early warning signs and makes determinations of genocide and other international crimes. A commitment to genocide determination becomes the bridge to a more comprehensive genocide response.

1   GENOCIDE PREVENTION

Prevention of genocide remains a promise yet to be fulfilled. While the Genocide Convention imposes an obligation upon states to prevent genocide, there is a significant gap between the duties under the Genocide Convention and their implementation, let alone successful enforcement. The section which follows discusses the issues which we have identified as the main challenges in genocide prevention, namely: (1) the lack of comprehensive predictive mechanisms to identify risk factors and early warning signs of impending genocides; (2) the absence of mechanisms for genocide analysis and determination; and (3) the *too little and too late* responses to the serious risk of genocide.

1.1   The Lack of Comprehensive Monitoring Mechanisms

Generally, states do not have comprehensive monitoring mechanisms that would enable them to fulfil their duty to prevent genocide, neither mechanisms for risk assessment[4] or early warning monitoring.[5] We have considered in what now follows some examples of the approaches some states take to monitoring.

1.1.1   United Kingdom

The UK Government does not have comprehensive mechanisms for the monitoring of risk factors or early warnings, whether of genocide or any other atrocity crimes. According to the UK Government, the issue of atrocity crimes is covered by its generic responses to conflict and instability. It argues that given that the majority of atrocities occur in and around conflict, the UK simply needs to dedicate significant resources to addressing conflict and instability by means of a comprehensive cross-government response. Atrocity crimes, including crimes against humanity and genocide, can be perpetrated outside of conflict scenarios, so this approach is flawed. The crimes being committed in China and North Korea are prime example of this. Responding to conflicts and responding to atrocity crimes require two different (even though sometimes overlapping) approaches.

Within this focus on scenarios involving conflict the UK Government contends that it uses early warning mechanisms to identify countries at risk of instability, conflict, and atrocities. Crucially we need to understand what are these early warning mechanisms used to identify countries at risk of atrocities and what are the frameworks and the methodology used. The UK claims it uses the Joint Analysis of Conflict and Stability (JACS) which includes a section on atrocity crimes. This is not a specific framework of analysis of atrocity crimes and should not be used as such. Furthermore, it was not until March 2021, that the guidance was updated to include a section on atrocity crimes. To this day the document is not public and as such—it is difficult to assess whether it is fit for purpose.

---

[4] 'Risk assessment focuses on the general structural elements of a society that affect its likelihood of experiencing significant human rights violations. These elements may include, inter alia, political regime type (e.g. autocratic, democratic), prior history of political instability, degree of integration into the global economy, and levels of state-led discrimination.' Ernesto Verdeja, 'Predicting Genocide and Mass Atrocities' (2016) 9 *Genocide Studies and Prevention: An International Journal* 3: 14.

[5] 'Early warning focuses on the mid- and short-term factors that make violence likely. This includes attempts to identify the escalation of instability and whether it may tip into large-scale, sustained violence.' Ernesto Verdeja, 'Predicting Genocide and Mass Atrocities' (2016) 9 *Genocide Studies and Prevention: An International Journal* 3: 23.

In scrutinising this further, Parliamentary questions reveal that the UK Government does not undertake its own monitoring of risk factors or early warnings. In 2021, Lord Alton wrote to the government asking whether, further to their framework for the analysis of the early warning signs of genocide, what assessment they have made of (1) the early warning signs of atrocity crimes in Afghanistan, and (2) the risk of genocide against the Hazaras. The government's response referred only to the UK's long-standing position on leaving the issue of genocide response to courts. It failed to respond to the question asked.[6] If the UK wishes to rely on the flawed argument that it does not have to make the determination of genocide, it must nevertheless conduct its own analysis of the serious risk of genocide and ultimately that must involve monitoring and analysis of risk factors or early warnings. The government has failed to respond to whether it conducts such monitoring and analysis of the serious risk of genocide. In 2022, further questions were asked in relation to Ethiopia, China, Iraq and Burma/Myanmar.

In 2019, the UK Government accepted a recommendation to: *'ensure that there are mechanisms in place to facilitate an immediate response to atrocity crimes, including genocide through activities such as setting up early warning mechanisms to identify countries at risk of atrocities, diplomacy to help de-escalate tensions and resolve disputes, and developing support to help with upstream prevention work. Recognising that the ultimate determination of genocide must be legal not political and respecting the UK's long held policy in this area, the FCO should nonetheless determine its policy in accordance with the legal framework and should be willing to make public statements condemning such atrocities.'*[7] To date, the Government has failed to implement it.

---

[6] 'It is the long-standing policy of the British Government that any judgment as to whether genocide has occurred is a matter for a competent national or international court, rather than for governments or non-judicial bodies. As Minister for Human Rights, I made clear in my address to the UN Human Rights Council on 24 August, the UK is committed to protecting the human rights of all Afghan people. This commitment extends to all ethnic and religious groups, including the Hazara community. The UK also led work on the recent UN Security Council resolution 2593, which made clear the Security Council's intent to Taliban actions, including their respect for human rights.' HL Deb, 29 September 2021, cW.

[7] Recommendation 7 of the Bishop of Truro Review. Available at: https://christianpersecutionreview.org.uk/recommendations/.

1.1.2   United States

Over the years, the United States has made progress in its legal and normative commitments to conceptualising and developing its infrastructure for preventing genocide and other international crimes. The 1997 National Security Strategy was the first step in the direction of developing a policy on atrocity prevention.[8] However, despite the commitment to developing its approach, in 2001, Samantha Power considered that the US *'national interest remain[ed] narrowly constructed to exclude stopping genocide.'*[9] She added that officials in the Bush Administration had admitted that the United States is as unprepared and unwilling to stop genocide today as it was seven years ago. *'Genocide could happen again tomorrow,'* one said, *'and we wouldn't respond any differently.'*[10] In 2008, a bipartisan group led by former Secretary of State Madeleine Albright (Democrat) and former Secretary of Defense William Cohen (Republican) published a policy on preventing genocide which was formulated around the principle that atrocity prevention should be inherently ingrained in both US values and interests.[11] The report provides a number of concrete steps which the US Government could take to address genocide, including the assignment of resources to match priorities and the creation of a comprehensive strategy. According to them, such a comprehensive strategy includes:

> *Early Warning: Assessing Risks and Triggering Action*
> The first step toward prevention is building a reliable process for assessing risks and generating early warning of potential atrocities. We recommend that the director of national intelligence initiate the preparation of a national intelligence estimate on worldwide risks of genocide and mass atrocities, and that the results be included in annual testimony to Congress on threats to US national security. acute warning of potential genocide or mass atrocities must be made an "automatic trigger" of policy review.

---

[8] The White House, *A National Security Strategy for a New Century* (1997). Available at: https://nssarchive.us/NSSR/1997.pdf.

[9] Samantha Power, 'Bystanders to Genocide' (September 2001) *The Atlantic* 106.

[10] Ibid.

[11] Madeleine K. Albright and William S. Cohen, Preventing Genocide: *A Blueprint for US Policymakers* (2008). Available at: https://www.ushmm.org/m/pdfs/20081124-genocide-prevention-report.pdf.

Early Prevention: Engaging Before the Crisis
Efforts to prevent genocide should begin well before a crisis has erupted. with international partners, we must engage leaders, develop institutions, and strengthen civil society within high-risk countries. (…) Preventive Diplomacy: Halting and Reversing Escalation. Even when signs of preparation for genocide are apparent, there are opportunities to alter leaders' decisions, interrupt their plans, and halt and reverse escalation toward mass atrocities. we recommend the creation of a new high-level interagency body—an atrocities Prevention Committee—dedicated to responding to such threats. (…) This new committee should prepare interagency genocide prevention and response plans for high-risk situations.

Employing Military Options
(…) Military options are especially relevant when opportunities for prevention have been lost, but they can also play an important role in deterring and suppressing violence. We recommend that genocide prevention and response be incorporated into national policy guidance and planning for the military and into defence doctrine and training. The United States should redouble its support for international partners such as the United Nations and the African Union to build their capacities to deploy effective military responses to mass atrocities.

International Action: Strengthening Norms and Institutions
The United States should be a leader in preventing genocide and mass atrocities, but we cannot succeed alone. America has an interest in promoting strong global norms against genocide so that sovereignty cannot be used as a shield. We must also make international and regional institutions more effective vehicles for preventing mass atrocities. We recommend that the United States launch a diplomatic initiative to create an international network for information sharing and coordinated action to prevent genocide.'[12]

In 2011, President Obama issued a presidential study directive on Mass Atrocities (PSD-10) which declared that *'preventing mass atrocities and genocide is a core national security interest and a core moral responsibility of the United States.'*[13] The PSD-10 called for the establishment of the

---

[12] Ibid.

[13] The White House Office of the Press Secretary, *Presidential Study Directive on Mass Atrocities* (4 August 2011). Available at: https://obamawhitehouse.archives.gov/the-press-office/2011/08/04/presidential-study-directive-mass-atrocities.

Atrocities Prevention Board (APB) within the White House to *'coordinate a whole of government approach to preventing' atrocity crimes.*[14] The responsibilities, structure, and protocols of the APB were then further elaborated in President Obama's Executive Order 13,729.[15]

Among the most relevant laws in the United States are the Syrian War Crimes Accountability Act of 2017 and the Elie Wiesel Genocide and Atrocities Prevention Act of 2018. The Syrian Accountability Act requires, among other provisions *'a report on, and to authorise technical assistance for, accountability for war crimes, crimes against humanity, and genocide in Syria.'* The Elie Wiesel Genocide and Atrocities Prevention Act (the Elie Wiesel Act) is to *'prevent acts of genocide and other atrocity crimes, which threaten national and international security, by enhancing United States Government capacities to prevent, mitigate, and respond to such crises.'*

The Elie Wiesel Act was first introduced in early 2017 by Reps. Joe Crowley and Ann Wagner, and by Sens. Ben Cardin and Todd Young. The Elie Wiesel Act passed final votes in the House of Representatives and the Senate in December 2018. On 14 January 2019, President Trump signed the Elie Wiesel Act into law. The Elie Wiesel Act, among other things, prioritises the prevention of genocide and other mass atrocities as a matter of national security interest and ensure that foreign service officers receive adequate training in conflict and atrocity prevention. It requires a report to Congress within 180 days, and annually thereafter for the following six years. It also requires the US State Department to deliver training to foreign service officers.

The final provisions, as signed into law, differed significantly from the original document. At its introduction in 2017, the draft act had called upon the President to instruct the US State Department to establish a Mass Atrocities Task Force, a new mechanism aimed at strengthening US efforts at atrocity prevention and response. It encouraged the Director of National Intelligence to include in his or her annual testimony to Congress on threats to US national security: *(1) a review of countries and regions at risk of atrocity crimes; and (2) specific countries and regions at immediate risk of atrocity crimes, including most likely pathways*

---

[14] Ibid.

[15] Executive Order No. 13,729, 81 *Federal Regulation* 32,611 (18 May 2016). Available at: https://www.federalregister.gov/documents/2016/05/23/2016-12307/a-comprehensive-approach-to-atrocity-prevention-and-response.

to violence, specific risk factors, potential perpetrators, and at-risk target groups.' However, this provision did not make it into the final document. Nor did the provision establishing a Complex Crises Fund become law. The provision had aimed to *'enable the State Department and the US Agency for International Development to support programs and activities to prevent or respond to emerging or unforeseen foreign challenges and complex crises overseas, including potential atrocity crimes. Fund amounts may not be expended for lethal assistance or to respond to natural disasters.'* Despite being a lighter version of the 2017 document, the potential of the Elie Wiesel Act is welcome and an incremental move in the right direction.

In particular, the reporting requirement imposed by the Elie Wiesel Act is an important step to ensure more transparency and accountability in the operation of the US atrocity prevention strategy.

A good example of this can be seen in the 2020 report which highlights steps the US Administration has taken to prevent and respond to atrocities between 2019 and 2020, including the enhancement of *'its existing data-driven, global atrocity early warning assessments of 99 countries by identifying ongoing atrocities and countries at risk of atrocities.'*[16] To undertake this task, the US Government uses State's Atrocity Early Warning Assessment alongside the US Holocaust Memorial Museum's Early Warning Project and the Intelligence Community's Annual Mass Atrocities Risk Assessment. Furthermore, in February 2020, the US State Department launched its first online Mass Atrocity Prevention course. According to the report, 'as a result, Foreign Service Officers and other state personnel trained in atrocity prevention increased by 20-fold in the past year.'[17]

The 2021 report specifically highlights countries of concern and efforts undertaken by the Atrocity Early Warning Task Force to prevent and respond to atrocities from July 2020 to May 2021.[18] This includes a response to the atrocities in Burma/Myanmar, China, Ethiopia, Iraq and Syria, and South Sudan. In 2021, the State Department also expanded its quarterly early warning assessment to cover 153 countries—up from 99 countries.

[16] See: https://www.state.gov/2020-Report-to-Congress-Pursuant-to-Section-5-of-the-Elie-Wiesel-Genocide-and-Atrocities-Prevention-Act-of-2018.

[17] Ibid.

[18] See: https://www.state.gov/2021-report-to-congress-pursuant-to-section-5-of-the-elie-wiesel-genocide-and-atrocities-prevention-act-of-2018.

1.1.3   Germany

In June 2017, the German Government adopted the *'Guidelines on Preventing Crises, Resolving Conflicts, Building Peace,'* a policy document aimed at addressing—among other things—atrocity crimes.[19] Commenting on the issue of early warning, the guideline states that:

> Early warning is a crucial basis for early and resolute crisis prevention measures. It makes it possible to reduce preventable surprises and to better prepare policymakers for possible escalations. This necessitates capabilities for the targeted observation of countries and regions. The Federal Government will hone its instruments of analysis with a view to keeping abreast of political, economic and structural developments that are likely to promote the emergence or aggravation of crises. It is important, however, to be realistic: even with excellent early warning mechanisms, it will not always be possible to predict crises in sufficient detail.[20]

It further adds that:

> In early warning, the Federal Government relies first and foremost on the observation of indicators in the areas of politics, economics, and society (e.g., the status and protection of human rights, political and social participation, the poverty rate, migratory pressure, prices and economic trends or social inequality, including ethnic, religious and gender specific indicators). For these efforts, the Federal Government uses targeted reporting received from German missions abroad and our partners from international organisations, civil society, the media, and academia in the field, as well as from a host of other sources. The individual departments of the Federal Government will increase their efforts to pool the findings obtained from their respective instruments of analysis depending on the situation at hand. The Federal Government will continue to develop its early warning instruments and expand its relevant international network. This will also involve methods of strategic forecasting, including scenario planning. The Federal Government's inter-ministerial "Horizon Scanning" working group, which meets either for a specific situation or otherwise at least every six months, will pro mote joint situation assessments of potential crises—even on issues

---

[19] Sarah B. and Philipp R. 'Germany's Politics and Bureaucracy for Preventing Atrocities' (2018) *Genocide Studies and Prevention: An International Journal* 20.

[20] See: https://www.auswaertiges-amt.de/blob/1214246/057f794cd3593763ea556 897972574fd/preventing-crises-data.pdf.

exceeding the narrow framework of foreign, development and security policy.[21]

1.1.4 The Great Lakes Region

The International Conference on the Great Lakes Region (ICGLR) is an intergovernmental body developed to address instability and conflict in Africa's Great Lakes Region. In 2006, its Member States[22] ratified the Protocol for the Prevention and Punishment of the Crime of Genocide, War Crimes, Crimes Against Humanity and All Forms of Discrimination (ICGLR Protocol).[23] The ICGLR Protocol reaffirms the obligations of its Member States to address genocide, crimes against humanity and war crimes, and calls upon them to establish a regional committee to help with this task. The Regional Committee, established in 2010, subsequently called upon the ICGLR Member States to establish their own National Committees to give effect to the obligation to prevent atrocity crimes.

In line with this recommendation, Kenya, Tanzania, and Uganda have established such National Committees. Their mandates include:

1. Regular monitoring of situations and processes that could lead to [genocide, crimes against humanity, war crimes];
2. The collection and analysis of information related to the above crimes;
3. Alerting the government and proper authorities in a timely fashion to undertake immediate measures to prevent the commission of the above crimes;
4. Recommending measures to effectively prevent the above crimes;
5. Fighting against impunity for the above crimes;
6. Raising awareness of the processes of these crimes and educating others about prevention to further peace and reconciliation programmes;

---

[21] Ibid.

[22] Angola, Burundi, Central African Republic, Congo, Democratic Republic of the Congo, Kenya, Rwanda, South Sudan, Sudan, Tanzania, Uganda, and Zambia.

[23] See: https://www.icglr-rtf.org/publication/view/protocol-for-the-prevention-of-the-crime-of-genocide-war-crimes-and-crimes-against-humanity-and-all-forms-of-discrimination/.

7. Recommending policies and measures to guarantee the rights of victims of such crimes to truth, justice, compensation, and rehabilitation; and
8. Carrying out any further task the Minister of Justice may entrust to the Committee under its mandate.[24]

This summary is not a complete analysis of the mechanisms available in the countries listed, but focuses on some of the most significant approaches, policies, mechanisms, laws. Notably, despite the pre-existing obligations in the Genocide Convention and the associated obligations to prevent and punish, which have been in existence for over seven decades, these are relatively new initiatives.

1.1.5   Other Initiatives

While state actors have been failing to identify the risk of genocide, international, regional organisations, and non-state actors have been filling the gap. For example, the UN Office of the Special Adviser on the Prevention of Genocide was established in 2004 to *'collect existing information, in particular from within the United Nations system, on massive and serious violations of human rights and international humanitarian law of ethnic and racial origin that, if not prevented or halted, might lead to genocide; act as a mechanism of early warning to the Secretary-General, and through him to the Security Council, by bringing to their attention situations that could potentially result in genocide; make recommendations to the Security Council, through the Secretary-General, on actions to prevent or halt genocide; and liaise with the United Nations system on activities for the prevention of genocide and work to enhance the United Nations' capacity to analyse and manage information regarding genocide or related crimes.'*[25] In 2010, the office was expanded to include the promotion of the Responsibility to Protect.

In 2014, the UN Office on Genocide Prevention and the Responsibility to Protect published the UN Framework of Analysis for Atrocity Crimes. It contained a list of 14 risk factors for atrocity crimes and several

---

[24] The Auschwitz Institute, National Mechanisms for the Prevention of Genocide and other Atrocity Crimes: Effective and Sustainable Prevention Begins at Home (2015). Available at: http://www.auschwitzinstitute.org/wp-content/uploads/2015/06/AIPR_N ational_Mech_Booklet_2015.pdf.

[25] See: https://www.un.org/en/genocideprevention/office-mandate.shtml.

indicators for each of the risk factors.[26] The eight common risk factors across mass atrocity crimes are: armed conflict or other forms of instability; a record of serious violations of international human rights and humanitarian law; weakness of state structures, motives or incentives; capacity to commit atrocity crimes; absence of mitigating factors; enabling circumstances or preparatory action and triggering factors.[27]

Similarly, several regional organisations conduct some early warning monitoring, including the Organization for Security and Cooperation in Europe (OSCE),[28] the EU Policy and Planning Unit,[29] and the Continental Early Warning System in the African Union.[30]

Among the initiatives taken by non-state actors is the Early Warning Project, a joint initiative of the Simon-Skjodt Centre for the Prevention of Genocide at the US Holocaust Memorial Museum and the Dickey Centre for International Understanding at Dartmouth College. It draws on cutting-edge forecasting methodology to identify countries at risk of the onset of mass killing.[31] Others, as for example *Genocide Watch*, founded by Gregory Stanton, provide regular analysis of situations measured against its established Ten Stages of Genocide.

In 2011, the Jacob Blaustein Institute for the Advancement of Human Rights, in cooperation with the Office of the UN Special Adviser for the Prevention of Genocide, published the Compilation of Risk Factors and Legal Norms for the Prevention of Genocide (the Compilation), identifying 22 risk factors specific to genocide under two sub-groups: (1) discrimination-related risk factors and (2) risk factors related to violations of the right to life and personal integrity.[32] An analysis of risk factors

---

[26] United Nations, Framework of Analysis for Atrocity Crimes—A tool for prevention, 2014. Available at: https://www.refworld.org/docid/548afd5f4.html.

[27] See Appendix A.

[28] See: OSCE. *Early Warning and Early Action*. Available at: www.osce.org/secret ariat/107485.

[29] See: EU Policy and Planning Unit, The Early Warning and Conflict Prevention Capability of the Council of the European Union. Available at: www.ifp-ew.eu/pdf/061 1prelisbon.pdf.

[30] See: African Union, Continental Early Warning System. Available at: www.peaceau. org/uploads/early-warning-system-1.pdf.

[31] See for example: Ernesto Verdeja, 'Predicting Genocide and Mass Atrocities' (2016) 9 *Genocide Studies and Prevention: An International Journal* 3: 13–32.

[32] See Appendix B.

should help to identify situations posing a serious risk of genocide which in turn should trigger the duty to prevent.

Independent of the work involving non-state actors, states should have in place comprehensive monitoring mechanisms capable of collecting data on situations of concern. With a few exceptions, where such domestic mechanisms generally do not exist, states rely on external bodies, whether international bodies, research centres, NGOs, etc. These come with their own challenges and limitations and are not a substitute for the commitment of governments and a comprehensive strategy.

States must introduce comprehensive domestic mechanisms to monitor situations of concern. As such,

> the very first thing which a state must do to fulfil its obligations to prevent is to be able to identify whether or not a genocide risk factor is present. This will require them to (1) establish a national mechanism that is mandated to conduct periodic risk assessments of the basis of the UN Atrocity Crimes Framework or another risk factors framework. This will need to be independent and properly funded; (2) There must be an effective data collection system within, or capable of monitoring from outside, the affected country to establish whether genocide risk factors are present; and (3) there must be open and free exchange between the national entity, civil society, and independent media.[33]

1.2   No Mechanisms for Genocide Analysis and Determination

Despite there being no mandatory requirement in the Genocide Convention to introduce a mechanism that would enable it to prevent genocide, if states are to comply with the more recent jurisprudence of the ICJ, they must conduct their own monitoring, but also conduct analysis and determination.

There is no prescribed way for doing this and different states have taken varying approaches. A good starting point would be to adopt the two main frameworks for the assessment of risk factors of genocide. Failure of states to do anything cannot be justified, not least because international bodies are all too often impotent or incapable of acting. The response taken by individual states must be fully informed about the nature and severity of the atrocities.

---

[33] Erin Rosenberg, Presentation on 9th December 2020.

While mechanisms for monitoring are crucial, they are of little assistance if states do not have in place comprehensive mechanisms for genocide analysis and determination.

Where a state does not analyse the serious risk or genocide and does not recognise the atrocities as genocide, by default, it will fail to take and use all means reasonably available to them to prevent the genocide from occurring. To be clear, genocide determination refers here to an interim determination of genocide and not to individual criminal responsibility that is to be determined by domestic criminal courts or international criminal tribunals nor does it refer to state responsibility (to be determined by, e.g. the ICJ).

In Chapter 2, Sect. 4, we cite some examples of how a few states have approached the issue.

However, as we explained in connection with the UK, some states continue to delegate the duty to act to bodies that were never to be tasked with this important role, relying on the argument that it is for international judicial systems to make such a determination, an argument that was challenged by the Dutch Government.[34]

Genocide determination is a crucial step to ensure that states fulfil their indivisible duties under the Genocide Convention and is a pre-requisite of states triggering their duty to prevent. As the ICJ confirmed,

> a state's obligation to prevent, and the corresponding duty to act, arise at the instant that the state learns of, or should normally have learned of, the existence of a serious risk that genocide will be committed. From that moment onwards, if the state has available to it means likely to have a deterrent effect on those suspected of preparing genocide, or reasonably suspected of harbouring specific intent (*dolus specialis*), it is under a duty to make such use of these means as the circumstances permit.[35]

For a state to be able to learn of the serious risk, a state must be in a position to conduct its own analysis of the risk factors and early warnings of genocide and then to determine the existence of a serious risk, or indeed, of a genocide already underway. Such an analysis would incline

---

[34] Dutch Government's letter of 22 December 2017. Available at: https://www.worldw atchmonitor.org/2018/01/netherlands-joins-un-security-council-shine-light-genocide/.

[35] *Application of the Convention on the Prevention and Punishment of the Crime of Genocide (Bosnia and Herzegovina v Serbia and Montenegro)*, 2007 Judgment, 431.

consideration of the UN Framework of Analysis for Atrocity Crimes, and the Jacob Blaustein Institute for the Advancement of Human Rights' Compilation of Risk Factors and Legal Norms for the Prevention of Genocide.

Genocide determination is a pre-requisite for Article VIII action. Article VIII of the Genocide Convention states that: '*any Contracting Party may call upon the competent organs of the United Nations to take such action under the Charter of the United Nations as they consider appropriate for the prevention and suppression of acts of genocide or any of the other acts enumerated in article III.*' Again, this is to be triggered by states. As such, a state must make its own determination to inform itself whether the situation justifies triggering Article VIII.

While many states, such as the UK, continue to rely on the argument that it is for international judicial bodies to determine genocide (which is correct only in relation to the issue of '*state responsibility*'), the UK has never engaged international judicial bodies to make such a determination. In the case of the atrocities against the Rohingya, it was The Gambia that initiated the proceedings before the ICJ. Canada and the Netherlands supported the initiative, while the UK simply tells us it '*monitors.*' In the case of Daesh atrocities, the UK authored the UN Security Council Resolution 2379 which prevented a determination by international judicial bodies relying on Iraqi domestic courts—which cannot make such a determination even in cases of individual criminal responsibility as the Iraqi penal code does not criminalise genocide.

In each of the last six years, and again in 2022, Lord Alton has introduced a Private Members Bill, the Genocide Determination Bill, and during the passage of the 2021 Trade Act he moved an amendment which became known as the '*Genocide Amendment.*' We now consider the process which these legislative proposals went through.

1.2.1   *The Case of the Daesh Genocide*

In March 2016, Lord Forsyth, Baroness Kennedy QC of The Shaws, Baroness Cox, and other Peers tabled an amendment to the Immigration Bill. It was in response to the unfolding genocide against Yazidis and other minorities in northern Syria and Iraq. The Government resisted the amendment and repeatedly told the House that genocide was a matter for the courts. In the House of Commons, Fiona Bruce MP, a lawyer, tabled a motion declaring those events to be a genocide, in line with the legal definition of genocide.[36] Although the House passed it with overwhelming all-party support, the UK Government again resisted it, saying that only international courts could determine a genocide. This is a circular argument—indeed, a vicious circular argument.

A similar initiative, although with a much broader focus, was proposed by Lord Alton in his Genocide Determination Bill. This Private Members' Bill would have allowed relevant actors to apply to the High Court to make a determination of genocide, and in such a case, for the Secretary of State to take follow up steps, including initiating a UN Security Council resolution referring the situation to the International Criminal Court or among other things, to establish an *ad-hoc* tribunal.[37]

1.2.2 *The Case of the Chinese Government's Genocide Against the Uyghurs*

In 2020/2021, cross-party amendment, the so-called *Genocide Amendment* to the Trade Bill, was tabled by Lord Alton, Baroness Kennedy QC, and Lord Forsyth. The amendment incorporated the thinking behind the Genocide Determination Bill and aimed to equip the High Court to make a determination of genocide.[38] As the amendment was to the Trade Bill, and to keep it within scope, the *Genocide Amendment* had to narrowly become operative where a trading partner (subject to bilateral trade agreement) was credibly accused of genocide.

The *Genocide Amendment* received significant House of Lords' support (287 to 161), with the majority of the House clear that it did not want the UK to trade with states committing genocide. On 19 January 2021, the *Genocide Amendment* was considered by the House of Commons. After an animated debate, during which the *Genocide Amendment* was given significant bipartisan support, it was narrowly defeated by 319 to 308.[39] Supporters included 34 Conservative rebels. On return to the House of Lords it was again agreed and returned to

---

[36] See EDM: https://edm.parliament.uk/early-day-motion/49597.

[37] See more: https://services.parliament.uk/Bills/2019-21/genocidedeterminationbill.html.

[38] See more: https://hansard.parliament.uk/Lords/2020-12-07/division/707DD43F-E4E5-4F63-AA9E-8B41FCE483C1/TradeBill?outputType=Names.

[39] UK House of Commons, Trade Bill, Division 202, 19 January 2021. Available at: https://hansard.parliament.uk/Commons/2021-01-19/division/DF685BE5-5E28-4897-AE8C-035334045CB1/TradeBill?outputType=Names.

the House of Commons during 'ping-pong.' The government replaced the Lords amendment with a compromise proposal mandating Select Committees of either House to consider, in the context of certain trade agreements, evidence of genocide but declining to give UK courts a role in predeterminations.

The UK Government thwarted the *Genocide Amendment* and declined to meet with its movers—who had made clear their willingness to work with the government on modifying the amendment. More puzzling still, even though the Minister for Trade Policy had received a refined version of the amendment in advance of the debate, he did not appear to be familiar with it. Despite agreeing that the *Genocide Amendment* would become relevant only in a very few cases (ultimately, genocide does not happen that often), the government opposed it in both Houses and clung to the fiction that courts would make determinations—without empowering one to do so. Cynics pointed out that it was the time-honoured way of ensuring no embarrassment would be caused to bilateral relations with states with whom the UK wants to engage in trade.

Among the claims made by the government were that giving this additional power to the High Court would affect the separation of powers; would enable judicial activism; clog up courts; and that the amendment, being very limited in scope, would amount to virtue signalling alone. All these concerns were addressed in the debates in both Houses, and in further versions of the amendment. The refined amendment tabled by Lord Alton clarified that, while it gave power to the High Court to make a determination of genocide, such a determination would not automatically revoke the trade deal in question. Instead, once the determination of genocide was made, the Lord Chancellor would bring the determination to both Houses of Parliament and a Minister of the Crown would arrange for the motion to be debated in each House. The government would then be required to set out its course of action, which might include a withdrawal or termination of the trade agreement. Thus, the *Genocide Amendment* respected the separation of powers. The *Genocide Amendment* was also very limited in scope, and much narrower than the Genocide Determination Bill. It was also specifically tailored to the Trade Bill, and specifically introduced a mechanism ensuring that the UK does not trade with states perpetrating genocide, and so become complicit in the genocide of other states. Its narrow scope meant that it would not necessarily clog up the judicial system with litigation. Despite these clarifications, the government refused to endorse the amendment.

The only conclusion to draw—albeit an unspoken one—is that the UK Government does not want to be constrained in matters of trade, even in cases of genocide. During the House of Lords debate, the government was called to rethink its trade relationship with China, which stands accused of committing genocide against the Uyghurs. Shortly before the vote on one of the versions of the amendment, the Minister, in a last attempt to persuade members to vote against the *Genocide Amendment*, reminded the House of the value of UK's trade with China: '*UK/China trade is currently worth approximately £76 billion. China is our fourth-largest trading partner, the sixth-largest export market and the third-largest import market.*'[40] This hints at a prioritisation of trade over the human rights of communities targeted for annihilation, and despite claims that it was not contemplating a *free trade* agreement with China, this was a skilled way of avoiding the need to outline the many bilateral trade deals with a state accused of genocide.

On 9 February 2021, the House of Commons voted on an amendment to the Trade Bill tabled by Sir Robert Neill MP that '*empowers*' Parliamentary committees to make the determination of genocide. The amendment passed with 318 to 303. The result came hours after the government coupled two unrelated amendments together (Lord Alton's *Genocide Amendment* and Lord Collins' human rights due diligence amendment) and after reports of 'bullying' new Tory MPs into compliance.

The Neill amendment, now known as Section 3 of the Trade Act 2021, allows a responsible committee of the House of Lords or the House of Commons to publish a report which '*(a) states that there exist credible reports of genocide in the territory of a prospective FTA counter-party, and (b) confirms that, in preparing the report, the committee has taken such evidence as it considers appropriate.*' If, after receiving a response from the Secretary of State, the committee is not satisfied by the Secretary of State's response then it may set out the wording of a motion to be moved in the House of Commons. The Minister of the Crown must then make arrangements for the motion to be debated and voted on.

Neill's amendment, which was fully supported by the government, means that the UK Government will, seemingly, abandon its almost 50-year policy of leaving the question of genocide determination to the courts without clarifying why, all of a sudden, the courts are incapable of adjudicating on an international crime. Over the years, as Daesh was targeting Yazidis, Christians, and others for destruction, the Burmese

[40] House of Commons Deb, 19 January 2021, c1086.

army was targeting the Rohingyas, and the Chinese Government has allegedly been targeting the Uyghurs, the UK Government has defended its long-standing policy, suggesting, contrary to international law, that is unable to take any steps until a court had ruled on the matter. The UK Government now argues that, after all, they have found a way for politicians to determine the matter and act upon that determination.

This might have been, on the face of it, a welcome first step towards a comprehensive atrocity prevention framework. A leaked document, however, suggests that the UK Government is willing to abandon its long-standing policy not because it is willing to act on a recommendation but because it still believes that a High Court determination, *would be impossible for the Government to ignore.'* In order to ensure continued ignorance, all the Neill amendment does is allow the Foreign Affairs Committee or a House of Lords committee to make a declaration and then Parliament to possibly make a declaration in response. The UK Government could still choose to ignore it stating that only a court can make such a declaration.

The UK Government's position is not connected in any way to the UK's continuing duty to prevent genocide the instant it learns or should have learned of a serious risk.

Apart from the bad intentions behind the UK Government promoted Neill amendment, it remains the case that responsible Parliamentary committees, such as the Foreign Affairs Committee, already have powers of assessment and to make recommendations. The Foreign Affairs Committee found credible evidence of genocide in its 2016 reports on the Daesh atrocities, in its 2017 report on the Burmese's military atrocities, and most recently in its 2020 report on the alleged Chinese Government atrocities. In relation to the Yazidis and the Uyghurs, there was even a motion passed in Parliament. The UK Government simply rejected those decisions of Parliament. The Neill amendment did not alter this contempt of Parliament.

The Neill's amendment was not an alternative to the *Genocide Amendment* or the Genocide Determination Bill. It simply preserves the status quo and nothing more. It gives little hope, to survivors or victims, or that we will turn the tide of the failed responses to genocide.

1.3   'Too Little and Too Late' Responses to Genocide

Inevitably, where states fail to establish comprehensive domestic monitoring mechanisms and fail to create structures for genocide analysis and determination, those states will not be able to respond to the atrocities; be unable to prevent such atrocities; and be unable to make informed responses. This has been the issue in every case of genocidal atrocities that we have discussed in this book. For example, in October 2020, it became obvious that the Ethiopian region of Tigray was being subjected to appalling acts of violence involving both Ethiopian and Eritrean militias. As we outlined in the preceding chapter, the authors alerted the FCDO about their concerns and drew the attention of the FCDO to accounts of fleeing refugees. One woman described systematic rape, another disembodiment and other war crimes. It took 18 months to get some substantive response.

But the UK Government did take one welcome step: the Magnitsky sanctions. These sanctions are a relatively new mechanism but gaining international support very quickly. The initiative was launched by US financier Bill Browder, and named after his friend, Sergei Magnitsky, a Russian tax adviser who uncovered tax fraud perpetrated on a vast scale, implicating Russian officials. He was imprisoned and tortured to death, and Browder has subsequently dedicated himself to the introduction of laws around the world named after Magnitsky and freezing the property interests of persons involved in serious human rights abuse or corruption.

Such sanctions are a recognised instrument of foreign policy that governments often use to pressurise perpetrators, or the state involved, hoping to bring them into compliance with international law or as a means of condemning specific acts. What such sanctions actually achieve and how they are able to change the situation of the persecuted communities is an open question and the answer may depend on a variety of factors, including strengthened parliamentary oversight. It is difficult to see how, for example, the freezing of a few individuals' UK-based assets can fundamentally change the situation faced by the targeted communities. However, such targeted sanctions do send a signal. Political semaphore has a place in putting violators on notice. Even if sanctions produce only small changes, they remain a useful diplomatic tool and way to condemn individuals or groups who have authorised or been complicit in atrocities—and should be seen as the opening scene in a play which has its conclusion in prosecutions in courts of law. The next steps will be to consider how the frozen assets could be repurposed to assists victims of atrocities.

2   Genocide Punishment

We fail to predict and unsurprisingly we then fail to prevent genocide; but also, we do not cover ourselves in glory when it comes to the prosecution and punishment of the perpetrators of genocide. The challenges include: (1) a failure to investigate and to prosecute the perpetrators using domestic mechanisms, either in the country where the atrocities had occurred or in other countries using the principle of universal jurisdiction; and (2) the failure to utilise existing international tribunals or to establish new judicial mechanisms.

Under the Genocide Convention, states have a duty to punish the crime of genocide. As explained in Chapter 2, the duty to punish requires states to enact laws that would give effect to the Genocide Convention. Many states have done so by way of introducing the crime of genocide into their domestic penal codes. However, using the legislation to bring the perpetrators to account is an issue that remains badly neglected.

One day, victims of genocide will seek the prosecution of governments which have failed to meet their legal obligations under international treaties to which they are a party. Such a course will only be successful if it can be demonstrated that governments had been given evidence of atrocity crimes but had chosen—for political reasons, economic advantages, or other—to ignore the evidence. States with access to the highest reaches of global power—such as membership of the UN Security Council, will be especially vulnerable to such charges.

2.1   The Failure to Investigate and Prosecute the Perpetrators Using Domestic Mechanisms

In response to the atrocities which we have discussed in a range of countries, we have seen two significant trends, (1) of atrocities not being prosecuted in the country where the atrocities had been perpetrated and (2) of atrocities not being prosecuted in other countries, using the principle of universal jurisdiction.

In many cases, and especially where the state in question has been complicit in the genocide, it is clear that the state may not wish to prosecute the perpetrators. By investigating and prosecuting such crimes the trail might well lead to the state's own involvement in the acts. This should not prevent future governments from initiating prosecutions.

Under the principle of universal jurisdiction, states can investigate and prosecute the crime of genocide, and other crimes (including crimes against humanity and war crimes). Several states have relied on the principle of universal jurisdiction to address the issue of impunity in other states. Among those which have had recourse to universal jurisdiction are Germany, Austria, Belgium, Canada, Denmark, France, Sweden, the Netherlands, and the US. The offences and crimes had occurred in Afghanistan, Iraq, Uganda, Rwanda, Sierra Leone, DRC, Chad, and the former Yugoslavia. Other states have established specialised war crime units—domestic mechanisms designated for investigating and prosecuting genocide, crimes against humanity, and war crimes.

2.2   The Failure to Engage Existing International Tribunals or to Establish New Judicial Mechanisms

The ICC and ICJ are the only permanent international courts of relevance here. There is a significant difference between the ICJ and the ICC and other international criminal tribunals. The ICC is a criminal court that prosecutes individuals. It is the only permanent international criminal tribunal. As it is treaty-bound, its jurisdiction is limited. The ICJ is the principal judicial organ of the United Nations. The main aim of the ICJ is to peacefully settle disputes between states and to issue advisory legal opinions in response to requests submitted by the UN General Assembly, the UN Security Council, other competent organs, and specialised agencies. The ICJ hears legal disputes relating to international law and provides authoritative judgments. The ICJ can also adjudicate on matters under (Articles VIII and IX of) the Genocide Convention.

The ICC's genesis in the Rome Statute is one of its most significant weaknesses. Many states which stand accused of genocidal and other atrocities are not parties to the Rome Statute, and consequently they fall outside of the ICC's mandate. Theoretically, the UN Security Council may refer situations occurring in countries which are not signatories to the Rome Statute to the ICC—countries in which the ICC does not otherwise have the required jurisdiction. In reality, this has only happened twice—in the case of Darfur and Libya. States may also refer situations of concern to the ICC. However, this power is limited to cases where the state allegedly perpetrating international crimes is already a party to the

Rome Statute and, in practice, this power has been used for self-referrals, except in the case of Ukraine in 2022.

In instances where the ICC is unable to extend its reach, the UN Security Council may establish an *ad-hoc* tribunal to prosecute the perpetrators. The UN Security Council used this approach to enable prosecutions following the genocides in Rwanda and Bosnia.[41] However, since the creation of the ICC, the UN Security Council has not subsequently used this approach again. Indeed, the whole point of creating the ICC was to empower it to deal with such issues and to remove the responsibility from the UN Security Council.

The challenges posed by the issue of the lack of an international judicial mechanism to deal with the crime of genocide was anticipated at the time of the drafting of the Genocide Convention. The Polish representative emphasised that while Article VI foresaw the possibility of an international tribunal, such an international tribunal was a chimera:

> Such a tribunal did not exist; it was problematical whether it would even be set up in the future. The inclusion of such a principle in the convention constituted at least a moral obligation on the parties to the convention, although they could not know precisely what had been meant. The creation of an effective international penal tribunal had to be based upon a compulsory, not on optional, jurisdiction. That implied that it would have to be based on principles contrary to those governing the Statute of the International Court of Justice. No decision had been taken as to the competence or the jurisdictional powers of the proposed tribunal and, in particular, whether it should supersede or merely supplement competence and jurisdiction of national tribunals...
>
> An international penal jurisdiction was possible in practice only when an international executive power existed having substantial means of enforcement at its disposal. The inclusion of the principle of an international penal tribunal, in article VI, might well constitute an intervention in the internal affairs of states and a violation of their sovereignty; perhaps that had been the intention. It was impossible to accept in advance an international penal court which did not exist, which had not been formally proposed or even discussed, and which might never even come into being.[42]

[41] See: Chapter 2, Sect. 1.3.

[42] UN GA, PPCG, December 1948.

Atrocity crimes such as genocide must be duly investigated and prosecuted, whenever and wherever they occur. The alternative of doing
precious little sends the message that you can get away with genocide.
This was the very question which Raphael Lemkin wanted us to address
when he said: *'Why is the killing of a million a lesser crime than the killing
of an individual?'* Investigations and prosecutions may be undertaken
by domestic courts and, wherever possible, international tribunals. The
benefit of engaging both should always be considered and explored in
every instance.

3   The Challenges

There are several UN resolutions, conventions, etc. to which member
states are parties, and yet none appear to have enforcement mechanisms
in practice, begging the question, what's the point of it all? In the case
of international law governing trade and commerce, shipping, etc. there
is a much higher likelihood that international law and conventions will
be enforced, so it is possible, if there's self-interest, and political will. As
events in Ukraine have demonstrated, this needs to be addressed as a
matter of urgency.

Apart from the issues which we have just raised, and even if these
are addressed, the two elephants in the room remain, namely, that the
Genocide Convention is a weak toothless treaty and generally there is no
political will to engage on the issue of genocide.

3.1   The Toothless Treaty—'Simply Not Up to the Job'

On 13 October 2020, during a debate on the *Genocide Amendment* to
the Trade Bill, Lord Hope of Craighead, a retired Scottish judge who
served as the first Deputy President of the Supreme Court of the United
Kingdom, provided an excoriating critique of the ineffectiveness of the
Genocide Convention:

> The [Genocide Convention] now seems, with hindsight, to be a deplorably
> weak instrument for dealing with the challenges we face today. It was
> indeed the first such treaty of the modern era, but it is simply not up
> to the job.
> It was conceived in the mid-1940s as a reaction against the Holo-
> caust that the Nazis' policy of extermination had created in Europe. It

was assumed that it would be enough to require the contracting parties
to enact the necessary legislation and, having done so, to require them to
bring those within their jurisdiction who were charged with genocide to
trial. But we can now see, in today's world, how ineffective and perhaps
naive this relatively simple Convention is...'

What then makes the Genocide Convention one of the weakest treaties
and not up to the job of addressing the crime of genocide?

3.1.1   The Gap Between the Duties and Implementation

As we argued earlier, the scope of the duties laid down in the Genocide
Convention, and amplified and augmented in the jurisprudence of the
ICJ, are clear. Yet, states shy away from recognising situations which pose
a serious risk of genocide and their concomitant duty to then prevent
genocide and/or to initiate prosecutions, especially when there is an
absence of international actors to initiate these proceedings. Pretending
that there are effective international remedies is self-serving and deceptive.

In order to fill this lacuna, states need to take the ownership required
by the Genocide Convention and develop appropriate architecture to
inform their response. While such a determination by international bodies
may be thought to have more legitimacy, in comparison to one state
making such a determination, there is nothing to prevent a state from
making such a determination. Indeed, making such a determination will
ensure that a state is able to fulfil its obligations under the Genocide
Convention. Waiting for hobbled international institutions to act is like
waiting for Godot—and, while waiting, millions of people suffer the
consequences.

3.1.2   No Oversight Over States' Implementation of Their Duties

What are the consequences of states not fulfilling their duties under the
Genocide Convention? Where a state is in breach of its duties, such states
may face reputational damage and adverse criticism. The ICJ has power to
pronounce on whether a state is in breach of its duties under the Genocide
Convention. In accordance with Article IX of the Convention, a state
party to the Convention may bring another state party before the ICJ for
its failure to apply, interpret, or fulfil its duties under the Convention.

In practice, this rarely happens. Some of the recent cases include the
proceedings brought by the Gambia against Burma/Myanmar, and of
Ukraine against Russia. However, if the other cases we have highlighted

are also genocidal, and have been met with a wholly inadequate response, we might expect to see more cases being brought before the ICJ citing Article IX. If it is concluded that recourse to Article IX is not a viable proposition it may leave a gaping hole in the enforceability of the Genocide Convention. The question would then be, is there a way around this difficulty?

3.2   The Lack of Political Will

While the Genocide Convention places crucial duties on states, it does not prescribe how they should fulfil their obligations. While this approach allows for flexibility, it also allows states to take a very minimalistic approach to fulfilling their duties—and a minimalist approach is the last thing needed by besieged and benighted communities facing genocide. These targeted communities are the very people whom the Genocide Convention was supposed to protect.

Chamberlain's disinterested description of Czechoslovakia as a *'faraway country about which we know very little'* finds its echo in the thought that *'genocide happens far from home'* and is a foreign policy challenge for others to sort out. Genocide may be the crime above all crimes but in the hierarchy of political concerns it is not a top priority. Politicians in democracies listen to their voters and if the people who choose the elected representatives do not make it an issue, do not demonstrate that they want something done about the failure to deter genocides, then nothing much will be done. In turn, this begs the question, how can we engage the general public to become much more genocide aware and to lobby politicians to act?

Media outlets report on genocide, but mostly when it has already happened. Nothing makes the headlines more than the bodies on the streets. Early warning signs and risk factors of genocide never get the same attention. Only a focus on early warning signs and risk factors of genocide can help prevent the occurrence of the crime: when bodies are on the street it is too late. We will have failed to prevent the genocide.

The same lack of political will is also visible at an international level—especially at the United Nations. The international polity is badly compromised and corrupted. States fail to raise the spectre of genocide fearful of jeopardising their relationships with the state accused of genocide—and are frequently indebted to and quite literally in the pocket of the perpetrator.

The political will to enforce international law can be found when commercial, interests are involved and international trade law is breached, and yet not when human rights are ignored. The late US Senator Paul Simon said that *'If every member of the House and Senate had received 100 letters from people back home saying we have to do something about Rwanda, then I think the response would have been different.'*[43]

Another reason states remain silent about the infringement of human rights law elsewhere is that they fear the spotlight might one day be turned on them, focusing on their current or historic misdeeds, a fact exploited by the Chinese Government, who are always primed to remind the United States about its treatment of, for example, Native Americans.

However, the current lack of political will may change. Juan E. Mendez, the former UN Special Rapporteur on Torture and Other Cruel, Inhuman or Degrading Treatment or Punishment, himself a survivor of torture during Argentina's dirty war, said that *'you must be like a grain of sand in the eye of the decision-makers. Remind them constantly of their international legal obligations. Never let them forget that they have an obligation to act when massive human rights abuses and genocide take place.'*[44]

Policies concerning genocide never, or rarely, feature in political manifestos or in appeals to the electorate. It is not a subject to which politicians have given sufficient prominence. Even a minimalist approach might be preferable to complete inaction.

In due course, political parties must come forward with Manifesto commitments to enact the Genocide Determination Bill, to replace simple mantras and empty political determinations with formal processes and to tie them to meaningful government action. And we must make this an issue about which the public will demand to know the position of their candidates and political parties seeking their votes. Then, we will not only uphold the letter of the Genocide Convention but finally its spirit. Hopefully, this book will make a small contribution to changing that.

---

[43] As cited in Samantha Power, *A Problem from Hell: America in the Age of Genocide* (Flamingo, 2010) 377.

[44] As cited by Waging Peace. See: https://wagingpeace.info/activities/atrocity-preven tion/.

4   BRIDGING THE GAP IN THE RESPONSES TO GENOCIDE

There is already some evidence that the campaigns in Parliament are increasing political awareness and a willingness to act.

In response to the ongoing failures to address genocide, on 9 December 2021, for the International Day of Commemoration and Dignity of the Victims of the Crime of Genocide and of the Prevention of this Crime, British politicians launched *The Westminster Declaration on Bridging the Gap in Genocide Responses* (*The Westminster Declaration*), a document to be used as a blueprint to address the current shortfalls. *The Westminster Declaration* call upon states to:

> *Monitor:* states must introduce domestic mechanisms for monitoring early warning signs of atrocity crimes. The duties under the Genocide Convention are states' duties. In order to be able to implement them, states must have comprehensive monitoring mechanisms in place that will enable them to be informed and act accordingly. Such monitoring should be done by a specially designated and trained team.

> *Analyse:* states must introduce comprehensive frameworks for real-time documentation, investigation, and analysis of atrocity crimes as well as preservation of evidence relating to atrocity crimes. The team should analyse the serious risk of genocide, as required by the ICJ.

> *Recognise:* states must acknowledge and recognise the nature, scope and scale of atrocities for what they are. It is not enough for states to use euphemisms and call atrocity crimes 'human rights violations' or 'industrial-scale human rights violations.' States must be cautious with making such determinations but must not shy away from making the determination in the light of evidence.

> *Cooperate:* states must establish cross-departmental teams to formulate response plans and act upon the findings. Such crimes as genocide require multi-layered responses and engagement of many different departments, including the Foreign Office, the Ministry of Defence, and others.

Respond: states must implement the recommended responses using best endeavours, expeditiously and with care.

Oversee: states must oversee the implementation of the recommendations and evaluate their impact.

Adjust: states must adjust the implementation of recommended responses to reflect the effectiveness of the steps as well as adherence to obligations under the Genocide Convention.

Assist: states must provide assistance to victims and survivors, including by creating a special fund to assist victims and survivors of genocide. This includes ensuring access to effective remedies and reparations.

Take ownership: states must appoint a Special Envoy on Genocide and other International Crimes to take ownership over the work on genocide and other international crimes. This does not change the fact that the task is a job for many. Each individual involved in this work must be adequately trained and equipped to conduct the task.

END NOTE: HAVE WE BECOME PART OF 'AN ALIBI FOR INACTION'?

From time to time, the Foreign Office has been challenged to reprioritise its outdated view of itself and the United Kingdom's place in the world; to stop thinking it is still playing 'the Great Game'; and to use its muscle to pursue a policy shaped by more than self-interest and to be a world leader in forging new initiatives to combat conflict and atrocity crimes. In 1997, when Robin Cook became Foreign Secretary, his brave attempt to shape an 'ethical' foreign policy was welcome but too short lived to embed itself into the DNA of many of our officials and Ministers.

More recently, Jeremy Hunt tried to recalibrate its priorities and met strong resistance from officials who simply pursue their own agendas. Cynically—and in a display of what they regard as 'subtle power'—by setting up a steeplechase which makes it virtually impossible to get a declaration of genocide (thus voiding Raphael Lemkin's intentions in the Genocide Convention), the Foreign Office has, down the years, known that they could go on wringing their hands while conducting business as usual with the perpetrators.

The 2021 *Genocide Amendment* achieved one major objective—to stir considerable debate both in Parliament and in the media about the way we deal with genocide. Significant organisations—ranging from the Jewish Board of Deputies and the Muslim Council of Britain to the International Bar Association—publicly endorsed the amendment. One former Minister who voted for the amendment told us: *'I knew that the argument*

© The Editor(s) (if applicable) and The Author(s), under exclusive
license to Springer Nature Switzerland AG 2022
E. U. Ochab and D. Alton, *State Responses to Crimes of Genocide*,
Rethinking Political Violence,
https://doi.org/10.1007/978-3-030-99162-3

that genocide determination was for the Courts, was the script provided by officials who don't want us to do anything. It became a trick to shut up Parliamentarians.'

By no means the end of the argument, the *Genocide Amendment* exposed the deficiencies of our response and the debate shone a light on a subject too long confined to the darkness. It also enabled Parliament to revisit the pioneering work of Rafael Lemkin. In 1959, he died exhausted and gaunt, having dedicated his life with ferocious energy to building international legal structures to prevent genocide from happening again. But, in recent years, the heat and urgency have gone out of the argument. The failure to live up to Lemkin's hopes was summed up by the resignation in 2017 of Carla Del Ponte, a renowned war crimes prosecutor, who quit the UN Commission of Inquiry into human rights abuses in Syria citing a *'lack of political will'* and criticising the UN Security Council which, in her words, *'does not want justice.'* This followed years of inertia from the international community in the face of crimes so unimaginably cruel that Del Ponte herself said she had never seen such crimes, even in Rwanda. In a vivid phrase, she said her role had become *'an alibi for inaction.'*

When a permanent member of the UN Security Council—in this case Russia—uses its right of veto to prevent war crimes being referred to the ICC, it graphically illustrates the broken-backed nature of the international justice system. Del Ponte's Syria Commission had no power to prosecute, but had amassed substantial evidence and a confidential list of names, believed to include actors from the highest echelons of the Syrian government and military. Del Ponte said: 'It was all about the inaction of the UN Security Council because if you look at all the reports we have published, we have obtained nothing in terms of justice. It is unbelievable... It's a disgrace for the international community and particularly for the security council.' Del Porte warned that people like her were becoming like window dressing with 'no powers, no possibility of seeking justice for the victims.'

The Commission had already interviewed more than 5000 witnesses, produced 13 reports, and prepared meticulous examples of war crimes. *'Justice must do its work because without justice there is no real peace, we know that from history.'* As this illustrates, in the face of ethnic and religious groups being wiped from the map, the UN Security Council and the ICC have been exposed as missing in action and the Genocide Convention allowed to become fading ink on decaying paper.

By contrast, in 1948, Lemkin's desire for justice, lasting peaceful cooperation, combined with the horror of war and the degradation of human life, provided the impetus for the creation of the Universal Declaration of Human Rights (UDHR) and the Genocide Convention. The political will was so strong that the actors of the day worked tirelessly and got the job done for the good of the many. It was the practice of law and politics at its best, and we can learn a great deal from that.

Recall that those principles are clear and that they rely on a notion of universal truth and on a concept of freedom that insists on the protection of the weak and the powerless. Those principles are, among others: that humanity has a shared dignity in simply being human; that we are both dependent and autonomous rational subjects; that at the heart of a thriving society and one comprised of flourishing individuals is the liberty to express all our human and rational capacities; and all that is good flows from recognising these foundational principles.

Today, we are facing a crisis in the upholding of the rule of law and international justice. There can be no bigger test than our response to the greatest injustices, including to the genocide in the Middle East; crimes against humanity documented by the UN in North Korea; genocide against the Rohingyas, Xinjiang's Uyghurs and Nigerian Christians. Add to that the impotence of the UN Security Council and the ICC.

The UK could make a start by surrendering its right of veto as a permanent member of the UN Security Council, and this where such a veto would have prevented a referral of genocide and crimes against humanity to the ICC. We are not asking for it to give up its right of veto on other questions. But on this specific issue it should invite the other permanent members of the UN Security Council to follow its lead. Let there be a vote in the UN Security Council and at least expose those who want to continue to get away with genocide. This is addition to the 'veto initiative', an initiative by Liechtenstein to ensure that when the UN Security Council reaches a dead end through using the veto, those blocking progress are held to account before the UN General Assembly.

Where is the political will of our forbearers for international justice? And to what horrors has our enfeebled response led?

Recall that at the beginning of 2014 in Northern Iraq, we saw the commencement of a new wave of mass beheadings of 'infidels.' People were thrown from high buildings, prisoners burned in metal cages, women raped, and homes looted. These atrocities then intensified in their number and scope.

On 3 August 2014, Daesh attacked Sinjar, killing thousands of Yazidis, abducting thousands of women and girls, and forcing the rest to flee. This attack on the Yazidis was followed by subsequent mass atrocities in the Nineveh Plains, where Christians were forced to flee or die. Daesh was responsible for murder, enslavement, deportation, the forcible transfer of populations, exploitation, abuse, abductions of women and children, forced marriage, and enforced disappearances.

In every sense, these atrocities, perpetrated against religious minorities, are crimes against humanity and genocide but, as we have documented, the UK and others have refused to name these crimes for what they are. It is a sleight of hand to say genocide determination is a matter for the courts, knowing that no process exists to give this effect—and then, without a trace of irony, say that such decisions should not be political.

One of our greatest political leaders took a different view.

In a live broadcast from London, in 1941, Winston Churchill said that the systematic slaughter of six million people was a *'crime without a name.'* Then, Lemkin gave it a name and crafted the Genocide Convention. But he expected the word to be matched by the deeds of political leaders. It never has been. We fail to predict genocide. We fail to prevent genocide. We fail to protect victims of genocide. And we fail to prosecute perpetrators of genocide.

On day 189 of the Nuremberg Trials into the crimes of the Holocaust, the French prosecutor, Auguste Champetier de Ribes, said the Holocaust was a *'crime so monstrous, so undreamt of in history through the Christian era up to the birth of Hitlerism, that the term "genocide" had to be coined to define it.'*

Implicit in Lemkin's genocide endeavour and Churchill's need to give such gross inhumanity a name was a determination to be deadly serious in confronting these monstrous crimes, along with upholding the centrality of fundamental human rights and human dignity: a *dignity of difference*, as the late Jonathan Sacks, Lord Sacks, the UK's former Chief Rabbi described it.

Central, too, was the upholding of just laws and the responsibilities that governments must have towards the vulnerable, the voiceless, the powerless, and the weak. Undoubtedly, we are today facing an existential crisis in how we fulfil our duties to uphold international law and to protect foundational freedoms.

We must insist that there are universal truths, as recognised in the very project of the UDHR and the Genocide Convention. Such truth is not merely the construct of the majority or the powerful, but the very foundation stone that enables both justice and a diverse, thriving, society. Our utilitarian relativism has proved a short-term gain for able or powerful actors but is dislodging those foundation stones: true justice rooted in truth. While we have used the prism of genocide and atrocity crimes to focus on this failure to protect humanity, to uphold justice, and to safeguard diversity, we are at pains to point to the canaries in the mine which warn us of how it all begins. Often it starts with violations of human rights through discrimination or persecution.

In 2019, in a debate on anti-Semitism, Lord Sacks told Parliament that *'the hate that begins with Jews never ends with Jews.'* Prior to the debate, and to mark Holocaust Memorial Day (January 27), Lord Alton met Helen Aronson, who survived the Holocaust as a teenager. A survivor of the Łódź ghetto in the Nazi occupied Poland, Helen Aronson said: *'It is vital that we do everything in our power to ensure that these things never happen again, anywhere in the world. Children must be allowed to grow up safe and secure and not be wrenched from their homes, like I was.'*

But who can doubt that perpetrators have become emboldened into believing that we are too weak or too disinterested to ever stop a repetition of what Helen Aronson experienced, or to hold those responsible to account?

What began with girls like Helen did not end there.

One year before meeting her, Lord Alton had told Parliament the story of a Christian family, a mother and 12-year-old daughter who were raped by Daesh militants, leading the father, who was forced to watch, to commit suicide. One refugee had described how she witnessed Daesh crucify her husband on the door to their home. On 16 April 2018, *The Times* reported on how Rita Habib had been tortured, and raped by four different 'owners', and enslaved for three years, as part of the Daesh genocide. A 16-year-old Yazidi girl, Ekhlas, met with Lord Alton and described crucifixions, beheadings, systematic rape, and mass graves. The crucifixion and death of one young man was boastfully posted on the internet. He was crucified for wearing a cross. From the same town, local girls were taken as sex slaves. Daesh returned their body parts to the front door of their parents' homes with a videotape of them being raped.

An Iraqi Yazidi MP, Vian Dakhil, wept as she described to parliamentarians how a baby was butchered and fed to its own unwitting mother by Daesh, which had taken the mother as a sex slave. She then described the rape and death of a 10-year-old girl in front of her father and five sisters. Such nauseating obscenity and barbarism breaks hearts but should also stir consciences. Imagine for a moment that this was your daughter, your sister, or your wife. Zainab Bangura, then United Nations special representative on sexual violence in conflict, authenticated reports of

Christian and Yazidi females—girls aged one to seven—being sold, with the youngest carrying the highest price tag.

In a leading article in *The Times* of 28 March 2016 asserted that Christians were facing '*nothing less than genocide* (…) Christians are victims of genocidal terror' and that 'Christians from the Middle East have a moral and legal claim to western asylum based on the recent rulings that the wholesale destruction of their communities now amounts to nothing less than genocide. That crime, most hideously demonstrated by the Nazis, now enjoins others to take active steps to protect the victims.' The Daily Telegraph concurred and trenchantly pointed out: 'America has finally acknowledged that Christians and other religious minorities are being butchered in the Middle East. Why does the UK government not do the same?'

In 2016, David Cameron had agreed that '*there is a very strong case here for saying that it is genocide, and I hope that it will be portrayed and spoken of as such.*' But his government never did. Although *everyone* affected by war suffers, it is instructive that under his Government's Syrian vulnerable persons scheme less than 1% of those helped came from the minorities directly affected by genocide. Either genocide is the crime above all crimes, or it is not—and that should be reflected in the entirety of government responses.

The veteran diplomat, Dr. Richard Haass, is right that in a world of bad options '*not acting can be every bit as consequential as acting,*' while, undoubtedly, if you turn a blind eye or walk away, don't be surprised when you are bitten too.

In truth, there is simply far too much genocide denial. Officials and Ministers say, '*It is clearly a matter for judicial authorities to determine whether a genocide has taken place,*' and then fail to put in place a mechanism for doing that. Then, they insist that '*Perpetrators will pay the price*' and tell us about '*the long arm of justice*' promising that one day those responsible will be tried. But as Gladstone once observed, '*justice delayed is justice denied.*'

Failure to speak and failure to act—followed by unconscionable delays and inactivity—is a green light to the predators, to the world's tyrants, to lawless militias, to totalitarian regimes, and to hate-filled ideologues, who despise difference and believe that religious minorities are a curse, not a blessing. Until we do as Lemkin intended and bring to justice mass murderers—who need to face their own Nuremburg Moment—it simply re-enforces their belief that they can sleep easily in their beds.

For as long as countries such as Russia and China use their UN Security Council vetoes to prevent justice being done, like-minded nations should by-pass it and establish *ad-hoc* tribunals and mechanisms of their own.

And we need to be more outspoken and clear-headed about the subversion of international institutions. In a contemptuous display of arrogance, the Chinese Government has imposed itself as a member of the UN Human Rights Council. Given that show trials, torture of prisoners, and executions are among its hallmarks, along with its appalling treatment of Muslim Uyghurs, Christians, Tibetan Buddhists, and Falun Gong, the Chinese Government will prevent the UN Human Rights Council from ever taking any action against it. The watchdog and the burglar have the same identity.

The crimes of which we speak include murder; extermination; imprisonment; or other severe deprivation of physical liberty in violation of fundamental rules of international law; torture; rape and other forms of sexual violence of comparable gravity; persecution on racial, national, ethnic, cultural, or religious grounds, and enforced disappearance, that are universally recognised as impermissible under international law. But as the world falls into the 'Thucydides Trap' and assumes that the rising power of authoritarian China will displace the United States and liberal democracies, it creates weakness and impotent dependency in the face of such evil.

President Xi Jinping has made it clear that he wants to make the world safe for authoritarianism and the Chinese Government is using its power on the UN Security Council and the UN Human Rights Council to achieve this. It is also using economic muscle and leverage to increasingly turn developing countries into vassal states. If this means protecting its dependent states by turning the spotlight away from atrocity crimes within their jurisdictions, it will do so—just as it seeks to turn the spotlight away from atrocities closer to home. And other authoritarian states then emulate it.

In the face of such suffering, the idea that there is nothing we can do is defeatist and absurd—and an insult to the memory of Raphael Lemkin.

Individual states should instruct their intelligence agencies to gather diplomatic intelligence and evidence of persecution, of war crimes, of emerging crimes against humanity and genocide and governments should better train and equip local embassy staff with in-depth knowledge of ethnic and religious history; persecution; and the diverse cultures of the countries where they serve. And democracies must stand together in calling out the perpetrators. They need to disprove Lenin's belief that capitalist countries would sell you the rope with which you intend to hang them and that our democratic leaders are weak, *'useful idiots.'*

When in 1948 the United States, the UK, and other major powers passed the UDHR, it was one day after the promulgation of the Genocide Convention. Raphael Lemkin wondered if part of the driver behind the timing was to distract attention from the Genocide Convention. Either way, after Lemkin's death in 1959, no one did anything with the Genocide Convention until the mid-sixties.

Significantly, from 1953 to 1967, not a single US Senate voice was raised calling for the United States to ratify the Genocide Convention— 14 years of silence. And not much was said in the UK, or elsewhere, either. But then Senator William Proxmire came on the scene. He was an economically conservative Democrat who stood for election to the US Senate three times and lost three times. When attacked for being a 'loser,' he said he'd be happy to represent *'all the losers,'* not a bad aspiration if it paves the way for a successful conclusion.

In 1957, after Proxmire was finally elected, a friend introduced him to Lemkin's legacy. As Senator for Wisconsin, in 1967, Proxmire stood before the Senate and told them that lack of ratification was a national disgrace. From 1967 until 1986, he then spoke on the subject *every single day* on which the Senate was in session, using almost every Bill available, to make the case for ratification. He was often caricatured as an irritating gadfly, but there's a lot to be said for the awkward squad in politics. Every speech was a new one and, more often than not, given to an almost empty floor. For 20 years, he returned to his theme—a total of 3211 times.

On 11 February 1986, the Senate finally ratified the Convention by a vote of 83–11. It was called the *'Proxmire law.'* When wondering what we can do, and how we should act, Proxmire's successors need to return to the fray. Ask yourself, in how many policy fields would parliamentarians be content to pass critical legislation intended to unlock a freedom, or to mitigate a risk at home or abroad, that they then never seek to use or ensure is implemented? And, in the long run, by using the tools available to us it helps in at least two ways: first, it is to do the right thing in the face of persecution. Second, it serves humanity's interests.

Consider how the Rwandan genocide has contributed to the instability of the Congo and Central Africa. Consider how the tensions in Nigeria put the stability of a country that will be among the world's largest countries by 2050 at risk—an asset-rich country made weak by genocide and religious conflicts. Consider how religious persecution from Eritrea to Pakistan, North Korea to Sudan, adds vast numbers to the 70 million displaced people and refugees and how persecution, gross and egregious human rights violations, crimes against humanity, and genocide correlate to the hobbled economies of the countries from which they flee on every level, which democratic nations want to serve the world's best interests would surely want to get this right. In the long term, getting this right saves both lives and resources. Those societies which are free of genocide, endless conflict, and outright persecution are the most prosperous and the least dependant on foreign aid. Their people are also able to lead happier and better lives. In such societies, our inhumanity can be displaced by kinder, gentler values based on an affirmation of the dignity and rights of every human being.

Judge Thomas Buergenthal, as a young boy, was incarcerated in Auschwitz—a victim of the genocide against Europe's Jews. He survived the Shoah. Judge Buergenthal throws down this challenge to each of us who greet contemporary stories of genocide with incomprehension and incredulity:

> The human mind is simply not able to grasp this terrible truth: a nation transformed into a killing machine programmed to destroy millions of innocent human beings for no reason other than that they were different ... If we humans can so easily wash the blood of our fellow humans off our hands, then what hope is there for sparing future generations from a repeat of the genocides and mass killings of the past? ... one cannot hope to protect mankind from crimes such as those that were visited upon us unless one struggles to break the cycle of hatred and violence that invariably leads to ever more suffering by innocent human beings.

In responding to Buergenthal's challenge to break the cycle of hatred and Lemkin's hopes for humanity—for the *genos*—by creating the architecture to deal with the drivers of atrocity crimes, and especially genocide, it will require a recalibrating of our policies and resources—and much greater political will in concluding the unfinished business of 1948. This is why we decided to publish this book.

APPENDIX A: THE UN OFFICE ON GENOCIDE PREVENTION AND THE RESPONSIBILITY TO PROTECT FRAMEWORK OF ANALYSIS FOR ATROCITY CRIMES (EXTRACTS)

Risk Factor 9
Indicators

9.1 Past or present serious discriminatory, segregational, restrictive or exclusionary practices, policies, or legislation against protected groups.

9.2 Denial of the existence of protected groups or of recognition of elements of their identity.

9.3 History of atrocity crimes committed with impunity against protected groups.

9.4 Past or present serious tensions or conflicts between protected groups or with the state, with regard to access to rights and resources, socioeconomic disparities, participation in decision making processes, security, expressions of group identity or to perceptions about the targeted group.

9.5 Past or present serious tensions or conflicts involving other types of groups (political, social, cultural, geographical, etc.) that could develop along national, ethnical, racial, or religious lines.

9.6 Lack of national mechanisms or initiatives to deal with identity-based tensions or conflict.

© The Editor(s) (if applicable) and The Author(s), under exclusive license to Springer Nature Switzerland AG 2022
E. U. Ochab and D. Alton, *State Responses to Crimes of Genocide*,
Rethinking Political Violence,
https://doi.org/10.1007/978-3-030-99162-3

Risk Factor 9
Indicators

10.1 Official documents, political manifests, media records, or any other documentation through which a direct intent, or incitement, to target a protected group is revealed, or can be inferred in a way that the implicit message could reasonably lead to acts of destruction against that group.

10.2 Targeted physical elimination, rapid or gradual, of members of a protected group, including only selected parts of it, which could bring about the destruction of the group.

10.3 Widespread or systematic discriminatory or targeted practices or violence against the lives, freedom or physical and moral integrity of a protected group, even if not yet reaching the level of elimination.

10.4 Development of policies or measures that seriously affect the reproductive rights of women, or that contemplate the separation or forcible transfer of children belonging to protected groups.

10.5 Resort to methods or practices of violence that are particularly harmful against or that dehumanise a protected group, that reveal an intention to cause humiliation, fear or terror to fragment the group, or that reveal an intention to change its identity.

10.6 Resort to means of violence that are particularly harmful or prohibited under international law, including prohibited weapons, against a protected group.

10.7 Expressions of public euphoria at having control over a protected group and its existence.

10.8 Attacks against or destruction of homes, farms, businesses, or other livelihoods of a protected group and/or of their cultural or religious symbols and property.

Appendix B: The Compilation of Risk Factors and Legal Norms for the Prevention of Genocide (Extracts)

Life Integrity Violations

1. The systematic subjection of members of a particular group to forced labour.
2. The systematic forcible transfer of children of a particular group from their families to individuals with a different identity for the purpose of changing their identity and assimilating them into another group.
3. The systematic forced marriage of women, enforced sterilisation, forced pregnancy, the prevention of births of children from a particular group, and other acts aimed at destroying a particular group in whole or in part, including although not limited to bans on intermarriage or forced marriage to individuals from the state-privileged identity/ies.
4. The deliberate destruction of subsistence food and medical supplies, including humanitarian aid, and/or the blocking of access to such supplies, with the intent to destroy a particular group in whole or in part.
5. The systematic arbitrary detention of members of a particular group, including their community leaders.
6. Systematic torture of members of a particular group on the basis of their membership in such a group.

© The Editor(s) (if applicable) and The Author(s), under exclusive license to Springer Nature Switzerland AG 2022
E. U. Ochab and D. Alton, *State Responses to Crimes of Genocide*, Rethinking Political Violence, https://doi.org/10.1007/978-3-030-99162-3

7. The systematic use of rape and sexual violence, including the incitement thereof, targeting members of a particular group.

8. The systematic forcible transfer from their habitual place of residence of members of a particular group with little or no warning, compensation or administrative or legal recourse or review, including although not limited to the creation of ghettos or segregated areas, the practice of ethnic cleansing.

9. The systematic killing of members of a particular group, as evidenced through extrajudicial, summary, and arbitrary executions, and/or as evidenced through the existence of mass graves resulting from such killings; enforced disappearances; and/or the targeting of community leaders and prominent intellectuals, professionals, educators, and religious leaders associated with a particular group.

10. The intentional targeting during armed conflict of civilian members of a particular group and of civilian sites inhabited by such civilians, calculated to destroy the particular group in whole or in part.

APPENDIX C: LETTER TO THE ICC PROSECUTOR ON THE SITUATION IN NIGERIA

6 August 2020

Dear Ms Bensouda,

Re: The Situation in Nigeria

Following a meeting with Mr Phakiso Mochochoko and the team working on the situation in Nigeria last week, and further to our previous correspondence (14 February; 25 June; 23 July), we write to draw your attention to a new report by UK-based Igbo Councillors, which cites evidence of escalating attacks against Christians and Igbo people (one of the three major tribes in Nigeria) in south-eastern states.

One of the helpful and constructive outcomes of our meeting with your colleagues was the suggestion that we continue to send you authenticated information which, while not directly relevant to the specific cases which you are assessing, will be information which you will be able to examine in due course. What follows is certainly illustrative of the culture of impunity which we discussed.

According to the report: 'During [the] period of strict lockdown.... [Fulani herders] have migrated in trailer and lorry loads with AK47s

© The Editor(s) (if applicable) and The Author(s), under exclusive license to Springer Nature Switzerland AG 2022
E. U. Ochab and D. Alton, *State Responses to Crimes of Genocide*,
Rethinking Political Violence,
https://doi.org/10.1007/978-3-030-99162-3

and other assorted weapons and ammunitions. They have taken occupation of the farmlands displacing the communities and causing havoc and damaging properties as well as senseless and traumatic killings of the villagers to take occupation of their lands and communities.' As of May 2020, 350 Igbo villages have reportedly been occupied by Fulani herders, as well as by Shuwa Arab mercenaries.

Their findings coincide with the launch of a report by the International Committee On Nigeria (ICON) and International Organization on Peace-building & Social Justice (PSJ), 'Nigeria's Silent Slaughter: Genocide in Nigeria and the Implications for the International Community,' which found that, since 2000, Fulani herders have killed 19,000 people (primarily Christian farmers) while Boko Haram have killed 43,000 people (the vast majority of women and children).

There is now a strong body of evidence to demonstrate a severe escalation of attacks by Islamist groups and a failure of the Nigerian courts to bring perpetrators to justice. We ask again, therefore, for an urgent review of the recently-submitted report by the UK All-Party Parliamentary Group on International Freedom of Religion or Belief, entitled 'Nigeria: Unfolding Genocide?' and to ensure that those responsible for these atrocities no longer oppress religious freedom with impunity.

Yours sincerely, Baroness Cox, Lord Alton of Liverpool

INDEX

© The Editor(s) (if applicable) and The Author(s), under exclusive
license to Springer Nature Switzerland AG 2022
E. U. Ochab and D. Alton, *State Responses to Crimes of Genocide*,
Rethinking Political Violence,
https://doi.org/10.1007/978-3-030-99162-3

Ingram Content Group UK Ltd.
Milton Keynes UK
UKHW022106040523
421248UK00006B/324